Writing History in the Medieval Islamic World

The Early and Medieval Islamic World

Published in collaboration with the Society for the Medieval Mediterranean

Society for the
Medieval Mediterranean

As recent scholarship resoundingly attests, the medieval Mediterranean and Middle East bore witness to a prolonged period of flourishing intellectual and cultural diversity. Seeking to contribute to this ever-more nuanced and contextual picture, *The Early and Medieval Islamic World* book series promotes innovative research on the period 500–1500 AD with the Islamic world, as it ebbed and flowed from Marrakesh to Palermo and Cairo to Kabul, as the central pivot. Thematic focus within this remit is broad, from the cultural and social to the political and economic, with preference given to studies of societies and cultures from a socio-historical perspective. It will foster a community of unique voices on the medieval Islamic world, shining light into its lesser-studied corners.

Series Editor
Professor Roy Mottahedeh, Harvard University

Advisors
Professor Amira Bennison, University of Cambridge
Professor Farhad Daftary, Institute of Ismaili Studies
Professor Simon Doubleday, Hofstra University
Professor Frank Griffel, Yale University
Professor Remke Kruk, Leiden University
Professor Beatrice Manz, Tufts University
Dr Bernard O'Kane, American University in Cairo
Professor Andrew Peacock, University of St Andrews
Dr Yossef Rapoport, Queen Mary University of London

New and Forthcoming Titles

Cross Veneration in the Medieval Islamic World: Christian Identity and Practice under Muslim Rule, Charles Tieszen (Fuller Theological Seminary/Simpson University)

Power and Knowledge in Medieval Islam: Shi'i and Sunni Encounters in Baghdad, Tariq al-Jamil (Swathmore College)

The Eastern Frontier: Limits of Empire in Late Antique and Early Medieval Central Asia, Robert Haug (University of Cincinnati)

Narrating Muslim Sicily: War and Peace in the Medieval Mediterranean World, William Granara (Harvard University)

Female Sexuality in the Early Medieval Islamic World: Gender and Sex in Arabic Literature, Pernilla Myrne (University of Gothenburg)

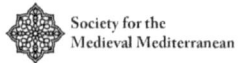

Writing History in the Medieval Islamic World

The Value of Chronicles as Archives

Fozia Bora

I.B. TAURIS
LONDON • NEW YORK • OXFORD • NEW DELHI • SYDNEY

I.B. TAURIS
Bloomsbury Publishing Plc
50 Bedford Square, London, WC1B 3DP, UK
1385 Broadway, New York, NY 10018, USA

BLOOMSBURY, I.B. TAURIS and the I.B. Tauris logo
are trademarks of Bloomsbury Publishing Plc

First published in Great Britain 2019
Paperback edition first published 2021

Cover design: Paul Smith, www.paulsmithdesign.com
Cover image 'Al-Harith Recognizes Abu Zayd in a Library in Basra', from a Maqamat of
al-Hariri, mid-13th century, Iraq. © Bibliothèque Nationale de France, Paris (Arabe3929).

A catalogue record for this book is available from the British Library.

A catalog record for this book is available from the Library of Congress.

ISBN: HB: 978-1-7845-3730-2
PB: 978-0-7556-3851-2
ePDF: 978-1-7867-3611-6
eBook: 978-1-7867-2605-6

Series: The Early and Medieval Islamic World

Typeset by Deanta Global Publishing Services, Chennai, India

For Y, S and L

Contents

List of Illustrations x
Acknowledgements xii
Abbreviations xiv
Note on Terminology, Transliteration and Dates xv

Introduction 1

Ibn al-Furāt: A hidden figure of Mamluk historiography 1
Inscribing with a date: Historiography as documentation 2
Reading Mamluk historians as archivists 2
Mamluk chronicles as documentary narratives 3
An archival turn in Mamluk letters 4
Capturing epistemic moments in Islamic history 5
New light on archival practices in the Mamluk chronicle 5
Epistemology or confession: The priorities of the Mamluk historian 6
The chapters and appendices of this book 7

1 The Archival Function of Historiography 11

Fatimid history refracted through a Mamluk lens 11
Documenting the past as archival exigency 13
Knowing through archives 14
Reversing traditional ways 17
Document–narrative bifurcations and symbiosis 18
The 'authenticity' debate in Arabic historiography 20
The archival ethos in an encyclopaedic age 21

2 An Exemplary Chronicle as Archive: Ibn al-Furāt's *Ta'rīkh al-duwal wa 'l-mulūk* 29

The material archive: Inside a fourteenth-century chronicle 30
Tracing the life of Ibn al-Furāt 36
Clean copy or draft: Ontology of the chronicle as archive 39
Reflections on the spatial textual archive 42

Ibn al-Furāt's contributions to later historiography 43
The afterlives of Ibn al-Furāt's textual archivalia 45
Archival casualties: Texts chosen and not chosen in Ibn al-Furāt's compilation 47

3 Fatimid Archivalia: Narratives and Documents in Late Fatimid Egypt 55

Dynastic, regional, confessional or social history: Framing the Fatimid past 56
The percolation of Fatimid-era chronicles into post-Fatimid accounts 58
A map of the scope and survival of late Fatimid historiography 59
The life cycles of Fatimid documents 64
The *imam* and his historians: Relations and tensions 66
Archival origins: Records from the court 68

4 Mamluk Archivalities: Late Fatimid History in Ibn al-Furāt's Chronicle 75

Ibn al-Furāt's archivalia: Sources from the Fatimid, Ayyubid and Mamluk eras 76
Illuminating archival choices: The sources adduced for comparison 78
Egyptian and Syrian traditions in a trans-metropolitan archival outlook 81
Modes of attribution in the chronicle: Archivality as conservation 83
Ibn al-Furāt's archival strategies 84

5 A Micro-Historical Analysis of Ibn al-Furāt's Archive (Part 1): Two Fatimid Vizierates 89

The vizierate of al-Afḍal 89
The vizierate of al-Ma'mūn al-Baṭā'iḥī 97

6 A Micro-Historical Analysis of Ibn al-Furāt's Archive (Part 2): Fatimid Caliphs and Viziers to the Rise of Ṣalāḥ al-Dīn 103

The caliphate of al-Āmir and the succession crisis after his death 104
The caliphate of al-Ḥāfiẓ and the vizierates of Kutayfāt, Hazārmard, Yānis, Ḥasan b. al-Ḥāfiẓ, Bahrām and Riḍwān 106
The caliphate of al-Ẓāfir and the vizierates of Ibn Maṣāl, Ibn al-Sālār and 'Abbās al-Ṣanhājī. Usāma b. Munqidh's sojourn in Egypt 109
The caliphate of al-Fā'iz and the vizierates of Ṭalā'i' b. Ruzzīk and al-'Ādil Ruzzīk. The rise of the vizier Shāwar 117
The vizierates of Shāwar and Ḍirghām. The arrival of Shīrkūh and the Syrian army in Egypt. Ṣalāḥ al-Dīn's acquisition of Bilbays and the siege of Alexandria 121

7 Concluding Remarks: The Value of Chronicles as Archives 129

Appendix A: Ibn al-Furāt's Use of Reports for Late Fatimid Egypt (1094–1166) 137
Appendix B: Diplomatic Edition of Selected Extracts from Ibn al-Furāt's *Ta'rīkh al-duwal*: Arabic Text 148
Appendix C: English Translation of Selected Extracts from *Ta'rīkh al-duwal* 175
Bibliography 223
Index 241

List of Illustrations

Figures

Ibn Ḥajar's autograph hadith work *al-Musalsalāt*, with additional lines at the end in Ibn al-Furāt's unmistakeable hand, praising God, verifying the hearing and reading of the text, giving Ibn Ḥajar his license, authorizing the text and ending with his signature. Reproduced with kind permission from Khayr al-Din al-Zirikli's *al-Aʿlām: qāmūs tarājīm li ashhar al-rijāl wa 'l-nisā' min al-ʿarab wa 'l-mustaʿribīn wa 'l-mustashrifīn*, 6:200, 15th edition in 8 vols (Beirut, 2002). © Dar El Ilm Lilmalayin, Beirut. 39

Figure 2.7 The location of the Madrasa al-Muʿizziyya in Fustat. Reproduced with permission from P. Casanova, 'Essai de reconstitution de la ville d'al-Fustat ou Misr' in *Mémoires de l'Institut français d'archéologie orientale, le Caire*, 1913, 107, reproduced in M. Ouerfelli, *Le Sucre Production, commercialisation et usages dans la Méditerranée médiévale* (Leiden, 2008), 281. © IFAO Cairo. 40

Figure 3.1 Vienna Cod. A. F. 117, vol. 3 of Ibn al-Furāt's *Taʾrīkh al-duwal wa 'l-mulūk*. A Fatimid-era eyewitness account (from line 8 onwards) is quoted by Ibn al-Furāt from *Akhbār al-dawla al-Miṣriyya wa mā jarā bayn al-mulūk wa 'l-khulafāʾ min al-fitan wa 'l-ḥurūb min ayyām al-Āmir ilā ayyām Shīrkūh*, a unique account of the years 1101–74 CE which is only known from Ibn al-Furāt. He received it without its author's name, and presents a sizeable extract of ten pages in all (MS Vienna AF 119 = Flügel 814, vol. 3, f. 185v). Reproduced with permission. © Österreichische Nationalbibliothek. 61

Table

Table 3.1 Historical narratives of the late Fatimid era 63

Acknowledgements

In a book about medieval Islamic historiography and archives, it's a profound pleasure as well as privilege to 'archivally' record thanks to supervisors, colleagues, friends and family members who helped to bring it to fruition. The doctoral thesis on which the empirical work of this book is based was guided by three gifted exemplars in the field of Islamic history, each of whom has wielded great influence on the discipline, and more personally on their students, including this one: Chase Robinson, Donald Richards and Judith Pfeiffer. My discussions with them over the years improved my research in countless perceptible and imperceptible ways, and they can take credit for making my experience of it deeply formative as well as enjoyable; the mistakes or shortcomings are my own.

In its roundabout journey to completion, the thesis preceding this book was at various stages enhanced by valuable advice from Jeremy Johns, Luke Treadwell and Michael Brett. The Arabic text benefited from the deep learning of Fareed Elshayyal. The Humanities Research Board of the British Academy funded my first years of graduate study, while Wolfson College, Oxford, the convivial home of my graduate studies, defrayed a number of research costs and provided me with a graduate award. The Muslim Academic Trust, under the direction of Tim Winter of the Cambridge University Faculty of Divinity, helped me with a generous grant, as did my benevolent parents-in-law, Jane and John; I'm deeply grateful to them all. Hisham Hellyer kindly went to considerable effort to procure manuscript material from the Dar al-Kutub al-Misriyya in Cairo. Further manuscripts from the Chester Beatty Library in Dublin, the Inebey Library in Bursa, the British Library and the National Libraries of France and Austria were (physically or digitally) acquired with financial help from the James Mew Fund at Oxford and the School of Languages, Cultures and Societies (LCS) at the University of Leeds, all of which helped to bring together a widely dispersed set of autographs. Talal and Yasmine al-Azem offered me, with enormous (and characteristic) kindness, a warm and hospitable home from home in Oxford countless times. Some preliminary work on the book was carried out in the libraries of the Markfield Institute of Higher Education and the Cambridge Muslim College, and I thank both institutions for their support.

The archival approach adopted in the book was articulated over the course of 2016 and 2017, during which I received beneficial feedback from Konrad Hirschler, an unfailingly helpful critical interlocutor of my ideas even in their earliest stages, who shared his time and insights generously. I benefited over those two years from the feedback of colleagues at an IMPAcT Colloquium at the Oriental Institute, Oxford University, kindly hosted by Judith Pfeiffer, at a workshop on 'Chronicles as Archives in Medieval Islamicate Contexts' held at the Leeds Humanities Research Institute funded by LCS and from a 'Chronicles as Archives' panel at the Leeds International

Medieval Congress. My warm thanks go to the participants of all these colloquia, in particular for critical conversations with or useful suggestions from Judith Pfeiffer, Talal al-Azem, Harry Munt, Arezou Azad, Erin Dailey, Daisy Livingston, Emilia Jamroziak and Hugh Kennedy, among others. Three anonymous readers of the book deserve my heartfelt gratitude for their incisive and helpful suggestions, especially in relation to the presentation of the archival argument. Their interventions remind me how much the wheels of academic scholarship are oiled by the unpaid and often anonymous labours of dedicated colleagues. Torsten Wollina suggested numerous improvements to an early draft. The whole manuscript was read by Chase Robinson and Erin Dailey, who generously offered stellar advice and valuable suggestions for improvement. The final draft was written during a half-year of research leave kindly supported by the research committee of LCS. At I. B. Tauris, Tom Stottor was a skilful editor, and focused and energetic in helping to steer the book to completion. Parts of Chapter 2 first appeared in the *Journal of Islamic Manuscripts* 3:2 (2012) as 'A Mamluk Historian's Holograph. Messages from a *Musawwada* of *Tarīkh*', published by Brill, and are reproduced here with permission.

I confess upfront that I can scarcely find words to thank my loving family that would be commensurate with their unstinting support. They keep my feet firmly planted, in the happiest way, in the present moment rather than the pre-modern Islamic world. My mother and late father are my inspirations in research, as in most things. Their integrity, courage and generosity have given me a great deal to live up to. My two children, Sulayman and Layla, have my affectionate thanks for sharing their mother's time with a fourteenth-century historian, a situation they have tolerated with patience and good humour. My deepest gratitude is to my partner Yaḥyā, whose birth name Jonathan translates from the Hebrew as 'God has given': I'm lucky to be a recipient of that gift.

Abbreviations

AI	*Annales Islamologiques*
AJSLL	*The American Journal of Semitic Languages and Literatures*
BIFAO	*Bulletin de l'Institut Français d'Archéologie Orientale*
BRISMES	*(Bulletin) British Society for Middle Eastern Studies*
BSOAS	*Bulletin of the School of Oriental and African Studies*
CSSH	*Comparative Studies in Society and History*
DI	*Der Islam*
EI	*Encyclopaedia of Islam*
*EI*²	*Encyclopaedia of Islam, Second Edition*
*EI*³	*Encyclopaedia of Islam, Third Edition*
IJMES	*International Journal of Middle Eastern Studies*
ILR	*International Library Review*
IQ	*The Islamic Quarterly*
IS	*Islamic Studies*
JAH	*Journal of African History*
JAIS	*Journal of Arabic and Islamic Studies*
JAOS	*Journal of the American Oriental Society*
JARCE	*Journal of the American Research Center in Egypt*
JESHO	*Journal of the Economic and Social History of the Orient*
JIM	*Journal of Islamic Manuscripts*
JIS	*Journal of Islamic Studies*
JMH	*Journal of Medieval History*
JRAS	*Journal of the Royal Asiatic Society*
JSS	*Journal of Semitic Studies*
MSR	*Mamluk Studies Review*
MW	*The Muslim World*
QSA	*Quaderni di Studi Arabi*
SI	*Studia Islamica*
WO	*Die Welt des Orients*
WZKM	*Wiener Zeitschrift für Kunde des Morgenlandes*
ZDMG	*Zeitschrift der Deutschen Morgenländischen Gesellschaft*

Note on Terminology, Transliteration and Dates

In this study of a medieval Islamic chronicle in its function as an archive, the clarification of several terms may prove useful to some readers. I refer to Ibn al-Furāt's book variously as a *chronicle* in regard to its genre, the annalistic form of Middle Period historiography; as a *text* meaning a literary construct; and as a *manuscript* (handwritten text), *codex* (book in manuscript form; plural: codices), *holograph* (text in the author's hand) and *autograph* (text authorized by its author) in discussions of its materiality.

The terms *Middle Period* and *medieval* are used in this book to refer to historiography produced during the Fatimid, Ayyubid and Mamluk periods of socio-political and intellectual history, which correspond roughly with the tenth to early sixteenth centuries of the Common Era.[1] That those terms, alongside *modern* and *premodern*, are Eurocentric in origin, and thus reductive in their application to Islamicate contexts, is a problematic given, and their use is not intended to reify a conceptualization of Islamic eras with reference to developments in Europe. Indeed, a forthcoming major study of Islamic world periodization argues that there were no 'Islamic Middle Ages' as such.[2] With due acknowledgement of this position, these terms are nonetheless retained in this book in view of their explanatory power in the absence of an agreed-upon endogenous temporal terminology. The latter continues to be slippery, elusive even, in light of the multiple temporalities and periodizations of Islamicate historiography explicated by Bashir and by Hirschler and Savant among others. In this, my usage of 'medieval' follows al-Azmeh and Hirschler more closely than the expansive recent definition offered in Musawi or the 'post late antique' medieval context delineated by Salaymeh.[3] For the purposes of this book's argument, therefore, the reader may understand 'medieval' and 'Middle Period' as referring in a specific sense to the Fatimid, Ayyubid and Mamluk periods. Meanwhile, the term *Islamicate* refers to the cultural complex 'centred on a lettered tradition', that is 'historically associated with Islam and the Muslims, both among Muslims themselves and … non-Muslims', as explained by Marshall Hodgson.[4]

The key term *archive*, used extensively in this study, is encapsulated in the following contemporary British definition as one of the many collections of documents or records that have been

> selected for permanent preservation because of their value as evidence or as a source for historical or other research. … Archives have value to nations and regions, organisations, communities and individual people. They provide evidence of activities which occurred in the past. They tell stories, document people and identity, and are valuable sources of information for research.[5]

While embracing this quintessential understanding of the archive, I make further occasional references to post-structuralist interpretations of the term that, if decontextualized in the present discussion, have recently inspired or facilitated new archival approaches in the contemporary humanities. The derivative terms *archivistics*, *archivality*, *archivalia* refer, respectively, to the theory, practice or methods of archival science; to the quality of being an archive and to material subsisting within an archive. The terms *epistemic archive* and *knowledge archive* are applied to Arabic historical texts *qua* collections of both items of information and of knowledge-making practice, while *episteme* denotes all of a system of knowledge discourses, a body of possible ideas and a crucible of knowledge production within a given epoch in a Foucauldian sense, with its well-recognized utility for the medieval Islamicate.[6]

Moving from the hermeneutic sphere to dynastic and confessional nomenclature, the term *Fatimid* refers to the branch of the Sevener Shiʿi movement that formed a dynasty in North Africa and Egypt between 909 and 1171, tracing the origin of its imamate to the Prophet Muḥammad through his youngest daughter Fāṭima (d. 632). The appellation *Ismaʿili*, not used by medieval adherents of the confession, denotes for both modern followers of the imams and recent commentators that branch of Shiʿism that identified its lineage through Ismail b. Jaʿfar al-Ṣādiq (d. 755), a direct descendant of the Prophet Muḥammad through Fāṭima's son Ḥusayn (d. 680), and his descendants ʿAlī Zayn al-ʿĀbidīn (d. 712) and Muḥammad al-Bāqir (d. 743).[7] In regard to discussions of Fatimid archivalia in Chapters 3 and 4, the phrase *Fatimid historiography* (as distinct from the 'Fatimid tradition of historiography') includes accounts written/recited by Egyptian and non-Egyptian witnesses to the events of the era, and goes beyond apologetical accounts of the polity to encompass the sum of narratives emanating from the milieu of Egypt under the Fatimids.

The Ismaʿilis' own name for their religious programme was the generic but revealing *al-daʿwa* (mission), an indication of their self-conception as a religious and political rival movement to the Sunni ʿAbbasid dynasty they hoped to supplant, the self-styled *dawla al-mubāraka* (blessed dynasty).[8] By *daʿwa*, as distinct from *dawla* (dynasty, polity, state), recent historians refer to the Fatimid Ismaʿili religious mission to preach, proselytize and convert non-Ismaʿilis, both to their formulations of Ismaʿili religious doctrine and, as a corollary, to acceptance of Fatimid political rule.

In regard to the analytical discussion of historical texts as archivalia at the heart of this study, it is worth noting that medieval sources present a nuanced and varied nomenclature regarding the Fatimid dynasty. Ibn al-Furāt's text does not generally use the terms 'Fatimid' or 'Ismaʿili', and eschews the epithets commonly applied to the dynasty by non-Ismaʿilis, such as Bāṭinī (esotericist), Qarmaṭī (follower of an Eastern Ismaʿili sect implacably opposed to the Fatimid line, named after its founder Ḥamdān Qarmaṭ, d. 933) or the abusive *malāḥida* (heretics).[9] While he uses the diminutive ʿUbaydī, he nonetheless refers to the Fatimid rulers as 'caliphs' and represents their caliphate as normative, the dynasty of the *Miṣriyyūn* (Egyptians),[10] a rare usage in the extant Arabic historiography of the Fatimid era, while the term *Bāṭinī* is reserved for the troublesome Niẓāriyya.[11] Meanwhile, the Twelver confessional affiliation is denoted *Imāmī* in a usage that contrasts with al-Maqrīzī's.[12] Like many medieval chroniclers and contemporary scholars, Ibn al-Furāt also refers to any given Fatimid ruler as both 'caliph' and 'imam', usually in accordance with the context in which he is mentioned: whether more emphatically political or religious.

Finally, the distinction between dynastic succession and the Fatimid doctrine of *continuing designation* requires elucidation. Despite hereditary modes of succession prevalent within the Umayyad and 'Abbasid houses, the Sunni theory of succession recognized a 'principle of "election"' that contrasted with the Shi'i notion of 'designation' of the imam. The Isma'ilis espoused the doctrine of continuing designation, in which each imam was to personally and formally name a successor, contrasting with Zaydis, who regarded the Prophet's designation of 'Alī as extending only to his grandsons Ḥasan and Ḥusayn, and Twelvers, who held that the Prophet had designated all twelve imams in advance.[13]

The transliteration of Arabic terms in this book uses the *Encyclopaedia of Islam* system, as modified in *IJMES*. Words commonly used in English, such as imam, Qur'an or hadith, are not presented with diacritical marks, for ease of reading. Well-known toponyms and proper nouns, such as the names of dynasties, are rendered in their Anglicized versions. Meanwhile, all dates are provided in the Common Era, at times augmented by Hijrī dates, in which case the latter appear first.

Notes

1 Defined by as occurring 'between the collapse of caliphal power in 334 [945] and the rise of the Ottoman and Safavid states around 900 [1494]': R. S. Humphreys, *Islamic History: A Framework for Inquiry* (Princeton, 1991), 129 (following Marshall Hodgson, *The Venture of Islam* (Chicago, 1977), 2:3).

2 T. Bauer, *Warum e skein islamisches Mittelalter gab* (Munich, 2018).

3 A. al-Azmeh, 'Muslim History: Reflections on Periodisation and Categorisation', *The Medieval History Journal* 1:2 (1998), 195–231, and K. Hirschler, *Medieval Arabic Historiography: Authors as Actors* (London and New York, 2006), ix–x; M. Musawi, *The Medieval Islamic Republic of Letters: Arabic Knowledge Construction* (Notre Dame, Indiana, 2015), 1; L. Salaymeh, *The Beginnings of Islamic Law: Late Antique Islamicate Legal Traditions* (Cambridge, 2016), 7–8; S. Bashir, 'On Islamic Time: Rethinking Chronology in the Historiography of Muslim Societies', *History and Theory* 53 (December 2014), 519–44; and K. Hirschler and S. Savant, 'What is in a Period? Arabic Historiography and Periodization', *Der Islam: Journal of the History and Culture of the Middle East* 91:1 (2014), 6–19.

4 Hodgson, *Venture*, 1:57.

5 http://www.nationalarchives.gov.uk/documents/information-management/archive-principles-and-practice-an-introduction-to-archives-for-non-archivists.pdf (accessed July 2017).

6 For instance throughout Musawi, *The Medieval Islamic Republic of Letters*; M. Foucault, *Les Mots et les choses* (1966), translated as *The Order of Things: An Archaeology of the Human Sciences* (Psychology Press, 2002); 224, 398, 419 &c.

7 F. Daftary, *The Isma'ilis: Their History and Doctrines* (Cambridge, 1990), 91; P. Walker, 'The Ismā'īlī Da'wa and the Fāṭimid caliphate', in C. Petry (ed.), *The Cambridge History of Egypt*, vol. 1 (Cambridge, 1998), 120–50, 121.

8 Dafary, *The Isma'ilis*, 93.

9 Cf. Ibn Taghrībirdī quoting Abū Shāma, Ibn al-Athīr and others (*Ibn Taghrībirdī, al-Nujūm al-zāhira fī mulūk Miṣr wa 'l-Qāhira*, ed. in 16 vols by M. H. Shams al-Dīn (Beirut, 1992), 5:324-6); cf. Daftary, *The Isma'ilis*, 93.

10 *Ta'rīkh al-duwal*, II:20b; III:215a, taken from Ibn Abī Ṭayy (d. 1233) and Shāfiʿ b. ʿAlī (d. 1330).

11 *Ta'rīkh al-duwal*, I:166a

12 P. E. Walker, 'Succession to Rule in the Shiʿite Caliphate', *JARCE* 32 (1995), 239–64, 32.

13 Walker, 'Succession', 3.

Introduction

Archival work turns archival materials into the building blocks of historical narratives. This process is by no means trivial. On the contrary, it is extraordinarily creative and constructive.

M. Friedrich, *The Birth of the Archive. A History of Knowledge* (2018), 199

Ibn al-Furāt: A hidden figure of Mamluk historiography

In the seminary-rich city of Cairo in the late fourteenth century, two men studied historiographical texts together. They knew this scholarly environment well, and had helped to create it, especially in the field of historiography. In a well-attested Arab-Muslim bibliophilic culture – both a trope and a truth, as recent studies indicate – Cairo and Damascus had developed into two of its most productive centres, where the love of books drew in scholars, readers and travellers from many walks of life.[1] Ibn Khaldūn (1332–1406), the older of the two men, was the author of what became by far the most widely acclaimed book of premodern Arabic historiography, while the younger historian, al-Maqrīzī (1364–1442), wrote over thirty books in the course of a prolific writing career, in which historiography was prominent.[2] The careers and literary output of the two historians have generated substantial scholarly interest, including editions of their main works and an ever-growing body of secondary literature. Behind them, however, stood a much lesser-known figure, a near-exact contemporary of Ibn Khaldūn's based in Cairo-Fustat, a *muḥaddith* (scholar of Prophetic traditions), historian and notary witness, in descending order of social prestige, who was known within scholarly networks in both Cairo and Damascus, but remained, as the biographical literature of the period shows, a relatively obscure figure throughout his life. Yet he wrote a major book of history, one of the most influential and methodologically revealing works of Middle Period historiography, which survives only in part, in the author's hand, as no subsequent copies were made, though his material was extensively utilized by later historians. This author was Nāṣir al-Dīn Muḥammad ibn ʿAbd al-Raḥīm ibn al-Furāt (1334–1405) and his book was *Taʾrīkh al-duwal wa ʾl-mulūk* (*The History of Dynasties and Kings*).[3] It is this forensic, document-laden tour de force of historiography that illustrates the argument of this book.

Inscribing with a date: Historiography as documentation

The writing of history in the premodern Islamicate world was commonly denoted by the Arabic verb *arrakha*, to 'inscribe with a date', an activity central to archival practice in a wide range of premodern and modern contexts.[4] In this study, I argue for a reconsideration of medieval Arabic historiography as a form of documentation, and a reading of resulting chronicles, a primary rubric of historical knowledge, as archives. Middle Period chronicles, a pre-eminent genre of Arabic historiography, can be seen to function as archives of both knowledge and knowledge-making practice, as storage spaces for deliberately preserved and strategically ordered reports that fulfil an unspoken brief of archivality as conservation. They are also texts constituted through a range of archival practices, bearing specific archival signs. The archival approach to historical narratives does not detract from immensely illuminating nascent research on documents per se, but rather emphasizes the seamless culture of archivality and documentation that permeates the medieval Islamic episteme within which chronicles were written. In short, I want to demonstrate that archivality is the heuristic key to Mamluk historical writing.

While Arabic terms for 'archive(s)' range, depending on social and temporal context, from *khizāna* (repository), *sijillāt* (registers), *maḥfuẓāt* ('preserved material', archivalia), *wathā'iq rasmiyya* (official documents) to *arshīf* (the Arabic transliteration of the French 'archive'), one term offers particular elucidation of the archival aspect of the medieval Arabic chronicle: *dīwān*. Ibn Khaldūn's major book of history, *Kitāb al-'ibar wa dīwān al-mubtada' wa al-khabar fī ayyām al-'arab wa al-'ajam wa al-barbar, wa man 'āṣarahum min dhawī al-sulṭān al-akbar* (*Book of Lessons and Archive of Early and Subsequent History, Dealing with the Political Events Concerning the Arabs, Non-Arabs, and Berbers, and the Supreme Rulers Who Were Contemporary with Them*, in Franz Rosenthal's translation),[5] uses the word *dīwān* to refer to an historiographical archive, a usage consistent with the use of *dīwān* for different categories of documentary archive by the renowned administrative historian al-Qalqashandī (1355–1418),[6] and widespread use of the term in Arabic letters to refer to an archive of poetry. Ibn Khaldūn's choice of the word articulates a key feature of the medieval Arabic chronicle, namely its function as an archive, the theme of the present study.

Reading Mamluk historians as archivists

As an analytical category applied to the study of the medieval Islamic chronicle, the archive – alongside the archival practices of historians – documents the specific strategies by which Mamluk historians gathered and marshalled copious numbers of books in diverse genres of both prose and poetry, in order to create meaningful new works with contemporary relevance and resonance, for the education and stimulation of present and future readers. In this conducive milieu, clues to the inherently archival nature of intellectual labour help us to understand a culture of textual production in which books in many genres, including Ibn al-Furāt's chronicle, were written by men (and rarely, women) of whom some honed an archival mindset through waged work in state bureaucracy, or in the apparatus of the multifaceted legal sphere. These were activities that attest the 'legal and notarial culture of Mamlūk urban society' as the normative setting in which chronicles were produced. In this environment, a 'documentary fabric ... sustained and facilitated medieval life' in its literary as well as social dimensions, as illustrated neatly by the small example of the legal and documentary journal of a fifteenth-century Damascene author, Ibn Ṭawq's (d. 1509) *al-Taʿlīq*, that 'often reads like a chronicle'.[7] A recent survey of Islamicate archival practices prior to the Ottoman era cites the examples of Abu 'l-Faḍl Bayhaqī (d. 1077) and ʿImād al-Dīn al-Iṣfahānī (d. 1201) as historians who used their access to administrative documents to flesh out their accounts of history.[8] At the same time, historians like Ibn al-Furāt, who had been inculcated in hadith study – with its emphasis on philological precision and its privileging of careful, individuated attribution, among other features – could, as Khalidi has noted, be expected to bring these qualities to their 'secular' works, to underscore the point that the Middle Period chronicle developed under the influence of, inter alia, several genres of a practical nature.[9]

The Middle Period chronicle examined in this study, in particular Ibn al-Furāt's account of the final century of Fatimid rule in *Taʾrīkh al-duwal wa 'l-mulūk*, presents both opportunity and resources for the present-day reader to engage systematically with the archival dimensions of the genre, as its author had collated many dozens of earlier and contemporary sources attesting the history of the Islamic Near East from Creation up to the final stages of his own life in 799/1396. The magnum opus of this Burji Mamluk historian is a self-reflexive patchwork quilt of historiography, which performs documentation as much as storytelling. The archival approach adopted in the present book is distinct from, yet complements, valuable studies on the literary and aesthetic dimensions of medieval Islamicate historiography, in which intelligible if porous lines are drawn, in Bauer's terminology, between pragmatic texts that address real-worldly issues and literary texts that are aesthetically driven and polyvalent within diverse contexts.[10] This book engages the reader in an epistemic journey of discovering the deeper value of the chronicle as an archive, and as a narrative-documentary record of historical and historiographical developments. In this process, the methodologies of archival studies offer a more crisp and compelling elucidation of the quasi-documentary and commemorative aspects of medieval Arabic historical writing as a practice devoted to supporting and creating memory, in Friedrich's terms, and to 'eternalizing' the past, than has often been appreciated.[11] These aims are achieved by authors like Ibn al-Furāt through a range of specific, locatable archival strategies, which I draw the reader's attention to in later chapters.

Mamluk chronicles as documentary narratives

Drawing from the comprehensive definition of 'archive' offered above, a key aspect of identifying the archivality of medieval Arabic chronicles is scrutiny of the evidentiary nature of historical texts that offer – separately or simultaneously – both documentary and narrative material. Moving from a general definition of the archive to the medieval Islamicate, this book draws on recent works that re-evaluate the nature and role of medieval Islamic archives, in particular the position formulated by Konrad Hirschler that the Mamluk archive is not merely 'a stable spatial entity and a product, but rather a multifaceted set of processes spread across the Mamluk realm'.[12] More specifically, I offer a micro-historical reading of Ibn al-Furāt's account of late Fatimid rule to demonstrate the key argument posited by Paulo Sartori that narrative sources can be treated as documentary material, for several reasons. One is that authorial manipulations are widely employed in genres conventionally separated as 'documentary' or 'narrative', so as to render the typological distinction between them dubious; a second reason is that historical texts often perform as evidence of past actions. Thus the presumption that 'documents alone can serve as evidences, whereas narrative/literary sources should be relegated to the sphere of fiction', is 'highly problematic and in urgent need of revision'.[13] Ibn al-Furat's chronicle reproduces documents, but is also a documentary-archival resource in itself.

An archival turn in Mamluk letters

The Mamluk era witnessed a turn towards archivality in administration and letters, as mapped by Hirschler, that wielded great influence on Mamluk historiography.[14] Within chronicles, the drive to create historical records for commemorative and 'identity-formation' purposes, that is, to map the contours of past and present society, and to locate noteworthy individuals and communities within them, stood as a counterweight to the social and political turbulence of Burji Mamluk urban elite life as recorded in the annalistic chronicles of Ibn al-Furāt, Ibn Khaldūn, al-Maqrīzi and a host of others. The two latter historians had deep and personal experience of this turbulence, during careers in which they were appointed to and dismissed from a variety of highly visible religio-legal positions in the state. A prominent characteristic of Mamluk urban life was the coexistence of social dynamism and precarity, attributable in part to the ruling military–civilian elite's massive investment in civic and intellectual institutions such as the madrasa, coupled with a penchant for confiscations and other financial depredations expressive of 'despotism, mismanagement and cruelty'.[15] With upward (or downward) mobility came a volatility often prevalent in scholarly professions as much as in sultanic or lower-level politics in civilian and military spheres. A range of fourteenth- and fifteenth-century chronicles offered an unfolding register of economic fluctuations, religio-legal controversies, environmental anomalies and domestic or foreign political developments and disputes.[16] Historiography in this context, chronicles alongside the biographical dictionaries, could offer a space for critique, for social-cum-intellectual catharsis in a positivist vein, yet also operated as a bulwark against lack of security, including the loss of books and documents, with archivality as its salient modus operandi.[17]

The prism of archive allows us to understand not just historiography in new ways but also broader trends in epistemology. Thus the study of medieval Arabic historiography promises to be invigorated by a more recent 'archival turn' in the study of history, which is multidisciplinary, global and explained and practised by a range of scholars of, inter alia, the Near Eastern and European pasts: Paulo Sartori, Markus Friedrich, Filippo de Vivo, Maria Pia Donato, Konrad Hirschler, Shannon McSheffrey and Tamer el-Leithy among others.[18] This up-and-coming mode of enquiry encompasses several founding axioms, including a recognition of the contingent and subjective nature of archives of every variety, scrutiny of the conditions that shape the creation of archives, and a move away from the concept of the archive as a necessarily fixed spatial entity towards emphasis on *archival practices* that suffuse the epistemic environments of many premodern societies, whether in the production of documents or in other modes of record-keeping. My argument uses Ibn al-Furāt's history to demonstrate that Arabic chronicles should be read as archives in themselves. In the Mamluk era, they were a vital form of documentation, repositories of shared (though not necessarily settled) memories of an often contested past and a unique means for the conscience-driven self-examination of literate communities in the premodern Arabophone world. In these books, irrespective of their size or stated focus, the authorial agencies of representing society, appraising hegemonic conduct, positing ideals, grinding personal axes and apportioning censure or praise could be exercised freely.[19]

Capturing epistemic moments in Islamic history

Conversely, the archival reading model adopted in this book pushes against the limits of reading medieval Arabic chronicles as tendentious narratives devised mainly for the pursuit of various religio-political causes. While some excellent studies have used chronicles to illuminate, for example, Mamluk socio-political dynamics effectively, there is also wide scope for examining in detail how chronicles reflect both the politics of their world and its vigorous, adaptable and catholic epistemic values.[20] Arabic historical texts can and should be read as radically revealing knowledge archives that capture epistemic moments in Islamic history: points in time for which the state of historical and historiographical knowledge can be charted and evaluated via scrutiny of the archival practices of their authors, as applied to a variety of source texts. In these epistemic moments, the archive concept is more than simply a trope, for it offers a hermeneutic framework with potentially wide applicability across various forms of historiography. This approach has been hinted at, and even obliquely pursued in some previous studies, in relation to the so-called Syrian school of historiography as a 'register of Muslim religious learning', and in regard to biographical dictionaries as 'comparable to the role of documentary sources in other traditions', in which they attest 'those informal relationships between individuals that secured the stability of Middle Eastern societies'.[21] In the present study, the primary focus is on the chronicle as a narrative and archival form, with additional reference to biographical monographs and administrative works from the Fatimid, Ayyubid and Mamluk eras that subsume and incorporate historical accounts.

New light on archival practices in the Mamluk chronicle

In re-evaluating Mamluk chronicles as archives recording valuable streams of knowledge, the analytical approach of this book builds initially upon Donald Little's micro-historical exploratory method of comparing historical accounts, an approach especially suited to the study of writing in general and archives in particular.[22] Little's aims are threefold: to draw out variations in Mamluk reports, similarities between them and establish a 'repertorium' of sources for particular epochs of history.[23] While incorporating these beneficial aims, I add as my principal objective the identification of the specific archival practices of Ibn al-Furāt, notably his gathering, prioritizing and rearranging of source material on late Fatimid history in *Ta'rīkh al-duwal*, with concerns of conservation, ease of reading, retrievability and space management very much in mind. Through this inductive analysis, the ultimate desiderata are a clearer picture of, first, the archival function of historiography as it is operationalized in steps and stages; and second, the tangible spatial epistemic archive (or repertorium, in Little's wording) in book form that results from this archival activity. This archive transmits material onwards to further chronicles *qua* archives, but remains in itself a repository of previously created records for present and future pedagogic, heuristic and recreational use. The uptake of material from Ibn al-Furāt's repository and its contribution to further chronicle-archives is a theme explored in Chapter 2.

Epistemology or confession: The priorities of the Mamluk historian

While pursuing dual aims of identifying and glossing both archive and archival practices, the textual analysis at the heart of this study alternates between descriptive and analytical modes in order to elucidate Ibn al-Furāt's method of discrimination between the sources (archival hierarchization), to ascertain the breadth of authorities he presses into service for each section (epistemic scope) and to appraise how much Fatimid-era material was available to him or his sources in each instance (archivality as conservation). In a departure from what a recent study of medieval Arabic authorship termed a 'polyphony' of texts characterized by 'double or multiple hermeneutic layers, multiply hidden authors, and authors in disguise',[24] Ibn al-Furāt's preference in *Ta'rīkh al-duwal* is to keep his informants' voices clear, separate and ideologically measurable. In this, he presents an alternative, if not a challenge, to the verdict proposed by Bernard Lewis and taken up by Michael Brett that the post-Fatimid Arabic literature on the Fatimids is 'highly apologetic, highly polemical in character, for and against the dynasty's religious and political claims'.[25] Furthermore, in reading Ibn al-Furāt's chronicle as a register also of socio-political and intellectual attitudes, his privileging of epistemic concerns over confessional ones comes to the fore, a point I return to later in this study.

The Mamluk historians' efforts to rebuild and synthesize Fatimid historiographical archivalia (a body of texts surveyed in Chapter 3), which forms the backdrop to Ibn al-Furāt's account of late Fatimid history, is an understudied phenomenon. For earlier phases of Fatimid Isma'ilism, significant textual work in the areas of the collation, edition and analysis of reports and chronicles has been carried out by A. F. Sayyid, M. Brett and H. Halm among others.[26] Overall, however, recent scholarship has paid scant attention to Fatimid-era historical accounts as they appear in later works. This is less attributable to a lack of interest in the subject than it is to the demands upon scholarly attention made by the contemporary history recorded in vast Ayyubid- and Mamluk-era compilations, not all of which have been published, and also to the fact that Fatimid historiography presents today's historian with an intriguing if rather knotty challenge. We have, on the one hand, ample material evidence attesting the Fatimids' dramatic and precipitous political ascent, which has engendered a substantial body of scholarship, for 'what is at stake is not the history of a marginal religious group in a peripheral area, but rather a centrally important, prolonged chapter in the history of Islam, with profound consequences for what came afterwards'.[27] On the other hand, the physical traces attesting the Fatimids' development of Egypt and its culture, in the forms of architecture, epigraphy, numismatics, glass weights, textiles embroidered with writing (*ṭirāz*) and *objets d'art*, offer but a skeletal outline of socio-political history at most, supplemented with sporadic atomistic insights.[28] For the wider trajectory of Fatimid rule in Egypt, and crucially, for its detail, we are reliant on reconstructions offered by Ayyubid and Mamluk chroniclers, including Ibn al-Furāt.[29]

Thus we are, in many ways, like Ibn al-Furāt's contemporary Ibn Khaldūn, 'at the mercy of the *akhbār*'.[30] However, given the multiplicity of earlier sources available to both authors, this is not an unhappy dependency, especially in light of the paradox expressed by al-Maqrīzī, who suggests in the *Itti'āẓ* that Egyptian books on the Fatimid caliphate were hard to find, even if both his *Itti'āẓ* and his *Khiṭaṭ*, like Ibn al-Furāt's *Ta'rīkh al-duwal*, subvert his argument and bear witness to the richness of the source base for the Fatimids available to the historians of their era and earlier.[31] That the present-day scholar has little or no independent access to most of these works is the real cause for regret.

The chapters and appendices of this book

As far as research priorities go, in 1995, Ulrich Haarmann argued convincingly that 'hardly anything is … more urgent in Mamluk studies than the systematic exploration of the literary (prose) writings of Mamluk authors', and to date, key aspects of historiography remain unexplored in the depth they deserve.[32] This study of Ibn al-Furāt's chronicle fits squarely into that endeavour. The operationalization of the archival approach forms a main theme of Chapter 1 that follows, which also contemplates the prospects and limits of present-day research into medieval Arabic historiography, chronicle writing in particular. I begin by delineating, briefly, the epistemic environment in which Ibn al-Furāt produced his account of late Fatimid history, then examine in more depth the elucidatory potential of the archival approach for re-framing historiography as documentation. This naturally engenders a discussion of the implications of the archival reading model for a hitherto largely fixed separation of 'narratives' and 'documents' in contemporary scholarship. The further strands of this chapter encompass the contribution of the archival approach to a field still marked by traces of an 'authenticity' debate in reading medieval Arabic sources, and the modes in which archivality is a necessary complement to, indeed component of, the encyclopaedism of Mamluk literary production.

In Chapter 2, I introduce the archive, that is, Ibn al-Furāt's chronicle as a set of codices carrying material signs of archivality. I then pursue the elusive details of the author's life and evaluate his place within the intellectual culture of Mamluk Cairo and (to a lesser extent) Damascus, while tracing the clandestine influence of his chronicle on contemporary and later historical texts, those of his peers as well as successors including Ibn Khaldūn and especially al-Maqrīzī. What I find is that the later (near-contemporary) sections of Ibn al-Furāt's chronicle are ubiquitous in more 'celebrated' accounts, but he is rarely if ever named. Chapter 3 audits the extent of historiographical and documentary production in late Fatimid Egypt, in order to evaluate the range of potential archivalia that Ibn al-Furāt and other post-Fatimid authors could draw on to populate their chronicle-archives. Chapter 4 sets the scene in historiographical terms for a move from broader arguments to the minutiae of Ibn al-Furat's text, and is followed by two chapters that offer detailed analyses of Ibn al-Furāt's accounts of the late Fatimid vizierate and caliphate, as compared with more than a dozen earlier, contemporary and later sources, chosen according to methodological criteria outlined in Chapter 4. The seventh and final chapter indicates the broader implications of this research for our understanding of medieval Islamic archivalities.

The three appendices provide textual and contextual information that, it is hoped, will help to pinion the archival argument to specific texts. Appendix A indexes the range of historical sources archived by Ibn al-Furāt for late Fatimid history. Appendix B provides a diplomatic edition[33] of unique extracts from Ibn al-Furāt's narrative on Fatimid historical events – that is, sections of text that are not available elsewhere in modern editions of works that are used by Ibn al-Furāt. Lastly, Appendix C offers an English translation of those extracts. Taken together, the chapters and appendices of the present book aim to pursue five components of an analytical matrix for archival study as delineated by Friedrich: the material/spatial aspects of the archive, in this case the archive of historiography; its modes of organization; its intended uses; the epistemic environment in which the archive plays a role and the connections between archival practice and conceptions of history and memorialization.[34] The fortuitous survival of Ibn al-Furāt's chronicle presents contemporary historians with both a wellspring of rich material and an ideal resource for deeper archival–historiographical enquiry.

Notes

1 For the more than 200 teaching institutions populating Cairo by the fifteenth century, see C. Petry, 'Scholastic Stasis in Medieval Islam Reconsidered: Mamluk Patronage in Cairo', *Poetics Today* 14:2 (1993), 323–48, 324; for the bibliomania of the medieval Islamic episteme, see E. Muhanna, *The World in a Book: Al-Nuwayri and the Islamic Encyclopedic Tradition* (New Jersey, 2017), 56; A. Ghersetti, Editor's introduction to 'The Book in Fact and Fiction in Pre-Modern Arabic Literature', A. Ghersetti and A. Metcalfe (eds), *JAIS* 12 (2012), 1–15, 13; M. Melvin-Koushki, 'Of Islamic Grammatology: Ibn Turka's Lettrist Metaphysics of Light', *al-'Usur al-Wusta* 24 (2016), 42–113, 46; cf. K. Hirschler, *Medieval Damascus: Plurality and Diversity in an Arabic Library* (Edinburgh, 2016), 3; N. Rabbat, 'Who Was al-Maqrizi? A Biographical Sketch', *MSR* 7:2 (2003), 1–19, 3.

2 F. Bauden, 'Taqī al-Dīn Aḥmad Ibn 'Alī al-Maqrīzī', in A. Mallett (ed.), *Medieval Muslim Historians and the Franks in the Levant* (Leiden and Boston, 2014), 161–200, 167–8; R. Irwin, *Ibn Khaldun. An Intellectual Biography* (New Jersey, 2018), 162–203; Rabbat, 'Who Was al-Maqrizi?', 11.

3 The chronicle's original title is *al-Ṭarīq al-wāḍiḥ al-maslūk ilā tarājim al-khulafā' wa 'l-mulūk*, which I do not use in this study in the interests of clarity, as the book is more widely known in most medieval and all secondary sources as *Ta'rīkh al-duwal wa 'l-mulūk*; cf. the description of the codices in Chapter 2. For not-yet stabilized book titles and variations in book titles, see Hirschler, *Medieval Damascus*, 135–7.

4 A verb with non-Arab roots, it refers primarily to the act of dating. Its original meaning has 'little to do with narrative': F. de Blois et al., *Ta'rīkh*, in *EI*²; S. Mejcher-Atassi and J. P. Schwartz, eds, *Archives, Museums and Collecting Practices in the Modern Arab World* (London, 2016), 33, n. 2; J. Harber, *Medieval Creation Commentary as Literary Interpretation* (Wisconsin, Madison, 1979), 254. Cf. L. Guo, 'History Writing', in R. Irwin (ed.), *The New Cambridge History of Islam* (Cambridge, 2010), 444–57; 444: '*ta'rīkh* conveys a sense of dating, whereas *khabar*, meaning "story, anecdote", bears no notion of fixation of time at all. Earlier historical reports were known as *akhbār*, whereas *ta'rīkh* came later to acquire a wider definition of "history" and "historical interpretation".'

5 Ibn Khaldūn, *The Muqaddimah: An Introduction to History*, trans. F. Rosenthal (New Jersey, 1967), 58.

6 *Selections from Subh al-A'shā by al-Qalqashandi, Clerk of the Mamluk Court: Egypt: "Seats of Government" and "Regulations of the Kingdom", From Early Islam to the Mamluks*, Tarek Galal Abdelhamid and Heba El-Toudy (eds) (London, 2017), 4.

7 T. el-Leithy, 'Living Documents, Dying Archives: Towards a Historical Anthropology of Medieval Arabic Archives', *al-Qanṭara: Revista de Estudios Arabes* 32:2 (2011), 389–434; 411–12.

8 J. Paul, 'Archival Practices in the Muslim World Prior to 1500', in A. Bausi et al. (eds), *Manuscripts and Archives: Comparative Views on Record-Keeping* (Berlin, 2018), 339–60; 350, n. 48.

9 T. Khalidi, *Arabic Historical Thought in the Classical Period* (Cambridge, 1994), 17–82.

10 T. Bauer, 'Mamluk Literature as a Means of Communication', in S. Conermann (ed.), *Ubi sumus? Quo vademus?: Mamluk Studies-State of the Art* (Göttingen, 2013), 23–56, 22–6; cf. S. Leder, *Story-Telling in the Framework of Non-Fictional Arabic Literature* (Wiesbaden, 1998), 34–60; J. S. Meisami, 'History as Literature', *Iranian Studies* 33:1/2 (2000), 15–30; K. Hirschler, *Medieval Arabic Historiography: Authors as Actors* (London and New York, 2006), 4–6; M. Hanaoka, *Authority and Identity in Medieval Islamic Historiography: Persian Histories from the Peripheries* (Cambridge, 2016), 1–3.

11 M. Friedrich, 'Epilogue: Archives and Archiving across Cultures – Towards a Matrix of Analysis', in Bausi, *Manuscripts and Archives*, 436, also citing F. Bauden.

12 K. Hirschler, 'From Archive to Archival Practices: Rethinking the Preservation of Mamluk Administrative Documents', *JAOS* 136:1 (2016), 1–28, 2.

13 P. Sartori, 'Seeing Like Khanate: On Archives, Cultures of Documentation, and Nineteenth-Century Khvarazm', *Journal of Persianate Studies* 9 (2016), 228–57; 235–8.

14 Ibid., 2–3.

15 U. Haarmann, 'Mamluk Studies: A Western Perspective', *Arab Journal for the Humanities* 13:51 (1995), 329–47; 331; see also idem, 'Mamluk Endowment Deeds as a Source for the History of Education in Late Medieval Egypt', *al-Abhath* 28 (1980), 31–47.

16 Petry, 'Scholastic Stasis', 330–1.

17 For the critical space offered by chronicles, see, for example, R. S. Humphreys, *Islamic History: A Framework for Inquiry* (New Jersey, 1991), ch. 5A, 136–47; Petry,

'Scholastic Stasis', *passim*; cf. Hirschler, *Medieval Arabic Historiography*, chapters three and six.

18 Sartori, 'Seeing Like Khanate'; Friedrich, 'Epilogue: Archives and Archiving'; F. de Vivo and M. P. Donato, eds, 'Scholarly Practices in the Archive (16th-18th centuries)', special issue of *Storia della Storiografia* 68 (2015); incl. joint Introduction, 15–20; Hirschler, 'From Archive to Archival Practices', 1–28; idem, 'Document Reuse in Medieval Arabic Manuscripts', *Comparative Oriental Manuscript Studies Bulletin* 3:1 (2017), 33–44; 'S. McSheffrey, 'Detective Fiction in the Archives: Court Records and the Uses of Law in Late Medieval England', *History Workshop Journal* 65:1 (2008), 65–78; el-Leithy, 'Living Documents, Dying Archives', 389–434.

19 Petry, 'Scholastic Stasis', 331–2.

20 Note the useful albeit brief discussion of sources in J. Van Steenburgen, *Order Out of Chaos: Patronage, Conflict and Mamluk Socio-Political Culture, 1341–1382* (Leiden, 2006), 8–14.

21 L. Guo, 'Mamluk Historiographic Studies: The State of the Art', *MSR* I (1997), 15–43, 38; K. Hirschler, 'Islam: The Arabic and Persian Traditions, Eleventh-Fifteenth Centuries', Ch. 13 of *The Oxford History of Historical Writing, Vol. 2: 400–1400*, ed. Sarah Foot and Chase F. Robinson (Oxford, 2012), 274.

22 On the potency of the 'micro-historical lens' for the study of archives, manuscripts and their histories, see Friedrich, 'Epilogue: Archives and Archiving', 430.

23 D. P. Little, *An Introduction to Mamluk Historiography: An Analysis of Arabic Annalistic and Biographical Sources for the Reign of Al-Malik-An-Nāṣir Muḥammad Ibn Qalā'ūn* (Stuttgart, 1970), 2–3.

24 L. Behzadi, 'Introduction: The Concept of Polyphony and the Author's Voice', in L. Behzadi and J. Hämeen-Anttila (eds), *Concepts of Authorship in Pre-Modern Arabic Texts* (Bamberg, 2016), 16.

25 M. Brett, *The Rise of the Fatimids: The World of the Mediterranean and the Middle East in the Fourth Century of the Hijra, Tenth Century CE* (Leiden, 2001), 8–9; Ibn Taghrībirdī's *al-Nujūm* is also one of a few later works that juxtapose conflicting accounts to weigh up their veracity.

26 For example, his excellent compilation of Ibn Ṭuwayr's (d. 1220) reports (1992) and also his edition of quotations from Ibn al-Ma'mūn al-Baṭāiḥī's chronicle as found in Ibn Muyassar's work, via al-Maqrīzī:

Passages de la Chronologie d'Egypte d'lbn al-Ma'mūn, Prince Jamāl al-Dīn Abū 'Alī Mūsā b. al-Ma'mūn al-Baṭā'iḥī, Textes arabes et etudes islamiques, vol. 21, ed. A. F. Sayyid (Cairo, 1983).

27 M. Bonner, review of M. Brett's *The Rise of the Fatimids*, *JAH* 44 (2003), 145–94, 147.

28 See Irene Bierman, *Writing Signs: The Fatimid Public Text* (Berkeley, California, 1998).

29 P. E. Walker, *Exploring an Islamic Empire: Fatimid History and Its Sources* (London, 2002), 94, discusses the limitations of the study of extant Fatimid objects as a means to discovering the political history of the dynasty.

30 M. Brett, 'The Way of the Nomad', *BSOAS* 58:2 (1995), 251–69, 255.

31 Al-Maqrīzī, *al-Mawā'iẓ wa 'l-i'tibār fī dhikr al-khiṭaṭ wa 'l-āthār* (also known as the *Khiṭaṭ*), partial edition in 4 vols by G. Wiet (Cairo, 1906, 1911), 3:346.

32 Haarmann, 'Mamluk Studies', 329–47, 345.

33 'A diplomatic edition is a typographical transcription of a manuscript, usually of a single surviving witness (unicum)': A. Gacek, *Arabic Manuscripts: A Vademecum for Readers* (Leiden, 2009), 93.

34 Friedrich, 'Epilogue: Archives and Archiving', 430.

1

The Archival Function of Historiography

Although no-one would disagree that the amount of Arabic historical writing reached an unprecedented level during the fourteenth and fifteenth centuries, ... we must admit that the state of our current knowledge of these developments, particularly the textual ones, is far from being exhaustive.
L. Guo, 'Mamluk Historiographic Studies: the State of the Art' (1997), 33

The archive is the repository of memories: individual and collective, official and unofficial, licit and illicit, legitimating and subversive.
H. Bradley, 'The seductions of the archive: voices lost and found' (1992), 2

Fatimid history refracted through a Mamluk lens

Towards the turn of the fifteenth century, the hadith scholar and notary witness based at al-Muʿizziyya *madrasa* in Mamluk Cairo-Fustat, Ibn al-Furāt, lifted his pen from a multi-volume chronicle of the Islamic world.[1] This was, by all accounts, not a voluntary cessation of work but an unwelcome disruption arising from the declining health of the author, who left his great chronicle unfinished.[2] Yet the magnitude of his achievement, if not obvious to those immediately around him, became clear over the course of time, as his book, a remarkably resourceful anthology of both extant and now lost historiographical resources, was a critical and – ultimately – highly influential link in the 'chain of text witnesses' attesting the history of recent as well as long-elapsed Arab world history. While a more detailed discussion of this author's life, as can be gleaned from the few sources that mention him, and the fortunes of his text, appears in the chapter that follows, it is worth noting at this juncture Ibn al-Furāt's special propensity for bringing together texts written by authors from a range of professional and confessional backgrounds in order to re-imagine, with the help of these documents and literary specimens, the history of bygone eras such as that of the Fatimids (909–1171). While a positivist reconstruction of Fatimid history is not pursued per se in the present study, in a context of patchy textual survival, a few observations about the epistemic backstory of textual risk, loss, recovery and rejuvenation through which Fatimid historiography came to be documented and preserved by post-Fatimid historians offers a useful point of departure.

Through a socially, culturally and administratively productive 200-year rule over Egypt and North Africa, the Fatimids were primary agents of the rapid metamorphosis of those regions from a politically unstable province of the rival ʿAbbasids into the architecturally and institutionally magnificent seat of their own empire. Despite the scale and sheer virtuosity of these achievements, however, the ruling family and its political elite left behind few enduring self-generated historiographical records in the forms of courtly chronicles or biographical works as a projection of their imperium, in the manner favoured by earlier Abbasid caliphs and later Ayyubid sultans. Between 957 when Qāḍī al-Nuʿmān (d. 974) wrote the *Iftitāḥ al-daʿwa wa ibtidāʾ al-dawla*, an account of the Fatimids' route to political power in North Africa, and the fifteenth century, during the course of which the Yemeni chief missionary (*dāʿī al-duʿāt*) Idrīs ʿImād al-Dīn (d. 1468) wrote his historical–theological digest *ʿUyūn al-akhbār*, of which three volumes deal with Fatimid history, there is no *comprehensive* official Ismaʿili history of the caliphate that we know of either as an extant work or as a source for later historians, though some fragments of earlier works remain.[3] The contrasting genealogies and histories of Fatimid Ismaʿilism and Twelver Shiʿism were well understood by al-Maqrīzī in fifteenth-century Cairo, who registers confessional developments over the course of his *oeuvre*.[4] Yet the late tenth-century Baghdad bookseller and bibliographer Ibn al-Nadīm seems unaware of any genre of Ismaʿili thought, which suggests that Qāḍī al-Nuʿmān was responsible for originating the Ismaʿili written corpus, rationalizing its nascent historical and theological narratives and creating a stable, recognizable Ismaʿili identity for the Fatimids.[5]

Fatimid history is thus largely promulgated by Ayyubid and Mamluk chroniclers such as Ibn Abī Ṭayy (d. 1233), Abū Shāma (d. 1268), Ibn al-Furāt (d. 1405), al-Maqrīzī (d. 1442) and Ibn Taghribirdi (d. 1470), to name several who preserve its original sources. These historians took up the task of representing and in some cases commemorating the Fatimid dynasty and its accomplishments – not least the creation of a North African Islamic metropolis and intellectual hub at Cairo – for their present and future reading and listening publics. This historiographical agency was developed and sustained notwithstanding the fact that Sunni and Twelver Shiʿi authors might be expected to regard the Ismaiʿili Fatimids as the proponents of a theological heresy, and as an expansionist imperial power that had threatened Sunni and, to a lesser extent, Twelver hegemony in their heartlands of Syria, Iraq, Hijaz and much of the Arab world.[6] It is in this interconfessional historiographic context that Ibn al-Furāt produced his autographs of *Taʾrīkh al-duwal wa ʾl-mulūk*. He cites his sources verbatim, allowing earlier textual witnesses to late Fatimid history, among other bodies of sources, to survive intact in the amber of his newer chronicle.

It is in such acts of preservation and onward transmission of sources that we see most clearly the role of Arabic historiographical works as archives: as multi-layered collections of literary reports that clarify and resolve, for contemporary readers with modern modes of inquiry, two critical areas of investigation. These are firstly the scope of medieval Arab historians' knowledge of their past, and secondly the criteria by which sources were selected, extracted, analysed and ordered into meaningful commentary in historiographical compendia, through an archival mindset and set of practices. As yet, Arabic historical works have not been construed as archives except in as much as they preserve documentary material.[7] Yet the value of these texts as intrinsically archival is substantiated through closer analysis of their synthetic composition:[8] alongside valuable documentation of the past, Mamluk historical works reveal vital clues about the epistemic values of their 'present'. Put another way, medieval Arabic chronicles embed intersecting temporal frames. They represent the past to a contemporary audience with a view to safeguarding historical memory for posterity, by carrying discrete areas of connotation: as 'records' (present use) and as 'commemorations' (future use) in pursuit of the 'eternalizing' of historical memory.[9]

Documenting the past as archival exigency

Of the many genres of writing developed by the savants of the medieval Arab-Islamic world of books, historiography – chronicles, biographical dictionaries, historical reports in a range of multidisciplinary works – came to be a prestigious activity. If not as deeply sanctioned within epistemic culture as religio-legal genres such as hadith commentaries or law treatises, the sheer volume and variety of historiographical works produced during the Ayyubid and Mamluk periods is testament to the intellectual value and social merit that generations of scholars, tasked with 'remembering' their past in order to secure their future,[10] attached to the production of detailed historical records.[11] Historiography was not a formal curriculum subject, with the exception of Prophetic biography, but it attracted substantial intellectual endeavour both within and outside the formal setting of teaching institutions: Mamluk recruits copied out historical treatises during their academic training, while established scholars, notably Ibn Khaldūn and al-Maqrīzī, lectured in Cairo on historiographical methods and features (e.g. timekeeping or *mīqāt*) or on specific texts (e.g. the *Muqaddima*), just as Abū Shāma and Ibn Wāṣil taught their respective historical books to students in Damascus, Hama and Cairo.[12] To put this in a longer perspective, more historiographical, biographical, administrative and geographical treatises were 'written in Cairo in the first half of the fifteenth century than in any other half-century period until the onset of modernity in the late nineteenth century'.[13] The appeal – and ubiquity – of historiography, especially in the fourteenth and fifteenth centuries, the heyday of the knowledge industry in the medieval Arabic-reading world, is further evidenced in the broad scope and savoir faire of many works inscribing history in a variety of rubrics, whether scholarly, popular or both.[14] From Ibn al-Ṣayrafī's (d. 1147) detailed monograph on administrative practice, informing al-Qalqashandī's (d. 1418) colossal clerical and epistolary handbook more than two centuries later – both of which present and elaborate historical events – to the court-centred yet sporadically dynasty-critical narratives of Ibn Ṭuwayr (d. 1220) and al-Maqrīzī (d. 1442) after him, to the vast corpus of general and specific biographical dictionaries surveyed by Auchterlonie and al-Qāḍī: historiographical composition reaching dizzying levels of magnitude and depth in the medieval Islamic episteme.[15] The products of this endeavour drew heavily on earlier literary models and prototypes, of which numerous extant manuscripts remain unedited and effectively out of the reach of potential readers, so that much empirical text-mapping work remains to be done.[16]

The Arabophone historians who contributed to this efflorescence of history-writing often employed a conventional prism, a largely though not wholly elitist view of historical developments and social agency,[17] which permeated chronicles, biographical dictionaries and works with an ostensible orientation towards administration, geography, prosopography and so on. At the heart of these books, which were invariably intertextual – where a 'whole web of texts is constantly and consciously paradigmatically and syntagmatically evoked, co-thought, quoted and reworked and re-interpreted with every phrase and sentence' – lay a noticeable quality of consistency in setting out (or taking for granted) the wider trajectories of Islamic history in universalistic mode, namely a Creation-to-the-present teleological framework, though the detail could vary enormously.[18] This metanarrative remained a stable backdrop within chronicles, despite massive political and social disruptions in the extra-textual world, whether due to dynastic change from Fatimid to Ayyubid or from Ayyubid to Mamluk rule, or intra-dynastic political upheavals that characterized all these eras, or the socially turbulent interplay between elite power politics and popular protests, all of which are documented, inscribed and often agonized or fought over in key chronicles and biographical works.[19] Research into the medieval Arabic past in both its social and epistemological aspects is richly facilitated by a virtually overwhelming wealth of historiographical texts that expound both the broad contours and atomistic detail of medieval Islamic history.

All of this acknowledged and appreciated, it is equally obvious that the deep obsession of Mamluk authors and their contemporary audiences with the pre-Mamluk past, evinced in various socio-cultural spheres including the ateliers of historians and the courts of sultans, has not been adequately excavated in modern scholarship. A primary direction of enquiry in recent decades has been, with some justification, the use of detailed diary-like Mamluk works for the examination of a positivist Mamluk history, usually contemporary and local, to the detriment of studying of Mamluk universal chronicles as repositories of key sources from pre-Mamluk eras.[20] Within this fertile epistemic context, Ibn al-Furāt's chronicle, with its broad inventory of named sources for past and contemporary eras, selections from which are presented in a diplomatic edition here for the first time, both demands and facilitates a shift in recent hypotheses about what Middle Period Arabic historiography intended to accomplish both in its own immediate contexts and for future generations of readers. *Ta'rīkh al-duwal wa 'l-mulūk*, viewed alongside other historical texts favouring similar rubrics, embodies the concept of historiography as archive: a chronicle sharply focused on socio-political history, yet also on the mechanics of history-writing and of knowledge creation. It also opens a productive pathway for the application of the archive framework to premodern Islamic historiography.

Knowing through archives

The archive as a concept has in recent years acquired the status of a privileged nexus of political, institutional, confessional and legal history, and a linchpin of the social orientation of individuals and communities. Crucially, the archival approach has allowed us to understand and analyse premodern societies in their own terms, and the formation and performance of 'identity' and 'community' in those spheres.[21] In post-Said criticism, the transfer and application of a largely European intellectual model to an Islamic past and its sources is not without the risk of Eurocentrism. At the same time, Friedrich has convincingly argued that in taking cross-cultural and premodern archivalities into consideration, we must note the fact that 'the history of archiving should be seen as crucial dimension of the history of writing', including the writing of history, and that archival practices were deeply embedded within the cultural production of many diverse societies interested in collecting and preserving their documents and manuscripts.[22] Indeed, in view of isomorphic tendencies in premodern knowledge-making practices in the European and Islamic worlds, el-Leithy, van Berkel, Hirschler and others have argued convincingly that archivistics, applied critically, reveal cultural self-fashioning in medieval Muslim social and intellectual life, restoring agency to the progenitors of archives. In the present context, 'knowing through archives'[23] offers a hermeneutic framework that promises to do justice to both *knowledge-accumulating tendencies* of medieval Muslim intellectuals – exemplified by their vast library holdings, their expansive higher education systems and their profuse literary outputs[24] – and also to less-examined *knowledge-sifting tendencies* within that same scholarship, in which the mass of material from earlier works, an overcrowded field by any reckoning, would be selected, trimmed, ordered, condensed and synthesized within new works.[25]

In this context Derrida's influential and transformative exposition of the archive as neither neutral nor objective, as significant for what is left out of it as for what is placed in it, and his invitation to examine the role of the archive in shaping – not merely recording – history, is powerful and relevant.[26] Mamluk historians would typically tread a precarious balance between relying on earlier sources and producing new interpretations. Through mapping an author's relationship with sources within a 'refractory archival landscape',[27] we can give shape to the processes underpinning the production of individual compendia of medieval Islamic history, and gain clearer insights into how the documentation and rearrangement of knowledge were planned and committed to paper.

The tracing of archival practices in the methodologies of medieval Arabic historical composition begs an immediate question of whether the resulting texts should be seen as archives of knowledge by design or by default. In other words, how conscious is the drive to produce a commemorative record, a repository of texts with future value and utility? To address this issue, scrutiny of the ordering of knowledge in other premodern settings, for example late antique historiography, can offer useful analogues. In an imperial context not wholly dissimilar to Ibn al-Furāt's Mamluk environment, König and Whitmarsh's breakdown of the steps involved in creating the 'discursive form' of knowledge in imperial conditions (whether the brokers of such knowledge support, subvert or even bypass the political project) is instructive: 'the typical modes of operation of the archive' rely upon the 'itemisation, analysis, ordering, hierarchization, synthesis, synopsis' of available texts.[28] Ibn al-Furāt crafts an archive of historical knowledge that employs this very range of techniques.

In the chapters that follow, I demonstrate that Ibn al-Furāt's chronicle, which is highly intelligible in its methodology, elucidates three epistemic facets of historiography, that is, concern for both knowledge and its modes of production and transmission. These aspects can be identified as firstly *textual*: reconstructions of history demonstrating knowledge creation in a primary sense, namely, a detailed record of the political vicissitudes of late Fatimid era, including the imam-army dialectic that both prolonged and undermined the late Fatimid imamate and imperium; secondly, *contextual*: indications of what a historian regarded as valuable and/or reliable knowledge according to the ideas or frameworks that had purchase at the time of writing, revealed by what is selected for or discarded from the narrative;[29] and thirdly, *metatextual*: self-reflexive glosses, often expressed subtly or implicitly within chronicles, on the works being consulted and evaluated.[30] These latter indications of deeper agenda within historiography, for instance the precept of *historia magistra vitae*, exemplify the self-conscious impulse to create a system of historical knowledge generating both positive and normative cultural meaning in contemporary society and for future generations. The study of Fatimid history was both worthwhile and pressing for a variety of reasons, including the dynasty's pivotal role in developing Egypt and their eventual eclipse by a series of aggressively ambitious military viziers, and the texts preserving their memory were deserving of archival conservation for the long term. Ibn al-Furāt's chronicle orchestrates, consciously or not, a range of archival signs and strategies – explored in detail in two subsequent chapters on the archive and its archivalia – that offer detailed demonstration of the doubly reflexive aspects of the chronicle as an archive.

The risk of conceptual overreach in using the archive framework to analyse history, historiography and epistemic values may be noted, yet the explanatory and commemorative features of medieval Arabic historical discourse, alongside its quality of double reflexivity, underpin the indispensable nature of taking the 'chronicle as archive' method to its analytical conclusion, by applying it consistently to the full range of levels at which historiographical texts speak to their readers. In this approach, the twin aspects of 'information-gathering' and 'archive-building' revealed by the typical medieval Arabic chronicle generate helpful synergy rather than tension. To adduce a brief example: in Ibn al-Furāt's discussion of the birth and survival of the putative Fatimid heir al-Ṭayyib (b. 524/1130), which instantiates the recording of this crisis in both its historical and historiographical implications, the archival reading model allows us access to a range of beneficial insights into contested historical events, historiographical controversy and confessional agendas, as well as offering helpful disclosures regarding the logistics of inclusion or exclusion of reports and the intellectual horizons and/or orientation of each text utilized in this section of Ibn al-Furāt's chronicle. This is over and above another valuable feature of Ibn al-Furāt's book: that it transmits and preserves accounts from works thereafter lost, which themselves constitute a historiographical archive in the sense of Chase Robinson's reference to Ibn al-Dawādārī's (d. c. 1335) chronicle as an 'archive' of lost sources.[31] The epistemic archive constructed by the collecting of books containing narratives and documents, followed by the gathering, selecting, itemizing, ordering and synthesizing of source materials, extends the life cycles of those materials, and populates an accessible repository for readers who can then dispense with consulting multiple volumes in order to gain an understanding of both the events and sources of history.

Reversing traditional ways

In 1980, in her book-length study of the *ta'rīkh* of Bayḥaqī, Marilyn Waldman called for 'a reversal of the traditional ways in which historical narratives have been used – not to demote them … to the role of confirming what hard evidence suggests, but rather to elevate them to the role of providing crucial evidence for a unique dimension of the history of language, culture, ideas, and communication'.[32] Her cri de cœur was entirely understandable and captures a set of axioms alluded to earlier: for too many years up to then and even since, Arabic historical texts have been utilized for a broad range of scholarly enquiry (political, institutional, cultural, confessional, intellectual, social, economic and local histories) – but rarely beyond a static hermeneutic paradigm: chronicles put to use, cautiously (in view of the alignments of their authors), to understand a 'factual' political and social history of the largely elite, largely urban developments within medieval Islam. However, that each of these texts, looked at through a synchronic rather than diachronic lens, also captures, wittingly or not, an epistemic stage in the intellectual culture of medieval Islamic cities and regions has been overlooked.

Waldman's call has borne some fruit in the thirty-five years since, as several new, progressive approaches to the historiography of Islam, especially medieval works of chronographic and prosopographic natures, have emerged in recent years. Tamer el-Leithy proposed, in a 2011 article, 'An outline for a research agenda of medieval Arabic archives, a historical inquiry in which we step beyond the evidence of today's physically intact and extant archives to a deeper forensic examination of the lives of documents and archives. … Such a project requires archivists to delve into narrative and biographical sources.'[33] Stephan Conermann, Konrad Hirschler and Syrinx Von Hees have discussed the use of *rijāl* and other works to found a new approach termed *historical anthropology*,[34] one key idea being that biographical dictionaries, which reach deeply into various strata of society,[35] function as biographical archives. Moreover, when authors of some major chronicles, such as Ibn al-Furāt, Ibn Taghribirdi and al-Maqrizi (in the *Sulūk*), write about recent or contemporary history, the last in diary-like fashion, historiography performs much less prescriptively than descriptively in as much as weaknesses, corruption and disasters at the individual, communal and institutional levels are represented in their unromantic and unsettling reality.[36] In this sense, historical narratives resist glossing over controversy, nor do they subsume honest scrutiny of socially subversive events to a normative framework: they clearly lend themselves to the notion of providing a 'data set' for the eras they represent, albeit information necessarily inflected with the intellectual and methodological predilections of each particular historian. In the case of Ibn al-Furāt's chronicle, his positivist 'data' archives include unique sources mobilized to create a nuanced, multifaceted reading of the succession crises beleaguering the Fatimids in the twelfth century.

Ibn al-Furāt's chronicle is peculiarly suited to an archival reading because, as we now know, holographs – original authorial versions of text in which methodological clues are not yet erased in acts of further copying or redacting – offer unique insights into textual strategies and interpretive pre-commitments.[37] This model of a near-complete text, with spaces left for additions to 'events' and/or obituary sections, differs markedly from the less ordered rough jottings and epitomes to be found, for example, in Maqrīzī's notebooks as discussed by Bauden, which are at a much earlier stage of the archival process. Far from being in their final form, they are thus much less open to analysis *qua* spatial archives,[38] but could bear fruitful examination in respect of their archival strategies when juxtaposed with completed works within al-Maqrīzī's extraordinarily wide-ranging oeuvre.[39] In offering a narrative that documents its own components and reflects on itself as a work of history, Ibn al-Furāt's book raises the prospect that the chronicle as an archive, replete with information and evidence of historiographic practice, performs both as a narrative and, as its less well-understood double, a documentary archive.

Document–narrative bifurcations and symbiosis

As several scholars have observed in a variety of critical contexts, for the premodern Near East, vast extant narrative source holdings were until recently, and partly erroneously, regarded as not at all matched by substantial documentary holdings as a spatial category of texts held in archives.[40] This acknowledged, clear boundaries between documents and narratives are obfuscated by the widespread appearance of documentary material in narrative works, for instance Ibn al-Furāt's reproduction of the marriage contract between the caliph al-Mustaʿlī (r. 1094–1101) and a daughter of al-Afḍal (d. 1121) as drawn from the work of late Fatimid and early Ayyubid administrator and historian Ibn Ṭuwayr (d. 1220).[41] To probe narrative-documentary interconnections further, Bauden's influential 2005 article on the state of Mamluk-era documentary studies is an illuminating starting point. Bauden defines documents as the 'authentic traces of tools necessary for the needs of daily life', and explicates in his first twelve pages several facets of both the structural and semiotic separateness and yet connectedness of various types of narratives and documents.[42]

Among Bauden's points of exposition is the foundational assumption that documents are regarded as 'impartial', which, we may note, contrasts strongly with recent understanding of the subjective nature of archives and documents.[43] He also weighs the potential for falsification in the copying of literary sources versus that of documents, and considers the widespread appearance of documents within chronicles, in which context Ibn al-Furāt is noted as a prolific exhibitor of documentary specimens in his book of history. Further, this article takes stock of the 'external' corroboration of documents within chronicles, the anthologies of documentary specimens collected and presented in clerical works, literary administrative texts as offering confirmation of real diplomatic practice, documentary scholarship as reliant upon contextual elucidation offered in literary and narrative works and the use of legal records in the narration of historical events. In sum, it becomes clear that documents and narratives are either complementary or can be fused within the same text. In a further revealing physical manifestation of the symbiosis of the two text types, it is evident, again from Bauden's major case study on al-Maqrizi's notebooks, that paper used for documents in medieval Arab societies could be redeployed for use in narrative works including historiography, a phenomenon also noted from earlier eras of Islamicate history,

Abbasid and Fatimid.[44] A recent edited volume on the use of legal documents as sources explicating the social history of Muslim societies draws out the mirrored relevance of documents and narratives in a variety of historical contexts ranging from early Islamic history to the contemporary era.[45] Anterior to the question of intertextuality, addressed in detail in further chapters, is the issue of the reciprocity of insights yielded by the two genres of texts.

Key conceptual and methodological questions still come to the fore in the conflation of narratives and documents within a single hermeneutic model. How, precisely, are narrative 'knowledge archives' distinct from documentary – administrative, legal, familial, institutional or confessional – archives? What are the justifications for treating historiographical works as archives, as quasi-documentary sources, when their contents, being 'witting' history, are contingent and plainly contradictory at times? What are the risks in blurring hitherto fixed boundaries between documentary and narrative material?

Both Arabic chronicles and biographical dictionaries frequently reveal that a taxonomy of rigid separation can be misapplied. As Robinson argues, 'An archival ethos – the desire to record and preserve copies of important documents – underpins a great deal of historical writing.'[46] At the same time, medieval Islamic documentary corpora are subject to shaping, selection and tendentious methodologies, as these are often performative archives designed to establish and maintain hierarchical relations between communities and institutions or authorities.[47] Salaymeh argued recently that those 'who maintain archives of documentary sources and those who compose documentary sources' are 'ideologically invested', and this 'subjectivity does not negate historical reliability'.[48] The strict disseverance of historiographical and documentary material is further subverted when we consider a point mentioned earlier, that a sizeable (as yet unquantified) subset of documentary material is extant *solely* within chronicles, as well as in legal literature and administrative manuals. So, is there any purchase left in the view that documentary specimens offer less partisan records than narrative material? Where documents are not available, chronicles have been shown in several recent works of scholarship as texts to be taken seriously for documenting historical developments.[49]

At the same time, narrative and documentary sources do not and could not always tell the same story, given the quite different ranges of social function of each category, and the study of these genres has therefore naturally bifurcated. Indeed the 'documentary turn' in studies of the medieval and early modern Islamicate continues to generate extremely well-justified scholarly interest in known and new documentary corpora, for example in the scattered and/or fragmentary texts recovered through scrutiny of document reuse in medieval Damascus, and in private archives in Ottoman Egypt, to name but two emerging valuable projects.[50] Further, a recent attempt was made, successfully, to bring together archaeological recoveries from Jordan with medieval narrative sources and documentary material in order to develop a rounded picture of Mamluk rule in Bilād al-Shām, in a methodological exercise relying on structural and functional differentiation between narrative and documentary sources. Yet while acknowledging the efficacy and significance of these kinds of approaches, it remains the case that the narrative-documentary relationship is a phenomenon of two halves:

on the one hand, documents and narratives are ontologically distinct categories of writing; on the other, within chronicles they are often structurally interfused, mutually contingent and assist in the interpretation of each within the other. In the present study of Ibn al-Furat's chronicle, I delve deeper into the simultaneously documentary and narratorial qualities of this work, which engenders a critique of the assumption that 'documents' constitute a self-explanatory category, having long been conflated with modern notions of 'legal documents' without any attempt to critically examine this categorization in heuristic terms, as decried by Sartori. Rather, narratives and documents share an essential characteristic, namely the desire to offer 'a coherent representation of an individual act [or acts] in the past'.[51]

Furthermore, and as reiterated earlier, narrative texts like Ibn al-Furāt's routinely assimilate documentary material. Where chronicles offer different versions of documents than originals that survive outside historiography, or where documents are offered in variant versions in later historical texts, these discrepancies are a matter of both historical and epistemic significance, as they reveal that some events were not recorded fully or carefully in historical sources, or did not command agreement, begging the question 'why not?' For example, in the historiographical dispute about the month of the year 413–414/1023 when the Fatimid regent Sitt al-Mulk died, Heinz Halm, relying solely on the encyclopaedist al-Nuwayrī (d. 1333), proffers a definitive date, while Marina Rustow, adducing evidence from a range of medieval witnesses including al-Musabbiḥī (d. 1030) and Yaḥyā al-Anṭākī (d. 1066), is justifiably more cautious.[52] In construing as archives the chronicles that discuss these details, we can move beyond the binaries of 'fixed' or 'not-fixed' to explain the discrepancy: the processes by which consensus formed or failed to form. Moving beyond Donald Little's valuable identification of similarities and differences between sources, the archival model establishes the epistemic choices of the historian and the subsequent shape of the tradition.[53] As epistemic archives, our sources thus have immeasurably more to offer than the outcomes of necessary empirical work in trying to settle a chronology of events and the reliability of sources.

The 'authenticity' debate in Arabic historiography

In embracing the archival approach to medieval Arabic chronicles, we are in some sense compelled to come to terms with key limitations and distortions engendered by an 'authenticity' debate in Arabic historiography which, though essential as a stage of epistemic and hermeneutical enquiry, has led to a restrained, at times morbidly conventional, field of investigation for these works. Problems of periodization persist, and criticisms levelled at formative period historiography leave their traces in the interpretation of much later works.[54] Meanwhile, source criticism too often remains the Holy Grail that forecloses other modes of enquiry.[55] Traces of this problem are evident in the way that Mamluk chronicles have been studied, in view of the difficulty of 'letting go' of the notion that historiography must be scoured and triangulated to secure 'objective facts'.[56] The ideological affiliations and resultant biases of Mamluk authors are not wholly underplayed in the secondary literature, especially of a positivist bent, and should not, arguably, be neglected in the process of analysis. Yet studying medieval chroniclers without reducing the value of their work to the limits of *their* affiliations is an increasingly well-recognized exigency of contemporary research.[57] A vastly more useful direction of enquiry is to look at these very alignments in a new, ethnographic light.

Medieval Arabic chronicles offer a plethora of materials permitting a historical ethnography of medieval Islamic societies, and not exclusively at the urban elite level.[58] In regarding annals, with their habitual incorporation of primary source documentation such as letters, reports and decrees, as archives, contemporary readers are well-positioned to recognize their multivalence, and can thus justifiably treat chronicles as primary witnesses for the epistemic concerns of their own eras, even if they are secondary sources for their pasts. Put another way, such texts build on both the reference culture (formative-era Islamic textual history) and the scribal culture (nascent intellectual shifts) of the Mamluk intellectual sphere, encompassing derivative *and* innovative forms of knowledge, and the interplay between the two. Ibn al-Furāt's chronicle, which documents the Islamic past by preserving formative 'reference culture' sources, and his present by engaging with post-formative 'scribal culture' sources, exemplifies this range of textual strategization. What he shows, in fact, is that Mamluk scribal culture in the realm of historiography is as creative as its 'reference culture' counterpart, as each historian innovated a particular combination of format, theme and writing style(s) within each new archival arrangement of history, a phenomenon best elaborated by Little in 1998. Chronicles with alternative formats, notably the seamless synthesis constructed via a process of 'diverse reading, note-taking and the preparation of summaries', exemplified by Ibn al-Athīr's *Kāmil* and the *Itti'āẓ* of al-Maqrīzī are also legible as archives of knowledge and knowledge-making practice, albeit ones that reveal less, overall, than their self-reflexive and compositionally disaggregated counterparts.[59] The archival aspects inhere in the collection of material that informs such works, even if that material is not signalled: the horizons or 'reach' of such a work can be deduced through comparison with cognate texts.

The post-Fatimid chronographers, including Ibn al-Furāt, were multidisciplinary in their approaches as storytellers, informants, polemicists/propagandists, critics of state and society and as expounders of a religious hermeneutics: they are self-evidently in pursuit of various political and at times confessional agendas, and their alignments, prejudices and manipulations are inscribed into their historiography. At the same time these alignments elucidate rather than obfuscate our understanding of their historiographical commentary. Medieval Arab historians typically claim *not* to be omniscient (despite the forensic detail they often provide, drawing on a multiplicity of sources), and their subjectivities are nuanced, varied and offer a particular epistemic register of change over time.[60]

The archival ethos in an encyclopaedic age

The embodiment of knowledge within the chronicles of fourteenth-century Egypt, when the ambit of works produced underwent noticeable expansion, relied on two essential processes.[61] The first of these is the procuring and assembling of a wide range of literary texts as a means to cultural self-understanding and thence self-representation, namely the *encyclopaedic age* concept developed by Khalidi and others and elucidated in depth in a recent study of al-Nuwayrī's (d. 1333) encyclopaedic anthology.[62] By itself, however, mapping the tendency of medieval Arab authors to collect diverse material for a 'great books' tradition of barely fathomable scope tells only part of the story.[63] To bring into focus how this material was ordered and brought to bear on the questions and exigencies of present-day experience requires scrutiny of the *archival ethos* characterizing the medieval Islamic episteme. This in turn throws a spotlight on the methods used to derive contemporary meaning from the reserves of accumulated knowledge.

To trace the roots of the phenomenon of archive building within Arabic historiography, we can usefully rewind to earlier Islamic epochs whence the 'archival mind' in early Islamic Egypt and the 'archival practices' of Abbasid Baghdad, examined by Petra Sijpestein and Maaike van Berkel respectively, are two excellent places to start.[64] These case studies illustrate the concern in premodern Islamic societies with creating records with practical, historiographic and commemorative significance.[65] For chronicle writing of the medieval period, the aforementioned discovery and discussion of Maqrīzī's notebooks by Bauden reveal the mechanics by which this especially resourceful and prolific author collected, selected and synthesized earlier historiographical (and prosopographic, topographic, theological, etc.) material.[66] Ibn al-Furāt's chronicle, predating Maqrīzī's works by only a few decades, typifies this archival proclivity by exposing its sifting of source material to leave in place the building blocks of his historiographic reconstruction.[67] This can be usefully characterized as a minimizing imperative that stands in contrast to – and simultaneously complements – the maximalist encyclopaedic tendency of medieval Arabic historiographical works.

This archival prism of analysis evidently benefits from the decoupling of archivistic enquiry from the notion of the archive as a necessarily fixed spatial entity. Hallaq, Chamberlain and Hirschler have each shown that scholarly practice in a variety of medieval Islamic settings is characterized by an archival mindset, and the resulting bodies of texts, whether documentary or narrative (chronicles, biographical dictionaries, legal case notes) are archival both functionally and with intentionality.[68] The archival practices that permeate modes of literary production in medieval Islamic cities were, moreover, a means to guard against narrative and documentary loss arising from natural and inexorable processes of attrition.[69] Hallaq explains the social and literary logic of legal document preservation in the form of the itinerant archive known as the *dīwān al-qāḍī*;[70] the same is true of chronicles, for which some material must be disregarded and systematically excluded in accordance with a historian's authorial and archival agendas, for other material to be successfully preserved and added to the historiographic archive, in a highly dynamic field of textual transmission and hermeneutical production. This *hierarchization*, one of the archival practices identified by König and Whitmarsh, which might also be termed prioritization, is conspicuous in the work of chronographers such as Ibn al-Furāt, who explicitly discuss the merits of some sources over others. Further, long-established features of Islamicate administrative practice and legal methodologies permeate the mechanics of chronicle writing: textual witness in historiography shares some of the form and function of legal witness, or at the least simulates it. *Isnād* as attribution of sources is a technical aspect of historiography firmly founded upon the disciplines of law and administration, but the journey of the typical chronicle from one redaction to another, or indeed from *musawwada* (draft: a complete copy not yet in the author's preferred final form)[71] to *mubayyaḍa* (fair copy) often results in the effacement of these technical features and methods. Ibn al-Furāt's text, in a clear and fortuitous contrast, makes them hyper-visible.

Notes

1 The Vienna series of the sole autograph manuscript of *Ta'rīkh al-duwal wa 'l-mulūk* (Cod. A. F. 117 et al.) is numbered volumes 1–9, which does not take into account earlier volumes in a separate autograph series on pre-Islamic and early Islamic history; cf. Chapter 2.

2 Ibn Ḥajar, *al-Durar al-kāmina*, ed. M. S. J. al-Ḥaqq in 5 vols (Cairo, 1966–7), 4:101.

3 Idrīs ʿImād al-Dīn, *ʿUyūn al-akhbār wa funūn al-āthār fī dhikr al-nabī al-muṣṭafā al-mukhtār wa waṣiyyuhu ʿAlī b. Abī Ṭālib qātil al-kuffār wa āluhumā al-a'imma al-aṭhār ʿalayhim ṣalawāt Allāh al-ʿazīz al-ghaffār*, vol. 7 edited with an English summary, introduction and notes by A. F. Sayyid as *The Fatimids and Their Successors in Yaman. The History of an Islamic Community* (London and New York, 2002). For a list of Ismaʿili personal memoirs, not histories proper, containing historical information, see Walker, *Exploring an Islamic Empire*, 193.

4 *Ittiʿāẓ*, 3:345–6.

5 D. J. Stewart, 'The Structure of the *Fihrist*: Ibn al-Nadīm as Historian of Islamic Legal and Theological Schools', *IJMES* 39 (2007), 369–87, 373; cf. Daftary, *The Isma'ilis*, 168–70. For al-Nuʿmān's approach to history, see J. E. Lindsay, 'Prophetic Parallels in Abu ʿAbd Allah al-Shiʿi's Mission among the Kutama Berbers', *IJMES* 24 (1992), 39–56.

6 Shainool Jiwa, 'Fatimid-Buyid Diplomacy during the Reign of al-ʿAzīz Billāh (365/975–386/996)', *JIS* 3:1 (1992), 57–71.

7 Note, for comparison, M. Friedrich's chapter on 'Sources: Archives in Historiography and Genealogy', in a pan-European perspective, in *The Birth of the Archive. A History of Knowledge*, trans. J. N. Dillon (Michigan, 2018), 166–200.

8 *Synthetic* here refers to its literal meaning of texts 'being placed together' rather than fused seamlessly.

9 Cf. Koselleck's formulation of multiple temporal frameworks governing the meaning of artefacts of history: R. Koselleck, 'Representation, Event, and Structure', in *Futures Past: On the Semantics of Historical Time* (2nd edition, Columbia, 2004), 105–14; Friedrich, 'Epilogue: Archives and Archiving', 436, n. 20.

10 El-Leithy, 390–1.

11 Though actual figures of works produced is elusive (see Hirschler, 'Islam: The Arabic and Persian Traditions', 281–2). D. P. Little's survey, 'Historiography of the Ayyubid and Mamluk epochs', in C. F. Petry (ed.), *The Cambridge History of Egypt*, vol. I (Cambridge, 1998), 412–44, reveals the striking breadth and diversity of this historiographical production, as a subset of the magisterial audit of premodern Islamic world historiography produced sixty years earlier by H. A. R. Gibb, 'Historiography', *Encyclopaedia of Islam*, First edition, Supplement (Leiden, 1938), 233–45.

12 R. Irwin, 'Mamluk History and Historians', in R. Allen and D. S. Richards (eds), *Arabic Literature in the Post-Classical Period* (Cambridge, 2006), 159–70, 159; W. J. Fischel, *Ibn Khaldūn in Egypt, His Public Functions and His Historical Research (1382–1406): A Study in Islamic Historiography* (Berkeley and Los Angeles, 1967), 28–9; Hirschler, *Medieval Arabic Historiography*, 12–13.
13 Rabbat, 'Who Was al-Maqrizi?, 1–19, 3.
14 Guo, 'Mamluk Historiographic Studies, 15–43; 33.
15 P. Auchterlonie, *Arabic Biographical Dictionaries: A Summary Guide and Bibliography* (Durham, 1987); W. al-Qāḍī, 'Biographical Dictionaries: Inner Structure and Cultural Significance', in G. N. Atiyeh (ed.), *The Book in the Islamic World. The Written Word and Communication in the Middle East* (New York, 1995), 93–122; 95.
16 Cf. Cl. Cahen, 'Editing Arabic Chronicles', *IS* (1962), 1–25; Guo, 'Mamluk Historiographic Studies'; M. Chamberlain, *Knowledge and Social Practice in Medieval Damascus 1190–1350* (Cambridge, 2002); K. Hirschler, '"Catching the Eel" – Documentary Evidence for Concepts of the Arabic Book in the Middle Period', *Journal of Arabic and Islamic Studies* 12 (2012), 224–34.
17 As J. König and T. Whitmarsh, *Ordering Knowledge in the Roman Empire* (Cambridge, 2007), 38, point out in the Roman epistemic context, the immanence of an imperial perspective in texts need not imply '"pro-imperial": the opposition between consolidation and challenging' social hierarchies is 'too crude', and Mamluk historians could be enormously varied and mobile in their political and religious alignments, as I demonstrate in detail in Chapters 5 and 6; cf. Petry, 'Scholastic Stasis', 331: 'While elites are the focus of most of a chronicler's exposition, the enumeration of the varied origins of those who clawed their way up to the highest echelons of authority or influence attests to a historian's keen awareness of the diversity to be found at even the highest rungs of society.'
18 J. Pfeiffer and M. Kropp, eds, *Theoretical Approaches to the Transmission and Edition of Oriental Manuscripts* (Würzburg, 2007), 10–11; C. F. Robinson, *Islamic Historiography* (Cambridge, 2003), 137, usefully delineates this teleological metahistory, often starting with Creation and ending in the author's own time.
19 A. Elbendary, 'The Historiography of Protest in Late Mamluk and Early Ottoman Egypt and Syria', *International Institute of Asian Studies Newsletter* 43:9 (2007), 9 and *Crowds and Sultans: Urban Protest in Late Medieval Egypt and Syria* (Cairo, 2016).
20 Walker, *Exploring an Islamic Empire*, delves into al-Maqrīzī's obsession with the Fatimids while Irwin, 'Mamluk History and Historians', 159–70, points up popular, scholarly and sultanic interest in Umayyad, Fatimid and other pre-Mamluk eras; Guo, 'Mamluk Historiographic Studies', delineates concerted moves to publish Mamluk studies of the Mamluk era.
21 De Vivo and Donato, 'Scholarly Practices in the Archive', 15.
22 Friedrich, 'Epilogue: Archives and Archiving', 421–5; idem, *Birth of the Archive*, Chapter 8: 'Sources: Archives in Historiography and Genealogy', 166–200.
23 R. C. Head, 'Preface: Historical Research on Archives and Knowledge Cultures: An Interdisciplinary Wave', *Archival Science* 10 (2010), 191–4; 193.
24 Hirschler, *Medieval Damascus*, 3, discusses the 2,000 books in the Ashrafiyya Library's catalogue, which dwarfed contemporaneous collections across Europe.
25 F. Rosenthal, '"Of Making Many Books There Is No End": The Classical Muslim View', in Atiyeh, *The Book in the Islamic World*, 33–55. For archives in modern Middle Eastern history, see O. El Shakry, 'History without Documents: The Vexed Archives of Decolonization in the Middle East', *The American Historical Review* 120:3 (2015), 920–34.

26 Cf. A. Mbembe, 'The Power of the Archive and Its Limits', in C. Hamilton et al. (eds), *Refiguring the Archive* (Dordrecht, 2002), 19–27.
27 Head, 'Preface', 193.
28 König and Whitmarsh, 38; cf. E. Muhanna, 'Why Was the Fourteenth Century a Century of Arabic Encyclopaedism?', Ch. 16 of *Encyclopaedism from Antiquity to the Renaissance*, ed. J. König and G. Woolf (Cambridge, 2013), 343–56.
29 M. Waldman, *Toward a Theory of Historical Narrative: A Case Study in Perso-Islamicate Historiography* (Columbus, Ohio, 1980), 6: Formal histories in the Islamicate 'whether contemporary with the periods they describe or not ... [are] pervaded by the views of the author and his age on writing history, on the meaning of history in general, and on the particular history that is the subject of the work', and 'an analysis of the structure and content of a work can add to an understanding of the values that lie behind it'.
30 This last term, used by Berque for the Koranic text but usually favoured by discourse analysts, captures perfectly the phenomenon of writing that reflects upon itself qua writing. J. Berque, 'The Koranic Text: From Revelation to Compilation', reprinted in *The Book in the Islamic World*, 24.
31 Robinson, *Islamic Historiography*, 167.
32 Waldman, *Toward a Theory*, 141.
33 El-Leithy, 'Living Documents', 431–2.
34 On 'anthropological history, history in anthropology, historical ethnography, and anthropology of history': M. Marshall, 'Engaging History: Historical Ethnography and Ethnology', *American Anthropologist* 96:4 (December 1994), 972–4; 972; in the Mamluk context: S. Von Hees, 'Mamlukology as Historical Anthropology. State of the Art and Future Perspectives', in Conermann, *Ubi sumus?*, 119–30; S. Conermann and T. Seidensticker, 'Some Remarks on Ibn Ṭawq's (d. 915/1509) Journal *al-Taʿlīq*', *Mamlūk Studies Review* 11:2 (2007), 121–36, 132–3; K. Hirschler, 'Studying Mamluk Historiography. From Source-Criticism to the Cultural Turn', in Conermann, *Ubi sumus?* 159–86; cf. el-Leithy's approach throughout his 'Living Documents'.
35 Hirschler, 'Studying Mamluk Historiography', 173.
36 S. G. Massoud, *The Chronicles and Annalistic Sources of the Early Mamluk Circassian Period* (Leiden, 2007).
37 W. al-Qāḍī, 'How Sacred Is the Text of an Arabic Medieval Manuscript?', in Pfeiffer and Kropp, *Theoretical Approaches*, 45, offers discussion of author drafts that were typically not 'the final form of the text'; cf. Hirschler, 'Studying Mamluk Historiography'.
38 A more detailed discussion of the status of Ibn al-Furāt's earliest volumes as 'drafts' or 'clean copies' follows in Chapter 2.
39 F. Bauden, 'Maqriziana I: Discovery of an Autograph Manuscript of al-Maqrīzī: Towards a Better Understanding of His Working Method Description: Section 1', *Mamlūk Studies Review* 7:2 (2003), 21–68, see especially 23. For two distinctive categories of writing, draft notebooks and 'manuscript-books', and their inherent fluidity, see Hirschler, '"Catching the Eel"...', 25.
40 *Pace* Little, 'The Use of Documents for the Study of Mamluk History', *MSR* 1 (1997), 1–13, 13, quoting Humphreys, *Islamic History*; cf. M. Rustow, 'A Petition to a Woman at the Fatimid Court (413–14 AH/1022–3 CE)', *BSOAS* 73:1 (2010), 1–27, and el-Leithy, 'Living Documents', who argue to the contrary.
41 *Taʾrīkh al-duwal*, I:164a, 28–31. A detailed elaboration of the differing heuristic potential of documents and narrative sources is offered in Little (1997), 8–13.
42 F. Bauden, 'Mamluk Era Documentary Studies: The State of the Art', *MSR* 10:1 (2005), 15–60.

43 McSheffrey, 'Detective Fiction', 67.

44 F. Bauden, 'Maqriziana I: Discovery of an Autograph Manuscript of al-Maqrīzī: Towards a Better Understanding of His Working Method Description: Section 1', *MSR* 7:2 (2003), 21–68; M. Rustow, 'Fatimid State, Documents, Serial Recyclers and the Cairo Geniza', Mellon Sawyer Seminar, University of Iowa (28 April 2017): https://www.youtube.com/watch?v=eM7FpQjGlvU (accessed September 2017); P. M. Sijpestein, 'The Archival Mind in Early Islamic Egypt: Two Arabic Papyri', in P. M. Sijpesteijn, L. Sundelin, S. Torallas Tovar and A. Zomeno (eds), *From al-Andalus to Khurasan: Documents from the Medieval Muslim World* (Leiden, 2006), 163–87; Hirschler, 'Document Reuse', 33–44.

45 M. van Berkel, L. Buskens and P. M. Sijpestein, eds, *Legal Documents as Sources for the History of Muslim Societies. Studies in Honour of Rudolph Peters* (Leiden, 2017).

46 Robinson, *Islamic Historiography*, 144.

47 Hirschler, 'Studying Mamluk Historiography', 176 and 'From Archive to Archival Practices', 6; el-Leithy, 'Living Documents'.

48 Salaymeh, *Beginnings*, 34.

49 For example, al-Musabbihi's chronicle and Geniza documents on Sitt al-Mulk's role as the receiver of petitions after al-Hakim's death; cf. Rustow, 'Petition', 1.

50 Hirschler, 'Document Reuse'; N. *Analysis of Arabic Annalistic*'s project on 'Private Archives in Ottoman and Contemporary Egypt': http://www.ifao.egnet.net/axes-2012/ecritures-langues-corpus/2012-archives-privees//#en (accessed October 2017).

51 P. Sartori, 'Seeing Like a Khanate: On Archives, Cultures of Documentation, and Nineteenth-Century Khvarazm', *Journal of Persianate Studies* 9 (2016), 228–57, 235–6.

52 H. Halm, 'Der Treuhander Gottes', *DI* 63 (1986), 11–72; Rustow, 'Petition', 1–27.

53 Exemplified in Little, *Introduction*.

54 *Pace* Hirschler, 'Islam: The Arabic and Persian Traditions', 277, Humphreys, 'Turning Points in Islamic Historical Practice', in Q. Edward Wang and Georg G. Iggers (eds), *Turning Points in Historiography: A Cross-Cultural Perspective*, (Woodbridge, 2002), 89–100, 94–6, and others, who argue that as historiographical tastes changed from the early to middle periods of Islamic history, so too has the nature of scholarship on these works. Nonetheless, new cultural and theory-driven approaches, underpinning a clear departure from vestiges of purely source-critical approaches of the past, are much needed and slowly coming to the fore, for example, Van Steenbergen et al., 'The Mamlukization of the Mamluk Sultanate? State Formation and the History of Fifteenth Century Egypt and Syria: Part I: Old Problems and New Trends', *History Compass* 14 (2016), 549–59.

55 Robinson, *Islamic Historiography*, final chapter.

56 T. Wollina, 'News and Rumor – Local Sources of Knowledge about the World', in S. Conermann (ed.), *Everything Is on the Move: The Mamluk Empire as a Node in (Trans-) Regional Networks* (Göttingen, 2014); 284–309; 284.

57 El-Leithy, 'Living Documents'.

58 For example, Elbendary, *Crowds and Sultans*, 2015.

59 Bauden, 'Taqī al-Dīn Aḥmad Ibn 'Alī al-Maqrīzī', 161–200, 170.

60 W. Fischel, 'Ibn Khaldūn's Use of Historical Sources', *Studia Islamica* 14 (1961), 109–19, 118–19; Irwin, 'Mamluk History and Historians', 159–70.

61 Li Guo, 'Mamluk Historographic Studies', 33; Muhanna, 'Why Was the Fourteenth Century …', 349.

62 Khalidi, *Arabic Historical Thought*, 183–4; a broader multi-genre discussion of medieval Arabic encyclopaedism is offered in U. Marzolph, 'Coining the Essentials: Arabic

Encyclopedias and Anthologies of the Pre-Modern Period', in A.-S. Goeing, A. T. Grafton and P. Michel (eds), *Collectors' Knowledge: What Is Kept, What Is Discarded* (Leiden, 2013), 32, and in Muhanna, 'Why Was the Fourteenth Century…'; Muhanna, *The World in a Book.*

63 Described vividly in Muhanna, *The World in a Book*, 5–6 and *passim.*

64 Sijpesteijn, 'The Archival Mind in Early Islamic Egypt', 163–87; M. van Berkel, 'Reconstructing Archival Practices in Abbasid Baghdad', *Journal of Abbasid Studies* 1 (2014): 7–22.

65 Friedrich, 'Epilogue: Archives and Archiving', 436.

66 Bauden, 'Maqriziana I' (part one), 1–12.

67 While Ibn al-Furāt apparently ceased to work on his chronicle c. 1400, al-Maqrīzi worked on his main body of works in the over thirty years or so years prior to his death in 1442: Rabbat, 'Who Was al-Maqrizi?', 18.

68 W. B. Hallaq, 'The "*qāḍī's dīwān (sijill)*" before the Ottomans', *BSOAS* 61:3 (1998), 415–36; Hirschler, 'From Archive to Archival Practices'.

69 Hirschler, 'From Archive to Archival Practices', 27.

70 Hallaq, 'The "*qāḍī's dīwān (sijill)*"', 419 and *passim*; Paul, 'Archival Practices', 353–4; C. Müller, 'The Power of the Pen: Cadis and Their Archives', in Bausi, *Manuscripts and Archives*, 361–85, 362–3.

71 Gacek, *Arabic Manuscripts*, 267.

2

An Exemplary Chronicle as Archive: Ibn al-Furāt's *Taʾrīkh al-duwal wa ʾl-mulūk*

Arabic manuscripts in the form of handwritten books have hitherto been studied first and foremost as vehicles of thought and not as objects in themselves.

A. Gacek, *Arabic Manuscripts – A Vademecum for Readers* (2009), x

We need to ... restore to documents their tactile physicality, which often contains various clues about the biography and social value of the document-as-object, especially in medieval society where various types of documents and texts were valued and revered, cherished and brandished, not only for their textual content, but also their physical attributes and authorizing stamp of their authors/creators.

T. el-Leithy, 'Living Documents, Dying Archives: Towards a Historical Anthropology of Medieval Arabic Archives' (2011), 432

Ibn al-Furāt's chronicle, widely known as *Taʾrīkh al-duwal wa ʾl-mulūk*, survives as two sets of non-overlapping autograph codices, one covering Biblical through Late Antique to early Islamic history in extant volumes, and the second devoted to the years 501–799/1107–1396. The latter set of codices, thought to be his fair copy of which nine volumes are extant, is largely housed in the Austrian National Library in Vienna, with additional volumes in Rabat and the Vatican. These I term Autograph A (AA). Five volumes from the earlier autograph series, possibly his draft, are located in London, Paris and Bursa and are denoted Autograph B (AB).[1] Ibn al-Furāt's original title for the chronicle, *al-Ṭarīq al-wāḍiḥ al-maslūk ilā tarājim al-khulafāʾ wa ʾl-mulūk*, is attested on the title page of each extant volume of AB, and in the author's own hand on the final page of four of these.[2]

The present chapter introduces this work in general, and the first three Vienna codices of AA – which host the discussion of late Fatimid history – in particular, as an archive in its material, spatial and textual dimensions. I take note of specific signs of archivality within the codices and take stock of the work as an accessible epistemic archive for both pre-Mamluk and Mamluk history. In light of the codex as a physical form allowing 'quick scanning back and forth across several pages' and hosting a 'discourse that privilege[s], indeed insist[s] upon, cross-referencing and non-linear reading'[3] – a format accommodating substantial quantities of text while ordering the material and expediting its retrieval – recognition of archival signs within

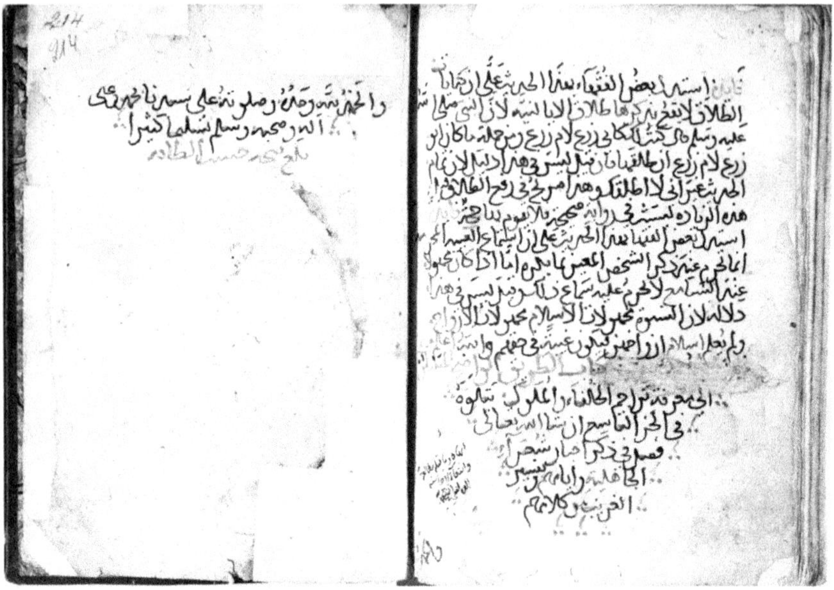

Figure 2.1 Paris MS Blochet 5990. Two pages (f. 213v and f. 214r) of a Paris volume of AB, with the first page giving Ibn al-Furāt's title for his chronicle in his own hand: *al-Ṭarīq al-wāḍiḥ al-maslūk ilā tarājim al-khulafāʾ wa ʾl-mulūk*.

Ibn al-Furāt's codices opens space for examination of the author's place within his epistemic environment, specifically how and to what extent his chronicle was accessed and exploited by later authors.

The material archive: Inside a fourteenth-century chronicle

As a corporeal object, Ibn al-Furāt's chronicle in both AA and AB is lucid in exhibiting signs of archivality: manuscript conventions and compositional signposts that signal the intention or execution of archival methods in history-writing, including selecting, itemizing, ordering and conserving material. In this aspect, the archival model of textual articulation and arrangement takes physical features common to codices of history and in other genres – the use of rubrication to mark the start and end of citations, *isikhrāj* (or *taʿqībāt*, catchwords) to ensure correct order of folios, headings and subheadings to indicate change of topic or sub-genre, the addition of glosses within margins, the alphabetization of obituary notices – and discloses their epistemic purposes: to secure, structure and clearly formulate a coherent, multi-sourced record of history.

The ongoing life cycle of this particular chronicle as a material archive begins with an ending: Ibn al-Furāt's suspension of writing at the end of 803/mid-1401 and the book's subsequent circulation after its sale by Ibn al-Furāt's son, who purportedly had no interest in historiography.[4] This is followed by stages in the use of the chronicle, or references to its usefulness, by a number of fifteenth- and sixteenth-century authors based in Cairo and Damascus, notably al-Maqrīzī (1364–1442), Ibn Ḥajar (1372–1449), Ibn Qāḍī Shuhba (1377–1448), al-Sakhāwī (1428–97) and Ibn Ṭūlūn (1475–1546).[5] The codices' later peregrinations remain unknown, however, and both autograph series were dispersed over the course of time. The next stage of intelligence for AA comes with Gustave Flügel's (d. 1870) identification of most of those volumes in the Austrian National Library catalogue of 1865.[6]

In AA, comprising the Vienna series of volumes of which the Rabat and Vatican volumes are integral components,[7] folio 1v in the first extant codex bears an undated colophon stating the following: *al-mujallad al-awwal min taʾrīkh/ al-duwal wa 'l-mulūk/ taʾlīf al-ʿālim/ al-wariʿ al-fāḍil ibn al-furāt al-ḥanafī/raḥimahu 'llāh/ mīm* (= *tamma*: a signing off term).[8] This notation should be juxtaposed with key information about Ibn al-Furāt's authorship of the Paris Blochet, Bursa and London volumes,[9] each of which starts with a *basmala* and ends with the author's confirmation of the book's title. Paris Blochet 5990, for instance, notes in its final lines Ibn al-Furāt's intention to devote the subsequent volume to the words and histories of the Jāhilī poets, which attests to his practice of claiming authorship clearly.[10] Returning to the earliest volume of AA, aside from the statement of Ibn al-Furāt's authorship in the colophon, along with another appearing in the author's preface to that same volume supplied below, there are no further attestations of authorship (*taṣdīq*), and the codices are without other formal signs of ownership, copying or changing hands in the forms of signatures, *waqf* seals or formulations, notices of transcription, reading, audition, transmission or loan statements.

While this codicological status quo for the earlier volumes of AA evidently restricts our prospects for adumbrating the chronicle's 'social codicology' in detail,[11] it must be noted that a work's claim to being an autograph is in the medieval Arabic bibliosphere rarely a fraudulent one, and a comparison of the handwriting of the codices with a reading and audition notice Ibn al-Furāt provides on an autograph hadith work of the savant, intermittent Shafiʿite chief justice (*qāḍī*) and renowned hadith scholar Ibn Ḥajar (Figure 2.5) provides incontrovertible evidence of the manuscript's identity as Ibn al-Furāt's autograph.[12] Further indications of AA's autographic nature include blank spaces left for extra information, death notices and obituaries.[13] Gaps are also left within individual biographies and between annals for Ibn al-Furāt or other readers/users to add detail as it became available, a common feature of codices that would change hands over the course of their life cycles.[14] Additions to the text in Ibn al-Furāt's hand appear in margins or are written above or between the original lines; these are not denoted as scholia (*hawāshī*) on the page but rather plug gaps in the narrative and attest that this was a work in progress.[15] Additional marginal notes and blocks of text of variable length, in two other different hands, also appear infrequently in some of the codices. The first volume of AA ends with the sealing off notation *tamma*; subsequent volumes, in which final folios are sometimes missing, dispense with this.[16]

In their material aspect, the AA volumes comprise 1893 folios in total of a large octave, nine inches by six, on yellowish Egyptian cotton paper, a more common paper type than the higher quality *sulṭānī* (chancery) paper at times repurposed for lengthy writing projects.[17] The hand is a polychrome (black and red) *naskh* script of twenty-three to thirty-four lines per page, with headings and many key words rendered in red.[18] Some folios are water-stained or worm-eaten, and each annal was originally bound as a separate fascicle. Following a blank recto in the first folio, the verso displays two Vienna library stamps.

The manuscript evidently endured vicissitudes in its journey to the present; along with missing sections of varying lengths, two volumes from the AA series largely housed in Vienna are located in Rabat and the Vatican respectively:

MS	Years Covered
Vienna I: AF117	501–21/1107–27
Vienna II: AF118	522–43/1128–48
Vienna III: AF119	544–62/1149–66
Vienna IV: AF120	563–67, 586–8, 591–9/1167–71, 1190–2, 1194–1202
Vienna V: AF121	600–24/1203–26
Rabat (no ref.)	625–38/1227–40
Vatican: V720	639–58/1241–59
Vienna VI: AF122	660–71/1261–72
Vienna VII: AF123	672–82/1273–83
Vienna VIII: AF124	683–96/1284–96
Vienna IX: AF125	789–99/1387–96

The following lacunae, for which we do not possess contextual explanation, are unaccounted for from the series:

568–85 (1172–89): 17 years; 589–90 (1193–3): 2 years; 659 (1260); 697–788 (1297–1386): 91 years.[19]

As for Autograph B, the known extant volumes comprise the following:[20]

'Patriarchs from Seth to Isaac' (vol. 3):	London, Brit. Mus. Or. 3007
'Sassanian kings to Jahili poets' (vol. 8):	Paris, Blochet 5990
'Early period' (vols. 9, 10, 11):	Bursa, Hussein Çelebi 782–84[21]

The London, Paris and Bursa volumes of AB all give the chronicle's correct title of *al-Ṭarīq al-wāḍiḥ al-maslūk ilā tarājim al-khulafā' wa 'l-mulūk* as Ibn al-Furāt renders it on the final folio of several volumes of AB. One further codex, Paris MS De Slane 1595, is a copy of a section of Ibn al-Furāt's account of early Islamic history made by another scribe, with corrections in Ibn al-Furāt's distinctive hand appearing in the margins of several folios, which was found at an unknown date in Damascus.[22] The two autograph series do not in the extant volumes cover the same eras of history, though it is quite possible that later volumes in AB overlap with AA. It would be impossible to say for sure unless these further volumes come to light.

In the opening volume of AA, the first page of narrative (2v) indicates with a *basmala* and preface that this is the beginning of a particular section of the work

Figure 2.2 Paris MS de Slane 1595. Two pages (f. 1v, f. 2r) of the codex Paris MS De Slane 1595, a scribal copy of a section of Ibn al-Furāt's account of early Islamic history, glossed in Ibn al-Furāt's distinctive hand appearing on the right margin of 1v.

recounting history from the year 501 AH, and that the volume is to cover the sixth Islamic century:[23]

> In the name of God, the All-Merciful, the Compassionate, the weak slave, hopeful of his Lord's pardon, full of errors, Muḥammad b. ʿAbd al-Rahīm b. ʿAlī b. Aḥmad b. Muḥammad b. ʿAbd al-ʿAzīz b. Muḥammad b. al-Furāt, the Ḥanafite student says:
>
> Chapter relating events of the start of the sixth century after the Emigration of our leader and our prophet Muḥammad the Messenger of God, the salutations and peace of God be upon him. Know that it is God Who guided us and you, and that the start of this blessed century was opened by God's month of al-Muḥarram, one of the months of the year 501, and the conclusion of this century is the end of the month of Dhu 'l-Ḥijja of the year 600. The length of this aforementioned century from start to finish is a hundred Islamic years. Know that God guided us and you, [and that] I relate at the beginning of the months of the years of this century that which occurred of: the caliphate of the caliph, the circumstances of his life, his death, his deposition and which of the rulers of Islam and others took possession of the countries and lands. [I relate] events from the domains of noblemen, judges, viziers, rulers and others. [I relate] the

> removal of he who was dismissed, the reason for his dismissal and [of] he whose circumstances changed because of this. I relate [the histories] of those whose affairs I was acquainted with: kings, noblemen, brave and retreating horsemen, the respectable descendants of the Prophet Muḥammad, judges, scholars, jurists, grammarians and poets. And I relate relevant [aspects] of their affairs, and their birth-dates.[24]

Within this elaboration of a fairly customary range of positivist socio-political concerns is an intriguing reference by Ibn al-Furāt's to his analytical approach to history-writing, expressed in the aim of examining the causal factors behind historical events ('the reasons for his dismissal'). The concern for reading events by examining causality communicates that the building of an epistemic archive of interpretation as well as source material is an explicit aim for Ibn al-Furāt. The uptake of the detailed later volumes of this chronicle, discussed presently, shows how his aim was met: the information and interpretations offered in his book were widely accessed, retrieved and (usually without attribution) reincorporated by later authors as the historiographic archive was recreated afresh within each 'new' work.

To return to the material features of the codices, the script is characterized by inconsistencies in orthography and a lack of points in many cases and occasional (uncorrected) cacographic errors. The author largely maintains his habit of supplying catchwords (*istikhrāj*, *taʿqībāt*) in the bottom left corner of each current page in both AA and AB, a typical and vital device for guaranteeing correct order of pages and meaning in a context in which manuscript pages were often separated and re-bound. The narrative within is presented both annalistically and topically. The archival aspect of annalistic dating, discussed in late antique documentary contexts but less so in Islamic narrative or documentary ones, resides in the structuring of information and sources for the twin aims of creating ease of access and ordering the material for semantic and temporal coherence.[25]

Ibn al-Furāt separates his chapters (typically, the individuals/places/dynasties/events to be reported) by rubricated bold headings, for example, 'Account of the vizier Shāwar's invitation to the Franks, their arrival in Egypt and their siege of Asad al-Dīn Shīrkūh at Bilbays',[26] with separate sections for obituaries. Alongside lemmata, red ink is regularly used for emphasis where a change of source occurs; for example, in the phrase *wa qāla fulān al-muʾarrikh*, *wa qāla* is rendered in red. For the end of the citations, *intahā kalāmuh*, the *intahā* is frequently in red. Other words for which rubrication is used include terms denoting accession to the caliphate, *wa būyiʿa*, and for a change of report within an annal, *wa fīhā* ['also in this year']. Finally, red ink is often used to accentuate key verbs and adverbs (e.g. *kāna*, *lammā*). The use of rubrication in manuscripts is attested from at least Late Antiquity and, in Islamicate contexts,[27] from Umayyad times, and its value as an explicit archival practice has been noted in non-Islamicate codicological contexts, for example, in relation to the eleventh-century tax and assets audit conducted by the Normans in Britain known as the Domesday Book, portions of which use rubrication.[28] In Ibn al-Furāt's chronicle, it reveals his patterning of his narrative, in both textual makeup and meaning, by means of analysis rather than synthesis: the semiotics of archivality are manifested

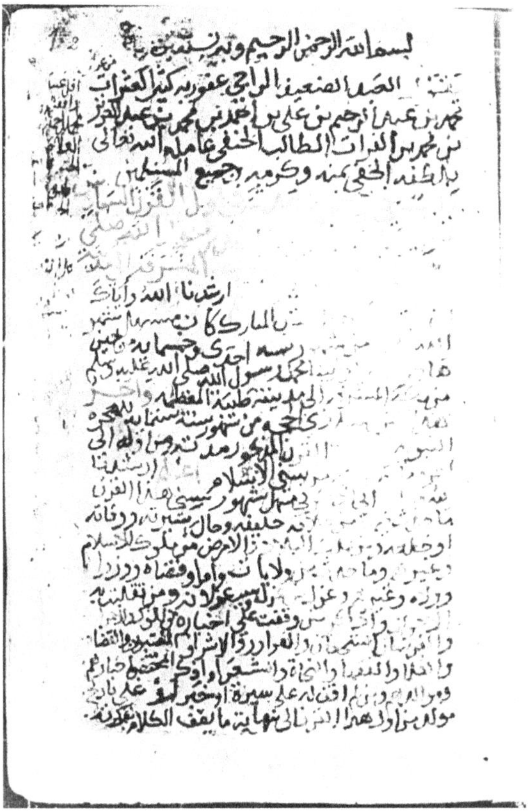

Figure 2.3 Vienna Cod. A. F. 117, vol. 1 of Ibn al-Furāt's *Ta'rīkh al-duwal wa 'l-mulūk*. The beginning of Ibn al-Furāt's introduction to his chronicle in his own hand. Starting with the *basmala* and necessary preliminary religious formulae, Ibn al-Furāt tells us from line 6 of this page up to line 6 of the subsequent page, what his subject matter will be, and which years he will cover in this volume, beginning with 501/1107 (MS Vienna AF 117 = Flügel 814, vol. 1, f. 2r).

in the itemizing of (i) source materials and (ii) moments of action, rather than integrating these aspects seamlessly.

The material signs of archivality in the codices can thus be summed up as follows: an atomized narrative is effected by the ruptures of changing of ink colour; a sense of layered textual richness is achieved by Ibn al-Furāt's saturating the narrative with a clearly signalled variety of reports, augmented by addenda in margins or above and between lines; at the same time, coherence is achieved through thematic organization in which ordered reports advance a positivist narrative of history; finally, a care to secure correct sequence of the folios via catchwords guarantees that the author's archival ordering of material is not disrupted in the acts of transmission or reading. The codicological features here, by no means unique to Ibn al-Furāt, operationalize the

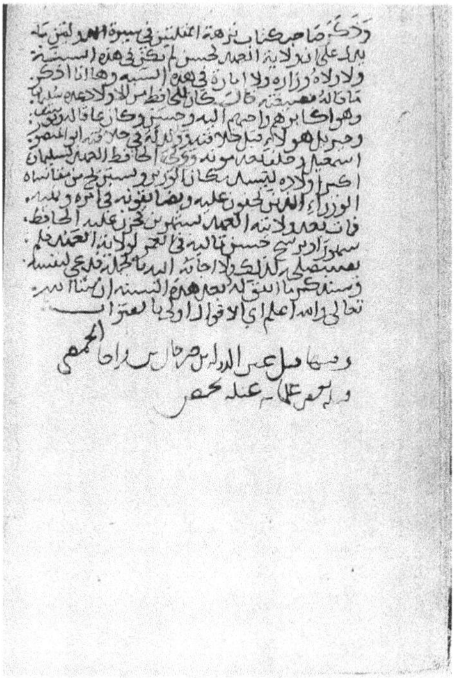

Figure 2.4 Vienna Cod. A. F. 117, vol. 2 of Ibn al-Furāt's *Ta'rīkh al-duwal wa 'l-mulūk*. A page of obituaries. The lower half of the page has remained blank and a later owner or reader has written two lines of additional information for the year 526/1121. The page begins with a quotation from the lost Fatimid chronicle *Nuzhat al-muqlatayn* of Ibn Ṭuwayr (d. 1220) (MS Vienna AF 118 = Flügel 814, vol. 2, f. 44v).

archivality of his approach in helpful and distinctive ways.[29] The chronicle brought into being by dint of these archival strategies is an epistemic archive that provided a reserve of historiographically valuable material to later authors.

Tracing the life of Ibn al-Furāt

Further redactions of the later volumes of Ibn al-Furāt's chronicle are notably few: the only one known is a series of extracts made from *Ta'rīkh al-duwal* by the Damascene Ibn Qāḍī Shuhba (d. 1448), extant in a unicum MS in the Chester Beatty Library in Dublin,[30] comprising a selection of reports collected, transmitted and penned by Ibn al-Furāt for the twenty-year period 773–93/1371–90, in Ibn Qāḍī Shuhba's hand. These are the only known verbatim (if sometimes summarized), attributed reproductions of Ibn al-Furāt's history available in Mamluk historiography aside from general attributions to Ibn al-Furāt such as one by Ibn Ḥajar in the preface to his *Inbā' al-ghumr*,[31] and have been used extensively in Massoud's recent study.[32] The Chester Beatty MS, *al-Muntaqā*

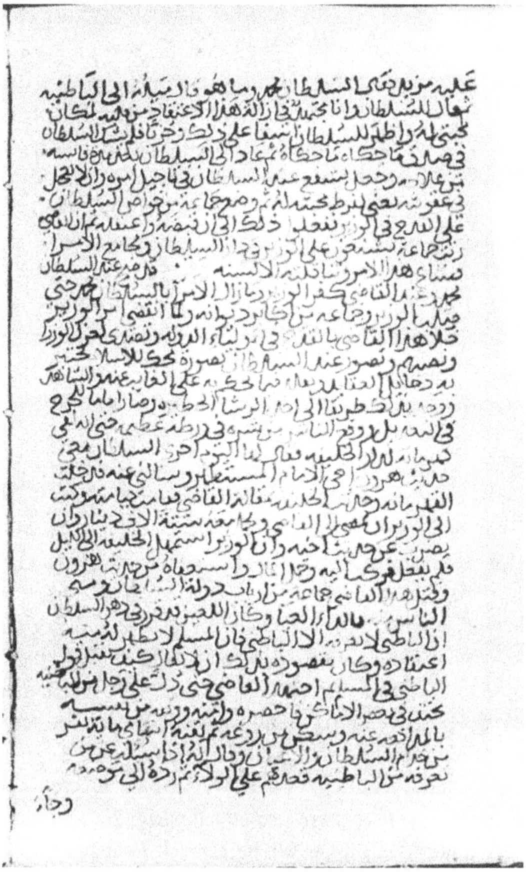

Figure 2.5 Vienna Cod. A. F. 117, vol. 1 of Ibn al-Furāt's *Ta'rīkh al-duwal wa 'l-mulūk*. The use of catchwords. Many folios such as this one show the author's use of *ta'qība* or *istikhrāj*, the catchword supplied beneath the final line of a page, denoting the first word of the page to follow, and guaranteeing the correct order of the leaves (MS Vienna AF 117 = Flügel 814, vol. 1, f. 30v).

min Ta'rīkh Ibn al-Furāt, reveals that Ibn Qāḍī Shuhba was mainly interested in seeking quotations that supplemented his *Dhayl* to the Mamluk-focused history of his teacher, Ibn al-Ḥijjī (d. 1413).[33] Ibn Qāḍī Shuhba clearly borrows from Ibn al-Furāt extensively for perhaps half of the *Dhayl*, the other half being Ibn Qāḍī Shuhba's own original material mostly relating to intellectual history in Damascus. The *Dhayl* could possibly fill the gap left by AA of *Ta'rīkh al-duwal*, as it is likely to contain Ibn al-Furāt's reports for the missing years 698–789.

Ibn al-Furāt's chronicle as an archive capturing an epistemic moment in Mamluk historiography has been manifestly useful to both Egyptian and Syrian traditions of historiography, in which context it should be recalled that the Paris codex covering early Islamic history (11–19 AH), in the hand of a scribe but corrected by Ibn al-Furāt himself, was procured from Damascus.[34] The value of the work for Damascene authors can be attributed to textual and contextual factors: Ibn al-Furāt's account of events and obituaries offers detailed resources to the hadith-cum-historiography narratives popular in fifteenth-century Syria; moreover, Ibn al-Furāt had established his personal reputation as a *muḥaddith* there in the course of his studies. Four later authors who make explicit reference to Ibn al-Furāt's chronicle hail from both Cairo and Damascus as follows: Ibn Ḥajar (1372–1449, mainly based in Cairo), Ibn Qāḍī Shuhba (1377–1448, Damascus), al-Sakhāwī (1428–97, Cairo) and Ibn Ṭūlūn (1475–1546, Damascus). The first two rely on him as a source of historical reports for their own compositions, while the latter two describe his work and scholarship in *rijāl* contexts. The book's seemingly simultaneous Cairo and Damascus connections are revealing of its early travel through time and space, yet also cements the multi-spatial significance of many larger Middle Period universal chronicles, in contradistinction to specific iterations of historiography such as the 'restricted biographical dictionaries' focusing on, inter alia, a city, district or region.[35]

For his biography as a whole, medieval and modern sources providing the few known details of Ibn al-Furāt's life have been usefully collated by M. F. Elshayyal: Ibn Ḥajar (d. 1448), Ibn Taghrībirdī (d. 1470), al-Sakhāwī (d. 1497), al-Ṣuyūṭī (d. 1505), Ḥājjī Khalīfa (d. 1658), Ibn al-ʿImād (d. 1678), Ziriklī (d. 1893) and Brockelmann (d. 1956).[36] Of these, Ibn Ḥajar provides the earliest and most complete information. Ibn al-Furāt was born in Cairo in 807/1334 to a well-known family of intellectuals and spent his life teaching, issuing marriage contracts, officiating as a public notary and writing history. His education included specialization in the study of hadith and jurisprudence under notable scholars of his day, some of them in Syria (Abu 'l-Faraj Ibn ʿAbd al-Hādī, Abū Futūḥ al-Dallasī, Abū Bakr b. Sannāj and Abu 'l-Ḥasan al-Bandanījī); his hadith licenses were provided by the Damascene savants al-Mizzī (d. 1341) and al-Dhahabī (d. 1348) while he himself later provided authorization in hadith to the Cairene polymath Ibn Ḥajar.

Of scholarly institutions where he taught or worked, the Muʿizziyya school, probably the earliest established *madrasa* in Fusṭāṭ, is mentioned by name, and the city, two miles south of Cairo, was by the Mamluk era both connected with Cairo in terms of bureaucracy and scholarly networks, yet also stood as a 'less significant administrative unit with its own set of officials'.[38] Though endowed in 1256 by the first Mamluk sultan Aybak whose regnal title was al-Malik al-Muʿizz (r. 1250–7), and built using expensive materials purloined from the Rawḍa Citadel, the Shafiʿi school merits only passing reference in topographical works by Ibn al-Furāt's contemporaries Ibn Duqmāq and al-Maqrīzī, and fell into disrepair in the fifteenth century soon after the appearances of those references during a period of lootings and demolition.[39] Ibn al-Furāt held a professorship and position of *khaṭīb* (preacher) there; previous professors at the *madrasa* included a chief *qāḍī* and vizier.[40] Ibn al-Furāt was evidently well-integrated into the scholarly and social networks of Mamluk Cairo as well as Damascus, through his roles as a *muḥaddith* under whom Ibn Ḥajar among others had studied, and as a *mudarris* (professor), and in some sense typifies the religious scholar who turns his hand to literary pursuits.[41] At the same time, he made a living through the relatively mundane sinecure of public notary.[42] Unlike his independently wealthy contemporary Ibn Duqmāq (d. 1407), Ibn al-Furāt was not a man of leisure, and undertook banal

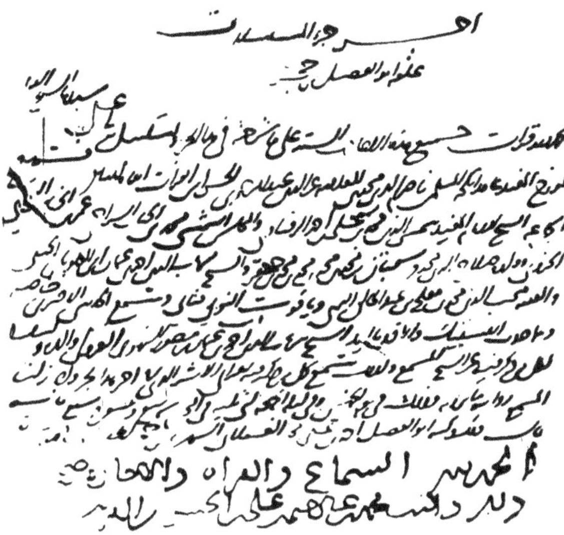

Figure 2.6 Ibn Ḥajar's autograph of *al-Musalsalāt*, with additional lines by Ibn al-Furāt. Facsimile provided by al-Ziriklī of a snippet from Ibn Ḥajar's autograph hadith work *al-Musalsalāt*, with additional lines at the end in Ibn al-Furāt's unmistakeable hand, praising God, verifying the hearing and reading of the text, giving Ibn Ḥajar his license, authorizing the text and ending with his signature.[37] Reproduced with kind permission from Khayr al-Din al-Zirikli's *al-A'lām: qāmūs tarājīm li ashhar al-rijāl wa 'l-nisā' min al-'arab wa 'l-musta'ribīn wa 'l-mustashrifīn*, 6:200, 15th edition in 8 vols (Beirut, 2002).

jobs in order to eke out a living.[43] Beyond this, we know little, as Ibn al-Furāt's life is only meagrely recorded in the biographical literature.[44]

Clean copy or draft: Ontology of the chronicle as archive

Despite the explicit references to Ibn al-Furāt's chronicle just mentioned, the work occupies a seemingly marginal space in the historiographic 'canon' of Circassian Cairo, notwithstanding substantial and growing evidence of its merit as either a repository or a conduit of sources for a host of later chroniclers. It is clear that a chronicle that seems impoverished in respect of completeness and multiplicity of copies still had a profound and traceable impact, as an archive of sources and interpretations, upon historiography in the early Burji realm and especially in Barqūq's Egypt (1382–89, 1390–99).[45]

Ibn al-Furāt's book has been widely referred to over the past few decades for its intricate elaboration of a positivist Mamluk history, with a reputation in the medieval sources for being both highly useful and weakly expressed, the latter an allusion to its author's adherence to the mixed-register 'Cairo narrative style'.[46] Such remarks are traceable to Ibn al-Furāt's student and contemporary Ibn Ḥajar (d. 1449), who

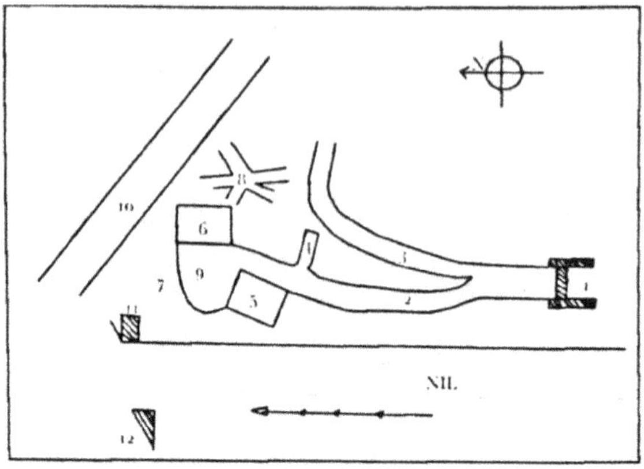

1. Bāb al-Qantara
2. Ḥārat al-Wāsimiyīn
3. Swīqat al-Barāġīth
4. Ḥārat al-ʿArab
5. al-Madrasa al-Muʿizziya
6. Dār al-Mulk
7. Sucreries du sultan
8. Ḥārat al-Maġānīn
9. Rahba
10. al-Sūq al-Kabīr
11. Funduq
12. Nilomètre

Figure 2.7 The location of the Madrasa al-Muʿizziyya in Fustat.

used the chronicle extensively in his own historiographical work, and thence to al-Sakhāwī (d. 1497) in the *Iʿlān* and other works.[47] Equally, it is well acknowledged in recent scholarship that there is a great deal more to be unearthed regarding the influence of *Ta'rīkh al-duwal* on al-Maqrīzī's *Kitāb al-sulūk*, a medieval and modern *source célèbre* for Mamluk rule, which draws from Ibn al-Furāt's earlier chronicle substantially and largely without attribution;[48] alternatively, al-Maqrīzī's debt to Ibn al-Furāt is acknowledged in his short monetary history.[49] Further, al-Maqrīzī's (d. 1442) handwriting has been identified on the front page of one volume of the manuscript.[50] In this aspect, Ibn al-Furāt is discernible as yet another influence on al-Maqrīzī, who is similarly careful not to judge the Fatimids harshly, and indeed presents a thoroughgoing defence of them in the *Ittiʿāẓ*, where they are designated *ḥunafā'* or 'believers in true religion'. In al-Maqrīzī's case, his sympathy would likely have been coloured by suggestions, later disproved, that he was descended from the Fatimids.[51] Al-Maqrīzī's *Ittiʿāẓ* contains at least seventeen passages close to or identical with reports found in *Ta'rīkh al-duwal*, some of them several pages long, though it appears in most cases that al-Maqrīzī summarizes Ibn al-Furāt's accounts.[52] Ibn al-Furāt provides for al-Maqrīzī a measure of detail and elaboration, for instance on the long stand-off between Shīrkūh and Shāwar outside the Gates of Cairo (559/1163), of which al-Maqrīzī would have found a basic outline from Ibn al-Athīr (for instance), but he transmits a lengthier account of it via Ibn al-Furāt, complete with an abundance of direct speech and details about gifts exchanged and numbers of days and specific persons involved.[53] Since Maqrīzī was born only thirty years after Ibn al-Furāt's birth in 1334, and both lived and worked in Cairo, it is very possible that they would have met. The value of Ibn al-Furāt's work was well known to the foremost historian-savant of the Mamluk era, and although never copied again as a whole work (to our knowledge), for indeed it was known then, as now, as an incomplete text, its authority is reified and inscribed in a range of medieval and modern discussions of medieval Islamicate history and historiography.[54] One may note also that Ibn Taghrībirdī's chronicle *al-Nujūm al-zāhira* borrows from *Ta'rīkh al-duwal* in some half a dozen instances independently of al-Maqrīzī's reading, thus cementing Ibn al-Furāt's centrality to the Mamluk tradition of chronicling the Fatimids.

In the estimation of the modern scholars Ashtor, Amitai and Massoud, Ibn al-Furāt is an unacknowledged saviour of modern understanding of the Bahri-to-Burji sub-era of Mamluk history alongside other periods of history,[55] and for the elaboration of recent Mamluk history, the reputation of Ibn al-Furāt's chronicle has long been secure. Its circulation is attested by the borrowings or references of al-Maqrīzī, Ibn Ḥajar, Ibn Qāḍī Shuhba, al-Jawharī, Ibn Iyās and possibly also Ibn Khaldūn, al-'Aynī, al-Malaṭī and Ibn Taghrībirdī.[56] In an account characterized by its candid political commentary, 'Ibn al-Furāt managed to convey the atmosphere of political volatility' of the times in his 'comprehensive coverage'.[57]

Some ambiguity about the nature of the chronicle as it was passed around Mamluk scholarly circles has persisted, due to the fact that Ibn Ḥajar, al-Sakhāwī and others described the work as a *musawwada*. In the words of al-Sakhāwī in his *I'lān*, a book devised to vindicate the discipline of history against its detractors,[58]

> Nāṣir al-Dīn Muḥammad b. 'Abd al-Rahīm b. 'Alī b. al-Furāt wrote an extensive history. The last three centuries (alone) were clean-copied (by the author) in about twenty volumes. The author's writing ended with the end of the year 803/1400-1. I suppose that if he had completed the work, it would have come to sixty (volumes). … The work was sold in a draft copy and was dispersed.[59]

A degree of confusion regarding the status of the extant codices has remained, as al-Sakhāwī describes the 'clean-copying' of three centuries' worth of historiography (a time frame that corresponds with the scope of the Vienna, Rabat and Vatican volumes: 501–799 AH), yet maintains that the draft copy was sold on. Citing Ibn Ḥajar, al-Sakhāwī also opines about the clean copying of twenty volumes in total,[60] while the later Ibn Ṭūlūn states that 'some of' the book was clean copied before death overtook the author, including volumes on the sixth to eighth Islamic centuries, which corresponds with the extant Vienna series *in toto*. This claim was repeated well over a century later by fellow Damascene Ibn 'Imād al-Ḥanbalī, author of a compendium offering a convenient reiteration of works by previous authors.[61]

A comparison of AA with AB throws light on the issue. The Vienna volumes (alongside those in Rabat and the Vatican) do indeed appear to be the fair copy of which the Blochet 5990, Hussein Çelebi 782–784 and Brit. Mus. Or. 3007 are the rough draft of earlier volumes covering Sassanid to early Islamic history. This is ascertained by the autographic handwriting in these volumes and by comparison of their relative paper sizes, numbers of lines per page, subject matter and titles. Taken together, these features confirm assertions in medieval sources that Ibn al-Furāt only clean copied later volumes, including what became AA. Overall, therefore, the verdict of clean copy for the Vienna volumes, including those covering late Fatimid history, carries the weight of authors both contemporary with and considerably later than Ibn al-Furāt, in both Damascus and Cairo, despite ostensibly contrary assertions.

The identity of AA as either part of the clean copy or the author's draft is in archival terms significant: if this was a *musawwada* as (near-) contemporary scholars assert, the refinement leading to a clean copy might risk erasing some key archival signs such as signalling authorship and detailed attribution. Although a clear citation practice is visible even in the draft volumes of AB, we cannot be certain whether or to what extent any details might be rendered invisible in the process of refinement. In sum, given the substantial evidence that the AA volumes are the author's *mubayyaḍa*, the material archival features of the codices should be regarded as inscribed by design in an Ur-text, the authorial version intended for circulation.

Reflections on the spatial textual archive

While Ibn al-Furāt's history offers some forty reports or clusters of reports on late Fatimid rule, it is not, as a universal chronicle, solely devoted to the history of that dynasty. Also present are accounts of a range of Islamic dynasties and political elites within relevant annals, including the Saljuqs, Zirids of Ifriqiya, Burids of Damascus, Almohads, Nizari Ismaʿilis of Alamut, Zengids, Ayyubids, Mongols, Mamluks and others including – unusually – dynasties of the Latin West.[62] Episodes from their histories are narrated/documented mainly through historical reports, extracts of poems and some documents for 'past' history, and a mixture of reports, poetic extracts and many more documents for 'present' history. Each volume in the series as a whole covers between ten and twenty years of history in c. 400 to 500 pages (200 to 250 folios.)

In the first of the initial three volumes covering late Fatimid history, the narrative on the Fatimids takes up approximately 10 per cent of the total number of reports; in the second, Fatimid entries account for about 15 per cent; while by the third volume, the Fatimid reports constitute about a fifth of the whole, yet conversely take up a little less than half of the available space since these extracts are lengthy and usually more detailed than those appearing in earlier volumes.[63] In the allocation of space in the manuscript, Fatimid reports occupy some seven folios in the first volume (recording the years c. 1107–27), fourteen folios in the second volume (recording 1128–48) and approximately forty-eight folios in the third volume (recording 1149–66), of which just the five years 1162–6 occupy some twenty-six folios.

Within these Fatimid-related reports, about 55 per cent is unique material from original sources for the late Fatimids; that is, reports not found elsewhere in the known Arabic historiography of the dynasty, overwhelmingly comprised of original Fatimid-era and Ayyubid-preserved Fatimid-era reports. Alongside this is a much smaller portion of unique Mamluk-era sources for the period transmitted mainly via Shāfiʿ b. ʿAlī (d. 1330), in a clear case of archival conservation, in which Ibn al-Furāt is the only author to carry this material, or its sole conduit for later historians. Another 15 per cent is from well-known chronicles (all of which are accessible today as published editions), while the remaining 30 per cent is either from unacknowledged sources or conflated accounts designated as taken 'from the books/people of history' or the like. In other words, unique and early extracts for the Fatimids predominate within Ibn al-Furāt's chronicle, a feature that emphasizes his archival criteria of inclusion.

A notable inference on the issue of inclusion is that the Fatimids play a small role in the narrative of the first two volumes, in which Saljuq history is dominant, but by the third volume, it is the Isma'ili dynasty that takes up more space than any other. Each temporal or spatial unit of history is treated via a consistent method, by means of attributed quotation, and each year ends with a list of alphabetized obituary notices for political leaders, religious scholars and other notables, as noted by Ibn al-Furāt in his preface.

The progressively greater attention Ibn al-Furāt accords the Fatimids over the course of the three volumes indicates firstly the profusion of sources that becomes available to Ibn al-Furāt for the final years of Fatimid rule, as revealed by his wider range of references. Secondly, the increasing depth and detail can be connected with the changing nature of his enterprise, from an account of late Fatimid history set against a larger canvas of Islamic world history, in which their importance is largely regional, to one in which the dynasty's connection with Islamic world developments include the processes by which Ṣalāḥ al-Dīn assumes a hegemonic role. While Ibn al-Furāt's broader aim, as his preface spells out, is a universal account of Islamic history, distinct from the specific thematic effort of al-Maqrīzī's *Ittiʿāẓ*, for example, a pattern of increasing prolixity that continues through the nine-volume AA series of *Taʾrīkh al-duwal* means that by the time the author reaches the events of his own era in later volumes, his chronicle recounts history on a virtually day-to-day basis and is consequently narrated in much greater detail.

The first three unpublished codices of *Taʾrīkh al-duwal* in AA cover most of the history of the Fatimids in the twelfth century up to and including the year 562/1166, in 106 partitioned reports. The third volume ends with events of the year 562/1166 when the Egyptians, Syrians and Franks are on the verge of agreeing a truce.[64] From there, the remainder of Fatimid rule in Egypt (563–567/1167–71) is covered in the fourth (published) volume of Ibn al-Furāt's chronicle.[65] A reference in the first volume (I: 165a) to previous reports on Badr's vizierate (r. 1073–94) points to earlier volumes that also recorded Fatimid history but are not extant in either autograph series.

Ibn al-Furāt's contributions to later historiography

In light of the intentions stated in his preface, Ibn al-Furāt's rubric does not break the mould of the medieval Arabic universal chronicle but rather works within a tried, tested and enduring formula for the summation of long-elapsed and more recent history.[66] Yet as a resource for reformulating the positivist history of Islamic societies, the key mode in which his work has been appreciated to date, the chronicle has in recent years received notable recognition from contemporary scholars as the extent of his influence on the Mamluk historiographical tradition is better understood. In his study of Circassian-era historiography, S. Massoud writes that 'no history ... of the early Circassian period can be written without reference to *Ta'rīkh al-duwal*'.[67] As far back as the 1930s, Cl. Cahen had pointed out the chronicle's significance for the history of the Fatimids.[68] As a 'master-historian of tremendous significance' (in R. Amitai's reckoning),[69] Ibn al-Furāt is also medieval Arabic historiography's 'unsung hero'.[70] E. Ashtor writes that 'the importance of the *Ta'rīkh al-duwal wa 'l-Mulūk* stems from the fact that it is perhaps the most comprehensive work among the numerous chronicles written in the Mamluk period',[71] while Irwin argues that Ibn al-Furāt had a 'mastery of source materials' and was 'the most professional of his contemporaries', a 'highly-efficient collator of earlier sources' who became a 'favourite (and often unacknowledged) source for the chroniclers who came after him'.[72]

The lack of copies of Ibn al-Furāt's chronicle is not suggestive of great acclaim in his lifetime or in the decades that followed. Yet Ibn al-Furāt clearly established his reputation to some degree early on in the Burji Mamluk era, as is discernible in patterns of borrowing to and from his chronicle verified by Little, Bacharach, Ashtor and Massoud. His integrity as a commentator on the events of his own era is proven by his sitting atop the stemma one may devise to illustrate the presence of his material in later works, alongside his colleague and friend Ibn Duqmāq,[73] as Bacharach has done in his search for hard economic data in the chronicles of Burji/Circassian historians. Here, we see that Ibn al-Furāt and the younger Ibn Duqmāq – who was born some fifteen years later than him in 1349 and died some months after him in 1407 – were the sources or conduits for historical information presented via several chains of transmission. In Ibn al-Furāt's case, these include the transfer of reports and information to al-Maqrīzī followed by Ibn Taghrībirḍi through to others, and to Ibn Ḥajar through to al-Suyūṭī via al-Sakhāwī.[74] That Ibn al-Furāt's detailed later volumes carried textual and archival authority early on is not a controversial point. A conundrum that does arise in this transmissional context, however, is the issue of whether he borrowed from some sources without attribution, notwithstanding his habit of 'showcasing' his sources in most cases for 'past' history, as this might be seen to detract from the diligence and precision of his archival practice.

There are two views on this issue, the first propounded by Sobernheim and Little, who aver that Ibn al-Furāt relied heavily on his predecessor al-Nuwayri, but does not acknowledge the obligation.[75] On the other hand, Ashtor's defence of Ibn al-Furāt's originality, and his care to explicitly recognize literary and archival debt, the second viewpoint on his method, appears convincing: in cases where he relies on the work of another chronicle for his outline of history; for instance Ibn Duqmāq's *Nuzhat al-anām* for the events of their lifetime, it is clear from Massoud's recent in-depth study of patterns of borrowing that Ibn al-Furāt added 'his own massive material', and in Ashtor's view followed his forbears in their choice of chronicles but made his own extracts and arrangements.[76] Not surprisingly, in Massoud's estimation *Ta'rīkh al-duwal* is 'superior to all other chronicles in terms of its wealth of information ... [containing] a substantial number of in-depth additional data that appear to be original'. While his life circumstances were modest, his 'belonging to a well-known family and the close contacts he might have established with certain sectors of the population and the government in his capacity as legal witness and *khaṭīb* could have afforded him ample opportunities to observe the society in which he lived'.[77]

It is this capacity to use his contacts in a resourceful manner that lies behind the centrality of Ibn al-Furāt's chronicle to al-Maqrīzī's *Sulūk* up to the turn of the fifteenth century, within which several passages criticizing Barqūq and his successors were lifted verbatim from *Ta ʾrīkh al-duwal*, proving that as an epistemic archive, it was razor sharp in its observation if not invective, and a highly effective resource.[78] Amitai also points out that a 'systematic comparison' between the *Sulūk* and *Ta'rīkh al-duwal* 'for twenty-two years of annals (AH 658-80), shows that, for this period at least, al-Maqrizi's work is virtually a précis of Ibn al-Furat's vast chronicle', though Ibn al-Furāt evinces diligence and precision, while al-Maqrīzī's use of sources is 'haphazard',[79] which can be read as a vindication of Ibn al-Furāt's archival standards.

Such verdicts on Ibn al-Furāt's book establish its powerful immanence within Mamluk historiography, despite the paucity of named citations from his chronicle in later works. The exception to its covert presence in later annalistic works are the extracts made by Ibn Qāḍī Shuhba, who might well have worked from a second copy given that authors in both Cairo and Damascus seem to have had roughly contemporaneous access to it. One might speculate that the chronicle did not gain prominence from extensive copying in its day or thereafter because of the relatively modest circumstances of the author as compared with other chroniclers of his generation or just after, such as Ibn Khaldun, al-Maqrīzī, Ibn Taghrībirdī, al-ʿAynī and others; after all, while professional copyists were not in short supply, the copying of books required funding and/or patronage and a degree of social prestige.[80] The chronicle's epistemic authority is nonetheless deeply inscribed within more renowned texts: its 'list of borrowers' is 'actually quite long and extends over a period of a century'.[81] The sheer volume of relevant topical material within its pages, offered as a material and spatial archive, rendered it a quintessential prism for the refraction of Circassian history as a whole in the works of historians of his own era and later, as it 'contains more accounts of political events than any other contemporary source, and it also outdoes these with regard to social and religious affairs'.[82]

The afterlives of Ibn al-Furāt's textual archivalia

To return to the proposition that the codex form accommodates and encourages cross-referencing and non-linear reading, Ibn al-Furāt's 'chronicle as archive' exemplifies the historical compilation that is organized so as to aid the retrieval of information. Some of the more obscure historical sources of late Fatimid history used by Ibn al-Furāt gain textual accessibility by means of his incorporation of them as usually compact, thus easily digestible, extracts. For authors such as the late Fatimid/Ayyubid Ibn Ṭuwayr (d. 1220) and Ibn Abī Ṭayy (d. 1233), to whom we return in two subsequent chapters, Ibn al-Furāt was an historiographical custodian, a preserver of texts that would most likely have fallen into oblivion or something very like it but for his archival conservation of sizeable sections of their books.

In this context, it is worth noting that alongside appreciation of Ibn al-Furāt's chronicle as a resource for presenting a detailed outline and reconstruction of history, Ashtor in particular has drawn attention to what we may call Ibn al-Furāt's archival proclivities. In a comprehensive discussion of the importance of *Ta'rīkh al-duwal* for, inter alia, the history of the Crusades (as recognized by the handful of nineteenth-century French scholars who utilized his contribution to recording that series of conflicts), as well as for the history of Baybars' reign (1260–77), Ashtor notes that Ibn al-Furāt adduces exactly dated documents procured from formal archives since lost.[83] This is a prima facie case of the extension of the life cycles of such documents via their archival incorporation in subsequent historiography. Ashtor draws attention to Ibn al-Furāt's propensity to offer alternative reports of a single incident,[84] to note discrepancies in the dates offered in his sources, his giving priority to 'the most ancient source' for particular persons or events and his interspersing the historical account with detailed and informative digressions – for instance on the history of a city mentioned in a report, or on a legal development – all of which constitute a 'successful modification of the annalistic style'.[85] In point of fact it is the depth and scope of epistemic concern that is modified here: the archivality of selecting, prioritizing and sequencing remain integral to Ibnal-Furāt's historiographic practice.

This degree of historiographical intelligence is not unique to Ibn al-Furāt. His contemporary Ibn Khaldūn engaged the history of non-Muslim peoples in the sixth part of his seven-volume *Kitāb al-ʿibar* with a similar level of rigour, as argued by W. J. Fischel. Ibn Khaldūn procures unusual sources for this history, compares and cross-checks them, noting their similarities and differences, evaluates their claims to veracity and includes 'an abundance of documentary evidence' available to a political figure with access to state archives.[86] Taken together with al-Maqrīzī's working habits for several books including the *Khiṭaṭ* (a topography assimilating a great amount of historical information and insight), we can discern a pattern in the works of late fourteenth-/early fifteenth-century Cairo historians: resourcefulness, rigour, forensic analysis and archival methods. These are the hallmarks of archival historiography.

In further demonstration of his resourcefulness, one may note the breadth of reference of each volume of Ibn al-Furāt's chronicle. In his sixth volume recounting 660–71/1261–72, Ibn al-Furāt uses twenty-seven prose sources as listed by Ashtor, which encompass a wide range of political, confessional and geographical perspectives, and a span of author death dates ranging from 209/819 (Hishām al-Kalbī) to 809/1407 (Ibn Duqmāq, Ibn al-Furāt's contemporary). Meanwhile, for the portion of the Crusading period that fell between 641 and 676/1243 and 1277, Riley Smith discusses eleven prose sources among others. For the second volume of *Ta'rīkh al-duwal* in Autograph A, Elshayyal has identified twenty-three prose and poetry sources for the years 522–43/1128–48, which include universal chronicles, local histories, inventories of state treasures, geographical works and so on.[87] In his valuable source analysis, Elshayyal reveals that for this volume alone, of which about 30 out of almost 200 folios cover Fatimid history, Ibn al-Furāt uses these 23 sources in 533 separate quotations.

Of these, 363 are properly attributed, often with the beginnings and ends of extracts signalled, in a medieval equivalent of quotation marks, and 170 are not, but are easily traced. Some instances of unidentified extracts remain but on the whole, the volume recounts a small number of events from many sources and perspectives, including an otherwise unknown work by Ibn Duqmāq (d. 1407) entitled *al-Durr al-munaddad fī wafayāt aʿyān ummat Muḥammad*.[88] For the late Fatimid period, Ibn al-Furāt adduces fourteen prose sources just for this dynasty.[89]

In sum, Ibn al-Furāt enjoyed peculiar talent for procuring and exploiting a wide variety of textual witnesses for each period he wrote about, including reports or documents not found elsewhere in the historiographic sources,[90] and, like Ibn Khaldūn in his sixth volume of history in particular, evinces an elasticity of deployment by fusing genres and confessional/political perspectives, including Christian ones.[91] It is these features of his work that have brought Ibn al-Furāt considerable attention in the modern era of scholarship, including in studies that have touched on his ingenuity in collecting and absorbing atypical reports of particular events. A telling example of this is Le Strange's discovery of parallels between Ibn al-Furāt's account of the death of the last ʿAbbasid caliph in 1258 and three entirely independent European sources from separate narrative traditions, as well as a Persian one, in which company his book is unique among the Arabic sources.[92]

Of the post-Fatimid universal chronicles, Ibn al-Furāt's is the prominent example of a methodologically lucid repository-cum-inventory of earlier works, the provenance and contributions of which he marks exceptionally clearly, surpassing the analogous method of Abū Shāma before him, and paving the way for similar practices by al-ʿAynī and Ibn Taghrībirdī after him. In this sense, Ibn al-Furāt clarifies and focuses the intertextuality of Middle Period Arabic historiography as defined by Kropp and Pfeiffer, evincing an unusually deep appreciation for earlier authorities and securing their long-term preservation.

Archival casualties: Texts chosen and not chosen in Ibn al-Furāt's compilation

There is, of course, a hidden backstory to the archival process, one which a well-placed appreciation of Ibn al-Furāt's preservation and rearrangement of sources occludes. This is the rejection of material from his chronicle-archive: the debris of textual selection and transmission, the secret double in the 'chain of consumption'[93] of texts, namely the 'chain of sacrifice' of texts that do not make it into the archive, a process analogous to the discarding of documentary material as adumbrated in preliminary fashion by Paul, once its social value was eroded, ended or transmogrified.[94] This brings up the issue of survival bias[95] and its risk to a well-founded perception of how much historiography was produced in any given era of history of the medieval Islamicate, how much of this was further copied – a matter often determined by the wealth and/or social position of the author – and how many of such texts survive in themselves or as quotations in subsequent redactions or compilations.[96] The key to understanding this problem is to view it less as narrative and documentary loss and more as a constructive phenomenon of sublimation in recognition of textual obsolescence, by means of which the continuing relevance – or otherwise – of texts was evaluated, acted upon and reified within works addressed to newer (present and future) audiences. In other words, high quality textual witnesses were most likely be preserved in the dynamics of archival transmission, given the careful choices made (and often explained) by a self-reflexive historian like Ibn al-Furāt. To take an example from his *Ta'rīkh al-duwal*, Ibn al-Furāt preserves unique narrative and documentary reports from Ibn Ṭuwayr's (d. 1220) invaluable eyewitness account of late Fatimid rule, discussed below in Chapters 5 and 6, while other sections of the work are preserved by al-Maqrīzī. In selecting some parts, the rest are lost.[97] Crucially, however, the book as whole withstood the risk of oblivion as a result of the archival agency of later historians.

That said, one must resist the temptation to regard the annalist-archivist as an omniscient figure who has at his/her disposal all possible manner of archivalia from which to accept or reject archival material. Rather, authors were resourceful to varying degrees, and may or may not have had access to key historiographical works preserving the histories they intended to retell and document, and of course archived some texts that fell victim to subsequent 'ups and downs' of historiographical survival, as is the case for some earlier text witnesses used by Ibn al-Furāt that have not – to our knowledge – made it to the present day in extant books.[98]

Medieval Islamic archivalities were thus modulated by the variable social, economic, environmental and intellectual contingencies of pre-print eras, and by the exigencies of future upheavals. A major implication of this for a chronicle such as Ibn al-Furāt's is that it renders the work an even more valuable archive emerging from contexts of ostensibly 'arbitrary' survival. Contemporary scholars are rarely well-positioned to trace the processes by which particular individual (sets of) codices end up in the modern libraries in which many of them are now to be found. Nor do we necessarily have deep or detailed information about the largely opaque early modern world of manuscript collection by means of purchase, theft or appropriation, or the general material as well as epistemic confusion if not systematic violence of colonial depredations via which historical texts were often removed from their places of origin, early circulation and spaces of safekeeping, to be preserved in later-formed collections. In short, a general climate of textual precarity could be said to have prevailed for Oriental manuscripts in the premodern, early modern and colonial eras.[99] That Ibn al-Furāt's historiography survives largely as two autographic series of codices underlines this perilous, nerve-wracking and contingent set of conditions. At the same time this survival underscores the absolute criticality of the processes of archival preservation of historiography within new textual compilations.

Notes

1 G. Flügel, *Die Arabischen, Persischen und Türkischen Handschriften der Kaiserlich-Koeniglichen Hofbibiliothek zu Wien*, II (Vienna, 1869), no. 814, 46–9; reference to the Rabat volume comes from al-Ziriklī (*al-A'lām* (Cairo, 1954–9), 6:631) and Cl. Cahen ('Ibn al-Furāt', *EI*[2], vol. 3, 1971, 768–9) who offer no full reference and the volume does not appear in the primary catalogue of the royal manuscript collection

of Rabat: A. Ammur and A. S. Binbin, *Kashshāf al-kutub al-makhṭūṭa bi 'l-khizānat al-ḥasaniyya* (Rabat, 2007); Vatican: A. Mai, *Codices Vaticani Orientali* (Rome, 1831): MS Arab 726, 607; E. Blochet, *Catalogue des manuscrits arabes des nouvelles acquisitions (1884–1924)* (Paris, 1925), 156; Bursa, Inebey Library: Huseyin Çelebî MSS 782–4 (further catalogue information appears to be not available for these volumes.) The correct title of the chronicle is attested in Ibn al-Furāt's hand in the London, Paris (Blochet) and two Bursa (HC783 and HC784) MSS discussed below.

2 Paris MS Blochet 5990, f. 213v; Khayr al-Din al-Zirikli, *al-A'lām: qāmūs tarājīm li ashhar al-rijāl wa 'l-nisā' min al-'arab wa 'l-musta'ribīn wa 'l-mustashrifīn*, 15th edition in 8 vols (Beirut, 2002), 6:200–1.

3 König and Whitmarsh, *Ordering Knowledge*, 34; Rustow, 'Fatimid State'.

4 Ibn Ḥajar, *al-Durar al-kāmina*, 4:101; al-Sakhāwī, *al-Ḍaw' al-lāmi' li ahl al-qarn al-tāsi'* (Cairo, 1355 H), 8:51.

5 I am grateful to an anonymous reviewer of this book for drawing my attention to Ibn Ṭūlūn's reference to Ibn al-Furāt's chronicle: *al-Ghuraf al-'aliyya fī tarājim muta'akhkhirī al-Ḥanafiyya*, Süleymaniye Library, MS Şehid Ali Paşa 1924, available online at https://f.hypotheses.org/wp-content/blogs.dir/3349/files/2016/12/Ibn-Tulun_Ghuraf-al-Aliyya.pdf, ed. T. Wollina (accessed October 2017), 38.

6 Flügel, 46–9; as I worked on Ibn al-Furāt's first three volumes, which are in very weak conservatorial condition, from microfilms, I have relied on Flügel's physical description of several features of the codices.

7 Flügel also indicates that the 'cut' of the first volume states (in a newer European hand) the following: *al-mujallad al-awwal min ta'rīkh Ibn al-Furāt bi khaṭṭi 'l-mu'allif*, a point repeated by Ahmed Taymūr (*Ta'rīkh al-duwal*, vol. IX, ed. Zurayk, editor's introduction, ي), which I could not verify from the microfilm of the first volume; for *tamma*: Gacek, *Arabic Manuscripts*, 75).

8 MS AF 117, f. 1v.

9 Paris MS Blochet 5990 has seventeen lines per page, while the Vienna series has a minimum of twenty-three and a maximum of thirty-four lines per page.

10 Paris MS Blochet 5990, ff. 1v, 213v.

11 Van Berkel et al., *Legal Documents*, 3.

12 al-Qāḍī, 'How Sacred …', 32.

13 These same signs and rubrics are present in the autograph Paris MS Blochet 5990, though I focus here on the Vienna series in which, inter alia, Fatimid to Mamluk history is covered.

14 A. Görke and K. Hirschler, *Manuscript Notes as Documentary Sources* (Würzburg, 2012), 9; al-Qāḍī, 'How Sacred…', 45.

15 A. Gacek, 'Taxonomy of Scribal Errors in Arabic Manuscripts', in Pfeiffer and Kropp, *Theoretical Approaches*, 217–35, 230.

16 Vienna AF117, 228r; cf. Paris MS Blochet f. 214r which has a sealing off statement in the author's hand.

17 Rustow, 'Fatimid State', identifies at least six different types of paper used in medieval Egypt from the Cairo Geniza fragments alone.

18 For comparison, while the Paris (Blochet), Bursa and London MSS have, as noted above, seventeen lines per page, they are in other respects similar to the Vienna volumes in showing rubrication, catchwords, titles and subheadings.

19 Though a thorough examination of Ibn Qāḍī Shuhba's selections from Ibn al-Furāt could perhaps fill some of this gap: D. Reisman, 'A Holograph MS of Ibn Qāḍī Shuhbah's *Dhayl*', *MSR* 2 (1998), 19–49; 39.

20 C. Brockelmann, *Geschichte der Arabischen Litteratur*, 2 vols (Leiden, 1943–9) and *Supplementbänden*, 3 vols (Leiden, 1937–42), II:61–2; *Supplement*, 50; Hajji Khalīfa, *Kashf al-ẓunūn ʿan asāmi ʾl-kutub wa ʾl-funūn*, 2 vols (Istanbul, 1941, 1943), II:104 (2104); I:27.

21 The Bursa, London and Paris (Blochet 5990) volumes are from one series; that is to say, the author's draft of his volumes on pre-Islamic and early Islamic history.

22 Paris MS Arabe 1595, ff. 1–138: ff. 1v, 6v, 22r, 45v, 55r, 77v, 90v; W. M. de Slane, *Catalogue des manuscrits arabes* (Paris, 1883–95), 301.

23 Paris MS Blochet 5990, f. 1v, Bursa HC 782 and Brit. Mus. Or 3007 all start with a *basmala*.

24 MS Wien AF 117, f. 2v; my translation.

25 T. Cornell, *The Beginnings of Rome: Italy and Rome from the Bronze Age to the Punic Wars* (c. 1000–264 BC) (London, 2012), 15.

26 *Taʾrīkh al-duwal*, III:192b.

27 Gacek, *Arabic Manuscripts*, 227–8.

28 D. Roffe, *Decoding Domesday* (Suffolk, 2015), 2.

29 Al-Qāḍī 2007, 33.

30 Chester Beatty MS Arab 4125, ff. 1–196; The rest of the MS offers selections from Ibn Duqmāq's (d. 1406) *Nuzhat al-anām*, and the work of unidentified fifteenth-century chronicler(s). Cf. Reisman, 'Holograph', 26–30.

31 J. L. Bacharach, 'Circassian Mamluk Historians and Their Quantitative Economic Data', *JARCE* 12 (1975), 75–87, 79.

32 Massoud, *Chronicles*.

33 Reisman, 'Holograph', 22–31.

34 De Slane, *Catalogue*, 301.

35 Al-Qāḍī, 'Biographical Dictionaries', 95.

36 M. F. Elshayyal, 'A Critical Edition of Volume II of *Taʾrikh al-duwal wa ʾl-Mulūk* by Muhammad b. ʿAbd al-Rahim b. ʿAli Ibn al-Furat', *IQ* 47 (2003), 197–216, 215, n. 3, provides full references to the known biographical entries on Ibn al-Furāt.

37 On Ziriklī's provision of autographs, see Humphreys, *Islamic History*, 28.

38 K. Stilt, *Islamic Law in Action: Authority, Discretion, and Everyday Experiences in Mamluk Egypt* (Oxford, 2011), 37.

39 G. Leiser, 'The Restoration of Sunnism in Egypt: Madrasas and Mudarrisūn 495–647/1101–1249', unpublished PhD dissertation (University of Pennsylvania, 1976), 289; N. O. Rabbat, *The Citadel of Cairo: A New Interpretation of Royal Mamluk Architecture* (Leiden, 1995), 92; D. Cortese and S. Calderini, *Women and the Fatimids in the World of Islam* (Edinburgh, 2006), 167; al-Maqrīzī, *Khiṭaṭ*, Bulaq edition, 2:165, l. 23; Ibn Duqmāq, *Kitāb al-intiṣār*, ed. K. Vollers, 2 vols (Cairo, 1891–2), 4:35; A. R. Guest and E. T. Richmond, 'Miṣr in the Fifteenth Century', *JRAS* (1903), 791–816, 809.

40 Leiser, 'Restoration', 289.

41 Bauer, 'Mamluk Literature', 23.

42 Historians 'either lived off inherited assets or plied mundane occupations to earn a living. Several wrote their huge compendiums "on the side" while … discharging juridical duties …': Petry, 'Scholastic Stasis', 332; cf. Leiser, 'Restoration', 419–20; for the life of another public notary and historian in Damascus, for comparison: S. Conermann, 'Ibn Ṭulūn (d. 955/1548) [*sic*]: Life and Works', *MSR* 8 (2004), 115–39; for lower-status scholarly roles in Mamluk society: J. Berkey, 'There Are ʿulamāʾ and Then There Are ʿulamāʾ: Minor Religious Institutions and Minor Religious Functionaries in Medieval Cairo', in R. E. Margariti, A. Sabra and P. M. Sijpesteijn (eds), *Histories of the Middle*

East Studies in Middle Eastern Society, Economy and Law in Honor of A. L. Udovitch (Leiden, 2011): 9–22; Bauer, 'Mamluk Literature', 23.

43 Massoud, *Chronicles*, 28, 34.

44 M. F. Elshayyal, 197–216, esp. 215, n. 3: Ibn Ḥajar (d. 1448), *Durar*, 4:101, *Inbā'*, 2:330; Ibn Taghrībirdī (d. 1470), *Manhal*, 1:145; al-Sakhāwī (d. 1497), *Ḍaw'*, 8:51, *I'lān*, trans. Rosenthal (1952), 497; al-Ṣuyūṭī (d. 1505), *Ḥusn al-muḥāḍara*, 1:320; Ḥājjī Khalīfa (d. 1658), *Kashf* 279; Ibn al-'Imād (d. 1678), *Shadharāt*, 7:72; Ziriklī (d. 1893), *A'lām*, 7:73; Kaḥḥāla, *Mu'jam*, 10:159 and Brockelmann (d. 1956), *GAL*, 2:50:61 and *Suppl.*, 2:50:49.

45 A 'large proportion' of the Arabic manuscript heritage succumbed to 'natural disasters, sweepings wars, frequent civil disturbances, personal or political actions, or simply … the passage of time' (al-Qadi, 'How Sacred …', 27).

46 A 'blending of colloquial and formal usages unique to the second half of the ninth/fifteenth century': Petry, 'Scholastic Stasis', 334. Ibn al-Furāt is an earlier exponent.

47 Ibn Ḥajar al-'Asqalānī, *al-Majma' al-mu'assas bi'l-mu'jam al-mufahras*, ed. Yusuf Abd al-Rahman al-Mar'ashli in 4 vols (Beirut, 1992–4), 2:516; al-Sakhāwī, *al-Ḍaw' al-lāmi'*, 8:51; idem, *al-I'lān bi 'l-tawbīkh li man dhamma 'l-ta'rīkh*, trans. Rosenthal (1952), 497.

48 *Kitāb al-sulūk li ma'rifa duwal wa al-mulūk*, 4 vols (Cairo, 1936–58, 1970–3); cf. n. 40.

49 *Shudhūr al-'uqūd fī dhikr al-nuqūd*, mentioned in Y. A. al-Mar'ashli *al-Majma' al-mu'assas*, 2:516, n. 1 and Ziriklī, *op. cit.*

50 G. Le Strange, 'The Story of the Death of the Last 'Abbāsid Caliph from the Vatican MS of Ibn al-Furāt', *JRAS* (1900), 293–300, 296, n. 1. Maqrīzī draws heavily on Ibn al-Furāt's history for his own history of the Mamluks, *Kitāb al-sulūk*, as noted by R. Amitai, *Mongols and Mamluks: The Mamluk-Īlkhānid War, 1260–1281* (Cambridge, 1995), 5, Massoud, *Chronicles*, 5, and others. Le Strange, *loc. cit.*, suggests that Maqrīzī owned Ibn al-Furāt's history for at least some period; for documentation of al-Maqrīzī's borrowings from Ibn al-Furāt for the events of 694/1294–5, see Little, *Introduction*, 73–5; and for the events of 778/1376–7 and 793/1390–1, see Massoud, *Chronicles*, chs. 1 and 2 (*passim*); further borrowings are indicated in: Amitai, *Mongols*, 43–59; Bacharach, 'Circassian Mamluk Historians', 76, 84.

51 P. E. Walker, 'Al-Maqrīzī and the Fatimids', *MSR* 7:2 (July 2003), 83–97, 85–7.

52 Al-Maqrīzī borrows or summarizes those 17 reports of Fatimid Egypt from volumes 2 and 3 of *Ta'rīkh al-duwal* for his *Itti'āẓ*, out of the total 106 discrete reports the first 3 volumes provide on the Fatimids. The number of reports presented by al-Maqrīzī is harder to enumerate as he does not in general mark the beginnings of quotations in the *Itti'āẓ*, virtually never marks their ends and conflates reports frequently.

53 Cf. *Ta'rīkh al-duwal*, III:191b–192a; *Itti'āẓ*, III:273–4; *al-Kāmil*, *sub anno* 559.

54 The medieval axiom, 'The closer [a] manuscript was to its author, and verifiably so, the greater was its value' (al-Qadi, 'How Sacred …', 42) still stands.

55 E. Ashtor, 'Some Unpublished Sources for the Bahri Period', in U. Heyd (ed.), *Studies in Islamic History and Civilisation* (Jerusalem, 1961), 11–30; Amitai, *Mongols*; Massoud, *Chronicles*.

56 Massoud, *Chronicles*, 34.

57 Ibid, 37; for a list of authorities used by Ibn al-Furāt for the Bahri period of Egyptian history alone: Ashtor, 'Some Unpublished Sources', 22–4.

58 *Al-I'lān bi 'l-tawbīkh li man dhamma 'l-ta'rīkh*, 497.

59 Ibid.

60 *Al-Ḍaw' al-lāmi'*, 8:51.

61 According to Ibn Ḥajar (Elshayyal, 200, citing *al-Durar al-kāmina*, 4:101); al-Sakhāwī, *al-Ḍaw' al-lāmi'*, 8:51; Ibn Ṭūlūn, *al-Ghuraf al-'aliyya*, ed. T. Wollina, 38; Ibn 'Imād al-Ḥanbalī, *Shadharāt*, 7:72.
62 Ashtor, 'Some Unpublished Sources', 14.
63 The range of subjects tackled by Mamluk chroniclers broadened as they reached times close to their own, including 'matters related to community and urban life including market prices, fires, murders, epidemics, floods and social relations': Elbendary, 'The Historiography of Protest', 9.
64 *Ta'rīkh al-duwal*, III:215a, b.
65 Ed. al-Shammā' (1968–9).
66 Defined as 'the history of the world, from Creation on', usually in annalistic or caliphal format (Robinson, *Islamic Historiography*, 135–7), in which an author would draw on … a few already existing chronicles for his account of events down to the most recent decades … , he would then complete his sources by writing a "continuation" (*dhayl*) based on a knowledge of events gained through direct participation, oral information gathered from friends, current official reports, etc.': Humphreys, *Islamic History*, 130–1.
67 Massoud, *Chronicles*, 34.
68 Cl. Cahen, 'Quelques chroniques anciennes relatives aux derniers Fatimides', *BIFAO* 37 (1937), 1–27, 1.
69 Amitai, 'Al-Maqrizi as a Historian of the Early Mamluk Sultanate (or: Is al-Maqrizi an Unrecognized Historiographical Villain?)', *MSR* 7:2 (2003), 99–118, 101.
70 R. Amitai, review of *The Cambridge History of Egypt, Vol. 1: Islamic Egypt, 640–1517*, ed. C. F. Petry in *JAOS* 121:4 (October–December 2001), 707–9, 709.
71 Ashtor, 'Some Unpublished Sources', 14.
72 Irwin, 'Mamluk History and Historians', 166.
73 According to al-Maqrīzī, Ibn al-Furāt and Ibn Duqmāq were friends, and the former borrowed from the latter (Massoud, *Chronicles*, 152).
74 Ibn Duqmāq was also an authority on early Mamluk history for his contemporaries, not least Ibn al-Furāt, but while the latter used Ibn Duqmāq's narrative for his own account of Circassian rule, he added very substantial quantities of further material to it: Massoud, *Chronicles*, 9.
75 Ashtor, 'Some Unpublished Sources', 21, n. 67; Little, *Introduction*, 73.
76 Massoud, *Chronicles*, 29.
77 Ibid., 36–7; Ibn Ḥajar did, however, regard Ibn al-Furāt as one of his teachers, not just a source for historical reports, and speaks of him highly respectfully: Van Steenbergen, *Order Out of Chaos*, 13.
78 W. C. Schultz, Review of Sami G. Massoud (2007): *Speculum* 84 (2009): 184–5.
79 R. Amitai, 'In the Aftermath of 'Ayn Jalut: The Beginnings of the Mamluk-Ilkhanid Cold War', *al-Masāq* 3 (1990), 12–13, 12–13; and *Mongols*, 129–30.
80 Al-Qadi, 'How Sacred …', 30–2; F. Déroche, 'The Copyists' Working Pace: Some Remarks towards a Reflexion on the Economy of the Book in the Islamic World', in Pfeiffer and Kropp, *Theoretical Approaches*, 203–13, 205.
81 Massoud, *Chronicles*, 34.
82 Ibid., 38.
83 Ashtor, 'Some Unpublished Sources', 14–18, 21–2.
84 Cf. Robinson, 148, citing Ibn al-Furāt's three variant accounts of the death of the Ayyubid sultan al-Malik al-Mu'aẓẓam (d. 1227).
85 Ashtor, 'Some Unpublished Sources', 17; Little, *Introduction*, 74.

86 Fischel, 'Ibn Khaldūn's Use of Historical Sources', 109–19, 118–19.
87 *Ayyubids, Mamlukes and Crusaders: Selections from the* Ta'rīkh al-duwal wa 'l-Mulūk *of Ibn al-Furāt*, two volumes, ed. U. and M. C. Lyons, with historical introduction and notes by J. S. C. Riley Smith (Cambridge, 1971), vii–xi; Elshayyal, 205–6.
88 Elshayyal, 203–4.
89 F. Bora, 'Mamluk Representations of Late Fatimid Egypt: The Survival of Fatimid-Era Historiography in Ibn al-Furāt's *Ta'rīkh al-duwal wa 'l-mulūk* (History of Dynasties and Kings)', DPhil thesis (Oxford, 2010), 92–6.
90 For instance the letter recording Kitbughā's accession to the sultanate in 1294: Little (1970), 74.
91 Ashtor, 'Some Unpublished Sources', 14; Cahen 1971.
92 Le Strange, 293–7; cf. Robinson, *Islamic Historiography*, 148.
93 L. Ryzova, 'The Good, the Bad, and the Ugly: Collector, Dealer and Academic in the Informal Used-paper Markets of Cairo', in S. Mejcher-Atassi and J.-P. Schwartz (eds), *Archives, Museums and Collecting Practices in the Modern Arab World* (London, 2011), 97–8.
94 Paul, 'Archival Practices', *passim*.
95 This is an understudied phenomenon: as of 2014, and since, there had been 'no research on the best practices for assessing survival bias in any corpus of manuscripts or printed books in Arabic script' according to D. A. Riedel's well-executed blog series about the history of Islamic books: https://researchblogs.cul.columbia.edu/islamicbooks/tag/survival-bias/ (accessed 10 November 2017).
96 Déroche, 'The Copyists' Working Pace'.
97 Reconstituted from these later quotations and others like it by A. F. Sayyid as follows: Ibn Ṭuwayr, *Nuzhat al-muqlatayn fī akhbār al-dawlatayn* (Beirut, 1992).
98 As mentioned above, in the earliest extant Vienna codex of AA, Ibn al-Furat refers (I:165a) to previous reports on Badr's vizierate (r. 1073–94) in an earlier volume that is no longer extant in either AA or AB.
99 Few collections in Europe, for example, offer detailed narratives of acquisition, though contents are often thoroughly described; see, for example, information on its Islamic world manuscripts offered by the Bodleian Library, Oxford: https://www.bodleian.ox.ac.uk/weston/finding-resources/guides/middleeast (accessed October 2017); Robert Jones, 'Piracy, War, and the Acquisition of Arabic Manuscripts in Renaissance Europe', *Manuscripts of the Middle East II* (1987): 96–110; see also Ryzova, 'The Good, the Bad, and the Ugly' and other fascinating chapters in this volume.

3

Fatimid Archivalia: Narratives and Documents in Late Fatimid Egypt

A famous anecdote is told … by Ibn Khallikān of how the great Imam and Caliph al-Mu'izz li-Dīn Allāh was challenged upon his entry into Cairo in 973 to prove his ancestry; his reply was to draw his sword as his nasab *or name, and throw down his gold coins as his* ḥasab *or ancestry … but the sword was called Dhu'l-Fiqār and the coins were stamped with an 'Alid legend.*

M. Brett, '*Lingua Franca* in the Mediterranean: John Wansborough and the Historiography of Medieval Egypt' (2001), 10

The 'logic and the semantics of the archive' are 'of memory and of the memorial, of conservation and of inscription'.

J. Derrida, *Archive Fever* (1995), 22

The written works from which Ibn al-Furāt and other post-Fatimid historians drew material for their historiographical archives are earlier works incorporating narratives and documents in order to explicate Fatimid history, including some key works written by Fatimid-era state officials with or without royal patronage. This literary activity serves to belie an essentializing assumption, made about Shi'i polities in general and about the Fatimids in particular, that the dynasty had little or no interest in the commemorative and archival value of historiography.[1] The nuances of framing 'Fatimid history' for medieval and contemporary historians forms a theme of the present chapter, alongside discussion of the extent of Fatimid-era material to be found in Ayyubid and Mamluk accounts and the archival mechanics of the process of transmission from one medieval text to another. This is followed by an audit of Fatimid 'historical' production of narratives and documents, from which later authors could select the texts that in turn become their archivalia. The discussion of sources from late Fatimid Egypt is not limited to the Fatimid tradition of historiography per se, that is, historiography produced for or on behalf of the ruling dynasty; rather, the focus is on historical books produced in the late Fatimid era, Isma'ili or not (a feature often hard to determine from the fragmentary narratives that remain). Key to this discussion is the issue of whether there was a hegemonic Fatimid 'canon' of works produced in proximity to the ruling family and its authority, and how much agency historians exercised, political or archival, with the caveats that not all canons are allied with ruling elites and, *pace* a dominant Foucauldian view, that not all archives are hegemonic.[2] From Fatimid archivalia there follows a brief excursus of key themes of Fatimid history as they appear in later works, as an appraisal of the uses that the historiographical archive is put to in reconstructing and analysing the late Fatimid era as elaborated by post-Fatimid authors including Ibn al-Furāt.

Dynastic, regional, confessional or social history: Framing the Fatimid past

In relation to Mamluk perspectives on Fatimid rule, it is taken as read that 'a comprehensive study of the Mamluk historiography of the Fatimid state remains an imperative', yet the task has yet to be undertaken on a large scale, chiefly due to its magnitude.[3] Ibn al-Furāt's recourse to, and archival preservation of past – often perished – texts in his formulation of late Fatimid history continues the work of predecessors from the Fatimid realm itself,[4] such as the Shafiʿite historian and early Fatimid-era official, al-Quḍāʿī (d. 1062). This author's digest (*mukhtaṣar*) of his universal chronicle, *ʿUyūn al-maʿārif*, extant in at least two redactions but not in its full form, contains several threads of information on early Fatimid history that were successfully archived and used in their more complete forms by at least nine major Ayyubid and Mamluk authors.[5] This reuse challenges an assumption, recently refuted in several studies, that Fatimid-era historiography did not survive the Ayyubid takeover of 1171 and its anti-Ismaʿili ideological aftermath, *pace* Lewis, Daftary, Halm and others.[6]

Whereas al-Quḍāʿī had offered an index of the political history of the earlier half of Fatimid rule in Egypt, where the author served in the office of the vizierate until his death in 1062, the first three unpublished volumes of Ibn al-Furāt's chronicle are occupied with accounts from the latter half of Fatimid rule in Egypt (viz. 1107–67, though with reference to past events from 1094), taking us up to a few years before the Fatimids' fall in 1171,[7] a period covering most of the second 'half' of the Fatimid era in Egypt, and the third of what may be termed the three phases of Fatimid rule.[8] Within this third and final age of Fatimid history, the forthcoming discussion focuses mainly on political affairs within Egypt, including the defence of Egypt's borders against Zengid and Crusader incursions.

A 'purely' political history of this caliphate and imamate, in which state (*dawla*) and religious mission (*daʿwa*) were structurally enmeshed, is in some sense elusive. Yet in another sense, Fatimid history constitutes a departure from the underlying pessimism of 'Shiʿite historiography' in which 'from the Shiʿite perspective, after the murder of the 'Ali and the withdrawal of his son and successor', history is but a 'long saga of crimes, misdeeds and oppressions' in Lewis's hardly neutral description.[9] A further methodological problem presented by Fatimid political history is that Fatimid statehood, once its locus had shifted to Egypt, began anew, and the previous sixty years of institutionalizing Fatimid rule in the Maghrib were superseded by the caliphate's attention to Egypt and the attempt to both establish themselves in and to reinvigorate that region. Unlike empires that collected territories or suzerainties from a central seat, the Fatimids' very capital moved once Jawhar (d. 992) had brought Egypt within their control in 969, in line with their imperial ambition. This political migration is clearly marked within historiography in distinctive ways: al-Quḍāʿī (d. 1062) writes of the Fatimid caliphs from al-Mahdī (d. 934) to al-Ẓāhir (d. 1036) in an Egypt-centred outlook. Even the brief extant *mukhtaṣar* (abridgement) of his chronicle mentions which of the Maghribi caliphs' children visited Egypt and what they did there, in locations from Fayyum to Alexandria to Fustat.[10] Meanwhile, the much later *Ittiʿāẓ al-ḥunafāʾ* of al-Maqrīzī (d. 1442), the only medieval work by a non-Ismaʿili devoted solely to Fatimid history, narrates the history of the Fatimid caliphate in both the Maghrib and Egypt. However, the work is one in a series of three separate histories of Egypt from the Islamic conquest to the author's own times, and in this sense the focus of the *Ittiʿāẓ* is Egyptian history too. Later still, Ibn Taghrībirdī (d. 1470) writes a universal Islamic chronicle in which, for the tenth to twelfth centuries, the year is reckoned according to the reigns of Fatimid caliphs, even if the annals also cover events in Islamic lands outside the Fatimid empire.

In contrast with this Egyptian frame of reference, the unique historical resource that is the Cairo Geniza,[11] the bulk of which deals with life in Fatimid and Ayyubid times, sheds light on a world of, inter alia, commercial transactions and communal and domestic relations that are much less circumscribed by regional borders. These papers serve as an unwitting archive, though conceived as an 'anti-archive' in that conservation for epistemic purposes is by default rather than design, and ordering of material is absent.[12] As a repository of miscellaneous records, they reveal personal networks transcending political boundaries, a feature that militates against the historiographical treatment of the Fatimid era purely in terms of Egyptian history.[13] Furthermore – and as an aside in the present context – as a repository that is non-hegemonic in its social function, the Geniza allows considerable scope for subaltern study of medieval Islamicate history.[14]

The history of the Fatimids could be approached as all of these: a dynastic history, a Mediterranean social history, a Shiʿi history and *the* Ismaʿili history par excellence; these perspectives are to a limited extent inscribed in a host of chronographic works. Yet with due acknowledgement of the immense, substantially untapped value of the Geniza papers for elucidating medieval Islamicate history, including history 'from below', modern historians cannot begin to understand late Fatimid socio-political developments without historiographical works that are rich in detail on these events, and also on the archival processes involved in their documentation.[15] Some material evidence for Fatimid history, for example the numismatic, is helpful but can also be potentially misleading if taken at face value: the first three Fatimid caliphs continued to mint coins with generic Sunni legends, and coins were often struck bearing the names of aspirants to the imamate rather than actual imams, for instance those struck in the name of Niẓār (d. 1097), the eldest son of al-Mustanṣir (d. 1094) who was passed over for the imamate in favour of his brother al-Mustaʿlī (d. 1101).[16] As for Ismaʿili works, no general histories proper are extant from the Egyptian phase of the caliphate.[17] This, too, leaves one to turn to the historical reports (*akhbār*) archived by Ayyubid and Mamluk authors, including Ibn al-Furāt.

The percolation of Fatimid-era chronicles into post-Fatimid accounts

While the Fatimid family had not *demonstrably* sponsored courtly historiography to a substantial or sustained degree after Qāḍī al-Nuʿmān's (d. 947) contributions, there were nonetheless a number of men within Fatimid Egypt, most of them servants of the state in some capacity, who wrote eyewitness accounts of Fatimid rule, some of which were likely official or semi-official in nature. The vestiges of these authors' works subsist in several later works of historiography, although clearly not all post-Fatimid authors had access to all or even the larger part of the most significant Fatimid-era historiographies, as one might expect in view of the selective transmission and dispersal pattern of *isnād*-based Islamic scholarship as a whole in the pre-printing age.[18]

More than a dozen Fatimid-era chronicles are known from later annals; it is predominantly through later references that we know of the books' existence. Apart from Ibn al-Ṣayrafī's (d. 1147) account of the Fatimid vizierate, a *mukhtaṣar* of al-Quḍāʿī's (d. 1062) multi-volume world history *ʿUyūn al-maʿārif* and three less comprehensive works by al-Anṭākī (d. 1066), Ibn Abi 'l-Ṣalt (d. 1134) and ʿUmāra al-Yamanī (d. 1175), these books do not survive as independent works today. Nonetheless, the use of Fatimid historiography in later compilations demonstrates that Arabic historiography from Fatimid to Mamluk times is marked more by continuity than disruption. Just as most Fatimid institutions, military, political, administrative and scholastic, were appropriated, albeit in an 'unsystematic' way,[19] by the Ayyubids in the late twelfth century and then again by the Mamluks after 1250, historiography, too, was to develop new strands while remaining firmly established on earlier bodies of reports.[20]

That continuity is encapsulated in the transmission of Fatimid-era historiography into Ayyubid works, which continued even as a new and prolific genre of works, centred around Ṣalāḥ al-Dīn's (d. 1193) campaigns and penned by a group of his close advisers and companions such as Qāḍī al-Fāḍil (d. 1200), Ibn Shaddād (d. 1235) and Abū Shāma (d. 1268), emerged. These, too, formed a main thread in Mamluk historiography of the thirteenth to fifteenth centuries, which absorbed and archived both sets of accounts. In fact, some of the main Mamluk authors to give Fatimid history a thoroughgoing narrative-documentary reconstruction, such as Ibn al-Furāt (d. 1405), al-Maqrīzī (d. 1442) and Ibn Taghrībirdī (d. 1470), reveal that the story of the last years of Fatimid rule was taken up by the chroniclers of Ṣalāḥ al-Dīn when they wrote of his early history, by which point some of the Fatimid-era accounts, including those by Ibn al-Ṣāyrafī (d. 1147) from the middle phase of Fatimid history and Ibn Ṭuwayr (1130–1220) from its final decades were either too early to contribute material or were preserved incomplete. ʿImād al-Dīn al-Iṣfahānī's (d. 1201) *al-Barq al-shāmī*, for instance, has an account of the last years of Fatimid rule (recounting 1166–93) which begins *after* many of Ibn al-Furāt's Fatimid-era sources cease to be used by him: the third volume of *Taʾrīkh al-duwal* ends in 1166/7.[21]

The complexities of the archival practices involved in transmission – the selecting, ordering and copying of historiographic material in Middle Period Arabic historiography – can be unravelled only piecemeal because of the temporal and geographic spread of authors and works, as Gibb's wide-ranging survey shows.[22] However, individual historiographic studies such as those by K. Hirschler and S. Massoud have the merit of throwing light on the processes of medieval Arabic historiographic transmission as a whole.[23] Modern studies thus reveal that Fatimid-era historiography produced by both Isma'ili and non-Isma'ili authors continued to be utilized by later authors in spite of its array of confessional perspectives, even if later compilers took differing underlying positions on whether Fatimid rule in Egypt had been a 'placing of Egypt on the world map', or an unholy interlude, or both.[24] The Mamluk historiographical archive shows a range of Fatimid-era authors whose works were exploited and preserved by at least some Ayyubid and Mamluk authors, whether their reports waxed lyrical about the Fatimids (such as Ibn al-Ṣayrafī's, d. 1147), were tonally 'neutral' about them (such as Ibn Ṭuwayr's, d. 1220) or took a pejorative anti-Fatimid view (such as al-Anṭākī's, d. 1066). One should note in this context that just as pro-Fatimid traditions made their way into later historiography, so too did anti-Isma'ili traditions exemplified by those of the late tenth-century 'Alid heresiographer and polemicist Akhū Muḥsin. His 'black legend', alleging a wholly different account of Fatimid origins than that generated by the dynasty, found its way into al-Nuwayri's, Ibn al-Dawādārī's and al-Maqrīzī's chronicles, though the latter challenged those views and presented the alternative even while he expressed them at length.[25] Each of these streams make their way into later chronicles, and further substantiate a picture of post-Fatimid historiography as a library of information and interpretation drawn together by means of a range of archival practices that will be isolated and discussed in the chapters that follow.

A map of the scope and survival of late Fatimid historiography

The historical outline of late Fatimid rule provided in detail in several major post-Fatimid chronicles is comprehensively informed by local narratives of historiography produced in Fatimid Egypt.[26] The following survey of the scope and survival of historiographical texts produced Fatimid Egypt, in particular the chronologically later portion of this corpus (post-1094), cannot constitute the whole sum of what was produced in that milieu. This acknowledged, the material that survives, whether a small or substantial part of late Fatimid historiography, is a rich vein of sources that promises to throw new light on the narratives and documents valued and used by later authors for record-keeping and commemorative purposes.[27]

Walker writes that 'for Fatimid history in general, the eyewitnesses whose accounts survive ... are the exception', and that 'few observers bothered to write an account of what they saw and heard, and of those that did, only a tiny handful [of texts] ever entered the public domain'.[28] While noting that this impression may result from survival bias, the overall dearth of eyewitness accounts is clear to see for the period of Fatimid historiography commencing with death of al-Mustanṣir (1094) and the ensuing Nizārī-Musta'lī split, up to the inception of Ayyubid rule proper between 1171 and 1174. Within this period, Sayyid's eighty-year 'third age' of the Fatimid caliphate, several eyewitness historiographical sources were available to later historians, though not all of them are extant.[29]

One of the earliest known post-Mustanṣir historical accounts is the lost *Risāla al-Miṣriyya* of the Andalusian Ibn Abi 'l-Ṣalt (1068–1134), who lived in Egypt between 1096 and 1112 under al-Afḍal's vizierate, spending three of those years in an Alexandrian prison on the vizier's orders, in which setting he composed works in the fields of medicine, philosophy and other subjects. Ibn Abi 'l-Ṣalt's eyewitness history of Egypt was produced during his later sojourn at the Tunisian court of the Zirid ʿAlī b. Yaḥyā. Some of his works are cited by later scholars, including Yāqūt al-Ḥamawī (d. 1229), al-Qifṭī (d. 1248) and Ibn Abī Uṣaybiʿa (d. 1269),[30] who preserve fragments of his writings. A small number of quotations from his history of Egypt, a 'description ... of the scholars and poets he met, and his assessment of the state of letters there in his time'[31] are provided by al-Maqrīzī.[32] His poetry, on the other hand, was widely known and is found in standard chronicles such as Ibn al-Athīr's *Kāmil*.[33]

Closer to the Fatimid administration were several authors who understood the Fatimid state in its later years well, and could convey an outline of its history and its ceremonial not only to al-Maqrīzī – who preserves much of this material – but also to several other historians, not all of whom wrote solely or primarily in Egypt. These historians, including Ibn al-Athīr (d. 1233) and Ibn Khallikān (d. 1282), did not all document their sources in the way the modern researcher might find helpful. The Fatimid insiders include the well-known historians Ibn al-Ṣayrafī (d. 1147), Ibn al-Ma'mūn al-Baṭā'iḥī (d. 1192) and Ibn Ṭuwayr (d. 1220), and more obscure figures to whom we only see briefest references in later works, such as al-Qurṭī (fl. c. 1160s), author of a history of Egypt up to his own day written for the vizier Shāwar (r. 1162, 1163–8). Another more fulsome account of the Fatimid caliphate, an important expression of the native Egyptian historiographical tradition but now lost, was written by the Fatimid administrator and *qāḍī* al-Muḥannak (or Ibn al-Muḥannak, d. 1154), a work I return to below.[34] Additional lesser-known historiographical treatises from the mid-to-late Fatimid period include four whose authors are not known: *Sīrat al-khalīfa al-Mustanṣir* (r. 1036–94), *Sīrat al-wazīr al-Yāzūrī* (r. c. 1049–58), *Sīrat al-wazīr al-Afḍal* (r. 1094–1121) and *Akhbār al-dawla al-Miṣriyya wa mā jarā bayn al-mulūk wa 'l-khulafā' min al-fitan wa 'l-ḥurūb min ayyām al-Āmir ilā ayyām Shīrkūh* (covering 1101–74), of which the last two, delineating events that appear in Ibn al-Furāt's compilation, feature in Chapter 4. That these authors' names are not recorded suggests that their works were not known well to Ayyubid and Mamluk compilers, and possibly survived only as singular autographs available to one or another later compiler like Ibn Ẓāfir (d. 1216), Ibn Muyassar (d. 1278), Ibn al-Furāt (d. 1405) or al-Maqrīzī (d. 1442), each of whom transmits extracts seemingly unavailable to others.

Of the better-known late Fatimid-era historians, three mentioned above were used by several later compilers: Ibn al-Ṣayrafī, Ibn al-Ma'mūn al-Baṭā'iḥī and Ibn Ṭuwayr. All three wrote directly from observations of events or records and were in a position to hear eyewitness testimony. They are thus united by their presence within the heart of the Fatimid courtly and administrative establishment, as were those forebears in whose tradition they might be said to have composed:[35] Ibn Zūlāq (d. 996), al-Musabbiḥī (d. 1029) and al-Quḍāʿī (d. 1062).[36] Of these last three, Ibn Zūlāq had written (now lost) biographies of the Fatimid general Jawhar and the first two Fatimid caliphs in Egypt, al-Muʿizz and al-ʿAzīz, while al-Musabbiḥī and al-Quḍāʿī served the Fatimids

Figure 3.1 Vienna Cod. A. F. 117, vol. 3 of Ibn al-Furāt's *Taʾrīkh al-duwal wa ʾl-mulūk*. A Fatimid-era eyewitness account (from line 8 onwards) is quoted by Ibn al-Furāt from *Akhbār al-dawla al-Miṣriyya wa mā jarā bayn al-mulūk wa ʾl-khulafāʾ min al-fitan wa ʾl-ḥurūb min ayyām al-Āmir ilā ayyām Shīrkūh*, a unique account of the years 1101–74 CE which is only known from Ibn al-Furāt. He received it without its author's name, and presents a sizeable extract of ten pages in all (MS Vienna AF 119 = Flügel 814, vol. 3, f. 185v).

directly in several official capacities, writing annalistic chronicles that survive only in part.[37] Though one could scarcely posit these historical texts as a 'tradition', in which reports from earlier histories would be transmitted in later historiographical archives (which, as far as may be detected in reports that remain, did not occur), there is no doubt that some semblance of what we may retrospectively term a 'Fatimid corpus' of historiographical works, pro-Fatimid and courtly in nature, was produced.

Indeed, a 'late Fatimid corpus' – though not a late Fatimid 'canon', with the hegemonic connotations of that term – may also be discerned from the traces that remain, from Ibn al-Ṣayrafī onwards, even earlier if reckoning from Ibn Abi ʾl-Ṣalt, a visitor to Fatimid Egypt who saw Fatimid political life first-hand. To this one could add, for the final years of Fatimid rule, eyewitnesses such as the emirs al-Idrīsī (fl. c. 1160s)[38] and Khalīl b. Khumārtakīn al-Ḥalabī (d. between 1194 and 1203) whose autobiographical accounts are preserved by the Shiʿi historian Ibn Abī Ṭayy (d. 1233) in Aleppo rather than Egypt. Though relative outsiders who did not emerge from the milieu of the Fatimid court, these authors' accounts do capture events at the heart of Fatimid political life, where they or their informants were present when several late Fatimid political struggles took place. Indeed, the emir Khalīl arrived in Egypt during the vizierate of his fellow Shiʿi Ṭalāʾiʿ b. Ruzzīk (r. 1154–61) and remained there for the rest of his life, giving him at least a ten-year stay in Egypt, which allowed him to pass first-hand reports to Ibn Abi Ṭayy and his father. Meanwhile, al-Idrīsī served as the vizier Ibn Maṣāl's envoy to Shīrkūh, and offers substantial reports to Ibn al-Furāt, while Khalīl provides one such report attesting the generosity of Ṭalāʾiʿ.[39]

Another eyewitness account is provided by Usāma b. Munqidh, discussed below. Meanwhile, Qāḍī al-Fāḍil's official court diary, the *Mutajaddidāt*, known well to al-Maqrīzī, has not survived intact. Though it sheds some light on late Fatimid rule, its content lies outside the scope of the years covered in this study (1107–66).[40] Yet another resource is the poetic *oeuvre* of ʿUmāra al-Yamanī, who versified the lives of the last Fatimid viziers and wrote idealized and fantastical homages to the role and qualities of the imam,[41] alongside memoirs that combine poetry and prose as vehicles for personal anecdotes. Much of ʿUmāra's verse refers and responds to contemporary political events, and represents the views of a late Fatimid courtly insider who wrote eulogies for and on behalf of the dynasty, despite harbouring ambivalence towards his Fatimid masters.[42] To bring together these works, whether surviving as traces, fragments or whole treatises, the trail of narratives transmitting from or to post-Mustanṣir Fatimid Egypt, as material for historiographical archives, would look like the table below (Table 3.1).[43]

Four of these were produced outside Fatimid Egypt, of which the history and memoirs of Ibn Abi 'l-Ṣalt and Usāma b. Munqidh respectively were apparently only available to al-Maqrīzī, although Ibn al-Furāt reproduces a portion of Usāma's verse epistles. The two emirs' testimonies are uniquely preserved by Ibn Abī Ṭayy and through him are transmitted by Abū Shāma and Ibn al-Furāt. In other words, these two sources exist (or migrate) outside Egypt and then return to Egypt via the Aleppan Ibn Abī Ṭayy (d. 1233) and the Damascene Abū Shāma (d. 1267). This leaves six prose sources produced in late Fatimid Egypt, and a body of poetry that does not fall into the genre of 'historiography' – if defined as a body of historical reports – but often records historical details. This last-mentioned poetical source was well known to later authors, but the remainder of the narratives listed above were known to only one or a handful of later historians, of the several dozen Egyptian and non-Egyptian Ayyubid and Mamluk authors summarized by Little in 1998 who wrote about Fatimid Egypt.

Whether or not one may trace a continuous tradition of Fatimid-era historiography for the final century or so of Fatimid history in Egypt, albeit one with significant gaps (the longest between al-Quḍāʿī (d. 1062) and Ibn al-Ṣayrafī (d. 1147)), the relationship between these early works, and indeed the lack of a discernible transmissional connection between them, prompts several questions. While most of the authors above were 'insiders' (many were Sunni, but served the Fatimid administration; it is hard to determine if any identified as Ismaiʿili), they seem to be either unaware or unengaged

Table 3.1 Historical narratives of the late Fatimid era

Author	Work(s)	Description
Ibn Abi 'l-Ṣalt (d. 1134)	*al-Risāla al-Miṣriyya*	Describes Egypt c. 1096–1110; lost; known to al-Maqrīzī
Ibn al-Ṣayrafī (d. 1147)	a history	Lost, known only to Ibn al-Dawādārī (d. 1334)
Ibn al-Ṣayrafī (d. 1147)	*al-Ishāra ilā man nāla 'l-wizāra* (or *Kitāb al-wuzarā'*)	history of Fatimid viziers from Ibn Killis (d. 991) to al-Baṭā'iḥī (d. 1125); extant; well-known to later authors including Ibn al-Furāt, al-Maqrīzī, al-Qalqashandī and al-Ṣuyūṭī
al-Muḥannak (d. 1154)	*Ta'rīkh khulafā' Miṣr*	Lost; known to Ibn Muyassar as an important source for his partially surviving *Akhbār Miṣr*, who possibly uses him for the periods 1047–1108 and 1120–58, and through Ibn Muyassar known to al-Maqrīzī
The emirs al-Idrīsī (fl. c. 1160s) and Khalīl b. Khumārtakīn al-Ḥalabī (d. between 1194 and 1203)		Provided eyewitness reports to the Aleppan Ibn Abī Ṭayy (d. 1233), who reproduces them in his *Ma'ādin al-dhahab*; they are then copied by Abū Shāma and Ibn al-Furāt
'Umāra al-Yamanī (d. 1175)	*Dīwān*, *al-Nukat al-'aṣriyya fī akhbār al-wuzarā' al-Miṣriyya*	Cover 1162–9; extant; known to many later authors, for example, Ibn Wāṣil, Abū Shāma, Ibn Khallikān, the Yemeni Idrīs 'Imād al-Dīn (d. 1468)
Usāma b. Munqidh (d. 1188)	*Kitāb al-i'tibār*	Covers parts of 1144–54 when the author lived in Fatimid Egypt; extant; known to Abū Shāma and possibly to al-Maqrīzī
Ibn al-Ma'mūn al-Baṭā'iḥī (d. 1192)	*Sīrat al-Ma'mūn*	Covers 1107–25, with special attention to the caliphate of al-Āmir (1101–30) and the vizierate of the author's father, Ibn al-Ma'mūn al-Baṭā'iḥī (r. 1121–5); lost; known to Ibn Ẓāfir, Ibn Muyassar, Ibn 'Abd al-Ẓāhir, al-Nuwayrī and al-Maqrīzī
Ibn Ṭuwayr (d. 1220)	*Nuzhat al-muqlatayn fī akhbār al-dawlatayn*	covers c. 1121–60; lost; known to Ibn al-Furāt, Ibn Khaldūn, Ibn Duqmāq, al-Qalqashandī, al-Maqrīzī, Ibn Ḥajar, Ibn al-Zayyāt and Ibn Taghrībirdī
Two anonymous treatises:		
	Sīrat al-wazīr al-Afḍal (r. 1094–1121)	Lost; known to Ibn Ẓāfir
	Akhbār al-dawla al-Miṣriyya wa mā jarā bayn al-mulūk wa 'l-khulafā' min al-fitan wa 'l-ḥurūb min ayyām al-Āmir ilā ayyām Shīrkūh	Extant fragment, which could be the whole, covers 1101–74; known to Ibn al-Furāt, to al-Maqrīzī via Ibn al-Furāt and possibly to Ibn Muyassar

with works by their predecessors. From the first century of Fatimid Egypt, al-Quḍāʿī's extant digest makes no references to Ibn Zūlāq or to al-Musabbiḥī. Nor, for the late Fatimid period, does the Fatimid portion of Ibn Ṭuwayr's account of Fatimid history draw upon the narratives of Ibn al-Ṣayrafī or Ibn al-Maʾmūn al-Baṭāʾiḥī, though both knew the workings of the state from within.

Overall, more historiography about Fatimid history was written than we thought, and in this, the twelfth century is richer in historical texts than the eleventh.[44] One may speculate whether substantial gaps in the broader historiographical archive of Fatimid Egypt is significant for determining the scope of a 'Fatimid corpus', an archive in itself which would contribute archivalia to later chronicles. One may also ponder the reasons behind these periods of seeming historiographical and archival silence. Is it due to the paucity of Fatimid authors, allied with their separation in time from one another, which would make contemporary collaboration of the kind later witnessed between the Mamluk-era Damascene historians al-Yunīnī (d. 1326), al-Birzālī (d. 1339) and al-Jazarī (d. 1338) impossible?[45] Or were individual works commissioned by caliphs or viziers for their edification or entertainment? Did historians see their forebears or their contemporaries as rivals, whose work could not be placed within their own historiographical archives? Did service under different rulers make a difference to particular approaches to composing a record of the dynasty? Or is the seeming lack of textual continuity between Fatimid sources an illusion created by our inability to consult fuller versions of perished Fatimid works? Did the divisions caused by periodic succession problems from 1094 through much of the twelfth century lead to interruptions in the archival record of historiography, as each ruler projected a new image of power and legitimacy, a process in which historians might be expected to play a part? This set of conditions might indeed thwart the prospect of a pan-Fatimid hegemonic projection within historiography. The paucity of records for al-ʿĀḍid (d. 1171), for instance, is remarkable compared with the fullness of those for Ṣalāh al-Dīn (d. 1193). Indeed, the records for al-Muʿizz, the caliph on whose behalf Egypt was conquered and who built Cairo and several of its major institutions, are scarcely better.

The life cycles of Fatimid documents

Though some of these questions could occupy chapter-length discussions of their own, several are broached in the textual analysis of Chapter 4. An underlying issue is whether or not any Fatimid-era works were 'official' or 'semi-official' compositions, relying for their information on one or more of several official channels of caliphal or vizieral authority. These include royal *khuṭbas* (Friday or festival sermons)[46] and, more significantly in view of their greater number and more pointedly political content, the ruler's decrees and royal/official correspondence (*sijillāt, mukhlaqāt*) through which public announcements were made, diplomacy carried out, news conveyed to sympathetic allies or clients abroad and petitions from the public answered. The *sijillāt* were the 'imperial announcements' and 'official instructive correspondence of the Caliphs [which the] Fatimid Imams used to guide their followers in religious matters, especially in various situations of emergency'. Al-Qalqashandī 'used the term in reference to documents issued by Fāṭimid caliphs, either conferring *iqṭāʿāt* on their subjects or appointing them to public office (*wilāyāt*)'; at the same time, '*sidjill* was also a general term for "document" especially during the Fāṭimid period'. As for *mukhlaqāt*, 'On the occasion of certain festivals, official documents, known as *mukhlaqāt*, were sent to the governors of the provinces.'[47] This category of sources, official Fatimid documents, is itself broad, divided by type and purpose and with varying survival patterns. It is also a corpus currently undergoing expansion in view of the evolving discovery, within Geniza collections, of state documents once de-acquisitioned by the Fatimid chancery and repurposed for a range of writings by Jewish communities in medieval Cairo, though the vast majority of these remain as yet unpublished.[48] In the context of a polity whose grandeur is performative and oral rather than inscribed within formal sacrosanct archives, the seemingly ephemeral nature of state documents as explained by Marina Rustow raises a fundamental question as to their archivality or lack thereof. At the same time, the reuse of valuable *sulṭānī* (government) paper, a finer quality of paper than several others identified from the Cairo Geniza, carries the implication that the documents of the Fatimid royal court were characterized by a degree of archivality in the sense of carrying potential for an afterlife, as manifested in their material value for literary reuse.[49] Thus the multifaceted archivality of Fatimid documents is recently being reconsidered as the chancery corpus buried within Geniza papers is slowly but surely excavated and examined. Nonetheless, preliminary readings of paper reuse in this context and in later documentary contexts indicate that the culture of documentation was an intrinsic and significant feature of the 'writerly culture' of the medieval Islamic episteme.[50] For the Fatimid era, el-Leithy helpfully points out, several 'examples suggest that there were systematic protocols for cancelling expired documents after they had been preserved and collected. As such, they remind us that such documents had a life cycle – indeed, that the "destruction" or discarding were not accidental events, but part of the deliberate and purposeful manner by which documents were handled.'[51]

I engage the question of how and to what degree Fatimid state documents had a prolonged life cycle within historiography, and how they may have informed and set the tone for individual specimens of Fatimid historiography – and thus entered the post-Fatimid archive – in the subsequent chapter, where I examine specific documents preserved by Ibn al-Ṣayrafī and Ibn Ṭuwayr, as archived by Ibn al-Furāt. Clearly, the official documents of Fatimid Egypt were pre-eminent vehicles for the dynasty's self-representation at home and abroad. They expressed the dynasty's continued will-to-legitimacy, their apologetic arguments[52] in the wake of succession problems and the projection of their royal and religious credentials as an imamate and an empire.

To attempt an audit of such documents as remain, a larger number than previously thought,[53] which 'provide solid evidence of how they were produced and recorded', we may note at the outset that they survive in several ways, as follows:

i. Original chancery documents preserved in an institutional or formal archive such as the decrees preserved at St. Catherine's Monastery in Sinai;
ii. Fatimid chancery documents discovered in the Cairo Geniza, both originals and copies (due to paper reuse);[54]

iii. Copies made within the chancery itself, for record-keeping purposes; these might also be further preserved in a repository such the Geniza;
iv. Copies preserved in a later literary or devotional sources, such as extant transcripts of letters from the caliph al-Mustanṣir to his Ṣulayḥid vassals in the Yemen preserved by the Tayyibi communities of Yemen and India, or the reminiscences, letters and other personal notes of the Fatimid chamberlain Jawdhar (fl. tenth century) transcribed by his secretary Abū ʿAlī Manṣūr al-ʿAzīzī al-Jawdharī.[55]

The main collections of these types of documents, which indicate a high degree of archivality immanent within the Fatimid chancery, within non-Muslim religious institutions[56] and within historiographical works, have been examined and in some cases collected and published over the years. Notable for their contributions to this endeavour are Stern, Goitein, Khan and Rustow for the first and second classes of documents,[57] and al-Hamdani and al-Shayyal for the third; preliminary work on the latter suggests they are accurate copies of the originals.[58] Al-Shayyal discovered some 110 copies of documents in 10 'major [mostly] Egyptian and Syrian works' including Ibn al-Ṣayrafī and al-Qalqashandī,[59] of which he published 23.[60]

The aggregate messages of these official statements, explicit and sub-textual, emanating from the variety of practical functions they performed as well as their imperial rhetoric, are powerful:

> The Fatimids followed the Abbasids in issuing decrees in response to petitions (*al-tawqīʿ ʿalā al-qiṣaṣ*), in principle in response to anyone in the realm and in practice anyone with connections. ... Each instance of petition and redress was also a performative occasion that allowed the caliph to establish himself as the highest protector of the weak and the dynasty as legitimate in the eyes of its subjects.[61]

Through their formulae as well as their pragmatic uses, the Fatimid caliph or his vizier would at every opportunity use such documents,[62] and others written for different purposes, alongside formal proclamations within *sijillāt* and *khuṭbas* (the latter delivered on the two feast-days and on Fridays in Ramaḍān) to reassert the caliph's role as the ultimate arbiter of disputes and the dispenser of justice in Fatimid domains. A proportion of these documents forms a key component of the Fatimid archivalia extant within post-Fatimid chronicles, which reveals their epistemic value as primary source witnesses to Fatimid political history.

The *imam* and his historians: Relations and tensions

It is clear that alongside the self-expression disclosed in the formulation of policy, the Fatimid government could use its organs and official documentation to express its views on a variety of political and social matters, to articulate the content and style of its management of the realm, and fashion itself and its responses (for instance, on the central question of succession to the imamate) as exigencies might demand. The statements made in these classes of documents (*sijillāt, mukhlaqāt*) were both initiated by the Fatimids, and written in response to petitions put forward to them, for example the often detailed issues from the special departments (*dīwāns*) dealing with the Fatimids' management of their own vast estates, and the responses to petitions from subjects, such as those requiring permission for the building of places of worship.[63] This dialogue with subjects, mediated by chancery officials, was in addition to the wide and ambitious *da'wa* programme carried out by Fatimid missionaries at home and abroad. With such extensive use of official proclamations and responses to their subjects' needs, did the Fatimid caliphs need to expressly harness the 'public relations' potential of historiography? Was the archival work of historians needed in order to record the achievements of the dynasty? Clearly, Qāḍī al-Nu'mān (d. 974) had played the role of official historian before the conquest of Egypt,[64] but within Fatimid Egypt, can we find a pro-Fatimid historiography, based upon the caliphate's version of social and historical developments as propounded in *sijillāt* and other documents issued by their various *dīwāns*?

The presence or absence of 'official' Fatimid historiography has been examined on several occasions by M. Brett,[65] who analysed the traces of earlier Egyptian material in the partially surviving chronicle of the early Mamluk author Ibn Muyassar (d. 1278), a history extant only in its digest produced by al-Maqrīzī, covering c. 1030–1171.[66] From Brett's close readings of Ibn Muyassar on a range of Fatimid-related events, including the Fatimids' decade-long dispute with the Zirids of Ifriqiya in the mid-eleventh century (1048–58), to their battles against the Crusaders at Ramla at the turn of the twelfth (1101–5), it is evident that Ibn Muyassar archived earlier Egyptian Fatimid sources, now lost, that were unavailable to earlier historians, notably Ibn al-Qalānisī (d. 1160) and Ibn al-Athīr (d. 1233), who cover those same events but had no access to the native Egyptian historiographical archive as Ibn Muyassar did. Brett makes a probabilistic argument that official *sijillāt* were the source on which Ibn Muyassar's sources relied. That a chronicle, perhaps the one(s) written by al-Muḥannak, from the centre of the Fatimid court, was the intermediate source for Ibn Muyassar is another point Brett proposes. This would indeed answer the puzzle of how Ibn Muyassar came to know the details of such pivotal events as al-Ma'mūn's convening of an assembly of Fatimid royals and state officials at the Fatimid Palace in 1122 to refute the Nizārī claim to the imamate and present a comprehensive justification of the Musta'lī-Āmirī line, supported by Niẓār's sister.[67] Meanwhile original Fatimid chancery issues that survived the fall of the Fatimids – on account of the institutional continuity from Fatimid through to Mamluk times – are offered by Brett as the likely source for al-Qalqashandī's reproductions of Fatimid-era documents.[68]

Crucial to the search for the sources of twelfth-century Fatimid history is Brett's suggestion that Ibn al-Ṣāyrafī may also have worked from a set of official annals even as he penned official letters and documents himself as head of the Fatimid chancery, an organ 'working as ever to generate a favourable version of events for public consumption'.[69] Ibn al-Ṣāyrafī was the foremost official wordsmith of the Fatimid era, author of the dynasty's decrees, their vizieral biographies and their annals. We might also characterize him as both a Musta'lian historian and *the* Afḍalite historian par excellence, for it was in homage to the latter that he composed one of his works, and he represents al-Afḍal's vizierate as sanctioned by al-Mustanṣir, a point elaborated in Chapter 4. Indeed, both al-Mustaʿlī and al-Afḍal who ruled in his name would have found the services of an historian with Ibn al-Ṣayrafī's range of literary skills to be an immeasurable asset, not just for writing significant legitimizing decrees on their behalf, as he was to do for al-Āmir later in his career, but for expounding the personality and achievements of a vizier such as the awe-inspiring al-Afḍal, whose stature within the state is indicated in Geniza documents, a relatively 'bottom-up' historical source compared with the 'top-down' perspectives expressed in many chronicles.[70]

Archival origins: Records from the court

Ibn al-Furāt's history cites Ibn al-Ṣayrafī's book of Fatimid viziers on a single occasion, to discuss al-Afḍal, who promoted Ibn al-Ṣayrafī to the headship of the chancery and was served by him until his (al-Afḍal's) death in 1121; he does not cite Ibn Muyassar at all. Yet through Ibn al-Ṣāyrafī, Ibn al-Furāt accesses an original Fatimid record, indeed draws upon other 'insiders', too, notably Ibn Ṭuwayr. The latter was a late Fatimid-era civil servant who provides Ibn al-Furāt with some twenty, often lengthy reports on the late Fatimids (compared with Ibn Abī Ṭayy, the next most frequently cited author by Ibn al-Furāt for the Fatimids, who is used on fifteen occasions.)

Ibn Ṭuwayr, who records history based upon official documentation, the author of these twenty reports archived in Ibn al-Furāt's account of twelfth-century Fatimid caliphs and viziers, is a little-known figure. Yet it is clear from sparse biographical details about him offered by al-Mundhirī (d. 1258), al-Dhahabī (d. 1348) and al-Ṣafadī (1363) that as a civil servant within the Bureau of Salaries under the final three and possibly the final four Fatimid caliphs, he would certainly have had access to documentation issued by the Fatimid chancery.[71] Indeed, Ibn Ṭuwayr provides more documentary material to later historians than Ibn al-Ṣayrafī's book of the vizierate, though we know from Ibn al-Ṣayrafī's other works, especially the *Qānūn*, that he had access to a full range of state archives and penned *sijills* himself, while also describing archival practice in some detail.[72] The preservation, via reproduction, of documents within historiography was not, then, dependent – in a primary sense – upon an aim of extolling the virtues of the Fatimid dynasty, but rather substantiated historical narratives with details derived from their own official channels of communication. At the same time, a historian's reliance on the latter source might result in a hegemonic discourse in a secondary sense, as a later discussion of Ibn Ṭuwayr's information on events leading up to and immediately after the death of al-Āmir, and the ensuing and ongoing succession crisis, reveals. In this light, the loss (or incompletion) of Ibn Ṭuwayr's section on the Ayyubids is unfortunate, since few individuals were as capable as he of providing an eyewitness comparison between the two polities, Fatimid and Ayyubid, in terms of historical events, documentary-archival practice and dynastic or vizieral self-representation. Qāḍī al-Fāḍil was in the similar position of having served both administrations, but spent most of his professional life working under Ṣalāḥ al-Dīn, while Ibn Ṭuwayr served the Fatimids for several decades; this length of service accounts for the specificity and range of information he offers that is not available via other means.

In the light of these considerations, one may note that 'serving the dynasty' remained a multifaceted occupation for men of the pen like Ibn al-Ṣayrafī and Ibn Ṭuwayr, and it is thus far from clear how much the latter's book could be said to represent an 'official' perspective on late Fatimid history. He does not eulogize the Fatimid viziers and caliphs he depicts in the manner of other authors we encounter below; at the same time, he offers a unique view of Fatimid ceremonial and civic life, including the contents of Fatimid-era documents, in which context he reveals the transmutation of documentary archives into narrative archives. The other eyewitnesses Ibn al-Furāt draws upon cannot be as clearly identified as offering 'a "Fatimid" view of Fatimid history'[73] as these two administrator-historians, although the anonymous treatise named *Akhbār al-dawla al-Miṣriyya* appears to come from the pen of a participant or at the very least first-hand observer of events at the palace and court of late Fatimid Egypt, specifically in its last decade.

From the Mamluk archive of Fatimid-era sources, it is far from clear that the late Fatimid caliphs and viziers had a close connection with the works of such chroniclers as remain, and indeed as the Fatimid state came closer to fragmentation, so too did the production of historical narratives archiving their history for posterity apparently cease to be produced altogether, until Ibn Ṭuwayr and to a lesser extent Qāḍī al-Fāḍil wrote ex post facto accounts mainly or wholly produced in Ṣalāḥ al-Dīn's Egypt. This is not to say that a close causal relationship between caliphal tenure and chronicle production might not have existed earlier in Fatimid Egypt: the question Brett raises regarding Ibn Muyassar's unique 'insider' information on Fatimid policies could usefully bear greater examination with detailed references to the sources in question, particularly the extracts that remain from al-Muḥannak.

For the Fatimid administration in its closing decades, however, once Ibn al-Ṣayrafī had ceased his service in a variety of literary and representational capacities, the Fatimid historiographical archive was similarly frail, and lacking the robustness of the early and authoritative narrative of the Fatimids' route to power penned by Qāḍī al-Nuʿmān in the years before the conquest of Egypt, or the courtly annals produced by al-Musabbiḥī under al-ʿAzīz, al-Ḥākim and al-Ẓāhir. ʿUmāra al-Yāmani contributed a body of panegyrics to the production of Fatimid-era literary works, though Fatimid viziers rather than caliphs took the lion's share of his attentions. Indeed, in the end ʿUmāra paid with his life for what looked, to the Fatimids' enemies, like his unwavering support for the dynasty. As far as chronicles went, however, so little remained that the eyewitness reports from non-Egyptians preserved by the Aleppan Ibn Abī Ṭayy gain special significance in both Ibn al-Furāt's and present-day understanding of the unravelling of Fatimid power in Egypt.

In this sense, therefore, firm conclusions about the archival discursive agency of the late Fatimid historian as it relates to the commissioning and entrusting agency of the late Fatimid caliph or vizier, whose image and policies the historian might be expected to explain or articulate, are elusive, especially in light of the paucity of both historical and historiographical information from late Fatimid Egypt on the question of how Fatimid ruler and Fatimid historian related to one another. A general observation could be made that historians could be expected to legitimize the rule of the caliphs or viziers who empowered them (via appointments and commissions) to undertake the task of keeping records for their tenure and record their legacies. But beyond this, the exploration of political–archival relations in late Fatimid Egypt fleshed-out further in Chapter 4 is necessarily limited to minutiae rather than a larger audit of the kind produced for later Mamluk Egypt by R. Irwin in 2006. The scale of this enquiry is circumscribed by the sporadic survival pattern of narrative and documentary sources for late Fatimid history. In archival terms, however, it is clear that Fatimid narrative and documentary corpora, rich and variegated as they originally were, deeply informed much later works. Numerous specimens of both literary texts and documents are often preserved solely via their integration into post-Fatimid narrative works including Ibn al-Furāt's chronicle.

Notes

1 The anecdote cited by Brett at the start of this chapter is widely cited in both medieval and modern sources, but is decried by the Isma'ili senior missionary and historian Idrīs 'Imād al-Dīn (d. 1468) as anti-Isma'ili propaganda: S. Jiwa, *The Founder of Cairo: The Fatimid Imam-Caliph Al-Mu'izz and His Era* (London, 2013), 263.

2 For a useful critique of a ubiquitous reading of archives that identifies them with political domination, see Sartori, 'Seeing Like Khanate', 231–5.

3 P. Sanders, 'Claiming the Past: Ghadīr Khumm and the Rise of Hafizi Historiography in Late Fatimid Egypt', *SI* 75 (1992), 81–104, 81.

4 For an analysis of what was written and what remains, see F. Daftary, *Isma'ili Literature* (London, 2004), 22–6, who argues that the Fatimids commissioned and produced numerous historiographical works.

5 For a detailed examination of Mamluk reports on the death of the Fatimid caliph al-Ḥākim (d. 1021), see F. Bora, 'An Historiographical Study of al-Quḍā'ī's *Ta'rīkh*', MPhil thesis (Oxford, 1998).

6 'With the exception of a few fragments, the Fatimid chronicles did not survive the downfall of the dynasty. The Sunni Ayyubids who succeeded the Fatimids in Egypt systematically destroyed the renowned Fatimid libraries at Cairo': F. Daftary, *A Short History of the Isma'ilis* (Edinburgh, 1998), 5. For a sample of modern scholars who propound the idea, see B. Lewis: 'Saladin and the Assassins', *BSOAS* 15:2 (1953), 239–45, 242; idem, review of *Die Chronik des Ibn ad-Dawādārī. Sechster Teil. Der Bericht über die Fatimiden* by Ṣalāḥ al-Dīn al-Munajjid, *BSOAS* 26:2 (1963), 429–31, 429; idem, Letter, 'The Vanished Library', *The New York Review of Books*, 37:14, 27 September 1990; H. Halm, *The Fatimids and Their Traditions of Learning* (London, 2001), 92–3; K. Thomson, *Politics and Power in Late Fatimid Egypt. The Reign of Caliph al-Mustansir* (London and New York, 2016), 1. For popular reiteration of that view, see, for example, *Rosicrucian Digest* 8:1 (2006), 8. Michael Brett asks the more pertinent question of why Fatimid chronicles survived the twelfth century, but not the fifteenth: '*Lingua Franca* in the Mediterranean: John Wansborough and the Historiography of Medieval Egypt', in H. Kennedy (ed.), *The Historiography of Islamic Egypt (c. 950–1800)* (Lieden, 2001), 1–11, 10–11. For a comprehensive analysis of this myth, see F. Bora, 'Did Salah al-Din Destroy the Fatimids' Books? An Historiographical Enquiry', *JRAS* 25:1 (2015), 21–39; cf. Hirschler, *Medieval Damascus*, 117.

7 The last five years of Fatimid Egypt, 1167–71, are covered in the published fourth volume of Ibn al-Furāt's chronicle: *Ta'rīkh al-duwal wa 'l-mulūk*, vol. 4, edited in two parts by M. H. al-Shammā' (1968), covering 563–87, but with significant lacunae.

8 These 'three ages' are the initial Maghribi caliphate based at Qayrawān (909–69), followed by stages of conquest and consolidation (969–1094) and the decline of the caliphate through its eclipse by the military vizierate (1094–1171). A. F. Sayyid, 'Lumieres nouvelles sur quelques sources de l'histoire Fatimide en Egypte', *AI* 13 (1977), 1–41, 19, denotes the last eighty years of Fatimid rule the 'third age' of the Fatimid caliphate beginning with the death of al-Mustanṣir in 1094, while Daftary, *The Isma'ilis*, 238, also begins a new chapter on Fatimid history with the year of al-Mustanṣir's death.

9 B. Lewis, 'Reflections on Islamic History', *From Babel to Dragomans: Interpreting the Middle East* (Oxford, 2004), 408.

10 See the epitome of the lost *'Uyūn al-ma'ārif* of al-Quḍā'ī, MS Pococke 270, Bodleian Library, Oxford; ff. 105a–108a.

11 This trove is ironically often regarded as 'the opposite of an archive': el-Leithy, 424.

12 By Friedrich's definition, the Genizas were counter-archival for not making their materials easily available, but were archival in intending long-term preservation of their contents: 'Epilogue: Archives and Archiving', 426.

13 S. D. Goitein, *A Mediterranean Society*, 5 vols (Berkeley and Los Angeles, 1967), 1:1; for more on counter-archival activity, see A. Hoffman and P. Cole, *Sacred Trash: The Lost and Found World of the Cairo Geniza* (New York, 2011), 13; cf. el-Leithy, 'Living Documents', Ryzova, 'The Good, the Bad, and the Ugly...'.

14 See for example Amitav Gosh's fascinating essay, 'The Slave of Ms. H. 6', Occasional Paper No. 125 (1990), Centre for Studies in Social Sciences, Calcutta.

15 Recent significant developments in Geniza research can be followed via, *inter alia*, the newsletter of the Princeton Geniza Lab: https://www.princeton.edu/~geniza/ (accessed October 2017).

16 For the Niẓārī coin: http://www.iis.ac.uk/view_article.asp?ContentID=105243 (accessed November 2017).

17 For the North African phase of the caliphate, H. Halm, *Das Reich des Mahdi* (Munich, 1991), translated by Michael Bonner as *The Empire of the Mahdi* (Leiden, 1996) and M. Brett, 'Fatimid Historiography: A Case Study – The Quarrel with the Zirids, 1048–58', in D. O. Morgan (ed.), *Medieval Historical Writing in the Christian and Islamic Worlds* (London, 1982), 47–59, examine its history and historiography. For the Fatimid Isma'ili *da'wa*, S. Jiwa, 'The Initial Destination of the Fatimid Caliphate: The Yemen or the Maghrib?', *BRISMES* 13:1 (1986), 15–26, begins with some useful pointers to primary sources from the different areas of missionary activity, especially 15–26.

18 On the endurance of traditionalism in historiography, and the use of the *khabar-isnād* (report and attribution): Robinson, *Islamic Historiography*, 92–3.

19 Y. Lev, 'Symbiotic Relations: Ulama and the Mamluk Sultans', *MSR* 13:1 (January 2009), 1–26, 5.

20 The literature on this issue is substantial but scattered; for continuities in the role of *waqf*: see S. A. Arjomand, 'The Law, Agency, and Policy in Medieval Islamic Society: Development of the Institutions of Learning from the Tenth to the Fifteenth Century', *CSSH* 41:2 (April 1999), 263–93, 281; for the pluralistic confessional conditions developed by the Fatimids which facilitated an Ayyubid takeover: P. Sanders, 'The Fatimid State, 969–1171', in Petry, *The Cambridge History of Egypt*, 151–74, 173–4; for the reliance of Mamluk institutions such as the military organization on Ayyubid models: R. S. Humphreys, 'The Emergence of the Mamluk Army I', *SI* 45 (1977), *passim*, discussing

D. Ayalon, 'Studies on the Structure of the Mamluk Army I', *BSOAS* 15:2 (1953); L. S. Northrup, 'The Baḥrī Mamlūk Sultanate 1250–1390', in Petry, *The Cambridge History of Egypt*, 242–89, 259; Y. Lev, *War and Society in the Eastern Mediterranean, 7th–15th Centuries* (Leiden, 1996), 5.

21 For more on this book, see H. A. R. Gibb, 'Al-Barq al-Shami: The History of Saladin by the Katib 'Imad al-Din al-Isfahani', *WZKM* 52 (1952–5), 93–115.

22 Gibb, 'Historiography', *EI*², 233–45.

23 Hirschler, *Medieval Arabic Historiography*; Massoud, *Chronicles*.

24 Bora, 'Mamluk Representations'.

25 *Khiṭaṭ*, 2:172–6; F. Daftary, *The Assassin Legends: Myths of the Isma'ilis* (London, 1994), 25ff.

26 For previous surveys of Fatimid historical texts, collected at different stages and through various strategies: A. R. Guest, 'A List of Writers, Books and Other Authorities Mentioned by El Maqrizi in His *Khiṭaṭ*', *JRAS* (1902), 103–25; Cahen, 'Quelques chroniques', Sayyid, 'Lumieres nouvelles' and Walker, *Exploring an Islamic Empire*.

27 Friedrich, 'Epilogue: Archives and Archiving', 436.

28 Walker, *Exploring an Islamic Empire*, 131–2.

29 Sayyid, 'Lumieres nouvelles', 19.

30 Ibid., 20; M. Comes, 'Umayya b. ʿAbd al- ʿAzīz, Abu 'l – Ṣalt al- Dānī al- Ishbīlī', *EI*².

31 Walker, *Exploring an Islamic Empire*, 147.

32 Sayyid, 'Lumieres nouvelles', 20; Guest, 118.

33 For example, *al-Kāmil*, trans. Richards, 1:310.

34 Cahen, 'Quelques chroniques', 5; Sayyid, 'Lumieres nouvelles', 22; Walker, *Exploring an Islamic Empire*, 148.

35 Ibn al-Ma'mūn did not appear to serve the Fatimid administration but, as the son of a vizier, attended state functions and had access to official documents: N. J. G. Kaptein, *Muhammad's Birthday Festival: Early History in the Central Muslim Lands and Development in the Muslim West Until the 10th/16th Century* (Leiden, 1993), 8.

36 Al-Maqrīzī takes his account of al-Mu'izz from Ibn Zūlāq, of whose history he possessed an autograph (P. E. Walker, *Orations of the Fatimid Caliphs: Festival Sermons of the Ismaili Imams* (London, 2009), 22) and his accounts of al-'Azīz, al-Ḥākim and al-Ẓāhir are from al-Musabbiḥī: A. F. Sayyid, edition of Ibn Muyassar's *Akhbār Miṣr: As Chronique d'Égypte* (Cairo, 1981), 50–1.

37 Sayyid, 'Lumieres nouvelles', 9–14; Walker, *Exploring an Islamic Empire*, 145.

38 Cahen, 'Quelques chroniques', 5.

39 *Ta'rīkh al-duwal*, III:150a, 212b.

40 Qāḍī al-Fāḍil's was appointed head of the Fatimid chancery in c. 1167; the precise dates for which he kept his diary are apparently not known: see C. Brockelmann, 'al-Ḳāḍī al-Fāḍil', *EI*².

41 P. Smoor, 'Umara's Odes Describing the Imam', *AI* 35 (2001), 549–626, 550.

42 See, for example, P. Smoor, 'Umara's Elegies and the Lamp of Loyalty', *AI* 34 (2000), 467–564.

43 For the lost history of Ibn al-Ṣāyrafī: Ibn al-Dawādārī (d. after 1335) quotes it for Fatimid caliphs from al-Qā'im to al-Ḥāfiẓ (i.e. for c. 934–1132), 'notably for panegyric poems in praise of the Fāṭimid caliphs', in his *Kanz al-durar*: see Shayyal, 'Ibn al-Ṣayrafī', *EI*². For Ibn Muyassar's use of al-Muhannak, see Walker, *Exploring an Islamic Empire*, 162. Ibn al-Zayyāt (d. 1411), author of a work on sacred journeys or *ziyārāt*: *Kitāb al-kawākib al-sayyāra fī tartīb al-ziyāra* (Cairo, 1907).

44 Walker, *Exploring an Islamic Empire*, 147–8.

45 Cf. L. Guo, *Early Mamluk Syrian Historiography: Al-Yūnīnī's Dhayl mir'āt al-zamān* (Leiden, 1998), 81 ff.
46 Walker, *Orations*, 92–3, 117.
47 Walker, 'Succession', 249; S. M. Stern, 'The Epistle of the Fatimid Caliph al-Āmir (*al-Hidāya al-Āmiriyya*): Its Date and Its Purpose', *JRAS* (1950), 20–31, 21; De Blois, Little, Faroqhi, 'Sidjill', *EI*[2]. *Mukhlaqāt*: Kaptein, 12, referencing both Ibn al-Ṣayrafī and Ibn Ṭuwayr, via the *Khiṭaṭ* of al-Maqrīzī.
48 Rustow, 'Fatimid State'.
49 Ibid.
50 Hirschler, 'Document Reuse' discusses the reuse of paper from Mamluk-era Damascene marriage contracts; Melvin-Koushka, 'Of Islamic Grammatology', 42–113, 46.
51 El-Leithy, 425. Cf. Jurgen Paul's similar argument in 'Archival Practices'.
52 See Stern, 'Epistle'; idem, 'The Succession to the Fatimid Imam al-Āmir, the Claims of the Later Fatimids to the Imamate, and the Rise of Ṭayyibi Isma'ilism', *Oriens* 4 (1951), 193–255.
53 Rustow, 'Petition'.
54 S. M. Stern, *Fatimid Decrees: Original Documents from the Fatimid Chancery* (London, 1964); S. D. Goitein, 'The Cairo Geniza as a Source for the History of Muslim Civilisation', *SI* 3 (1955), 75–91, 76, refers to 'about 20 pieces from the chancellery of the Fatimid caliphs' but the real number is much larger and as yet unquantified fully; cf. Rustow, 'Fatimid State'.
55 H. F. al-Hamdani, 'The Letters of Al-Mustanṣir bi'llāh', *BSOAS* 7:2 (1934), 307–24; Walker, *Exploring an Islamic Empire*, 113; al-Jawdharī's biography of Jawdhar, which includes the latter's letters and other archivalia, was published by H. Haji as *Inside the Immaculate Portal: A History from the Fatimid Archives* (London, 2012).
56 As examined in detail by el-Leithy.
57 Rustow, 'Petition', 2, n. 1. Cf. Paul, 'Archival Practices'.
58 An illuminating comparison by Geoffrey Khan between a rare archival transcript of a decree issued by the Fatimid caliph al-Ḥāfiẓ (r. 1131–49) (a copy made by a chancery official at the time of issue), found in the Taylor-Schechter Genizah collection, and the structure of archival copies reproduced by Ibn al-Ṣayrafī (d. 1147), reveals that the copy in the archive has the same wording *and* sense as the original decree; G. A. Khan, 'A Copy of a Decree from the Archives of the Fatimid Chancery in Egypt', *BSOAS* 49:3 (1986), 439–53, 441.
59 J. al-Shayyal, *Majmūʿāt al-wathā'iq al-fāṭimiyyīn: I wathā'iq al-khilāfa wa wilāyat al-ʿahd wa 'l-wizāra* (Cairo, 1958, reissued 1965); see also Rustow, 'Petition', 2, n. 1.
60 Walker, *Exploring an Islamic Empire*, 120.
61 Rustow, 'Petition', 5.
62 S. M. Stern, 'A Fāṭimid Decree of the Year 524/1130', *BSOAS* 23:3 (1960), 439–55, 446: several of the decrees mentioned are issued by viziers rather than caliphs; in fact, in al-Ḥākim's era, some were even issued by his half-sister Sitt al-Mulk: see Rustow, 'Petition', 1.
63 For example, D. S. Richards, 'A Fatimid Petition and 'Small Decree' from Sinai', *Israel Oriental Studies* 3 (1973), 140–58; Rustow, 'Petition', 1.
64 Qāḍī al-Nuʿmān's *Iftitāḥ al-daʿwa*, an official, caliph-commissioned history offering an authoritative account of the spread of Ismaʿilism in Yemen and across North Africa, dates from 957, some twelve years *before* the conquest of Egypt. For the fusion of genres in Ismaʿili literary/historical works, see C. E. Bosworth, 'A Medieval Islamic Prototype of the Fountain Pen', *JSS* 26:2 (1981), 229–34, 230; for historical elements

embedded in Isma'ili theological works, see F. Daftary, 'Isma'ili Historiography', *Encyclopaedia Iranica* 14 (2007–8), 176–8, 176.

65 *Inter alia* 'Fatimid Historiography'; review of A. F. Sayyid's edition of Ibn Muyassar's *Akhbār Miṣr*, *JRAS* 2 (1983), 293–5; 'The Battles of Ramla (1099–1105)', in U. Vermeulen and D. de Smet (eds), *Egypt and Syria in the Fatimid, Ayyubid and Mamluk Eras*, vol. I (Leuven, 1995), 17–37; Brett, '*Lingua Franca*', 1–11.

66 Brett, review of A. F. Sayyid.

67 See Daftary, *The Isma'ilis*, 245.

68 See Brett, '*Lingua Franca*', 9–11.

69 Ibid., 8.

70 In relation to al-Afḍal (r. 1094–1121), the Geniza sources do indeed support descriptions in historiographic sources such as Ibn al-Ṣayrafī's, regarding his conduct as an able and powerful ruler. Goitein, *Mediterranean Society*, III:348.

71 Sayyid, *Nuzhat*: Introduction, 10.

72 Hirschler, 'From Archive to Archival Practices', 44.

73 Sanders, 'Claiming the Past', 81.

4

Mamluk Archivalities: Late Fatimid History in Ibn al-Furāt's Chronicle

Archival thinking encourages a specific approach to knowledge, as manipulable, discrete fragments ... that are to be subjected to a process of analytical ordering.

J. König & T. Whitmarsh, *Ordering Knowledge in the Roman Empire* (2007), 35

Through archived documents, we are presented with pieces of time to be assembled, fragments of life to be placed in order, one after the other, in an attempt to formulate a story that acquires its coherence through the ability to craft links between the beginning and the end.

Achille Membe, 'The Power of the Archive and its Limits' (2002), 3

The archival function of Mamluk historiography as it pertains to the history of the Fatimid dynasty is manifested in two senses. Chronicles are repositories of reports that carry out a deliberate if unenunciated role of archival conservation, constructed through a range of archival strategies as revealed by particular archival signs. The approach of archivistics as a hermeneutic model brings into sharp relief the specific choices of Mamluk chronographers, and illuminates key features of the epistemic values that shaped their production of chronicles that served positive, normative, subversive, didactic and recreational purposes. The archival reading mode also allows exploration of what was discarded in the positive act of making a selection, that is to say, both conservation and exclusion of source material as twin aspects of choosing, reinvigorating and authorizing source material. Where Ibn al-Furāt uses otherwise perished sources, for example an anonymous treatise on the vizieral struggles of the final years of Fatimid rule, discussed presently, his chronicle plays a key role in the survival of this text, thus mitigating the long-term effects of textual loss engendered not simply by the passage of time but by acts of banal or routine but also symbolic epistemic violence in which literary corpora, documentary and narrative, were often a casualty.[1] Without indulging the counterfactual, it is safe to say that in the absence of documentary and narrative archival conservation within chronicles such as Ibn al-Furāt's, inquiry into such eras as the Fatimid would be poorly resourced. Indeed, the key issue of narrative and document reuse within chronicles as an essential procedure for extending the life cycles of historical reports should be evaluated alongside other forms of conservation in the medieval episteme, such as the recovery of library holdings in the context of political vicissitudes, as documented by Hirschler.[2] To adduce an example from the Fatimid era, the author Ibn al-Ma'mūn al-Baṭā'iḥī (d. 1192) used documents procured from his father, a Fatimid vizier between 1121 and 1125, for his book of history, in which process the copy in his book is the one that survives while the two copies originally prepared were destroyed in course of conflicts between his father and the Fatimid caliphs.[3] The chronicle as archive proves the resilience of narrative and documentary material over the Fatimid to Mamluk eras, in which the obsolescence, discarding, recovery and redeployment of texts – both for their content and for the media on which they were inscribed – were common features of the epistemic landscape of government, law, education and religious institutions, family affairs, trade, business, estate management and so on, of which several key aspects, in particular government and legal documents, were discussed recently by Jurgen Paul.[4] The archival aspect of documents reproduced within later books, particularly chronicles alongside bureaucratic manuals and legal literature, where they apparently survive in relatively healthier numbers than as independently surviving documentary collections,[5] is discussed in a Mamluk belletristic context by Bauer, who regards such documents' transition from a pragmatic to a literary textuality as offering them a 'second life'.[6] Meanwhile Paul has convincingly speculated that while loose folia were evidently frequently lost to posterity, books including chronicles, offering the 'protective envelope' of a codex, were 'routinely preserved'.[7]

Ibn al-Furāt's specific choices of text for his record of late Fatimid rule, and the archivality of his techniques, form the main subject matter of this chapter, preceded by an enumeration of his sources, the further sources adduced for comparison, remarks on the relevance or otherwise of distinctive Egyptian and Syrian schools of historiography and general preparatory comments on the stages of archivality in his approach.

Ibn al-Furāt's archivalia: Sources from the Fatimid, Ayyubid and Mamluk eras

While his chronicle, in familiar pattern, covers events across the central Islamic lands, Ibn al-Furāt appears to use distinct clusters of authors for specific areas of historiography, although a few, such as Ibn Khallikān, are ubiquitous throughout his work. For Fatimid rule, Ibn al-Furāt's prose sources are the following:

Fatimid-era sources (969–1171)

1. *Kitāb al-wuzarā' li 'l-dawla al-Fāṭimiyya bi 'l-Qāhira al-Mu'izziyya* (= *al-Ishāra ilā man nāla 'l-wizāra*) by Abu 'l-Qāsim 'Alī b. Munjib Ibn al-Ṣayrafī (1071–1147),[8] an administrator and author based in the Fatimid chancery for nearly fifty years from 1101, eventually becoming its head when promoted by the vizier Afḍal b. Badr (d. 1121). Two of his works have been published, including *al-Ishāra*, while a *mukhtaṣar* (abridgement) and continuation of an earlier Fatimid chronicle has not survived. He also wrote *Sijillāt* (official letters)[9] and *al-Qānūn fī diwān al-rasā'il* (a guide to chancery practice).[10]

2. *Nuzhat al-muqlatayn fī akhbār al-dawlatayn al-Fāṭimiyya wa 'l-Ṣalāḥiyya* by al-Murtaḍā al-Qayṣarānī Ibn Ṭuwayr (1130–1220),[11] a high-ranking Fatimid and Ayyubid official. His history of the two dynasties has not survived whole, but is used by several later authorities including al-Maqrīzī (d. 1442), and has been reconstituted from later quotations.
3. Accounts by al-Sharīf al-Idrīsī (via Ibn Abī Ṭayy): originally Aleppan, al-Idrīsī was an eyewitness to events of late Fatimid rule in Alexandria, and served as an Alexandrian envoy to the general Shīrkūh[12] as mentioned in Abū Shāma's extracts from Ibn Abī Ṭayy's work.[13] The narrative is first person: presumably, Ibn Abī Ṭayy heard it directly. Neither Ibn al-Furāt nor Abū Shāma mention that Ibn Abī Ṭayy provides the reports from al-Idrīsī, or cite the latter as al-Idrīsī's transmitter. It is, however, clear from both *Ta'rīkh al-duwal* and *al-Rawḍatayn* that Ibn Abī Ṭayy is the source for these and other eyewitness accounts of the power struggle between Shāwar and Asad al-Dīn Shīrkūh in c. 560–62/1164–6.
4. *Akhbār al-dawla al-Miṣriyya wa mā jarā bayn al-mulūk wa 'l-khulafā' min al-fitan wa 'l-ḥurūb min ayyām al-Āmir ilā ayyām Shīrkūh*, a work of unknown (complete) length and authorship, described as a 'small fragment' by Ibn al-Furāt (III: 185b). It is extant only in the extract provided in *Ta'rīkh al-duwal*, covering the years 1101–74, though al-Maqrīzī appears to summarize its contents in his *Khiṭaṭ*, and Ibn Muyassar, another keen collector of Fatimid traditions, may have been aware of its contents.[14]

Ayyubid-era sources (1171–1250)

5. *al-Muntaẓam fī ta'rīkh al-umam* by Ibn al-Jawzī (1114–1201),[15] a prolific Hanbalite author based in Baghdad, who created a new literary genre with this monumental historical–biographical work.
6. Khalīl b. Khumārtakīn al-Ḥalabī (d. between 1194 and 1203): an Imami Shi'i notable who was one of Ibn Abī Ṭayy's oral informants, having arrived in Egypt during the vizierate of his fellow Imami Shi'i Ṭalā'i' b. Ruzzīk (r. 1154–61). Having received a gift of 1,000 *dīnārs* from the vizier, he spent the rest of his life in Egypt.[16]
7. *Ma'ādin al-dhahab fī ta'rīkh al-mulūk wa 'l-khulafā' wa dhawi 'l-rutab* by Yaḥyā b. Ḥamīd al-Najjār al-Ḥalabī Ibn Abī Ṭayy (1180–1233), an Aleppan chronicler who was the only known Imami Shi'i historian of the Fatimids. His universal and Egyptian histories are now lost. As well as being central to Ibn al-Furāt's work, he was a key source for Abū Shāma in *al-Rawḍatayn*.[17]
8. *al-Kāmil fi 'l-ta'rīkh* by 'Izz al-Dīn Ibn al-Athīr (1160–1233), the Mosul-born author best known for this universal history and for an account of the Atabegs of Mosul, *al-Bāhir fī ta'rīkh atābakāt al-Mawṣil*.[18]
9. *Wafayāt al-a'yān* by Shams al-Dīn Abu 'l-'Abbās Aḥmad b. Muḥammad Ibn Khallikān (1211–82), who lived and worked as a senior judge and legal scholar in both Cairo and Damascus.[19] This work is a renowned biographical dictionary of personalities from Tulunid and Ikhshidid through to Ayyubid times, and is a popular reference point for Ibn al-Furāt throughout *Ta'rīkh al-duwal*.

10. *Akhbār al-duwal al-munqaṭiʿa* by Ibn Ẓāfir (1171–1216 or 1226), (quoted via Ibn Khallikān): the author was a secretary in the early Ayyubid chancery in Egypt, and produced a series of dynastic chronicles of which this and a section on the Samanids has been published.[20] The Fatimid portion, a discrete volume, was edited by André Ferré in 1972.[21]
11. *al-Taʾrīkh al-Manṣurī talkhīṣ al-kashf waʾl-bayān fī ḥawādith al-zamān*, (or *Taʾrīkh-i Mansūrī*) by Muḥammad b. ʿAlī Ibn Naẓīf al-Ḥamawī (d. 1240): an Ayyubid author described by Ibn al-Furāt as 'the scribe of al-Malik al-Ḥāfiẓ Arslān Shāh b. al-Malik al-ʿĀdil Sayf al-Dīn Abū Bakr b. Ayyūb' (*Taʾrīkh al-duwal* 3: 193b), whose Syria-focused chronicle survives as a unicum housed in St. Petersburg, edited by P. A. Gryaznevich.[22]
12. *Mufarrij al-kurūb fī akhbār Banī Ayyūb* by Jamāl al-Dīn Muḥammad Ibn Wāṣil (1208–98), an *ʿālim* and *qāḍī* whose chronicle was devoted to the Ayyubid dynasty.[23] The first three volumes go up to the reign of al-Malik al-Kāmil, Ṣalāḥ al-Dīn's nephew.

Mamluk-era sources (1250–1325)

13. *Naẓm al-sulūk fī taʾrīkh al-khulafāʾ wa ʾl-mulūk* by Nāṣir al-Dīn Shāfiʿ b. ʿAlī b. ʿAsākir b. al-ʿAsqalānī (1251–1330) who was, according to Ibn al-Furāt, the grandson (though some maintain the nephew)[24] of the *qāḍī* Muḥī al-Dīn Ibn ʿAbd al-Ẓāhir (d. 1292), the private secretary of Baybars and author of biographies of Mamluk sultans as well as a topographical work.[25] Shāfiʿ b. ʿAlī's career as a chancery clerk was cut short by being blinded in battle, which led to a long retirement devoted to scholarship. His history, also used by Ibn al-Furāt in later volumes of *Taʾrīkh al-duwal*, is thought to be a lost work, but his précis of his grandfather's biography of Baybars survives.[26] One of Shāfiʿ b. ʿAlī's main historiographical sources is his aforementioned uncle, Ibn ʿAbd al-Ẓāhir, who in turn quotes from earlier lost Egyptian authorities such as al-Quḍāʿī (d. 1062), for instance in his topography of Cairo.[27]
14. *Zubdat al-fikra fī taʾrīkh al-hijra* by Rukn al-Dīn Baybars al-Dawādār al-Manṣūrī (c. 1247–1325),[28] a Mamluk general and historian, initially the *mamlūk* of Qalāwūn, who went on to become head of the chancery. Baybars's personal history was linked with that of Qalāwūn: at one stage he was appointed the viceroy of Egypt (*nāʾib al-sulṭān*), second only to the sultan, but was later deposed and imprisoned in Alexandria. He wrote two main histories: *Zubdat al-fikra*, a partially surviving universal history, and an account of the Bahri Mamluks entitled *al-Tuḥfa al-mulūkiyya fī ʾl-dawla al-Turkiyya*,[29] and possibly also a history of caliphs.[30]

Illuminating archival choices: The sources adduced for comparison

The Mamluk chronicles above habitually transmit earlier reports in a non-uniform way. The authorial 'voice' is switched frequently between the compiler-archivist and his informants, and layers of reports are laid down at times in a seemingly haphazard manner, moving between the years in which an event might take place, or presenting a series of events within one of the annals in which a significant aspect of it occurred, as was common in earlier modes of Arabic historiography. These practices are discernible in Ibn al-Furāt's account of Fatimid history. Yet his selection, far from being arbitrary, reveals patterning and suggests rationales for his choices of reports for any particular incident. It is therefore germane at this juncture to scrutinize the sources of Ibn al-Furāt's sources, and to compare Ibn al-Furāt's account with relevant reports from works by authors who preserve some of the fullest, most original or methodologically distinct accounts of Fatimid Egypt, from Egyptian, Syrian and other historiographical traditions.[31] Donald Little's discussion of thirty-five historiographical sources from the Ayyubid and Mamluk eras sets the boundaries of the following survey, and to this I add two authors not included by Little because their accounts are more significant for the Fatimid period than for the Ayyubid or Mamluk, namely Ibn Ẓāfir (d. 1216 or 1226) and Ibn Muyassar (d. 1287).[32]

For authors who were near contemporaries of Ibn al-Furāt, Sami G. Massoud's synchronic study of the chroniclers who, like Ibn al-Furāt, straddle the Bahri and Burji eras of Mamluk history from the 1380s onwards, offers a useful resource for comparative analysis.[33] Of these fifteen or so historians, Ibn Khaldūn (d. 1406) and Ibn Duqmāq (d. 1407) are the closest contemporaries of Ibn al-Furāt to write on the Fatimids, albeit at varying lengths.[34] Both died within a year or two of Ibn al-Furāt's death in 1405; they are the main reference points for the question of how Ibn al-Furāt's materials and approach compare with concurrent efforts.[35]

An archival reading of source material within chronicles must remain open-ended rather than exhaustive due to the fact that some works are in manuscript form and present problems of access. That said, Ibn al-Furāt's conservation and reuse of Fatimid-era material is most usefully elucidated with reference to a finite yet securely established set of works by authors who wrote on late Fatimid Egypt. A list of their main relevant works now follows, although additional titles were consulted where the coverage of history made this appropriate:

Ibn Ẓāfir (d. 1216 or 1226), *Akhbār al-duwal al-munqaṭiʿa*
Ibn Muyassar (d. 1287), *Akhbār Miṣr*
al-Nuwayrī (d. 1333), *Nihāyat al-arab*
Ibn Khaldūn (d. 1406), *Kitāb al-ʿibar*
Ibn Duqmāq (d. 1407), *Nuzhat al-anām*
al-Maqrīzī (d. 1442), *Ittiʿāẓ al-ḥunafāʾ*, *Khiṭaṭ*
Ibn Taghrībirdī (d. 1470), *al-Nujūm al-zāhira*

These sources complement the above-mentioned twelve independent works that are explicit sources for *Taʾrīkh al-duwal*, either directly or through an intermediate source, and help to clarify Ibn al-Furāt's archival strategies and his specific choices of text. Some notable medieval chronicles do not feature in the forthcoming comparative archival analysis, while others do; it is perhaps apposite at this stage to indicate the limitations and/or historiographical potential of these sources, even briefly.

The inclusion of Isma'ili historiography in the analysis that follows, a key desideratum given that this material might offer a uniquely 'Fatimid' perspective on the dynasty's history, is made difficult by the fact that only one, albeit substantial, Isma'ili historiographical work covering some part of mid-to-late Fatimid history survives: the seven-volume historical digest *'Uyūn al-akhbār*[36] written by the head of the Ṭayyibī Isma'ili mission (*dā'ī muṭlaq*) in the Yemen, Idrīs 'Imād al-Dīn (d. 1468). In its final volume, this work narrates historical episodes from the lives of the caliphs al-Mustanṣir to al-Āmir; subsequent caliphs were regarded by Ṭayyibīs as usurpers of the imamate. While there is some (limited) overlap with events covered by Ibn al-Furāt's material on the Fatimids, Idrīs' book is written from the perspective of a partisan of a Ṭayyibī reading of Fatimid history, and while all the medieval chroniclers had confessional or political pre-commitments, the *'Uyūn al-akhbār* is noted by a number of modern scholars as unreliable in its provision of some information and dates, and in its tendentious reading of events, in particular the Ḥāfiẓī-Ṭayyibī schism of 1130 discussed below. That said, Idrīs preserves testimonies from eyewitnesses to late Fatimid history including the poet 'Umāra al-Yamanī (d. 1174), and also documents preserved in Yemen, such as some of the royal *sijillāt* dispatched to the Sulayhids over the reigns of al-Mustanṣir to al-Āmir and doctrinal works sent to the Yemen for safekeeping in the 1060s.[37] In archival terms, this book stands as an essential part of Idrīs' wide-ranging oeuvre capturing the intricacies of the Ṭayyibī mission that he served for over forty years, and whose legacy, largely concealed from non-Ṭayyibīs, he had full access to and preserved for later generations of both believers and/or historians. Where appropriate, I make brief allusions to the *'Uyūn* especially in regard to the contradictory information emanating from a range of medieval sources regarding the birth of al-Āmir's son and putative heir al-Ṭayyib.

Two authors of contemporary accounts of the Fatimid period, Baghdad-born chronicler Hilāl al-Ṣābī (d. 1056) and Antioch-based Egyptian Christian Yaḥyā al-Anṭākī (d. 1066), are omitted from the forthcoming analysis of sources because they report only the first half of Fatimid rule. Ibn Ṣa'īd al-Maghribī (d. 1286) does not preserve significant source material for late Fatimid history except for unique but brief Qayrawānī reports from the lost works of al-Rawḥī and al-Qurtī, which do not display extra intelligence about the Fatimid state.[38] Ibn al-Qalānisī (d. 1160) and Sibṭ b. al-Jawzī (d. 1256) both drew heavily on Hilāl's history for the Fatimid era up to Hilāl's own death, after which they concentrate more closely on the Crusades and events in Syria than Fatimid Egypt: they have a limited presence in the discussion as they provide snippets of valuable information from a Syrian angle not otherwise available to most Egyptian chroniclers, such as alternative views on Usāma b. Munqidh's involvement in the deaths of the caliph al-Ẓāfir and his family in 1154.[39] Conversely, the brief annalistic treatise known as *Bustān al-jāmi'* written around 1192 in Aleppo and attributed to 'Imād al-Dīn al-Iṣfahānī (d. 1201) by at least one of its editors, which reads like a skeletal draft to be later expanded into a fuller narrative of history, is referred to several times:[40] despite its sketchy content, there are references in the fragment to reports that are otherwise scarce in Ayyubid and Mamluk annalistic histories, which originate in both common and rare North Syrian accounts, for example those by Ibn al-Qalānisī, d. 1160, and al-'Aẓīmī, d. after 1160, respectively.[41]

By that same token, Ibn al-Dawādārī (d. after 1337) is not a main point of comparison because his annals comprise summary notes for the Fatimid caliphs and viziers, do not offer source attribution except for the occasional report from Ibn al-Athīr's *Kāmil* and do not provide unique information. Meanwhile al-Qalqashandī's (d. 1418) magnificent epistolary and administrative handbook *Ṣubḥ al-aʿshā* offers, at times, material of key historiographical significance, for example a letter purportedly written by the caliph al-Ḥāfiẓ to Roger II of Sicily, a unique specimen.[42] His documentary sources are referenced where appropriate, for instance in relation to the appointment of al-Ḥāfiẓ as the new *imam* in 1131.

In the vein of comparing types of historiography as well as bodies of reports, brief allusions to Ibn Wāṣil's (d. 1298) history of the Ayyubids, *Mufarrij al-kurūb*, are made in order to draw out the differences between an Ayyubid-centred view of late Fatimid rule and the Fatimid-focused accounts of Ibn Ẓāfir and Ibn Muyassar, for example. Finally, moving forward again to Mamluk views of Fatimid history, Badr al-Dīn al-ʿAynī's (d. 1451) *ʿIqd al-jumān* holds only limited material on the Fatimids, though he, like Ibn al-Furāt half a century before him, keeps a careful note of his sources.[43] Since al-ʿAynī was a contemporary and rival of al-Maqrīzī, and could broaden our picture of how and why al-Maqrīzī contrived to consult, conserve and reuse so many tenth-twelfth century histories, a subject that confounded other Egyptian historians,[44] this aspect of his oeuvre constitutes a promising subject for research in the future.[45]

Egyptian and Syrian traditions in a trans-metropolitan archival outlook

Inevitably, the geographical vantage point of earlier authors cited by Mamluk chroniclers have profound consequences for the ways in which they portray late Fatimid history, and Ibn al-Furāt's sources may be separated into geographical strands, Egyptian and non-Egyptian, particularly Syrian. The question of survival also bifurcates along Syrian and Egyptian lines to some degree. Of Ibn al-Furāt's fourteen prose authors/sources listed above, six are Egyptian: Ibn al-Ṣayrafī (d. 1147), Ibn Ṭuwayr (d. 1220), the Fatimid-era *Akhbār al-dawla al-Miṣriyya* (n.d.), Ibn Ẓāfir (d. 1216 or 1226), Shāfiʿ b. ʿAlī (d. 1330) and Baybars al-Manṣūrī (d. 1325); while two emirs, al-Idrīsī (n.d.) and Khalīl b. Khumārtakīn (d. between 1194 and 1203) lived in Egypt during the final decade of Fatimid rule. Two others are Syrian, namely Ibn Abī Ṭayy (d. 1233) and Ibn Naẓīf al-Ḥamawī (d. 1241). A further two authors lived in both Egypt and Syria and moved between the two, Ibn Khallikān (d. 1282) and Ibn Wāṣil (d. 1298), while the remaining two were based in Baghdad and Mosul respectively: Ibn al-Jawzī (d. 1201) and Ibn al-Athīr (d. 1233). Ten of the fourteen authors whose works are cited by Ibn al-Furāt are therefore located within Egypt, either permanently or temporarily. Of the Syrian sources, the most significant for Ibn al-Furāt's chronicle is undoubtedly Ibn Abī Ṭayy, whose eyewitness reports on the last years of Fatimid rule are often uniquely preserved by Ibn al-Furāt.

Yet a rigid distinction between Egyptian and Syrian 'schools' of Mamluk historiography has not been made in the forthcoming analysis, for two main reasons. The first is that the identification of the two distinct approaches of Egyptian and Syrian historiography by Guo and others rest substantially on differences in career paths, networking practices and subject matter of historians: chiefly contemporary 'ulama-focused history in Syria the form of the 'diary-chronicle', and preoccupation with sultanate politics in Egyptian historiography.[46] However, these distinctions do not prove useful for the more varied locations and types of historiography represented by Ibn al-Furāt's diverse sources for the late Fatimid era. Second, Ibn Abī Ṭayy's informants represent an unusual thread of accounts produced by non-Egyptians passing through or residing in Egypt and reporting its events to an Aleppan chronicler (or often his father) and thus cannot be said to offer a contemporary Syrian angle on events but rather give us a de facto Egyptian one. The two Aleppo-born emirs in question were not merely located in Egypt in the late Fatimid era but were participants in its history. One of them, Khalīl, remained there for ten years under the patronage of the vizier Ṭalā'i', while the other, al-Idrīsī, represented Fatimid viziers such as Ibn Maṣāl as an Egyptian envoy to Asad al-Dīn Shīrkūh in Damascus.[47] This, too, occludes any sense of completely distinct strands of Egyptian and Syrian historiographical reports among Ibn al-Furāt's primary eyewitness sources.

At the same time, the question of the survival of historical texts is a transregional, or more specifically a trans-metropolitan one, in which geography plays a significant role inasmuch as Syrian traditions were not subject to the same vicissitudes as some Egyptian reports scrutinized here.[48] A great many historiographical works clearly migrated from one region to another, and hence the textual witness of two Aleppo-born emirs that are transcribed outside Egypt but re-enter the Egyptian tradition via Ibn al-Furāt. The endurance of these reports is a separate issue to the survival of Egyptian accounts that remained in Egypt. Yet their emergence from late Fatimid Egypt demands that they be regarded as Fatimid-era sources among those that Ibn al-Furāt is able to draw upon. In short, they are not included in the argument made about the survival of Fatimid historical texts within Egypt, but *are* incorporated in the quantification of reports emanating from the late Fatimid milieu.

Finally, it will be noted that by the time Ibn al-Furāt reaches the last years depicted in the third volume of his chronicle, namely 1162–7, his informants include many non-Egyptian authors, including Ibn Wāṣil, Ibn Khallikān and Ibn Abī Ṭayy. Yet testimonies from Fatimid Egypt also make their presence in Ibn al-Furāt's account of these years. These take the form of the unique anonymous treatise called *Akhbār al-dawla al-Miṣriyya*, the verse of 'Umāra al-Yamanī and the emir al-Idrīsī's vivid first-person accounts from Cairo, Alexandria and Damascus, and his recounting events from proximity with both Shāwar and Shīrkūh. In addition, one might surmise that the four reports offered by Shāfi' b. 'Alī, a chancery clerk from Mamluk Egypt, might also be of Egyptian provenance given that his main source in his now-lost chronicle was his more famous uncle Ibn 'Abd al-Ẓāhir, who was known to cite and conserve Fatimid authorities.[49] In other words, although the Fatimid state was near its end and few if any narratives from within the Fatimid tradition were produced during these final years, Ibn al-Furāt nonetheless succeeded in procuring and reusing native sources to tell the late Fatimid story. Ibn Ṭuwayr, perhaps the last of the known and named Fatimid narrators, is no longer available for these years, but of the twenty-one or so identified reports for this era, eleven are non-Egyptian while ten are Egyptian, a fair balance of indigenous and external authorities that reflects the transregionality of Ibn al-Furāt's sources.

Modes of attribution in the chronicle: Archivality as conservation

A further question raised by an archival approach that deliberates upon the selection and synthesis of source material is how to ascertain that Ibn al-Furāt's citations from earlier sources are accurate, given that transmitters often adapted and revised received material while 'conserving' it; after all, al-Maqrīz's archival strategy included a penchant for radical epitomization of sources.[50] This is not to re-reify the 'authenticity' approach critiqued earlier, but to point up archivality as conservation. The first consideration here is the clear variation in the methodologies of text reuse between individual authors. Ibn al-Furāt's history is evidently a boon to the present-day researcher because of his tendency towards careful attribution. Yet he is far from being the only author to emphasize, for instance through the archival sign of rubrication, his acknowledgement of sources. Aside from Ibn al-Athīr, all the Ayyubid and Mamluk historians consulted in this analysis mention their sources in at least some instances. One implication of such attribution is that it facilitates direct comparison of two facets of historiography: information and sources. Such comparison is possible even where the format of arrangement varies. For example, the annalistic work of al-Nuwayrī can be usefully compared with the biographical dictionary of Ibn Khallikān because many of the same authorities are cited by each. Where a report from one source is independently reused by more than one later author, this elucidates the accuracy of the transmission and its conservatorial integrity.

In Ibn al-Furāt's case, examination of his citation strategy reveals that his extracts from works like Ibn Ṭuwayr's *Nuzhat al-muqlatayn* are close or identical to those made by al-Maqrīzī and other later authors, with few or no signs that the material has been reworked or abbreviated/expanded: in other words, we see reuse *as* conservation. Moreover, authors regularly select, arrange and preserve material independently of one another but in a complementary way. For instance al-Maqrīzī uses some extracts from Ibn Ṭuwayr that are identical with Ibn al-Furāt's, and others that do not feature in Ibn al-Furāt's work at all, rendering it unlikely that al-Maqrīzī receives Ibn Ṭuwayr's history only through Ibn al-Furāt. They are in effect – and in some sense by design in view of their archival practices – collaborators in the conservation of this corpus of reports. Despite the frequently tendentious rewriting of early reports common in earlier periods of Arab-Islamic historiography,[51] the use of attribution and *isnad* in the Ayyubid and Mamluk periods is an archival strategy that signals clearly to readers that original works of canonical status are conserved within the newer work they are reading.

Ibn al-Furāt's archival strategies

In his account of late Fatimid rule, Ibn al-Furāt employs a number of stratagems that may be usefully described as archival, in which endeavour he is both a creator and beneficiary (user) of the historiographic archive. These practices, some of which he shares with other chronographers such as Abū Shāma, include a resourceful collation of written materials, the isolation of salient information (reports, author names, book titles, clues to and appraisals of reliability), the copying of selected extracts *qua* retrieval and conservation, and careful management of epistemic storage space as he arranges individual texts to form a narrative. The silent obverse of selection, the discarding of source material discussed in Chapter 2, is another intrinsically archival practice in this methodology.

Further, Ibn al-Furāt curates extracts in order to narrate a new account clearly intended to preserve knowledge of late Fatimid history, which extends the life cycles of source materials and forestalls their potential descent into obscurity. As narrative texts of historiography are never formally de-acquisitioned, as state or other documents might be, they are therefore liable to suffer neglect, and thence risk of oblivion, as examples offered later in this chapter demonstrate.[52] Conversely, it is worth noting that assumptions about the obsolescence of medieval narrative and documentary texts, that is to say their limited 'shelf value', are revealed by such archival practices to be overly conjectural. Text reuse is an omnipresent feature of medieval Islamicate society in both material and semantic senses; it reveals that textual corpora in the orbit of the 'sophisticated documentary culture' of medieval Islamic letters, in Rustow's words, do not simply expire en masse (though some, for example, receipts, would elapse and become defunct) but could remain living texts that enjoyed afterlives where re-deployment was deemed practical or desirable in fresh epistemic contexts.[53]

Specifically, alongside the material signage of archivality explored in Chapter 2, the stages of archivality discernible in Ibn al-Furāt's recovery and reuse of historical reports for late Fatimid history broadly follow the pattern outlined earlier by König and Whitmarsh. To reiterate, these are practices of itemization, analysis, hierarchization, sequencing, space management, synthesis and conservation.[54] This range of strategies is next examined in detail, where historiographical accounts of each sub-era of late Fatimid history in *Tarīkh al-duwal* are compared with those of other Ayyubid and Mamluk authors covering, *grosso modo*, those same events.

Notes

1 El-Leithy, 'Living Documents'; Paul, 'Archival Practices'.
2 Hirschler, *Medieval Damascus*, 34, describes Fatimid texts conserved in the Ashrafiyya, traceable to the Fatimid royal collections sold on or dispersed after the inception of Ayyubid rule, a phenomenon discussed in detail in Bora, 'Salah al-Din'.
3 Bauden, 'Maqriziana IX', 46.
4 Paul, *op. cit.*
5 Paul, 'Archival Practices', 347, 357.

6 Bauer, 'Mamluk Literature', 25.
7 Paul, 'Archival Practices', 356–7.
8 Ed. A. Mukhlis (Cairo, 1924).
9 For those that are extant, see al-Shayyal, *Majmū'āt*.
10 Ed. A. F. Sayyid (Cairo, 1990).
11 Ed. A. F. Sayyid (Beirut, 1992).
12 Referred to by D. S. Richards, 'A Consideration of Two Sources for the Life of Saladin', *JSS* 25:1 (1980), 46–65, 150.
13 Vol. 1, 426 ff. of *al-Rawḍatayn*, ed. H. Ahmad in two parts (Cairo, 1956, 1962).
14 Cl. Cahen, 'Un récit inédit de vizirat de Dirgham', *AI* 8 (1969), 27–46, 28, n. 1.
15 Ed. M. A. Ata et al. (Beirut, 1992).
16 Cf. D. Morray, *An Ayyubid Notable and His World: Ibn Al-Adim and Aleppo as Portrayed in His Biographical Dictionary of People Associated with the City* (Leiden, 1994), 96–7.
17 *Kitāb al-rawḍatayn*, ed. in 5 vols, I. al-Zibaq (Beirut, 1997). For Ibn Abī Ṭayy's other works, see Elshayyal, 211.
18 *Al-Kāmil fi'l-ta'rīkh*, ed. Tornberg (1851–76, reprint: 1965–7); *al-Bāhir fi 'l-dawlat al-atābakiyya*, ed. A. A. Tulaymat (Cairo, 1963).
19 Ed. I. Abbas, 8 vols (Beirut, 1968–72).
20 For more on the Samanid section (in two parts), see L. Treadwell, 'Ibn Ẓāfir al-Azdī's account of the murder of the Samanid *amīr* Aḥmad b. Ismā'īl and the succession of his son, Naṣr', in C. Hillenbrand (ed.), *Studies in Honour of Clifford Edmund Bosworth, Vol. 2: The Sultan's Turret* (Leiden, 2000), 397–419, and 'The account of the Samanid dynasty in Ibn Ẓāfir al-Azdī's *Akhbār al-duwal al-munqaṭi'a*', *Iran* 43 (2005), 135–71.
21 *Akhbār al-duwal al-munqaṭi'a: La section consacrée aux Fāṭimides*, ed. A. Ferré (Cairo, 1972).
22 Moscow, 1963; for more on the significance of this work see A. Hartmann, 'A Unique Manuscript in the Asian Museum, St. Petersburg: The Syrian Chronicle *at-Ta'riḥ al-Manṣūrī* by Ibn Naẓīf al-Ḥamawī from the 7th AH/13th Century', in Vermeulen and de Smet, *Egypt and Syria in the Fatimid, Ayyubid and Mamluk Eras*, 89–100, 89–93.
23 Edited as follows: vols 1–3: ed. J. al-Shayyal (Cairo, 1953–60); vols 4–5: ed. S. A. Ashur and H. Rabie (Cairo, 1972–7).
24 Little, 'Historiography of the Ayyubid and Mamluk epochs', 421.
25 For more on the author, see P. M. Holt, 'A Chancery Clerk in Medieval Egypt', *The English Historical Review* 101:400 (July 1986), 671–9; and Little, 'Historiography of the Ayyubid and Mamluk epochs', 422.
26 Entitled *Ḥusn al-manāqib al-sirriyya*, ed. A. al-Khuwaytir (Riyad, 1976).
27 Ed. A. F. Sayyid (Cairo, 1996).
28 Ed. D. S. Richards (Beirut, 1998).
29 Ed. A. S. Hamdan (Cairo, 1987).
30 According to al-Sakhāwī: *Zubda*, Richards edition, XX.
31 Most of these are transmitters of some of the earliest Fatimid-era reports, either first-hand or through intermediaries.
32 Little, 'Historiography of the Ayyubid and Mamluk epochs'.
33 Massoud, *Chronicles*, esp. 14–38.
34 Another close contemporary, the Aleppo-born Ibn Ḥabīb al-Ḥalabī (d. 1406), who spent some years of his life as a chancery official in Cairo, wrote only Mamluk history: Massoud, *Chronicles*, 22.

35 Ibn al-Furāt's later volumes borrow from Ibn Duqmāq's narrative of Bahri Mamluk history, the *Nuzhat al-anām* (see Ashtor, 'Some Unpublished Sources', 19; Massoud, *Chronicles*, 152; Amitai, *Mongols*, 5). However, Ibn al-Furāt's information on the Fatimids is far more extensive than either Ibn Khaldūn's or Ibn Duqmāq's; the former mentions that his account of the Fatimids is derived from Ibn al-Athīr and Ibn Ṭuwayr, with a little addition from al-Musabbiḥī, but the narrative is a rather jerky summary occasionally beleaguered by factual mistakes. Meanwhile Ibn Duqmāq's surviving synopsis is noticeably devoid of detail or originality (Ibn Khaldūn: *Kitāb al-ʿibar*, Bulaq edition, 4:83; Ibn Duqmāq: 241–69). For Mamluk history, there are signs that Ibn Khaldūn borrowed from the other two authors (Massoud, *Chronicles*, 20).

36 Idrīs, *ʿUyūn.*

37 Ibid., 2–14.

38 Al-Rawḥī (n.d.) was also a transmitter of abbreviated reports from al-Quḍāʿī's (d. 1062) lost world history, *ʿUyūn al-maʿārif*; his late fifth-century epitome of that work going up to 1062, *Bulghat al-ẓurafāʾ fī akhbār al-anbiyāʾ wa ʾl-khulafāʾ*, is still in manuscript form, however: see MS Bodleian Marsh 46. On al-Rawḥī's problematic identity, see E. Kohlberg, *A Medieval Muslim Scholar at Work: Ibn Ṭāwūs and His Library* (Leiden, 1992), 360–1.

39 Both were Damascus-based, though Sibṭ was born and raised in Baghdad.

40 Ed. Cl. Cahen (*Bulletin d'Etudes Orientales*, 7–8, 1937–8) and U. A. Tadmuri (Beirut, 2002); the latter offers a more definite ascription of the work to ʿImād al-Dīn than the former. For a fuller discussion of the ascription, see Bora, 'Salah al-Din', 17, n. 80.

41 For the latter, see Cl. Cahen, 'La Chronique Abrégée, d'Al-ʿAzīmī', *JA* 230 (1938), 353–448, and al-ʿAẓīmī, *Taʾrīkh Ḥalab*, ed. I. Zarur (Damascus, 1984).

42 *Ṣubḥ al-aʿshā*, 7:458–63. For more on the letter, see M. Canard, 'Une lettre du Calife Fatimite Al-Hafiz (524–44/1130–49) à Roger II (Roi de Sicile)', in *Atti del Convegno Internaxionale di Studi Ruggeriani*, I (Palermo, 1955), 125–46.

43 Cf. Haarmann, 'Mamluk Studies', 338. The earliest published section known to me covers the Ayyubid period: *ʿIqd al-jumān fī taʾrīkh ahl al-zamān – al-ʿasr al-Ayyūbī*, ed. M. R. Mahmud (Cairo, 2003); see also Shayea al-Hajeri, 'Critical edition of the eleventh volume of *ʿIqd al-jumān fī tārīkh ahl al-zamān*, with particular reference to the historical fragments from the lost book of Muḥammad b. ʿAbd al-Malik al-Hamadhānī called: *ʿUnwān al-siyar fī maḥāsin ahl al-Badū waʾ l-Ḥaḍar* or *al-Maʿārif al-mutaʾkhkhira*', PhD Thesis, University of Edinburgh, 2007.

44 His *Khiṭaṭ*, for example, is replete with extracts from poets (such as Qāḍī al-Rashīd b. al-Zubayr, d. 1069), topographers (such as Ibn ʿAbd al-Ẓāhir, d. 1292) and historians (such as Abū ʿUmar al-Kindī, d. 961) whose works are no longer extant and not directly known to later historians like al-Jabartī (d. 1825), who complained that al-Maqrīzī referred to works by al-Musabbiḥī (d. 1029), Ibn Zūlāq (d. 996) and al-Quḍāʿī (d. 1062) that he (al-Jabartī) could not avail himself of. Cf. R. Gottheil, 'Al-Ḥasan ibn Ibrāhīm ibn Zūlāq', *JAOS* 28 (1907), 254–70, 270.

45 A. F. Broadbridge, 'Academic Rivalry and the Patronage System in Fifteenth-Century Egypt: al-ʿAynī, al-Maqrīzī, and Ibn Ḥajar al-ʿAsqalānī', *MSR* 3 (1999), 85–107, examines this question from the point of view of politics and contemporary history, though not of historiographic sources for earlier eras; see also D. P. Little, 'A Comparison of al-Maqrīzī and al-ʿAynī as Historians of Contemporary Events', *MSR* 7:2 (July 2003), 205–15.

46 Guo, 'Mamluk Historiographic Studies'; Elbendary, 'The Historiography of Protest', 9; Torsten Wollina, 'Ibn Ṭawq's Taʿlīq. An Ego-Document for Mamluk Studies', in Conermann, *Ubi sumus?*, 344.

47 *Ta'rīkh al-duwal*, III:212b.
48 Hirschler, *Medieval Damascus*, demonstrates this point comprehensively.
49 Cf. Brett, 'The Battles of Ramla', 21, on the lost chronicle of the early Mamluk historian Ibn Muyassar, which recounts 'a primarily Egyptian affair, drawing in principle upon Egyptian chronicles. . .'.
50 L. I. Conrad, 'Recovering Lost Texts: Some Methodological Issues', *JAOS* 113:2 (April–June 1993), 258–63, discusses an earlier period of Islamic historiography than Fatimid, Ayyubid and Mamluk, but similar issues prevailed in all: E. Landau-Tasseron, 'On the Reconstruction of Lost Sources', *al-Qanṭara* 25 (2004), 45–91; for al-Maqrīzī's epitomes: Bauden, *Maqriziana II*.
51 Khalidi, *Arabic Historical Thought*.
52 El-Leithy; Hirschler, 'Document Reuse'.
53 Rustow, 'Fatimid State'; Hirschler, 'Document Reuse'.
54 Konig and Whitmarsh, el-Leithy, Hirschler, 'Document Reuse'.

5

A Micro-Historical Analysis of Ibn al-Furāt's Archive (Part 1): Two Fatimid Vizierates

The opening section of the analysis below introduces many of Ibn al-Furāt's main sources, and is subdivided according to author for ease of perusal. Subsequent sections of this chapter and the next discuss alternative and/or supplementary reports in an integrated format. The topic of this chapter is an analysis of Ibn al-Furāt's discussion of the vizierates of al-Afḍal b. Badr al-Jamālī and al-Ma'mūn al-Baṭā'iḥī under three Fatimid caliphs, as follows:

Fatimid caliphs

al-Mustanṣir	(428–87/1036–94)
al-Musta'lī	(487–95/1094–1101)
al-Āmir	(495–525/1101–30)

Fatimid viziers

al-Afḍal	(485–515/1092–1121)
al-Ma'mūn al-Baṭā'iḥī	(515–19/1121–25)

The vizierate of al-Afḍal

[sub anno 515/1121]

Sources: For the life and career of al-Afḍal, Ibn al-Furāt turns to six main works:

- *Kitāb al-wuzarā' li 'l-dawla al-Fāṭimiyya bi 'l-Qāhira al-Mu'izziyya* or *al-Ishāra ilā man nāla 'l-wizāra* by Ibn al-Ṣayrafī (1071–1147)
- *Nuzhat al-muqlatayn fī akhbār al-dawlatayn* by Ibn Ṭuwayr (1130–1220)
- *Ma'ādin al-dhahab fī ta'rīkh al-mulūk wa 'l-khulafā' wa dhawi 'l-rutab* by Yaḥyā Ibn Abī Ṭayy (1180–1233).
- *al-Kāmil fi 'l-ta'rīkh* by Ibn al-Athīr (1160–1233)

- *Wafayāt al-aʿyān* by Ibn Khallikān (1211–82)
- *Akhbār al-duwal al-munqaṭiʿa* by Ibn Ẓāfir (1171–1216 or 1226), via Ibn Khallikān

Ibn al-Furāt's first choice of information on al-Afḍal is Ibn al-Ṣayrafī, who worked in the Fatimid chancery (*dīwān al-inshāʾ*) for over fifty years, from 1102 to 1147, becoming its head after his promotion by al-Afḍal; hence Ibn al-Furāt's appellation: *al-shaykh, tāj al-riyāsa*. The earliest available author to write al-Afḍal's life, Ibn al-Ṣayrafī was a devoted supporter of the vizier's rule, and dedicated one of his books to him.[1] Ibn al-Furāt cites Ibn al-Ṣayrafī's account of the Fatimid vizierate directly rather than through Ibn Khallikān or Ibn al-Athīr, both of whom also use Ibn al-Ṣayrafī's reports and constitute two further sources for Ibn al-Furāt. One clue to this unmediated recourse lies in the fact that Ibn al-Furāt preserves a different title of Ibn al-Ṣayrafī's work on the Fatimid vizierate than that cited by other historians quoting the work (and used for the modern published version),[2] notably Ibn Khallikān (viz. the latter's *al-Ishāra ilā man nāla 'l-wizāra*, as opposed to Ibn al-Furāt's *Kitāb al-wuzarāʾ li 'l-dawla al-Fāṭimiyya bi 'l-Qāhira al-Muʿizziyya*).[3] While variations on book titles were common in medieval Muslim scholarship, and books were often referred to by a description of contents rather than their most widely known titles (see, for example, the varying titles of al-Maqrīzī's *Ittiʿāẓ* rendered by al-Sakhāwī, al-Ṣuyūṭī and Ḥājjī Khalīfa),[4] Ibn al-Furāt gives us a full rhyming variant of the better-known title of Ibn al-Ṣayrafī's work. This suggests that he had possession of a different copy and possibly redaction from the one used by Ibn Khallikān (whose death date precedes Ibn al-Furāt's by 125 years) and from the sole extant version edited in 1925, which does not mention Ibn al-Furāt's version of the title. That more than one copy of Ibn al-Ṣayrafī's history of the Fatimid vizierate was in circulation (or available to some individual authors) in Mamluk Egypt is indicated. This source's ubiquity in later works also points to later compilers' preference for eyewitness accounts where they were available. This evinces the gravity of socio-political history in the minds of its practitioners, as expressed in the importance attached to the conservation of sources within the historiographic archive. That Ibn al-Furāt identifies a source by author name on some occasions and by the title of a work at others reveals that certain book titles had not stabilized by his time, or that an author was at that juncture more easily identifiable than his book, or vice versa.[5]

Other authors who reuse Ibn al-Ṣayrafī's works include al-Maqrīzī, al-Qalqashandī and al-Ṣuyūṭī. A further chronicle by Ibn al-Ṣayrafī is referred to by Ibn al-Dawādārī (d. c. 1336) in *Kanz al-durar*, who cites it for events up to 1130, but the work is not attested elsewhere.[6] Ibn al-Ṣayrafī's probably best-known extant work is *al-Qānūn fī dīwān al-rasāʾil*, a guide to chancery practice, a key source for al-Qalqashandī's (d. 1418) *Ṣubḥ al-aʿshā*. Neither of these are chronicles, but they reveal that the unbounded penchant for documentation and archivality in the medieval Islamic intellectual milieu encompassed administration, manuals devote thereto and historiography, which was in a number of cases composed by trained bureaucrats.[7]

Ibn al-Ṣayrafī's account of al-Afḍal's rule is, perhaps predictably, eulogistic, and portrays him as a ruler legitimized by the caliph al-Mustanṣir.[8] Since al-Afḍal had engineered al-Mustaʿlī's accession, their mutual attempts to accredit each other's rule reveals a far-reaching co-dependence between caliph and vizier. Al-Afḍal is described in the text as a clement master, an effective manager of the Fatimid state and a determined fighter against Crusaders. Ibn al-Furāt next turns to Ibn Ṭuwayr, a later Fatimid official, for his version of the life and death of al-Afḍal.

Ibn Ṭuwayr: *Nuzhat al-muqlatayn fi akhbār al-dawlatayn*

The chronicle of Ibn Ṭuwayr, his only known work, was known well by some Mamluk historians: Ibn Khaldūn (d. 1406), Ibn al-Zayyāt (d. 1411, author of a work on sacred journeys),[9] al-Qalqashandī (d. 1418), al-Maqrīzī (d. 1442) and Ibn Taghrībirdī (d. 1470) as well as Ibn al-Furāt.

The *Nuzhat* survives only as extracts archived in later works (usefully collated into a discrete modern volume)[10] and was conceived as an account of the Fatimid and Ayyubid dynasties, both of which the author served in their bureaux of salaries (*dīwān al-rawātib*).[11] No citations from the Ayyubid section of the work are extant (assuming that this section was written, as the title of the work rendered by Ibn al-Furāt and others suggests) and the Fatimid account was left incomplete.[12] Ibn Ṭuwayr, a Sunni, provides a detailed and unique record of Fatimid ceremonial, festival days, processions, the ranks and roles of state officials, the different treasuries maintained by the state and so on. It constitutes a source much valued by Ibn al-Furāt for its historiographical and ultimately archival significance in a textual field where this depth of information, and its conservation, were marked by rarity.

For al-Afḍal, Ibn Ṭuwayr provides a three-page report in which he applauds al-Afḍal's fierce and resolute battle against the Crusaders, but is forthright about the vizier's despotism (*istibdād*, 163b, l.26).[13] Ibn Ṭuwayr's attitude towards the Fatimids is clearly more ambivalent than Ibn al-Ṣayrafī's: both were employed by the Fatimid state, but Ibn al-Ṣayrafī was a more instrumental figure in the workings of that state than Ibn Ṭuwayr since he spent his life in its service, while Ibn Ṭuwayr witnessed the Ayyubid takeover and served the latter administration. We know from Ibn al-Ṣayrafī's other works, notably *Qānūn*, that he had access to a full range of state archives and indeed penned *sijill*s, or official decrees, himself. Ibn Ṭuwayr provides even more documentary material in his text than Ibn al-Ṣayrafī, underlining once again that historiography was in a key sense a quasi-documentary resource. Thus the loss (or incompletion) of Ibn Ṭuwayr's section on the Ayyubids is unfortunate: few individuals were as capable as he of eyewitness comparison between the two administrations.[14]

The historical accounts in Ibn Ṭuwayr's work cover the period from al-Āmir to al-Fā'iz (the first half of the twelfth century), and provide an ostensibly dispassionate narrative with little partiality for either caliphs or viziers. The reports cover several complex political power struggles which, if not experienced directly, Ibn Ṭuwayr would have heard about from eyewitnesses, either orally or through written accounts (though he does not name his sources), and thus forms an invaluable archive of the earliest available sources for this period of Fatimid rule. Ibn al-Furāt draws heavily on Ibn Ṭuwayr – in twenty out of a total of just over eighty separate reports in the Fatimid-related sections of *Ta'rīkh al-duwal* – for every ruler of Egypt, caliph and vizier, from the eras of al-Afḍal to al-Fā'iz (c. 1070–1154). That neither Ibn al-Furāt nor any other historian uses him after this time indicates that only this portion of the work was available to later historians; the remainder was either never written or lost.

Ibn Abī Ṭayy: *Maʿādin al-dhahab fi taʾrīkh al-mulūk wa ʾl-khulafāʾ wa dhawi ʾl-rutab*

Ibn al-Furāt's third source for the life of al-Afḍal is the Aleppan Ibn Abī Ṭayy, who differs from the two previous informants on several counts, the first of which is that he was not an eyewitness to the Fatimid era but rather related its history often on the authority of his Aleppo-based father, a man well-informed about the weakening of the Fatimid house and the rise of Ayyubid rule in Egypt first under Shīrkūh and then Ṣalāḥ al-Dīn. He was also unusual for being a Syrian eyewitness and author who recounted events in Egypt from the late Fatimid period.[15] In addition, Ibn Abī Ṭayy had met with local dignitaries from Fatimid and Ayyubid Egypt and collected, sifted and arranged their reports to create a unique repository of informants and information.[16] A Twelver Shiʿi, Ibn Abī Ṭayy was not used by many later authors but is a central source for Ibn al-Furāt, for Abu Shāma (d. 1267) in the *Rawḍatayn* and to a much lesser extent Ibn Khallikān, for events in locations ranging from Khurasan and Iraq to the Maghrib.[17]

For Ibn al-Furāt's chronicle, Ibn Abī Ṭayy is one of two most-cited sources (Ibn Ṭuwayr is the other) in terms of both numbers of quotations (15) and their length (often a whole page or several in the manuscript), which reveals the ingenuity of Ibn al-Furāt's hierarchization of sources and his management of textual space to give most prominence to historiographically rare but revealing authors. In the reconstruction of the Fatimid historiographic corpus, this cited material is of key significance: Ibn al-Furāt is one of only two post-Fatimid authors (alongside Abū Shāma) to preserve substantial extracts from a lost work by Ibn Abī Ṭayy that offers an archive of oral testimonies provided by at least three participants in late Fatimid history. The Aleppan also occasionally offers new information not available in other standard sources, for instance the indication that after al-Āmir's death in 1130, the Ṭayyibī *daʿwa* had, according to Ibn Abī Ṭayy's Yemeni sources, been carried out in Syria.[18] This penchant for accounts from personal witnesses whose reports then perform textual witness is a profound manifestation of both the heuristic and epistemological worth of primary evidence in post-Fatimid historiography. Conversely, it took the efforts of resourceful and self-aware historians with a notably archival instincts, like Abū Shāma and Ibn al-Furāt, to ensure that this material survives, in some form, until the present day.

On al-Afḍal's era, and especially in examining his death, Ibn Abī Ṭayy is characteristically thorough, looking at the events surrounding his murder from multiple angles and drawing out the agendas of the individuals involved. Ibn Abī Ṭayy's account of al-Afḍal is similar in length to that of Ibn Ṭuwayr (three and a half pages for the former, three for the latter), but while Ibn Ṭuwayr very usefully provides what appears as factual detail, such as the wording of the marriage contract that united the caliph al-Mustaʿlī with al-Afḍal's daughter – thus effacing the boundary between the offices of imamate and vizierate (I: 164a, 28–31) – Ibn Abī Ṭayy is more concerned with throwing light on the motives of those potentially responsible for al-Afḍal's assassination. Though he had less first-hand information about the life of al-Afḍal than either Ibn al-Ṣayrafī or Ibn Ṭuwayr before him, Ibn Abī Ṭayy evidently has the critical distance needed to examine the role of the caliph in the vizier's death. He reports the moral ambiguities in al-Āmir's situation (namely, his desire to be rid of a vizier who curtailed his power, and had amassed a great personal fortune from revenues intended for the state treasury), and weighs up the different possible causes of al-Afḍal's death, coming to the conclusion that the most probable explanation was that al-Āmir did not carry out the murder by his own hand but looked the other way when it was (conveniently) carried out by another.[19] This register of possible protagonists and motives for an assassination at the heart of the Fatimid political establishment points up the manner in which chronicles based on eyewitness accounts were often as concerned with 'reading' events as reporting them, and in this sense provide registers of interpretation as well as information. This penchant for analysis in a key source for Ibn al-Furāt manifests one of the governing principles of archivality within historiography: evaluation of archivalia prior to, or in the act of, their integration into the historiographic archive.

Ibn al-Athīr: *al-Kāmil fī 'l-ta'rīkh*, sub anno 515

Ibn al-Athīr's general chronicle, one of the fullest post-Ṭabarī accounts of Islamic history, is significant for many reasons, not least its comprehensiveness, which made him a popular source for dozens of later authors.[20] Ibn al-Furāt uses Ibn al-Athīr's reports at least fourteen times for the Fatimid sections of *Ta'rīkh al-duwal*, although of these, nine are attributed to '*al-ḥāfiẓ Ibn al-Athīr wa 'l-amīr Rukn al-Dīn Baybars* [al-Munṣūrī]' (d. 1325), which refers to the latter's *Zubdat al-fikra fī ta'rīkh al-hijra*. Baybars relied heavily on Ibn al-Athīr's *Kāmil* in his *Zubda* for all the events that Ibn al-Athīr's work covers (up to 629/1231, two years before the latter's death). In this, Ibn al-Furāt shows how exactly he likes to indicate the provenance of his material: in the precision of his archival mindset, he takes note of the identification between the two sources. This attention to detail in attribution brings into focus the weight attached by Ibn al-Furāt to inscribing not just knowledge but connections between its purveyors. The closeness with which Baybars follows Ibn al-Athīr's account is a feature of the *Zubda* that has been noted elsewhere[21] and finds clear and useful confirmation in *Ta'rīkh al-duwal* since only some parts of the *Zubda* are extant and available for cross-checking against the *Kāmil*.[22]

One could speculate that Ibn al-Furāt's rationale in citing the *Zubda* when he had simultaneous access to the *Kāmil* may be explained by the former work's higher status as a text penned by a Mamluk author. Regardless, he is keen to trace stages in the journeys of his source material. That said, scrutiny of this issue is difficult because the parts of the *Zubda* quoted in *Ta'rīkh al-duwal* have not survived independently. However, Ibn al-Furāt's citations correspond very closely with the relevant sections of the *Kāmil*, so one assumes that the *Zubda* and the *Kāmil* were identical (or nearly so) in these sections at least. The four manuscript fragments of the *Zubda* that deal with pre-Mamluk history, and could thus be compared with the *Kāmil* (whose author died in 1233), are in different locations and appear to be from different redactions of the work. One of those manuscripts, MS Bodleian Hunt 198, purports to be volume six of the *Zubda*, covering 936–1009 CE but on closer examination turns out to be a collage of different excerpts from past chronicles, one of which is obviously al-Ṭabarī's (up to f. 107) and the rest of seemingly indeterminate origin, and show little trace of direct copying from the *Kāmil*.

For al-Afḍal, Ibn al-Furāt states that he consults the *Kāmil* itself rather than Baybars's reworking of it. Ibn al-Athīr, who usually relates Fatimid history more briefly than he does affairs in other parts of the Near East to the west of Iran, especially Zengid and Buyid history, presents a typically terse and prosaic account of al-Afḍal's merits and faults. The only notable addition to the information provided by earlier chroniclers is a paragraph explaining why the Isma'ilis disliked al-Afḍal (though he was, nominally at least, Isma'ili himself; his father had been a pro-Fatimid Armenian Muslim before he made his home in Fatimid Egypt).[23]

Ibn al-Furāt's recourse to Ibn al-Athīr's *Kāmil* is attributable to its status as an authoritative source for early twelfth-century history, in spite of its author's pro-Zengid, pro-Nūr al-Dīn leanings. Notably, Ibn al-Furāt demonstrates fastidiousness in not turning to Ibn al-Athīr for events after the mid-twelfth century, when Nūr al-Dīn's interest in acquiring Egypt became more pronounced and in which period Ibn al-Athīr shows his partiality very clearly in the *Kāmil*. For the later parts of his account of Fatimid history, Ibn al-Furāt turns to several authors who had not informed the earlier part of the narrative; his discrimination between the available sources, a notable archival instinct as well as strategy, is significant for revealing that Ibn al-Furāt saw specific sources as authoritative for particular sequences of events. This historiographical acumen throws light on the mechanics of the 'encyclopaedic' tendency in Mamluk history-writing, and suggests that in reconstructing late Fatimid history, Ibn al-Furāt provides an index of the reliability of sources as he proceeds, in a process of analysis, hierarchization and ordering. As a masterful archivist, he prefers to use appropriate sources for each sub-era of history and historiography.

Ibn Khallikān: *Wafayāt al-a'yān* and Ibn Ẓāfir: *Akhbār al-duwal al-munqaṭi'a*

Ibn Khallikān, who was born forty years after the death of the last Fatimid caliph, offers biographical entries on rulers of Fatimid Egypt that are fascinating for transmitting florid, even sordid, descriptions about them that were then in circulation. While it is clear that several Fatimid caliphs and viziers were flamboyant characters (or portrayed as such in the earliest sources), it is equally clear that Ibn Khallikān, a lover of oddities, enjoyed recounting their more idiosyncratic characteristics. In fact, while biographies of caliphs are generally omitted from the *Wafayāt* (as are those of other well-known political-historical figures, such as the Prophetic companions and their successors), Ibn Khallikān offers several entries for Fatimid caliphs.[24]

Ibn al-Furāt uses some fifteen reports from the *Wafayāt*, at least once each for the most politically significant players in late Fatimid history, including three of the four caliphs and six of the ten viziers whose lives are recorded in *Ta'rīkh al-duwal*. That Ibn Khallikān had access to certain original Fatimid accounts now lost, in particular those of al-Musabbiḥī and Ibn Zūlāq, has been noted, but he does not name his sources with great consistency and it is thus often hard to determine the origin of his information, even for the colourful vignettes.[25]

For al-Afḍal, Ibn al-Furāt uses two reports by Ibn Khallikān, the first describing his murder, in a brief account that does not add to the details provided by earlier authors. The second, however, is a description of the treasures found at al-Afḍal's house after his assassination, attributed to Ibn Ẓāfir's (d. 1216 or 1226) *Akhbār al-duwal al-munqaṭiʿa*. The latter was one of a series of dynastic chronicles written by an early Ayyubid official in Egypt who witnessed life under the last years of the Fatimid era, of which the section on the Fatimids is one of two that have been published.[26] The two extant manuscripts cover several Islamic dynasties up to Ibn Ẓāfir's own times. Ibn Khallikān's recourse to Ibn Ẓāfir is significant because the latter drew upon the lost world history of al-Quḍāʿī (d. 1062) for early Fatimid history, and on ten other significant early Fatimid sources now lost, such as an otherwise unknown work called *Ṣīrat al-wazīr al-Afḍal* which had evidently survived until his own times.[27] In addition, Ibn Ẓāfir is himself a source for Ibn Muyassar (d. 1278),[28] another preserver of lost Fatimid histories, who continued the early Fatimid history of al-Musabbiḥī (d. 1029). Ibn Muyassar offers fragments of further lost works by al-Muḥannak (d. 1154) – whose history of the caliphs of Egypt went up to the rule of al-Ḥāfiz (d. 1149)[29] – and Ibn al-Ma'mūn al-Baṭā'iḥī (d. 1192). Between them, Ibn Ẓāfir and Ibn Muyassar bring to light the range of Fatimid-era historiography surviving into the thirteenth century and entering the late Ayyubid and early Mamluk historiographic archive.[30]

The list of al-Afḍal's treasures provided by Ibn Ẓāfir is detailed and presumably derived from one of the unnamed early sources he relies on for this period; the report immediately after is from the aforementioned *Ṣīrat al-wazīr al-Afḍal*, which modifies this list of treasures slightly. Ibn Muyassar has a different account of al-Afḍal's assets, but Ibn Ẓāfir's version goes on to inform the accounts of Ibn Khallikān and through him Ibn al-Furāṭ, whereas the slight modification from the *Ṣīrat al-wazīr al-Afḍal* finds its way into al-Nuwayrī's (d. 1332) *Nihāyat al-arab*. The latter author evidently got the information from Ibn Ẓāfir, to whom he attributes the report.[31]

Ibn al-Furāt's quotation from the *Wafayāt* differs in detail from the published version in being more concise, and there are slight changes in wording, though the divergence is not surprising given the number of redactions of the *Wafayāt* to have survived to the present day.[32] Ibn Khallikān's account also differs slightly from the published version of Ibn Ẓāfir's work (based on a single manuscript). This could indicate that Ibn al-Furāt and Ibn Khallikān did not copy carefully, which is not likely for the former given his fastidious citation practice and seemingly exact quotation of other sources that are easy to check against extant versions.[33] It is, however, a fairly safe assumption for the latter, in light of his habit of reworking of source material. Another explanation for the discrepancy is that Ibn al-Furāt had access to a different redaction of *Wafayāt al-aʿyān*, and Ibn Khallikān possibly to a different redaction of *Akhbār al-duwal al-munqaṭiʿa*, than extant versions of either work;[34] in other words, that more than one redaction of each was in circulation in the thirteenth and fourteenth centuries.

To recapitulate, the Mamluk historian Ibn al-Furāt narrated late Fatimid history with the help of multiple earlier sources including eyewitness accounts extant in his day. He makes use of twelve prose works, most cited as discrete reports whose beginnings, and often ends, are signalled, and he clearly uses critical judgement in deciding which authors to use (analysis), at what length (space management) and how to order the material (hierarchization). He starts out by using the earliest available source for al-Afḍal, from a man intimately acquainted with his life and career; this suggests that Ibn al-Furāt, like his successor al-Maqrīzī, favoured 'early and local' sources above others.[35] The subsequent report is also from a Fatimid-era historian, one with less partiality for al-Afḍal than Ibn al-Ṣayrafī, for whom, as his extant works indicate, the vizier was a personal mentor. From there, Ibn al-Furāt consults a Syrian Imami Shiʿite history of the Fatimids, in which the author relates on the authority of his well-informed father, followed by two authors better known to medieval and contemporary readers: Ibn al-Athīr and Ibn Khallikān, compilers of vast numbers of reports themselves, although Ibn al-Athīr rarely names his sources while Ibn Khallikān does so inconsistently.

Ibn al-Furāt's manner of referring to particular authors is also revealing of the regard in which he holds them: Ibn al-Athīr is invariably '*al-ḥāfiẓ Ibn al-Athīr*'; when his work is cited via Baybars al-Manṣūri, the latter is named '*al-amīr Rukn al-Din Baybars*'; meanwhile Ibn Khallikān is always given his title of '*qāḍī al-quḍāt*', and Ibn Abi Ṭayy is referred to as '*shaykh*', with his name given fully each time he is quoted (*ism*, *kunya* and several *nisbas*). Ibn al-Ṣāyrafī is offered the honourable appellation '*al-shaykh, tāj al-riyāsa*', whereas Ibn Ṭuwayr is never referred to by name; he is simply '*ṣāḥib Nuzhat al-muqlatayn*'. Such fidelity to detail in identifying authors and works on the part of authors from the Fatimid era or later is unusual in Middle Period chronicles, although al-Maqrīzī in his *Khiṭāṭ* comes close, while the *Ittiʿāẓ* does not regularly name sources. This recording of author names, titles and honorifics further reveals Ibn al-Furāt's precisely honed archival mindset. Rather than adopting uniform conventions, he uses the details available to him to identify the authors of his chosen archivalia with as much specificity as possible, in order to conserve signs of both their epistemic and social prestige and authority.

To return the *Wafayāt* which, as stated earlier, names sources only intermittently: its author Ibn Khallikān is adept at drawing out the bigger historical picture in his widely copied biographical work. For al-Afḍal, he supplies Ibn al-Furāt with an early assessment of the vizier's assets at the moment of his death, citing Ibn Ẓāfir, who had a copy of a life of al-Afḍal unknown to other authors. The account of al-Afḍal's wealth was a highly charged subject because the Jamali house of viziers, of which he was a second-generation scion (out of three), was instrumental in the eclipse of the Fatimid imamate by the military vizierate, even while it prolonged Fatimid authority. The Jamali viziers' assumption of various ceremonial roles, alluded to by Ibn al-Furāt, as well as their appropriation of public funds, were politically controversial matters, since they wrested power away from the Fatimid ruling family. Ibn al-Furāt is deeply aware of this moral quandary in a series of reports covering eight pages in the manuscript, which balance the portrayal of al-Afḍal's contributions to Egypt's military and domestic successes with his hubris and his provocation of the caliph's legitimate jealousy and anger.

The anthology of sources Ibn al-Furāt procures and exploits for his reconstruction and analysis of al-Afḍal's era, and his careful calibration of these diverse reports, documents the stages of archivality of his account, a fourteenth-century (Mamluk,

Sunni) record of twelfth-century (Fatimid, Isma'ili) history. In crafting a documentary-like narrative by reusing a range of primary and secondary textual witnesses, Ibn al-Furāt signals change of source clearly and consistently, and orders his material with clear consideration given to how much space to allocate to each informant. Taken together these signs and strategies are testament to the fact that the Middle Period Arabic chronicle was both an object of heuristic value and a vector of archivality in the Mamluk epistemic environment.

The vizierate of al-Ma'mūn al-Baṭā'iḥī

[sub annis 515/1121, 519/1125]

For his account of al-Ma'mūn's life and death, Ibn al-Furāt relies on the following:

- *Nuzhat al-muqlatayn* by Ibn Ṭuwayr
- *Ma'ādin al-dhahab* by Ibn Abī Ṭayy
- *al-Kāmil fī' l-ta'rīkh* by Ibn al-Athīr
- *Wafayāt al-a'yān* by Ibn Khallikān

As well as being a vizier, al-Ma'mūn is a significant figure in the historiographical landscape of the Fatimid era. He commissioned Ibn al-Ṣayrafī's history of Fatimid viziers, *al-Ishāra*, which includes a highly eulogistic account of al-Ma'mūn's vizierate.[36] Al-Ma'mūn was also the subject of a biography written by his son, although there remains doubt about whether this work was a general chronicle or a dedicated biography that incorporated contextual historical detail.[37] That two viziers, al-Afḍal and al-Ma'mūn, were the subjects of early biographical works which informed later chronicles indicates how much more powerful the Fatimid Viziers of the Pen and Sword were than most (if not all) of the Fatimid caliphs in the twelfth century, for whom no discrete biographies are attested.

The biography of al-Ma'mūn by his son is not used by Ibn al-Furāt in *Ta'rīkh al-duwal*, though it is cited by Maqrīzī in his *Khiṭaṭ*, and (in two passages) by al-Nuwayrī (d. 1332). The latter does not, however, use it for al-Ma'mūn's own life, for which Ibn Muyassar (d. 1278) is al-Nuwayrī's chief informant. One assumes that the version available to later historians did not include Ibn al-Ma'mūn's account of his father's death, since no one quotes him on that subject.[38] Another possibly early source on the life of al-Ma'mūn, an anonymous Paris MS consulted by Leila Imad in her study of the Fatimid vizierate, is apparently not referred to elsewhere; this work emphasizes useful contributions made by al-Ma'mūn to Fatimid governance.[39]

Ibn al-Furat writes about al-Ma'mūn's life in two sections. The first half-page report only identifies the vizier's name and title with the help of Ibn al-Athīr, Ibn Abī Ṭayy and Ibn Ṭuwayr and speculates on his origins for a few lines. Ibn al-Furāt then turns his attention to other matters, returning to al-Ma'mūn some forty folios later, where he offers a much fuller account of his life and career. This is not an unusual pattern of writing for Ibn al-Furāt (or indeed other chroniclers), who often introduces a subject in an annal in which a significant aspect of it took place, only to return to that theme later, usually in the annal of the death date of a protagonist. It is on his return to the subject that Ibn al-Furāt habitually follows through with exploring the relevant accounts and explanations that he deems worthy of inclusion.

Upon his return to the subject of al-Ma'mūn's vizierate, Ibn al-Furāt devotes six pages of text to the vizier, on the authority of the four authors on whom he largely relies for all the events up to 1154, the death year of the penultimate Fatimid caliph al-Fā'iz. After this point, the number and range of Ibn al-Furāt's sources for the Fatimids expand dramatically. The most striking feature of the whole series of reports is that none of the four sources agree on the chain of events that leads to al-Ma'mūn and his brothers being sentenced to death by the caliph.

Ibn al-Athīr (*al-Kāmil*, sub anno 519), the first author consulted, is the source for a page-long account in *Ta'rīkh al-duwal* informing us that al-Ma'mūn's father had been a spy for al-Afḍal. The report sets up a close relationship between the two men, which makes al-Ma'mūn's involvement in al-Afḍal's assassination appear cold-blooded and ambitious. Ibn al-Athīr reports that al-Āmir executed al-Ma'mūn for his involvement in a plot against the caliph's life, instigated by the latter's brother, Ja'far. (Ibn al-Athīr's account is copied by several later authors, including al-Nuwayrī, Ibn Khaldūn and al-Maqrīzī.) Ibn Khallikān, on the other hand, attributes al-Ma'mūn's execution to his tyrannical conduct, which threatened the caliph (*Wafayāt*, under 'al-Āmir bi Aḥkām Allāh'). Ibn Khallikān's report as copied in *Ta'rīkh al-duwal* is followed by an account from Ibn Abī Ṭayy in which al-Ma'mūn's death is at the hands of al-Āmir, but involves a supposedly bloodthirsty emir named Zurayk who harbours resentment against the vizier. This story appears to be whimsical, is otherwise unattested, and hyperbolically projects a picture of the Franks' fear of this emir's reputation, a not-uncommon trope in Crusades-era and later Arabic historiography. That the story is told by one of Ibn al-Furāt's favourite authorities may be the reason for its inclusion, for it otherwise appears as a red herring in the larger picture of why al-Āmir orders al-Ma'mūn and his brothers to be executed. In the multi-genre, mixed-register 'Cairo narrative style', the inclusion of apocryphal though entertaining stories were a sine qua non, and while not conventionally 'documentary', their presence is archival in preserving historiographical elements with potentially wide popular appeal.

Ibn Ṭuwayr provides an even longer report on al-Ma'mūn for Ibn al-Furāt, of more than three pages. In this, he describes vicissitudes in the relationship between the vizier and caliph in some detail, and ends with the caliph being persuaded to kill al-Ma'mūn and his brothers for their treacheries against him. Ibn Ṭuwayr is clearly well-informed about the precise dealings between al-Āmir and al-Ma'mūn, and includes the texts of *sijillāt* (official decrees) made by al-Āmir vis-à-vis his vizier.

The inclusion of these four sources alone by Ibn al-Furāt suggests that although some very early sources for the life of al-Ma'mūn were available to Ibn al-Furāt, he does not necessarily use them. Though he had Ibn al-Ṣayrafī's history, he does not copy from it for al-Ma'mūn. The earliest work he uses for this section is the account by Ibn Ṭuwayr, who was born in 1130, five years after al-Ma'mūn's death, but as a Fatimid civil servant would have had access to recent information about him. The reports by Ibn al-Athīr and Ibn Khallikān would certainly have relied on earlier unnamed materials. Other accounts of the life and death of al-Ma'mūn, namely those written or copied by Ibn Khaldūn, al-Nuwayrī, al-Maqrīzī (in both the *Itti'āẓ* and the *Khiṭaṭ*) and Ibn Taghrībirdī, rely on early *and* late authors, namely Ibn al-Ma'mūn al-Baṭā'iḥī (d. 1192) – who, as noted above, does not in extant extracts leave an account of his father's death – Ibn al-Athīr (d. 1233), Ibn Muyassar (d. 1278) and al-Dhahabi (d. 1348). But again, no consensus emerges as to the reasons for al-Ma'mūn's execution. Al-Nuwayrī (d. 1332) discusses the differences of dating offered by Ibn al-Athīr and Ibn Muyassar,[40] and in this context draws upon another non-extant work called *Kitāb al-bustān fī ḥawādith al-zamān*, which is presumably the *Bustān al-jāmi'* discussed earlier and mentioned by Ibn al-Dawādāri in *Kanz al-durar*,[41] but is seldom attested elsewhere.[42] Al-Maqrīzī offers the same report as Ibn Taghrībirdī, from *Kitāb al-bustān*, without naming his source.[43] Al-Dhahabī, who informs Ibn Taghrībirdī's account, simply attributes the execution of al-Ma'mūn and his brothers to al-Āmir's general cruelty and high-handedness.

The varied explanations for al-Ma'mūn's death that are itemized, analysed and ordered by Ibn al-Furāt suggest that where a clear and convincing authority for an event did not exist, later authors were forced to speculate, and these speculations are inscribed and archived in the historiographic record. Although Ibn Ṭuwayr transmits a detailed account, he is (for opaque reasons) not used by the five later authors – other than Ibn al-Furāt – who had access to his *Nuzhat*, including Ibn Khaldūn, al-Maqrīzī and Ibn Taghrībirdī.[44] Ibn al-Furāt's compilation and juxtaposition of these conflicting reports, in the order of Ibn al-Athīr – Ibn Abī Ṭayy – Ibn Ṭuwayr – Ibn Khallikān, reveal that the existence of eyewitness accounts did not foreclose the explanation of political events. Ibn al-Furāt himself appears undecided as to which account was the most plausible ('And God knows best as to which of these events took place', he says, III: 208, l.23), but the length at which Ibn Ṭuwayr is cited, in comparison with the three other authors, lends weight to his narrative, which is the earliest of those consulted by Ibn al-Furāt in a clear indication of his hierarchization of source material. One may note that two other works quoted on al-Ma'mūn's life, the book by his son and *Kitāb al-bustān* (written c. 1192), were available to some Mamluk compilers but not, presumably, to Ibn al-Furāt. Knowledge of late Fatimid and early Ayyubid works had not remotely died out by the Mamluk period but was certainly patchy, as the historiographic record in its archival dimension reveals. This suggests that some texts were not available in multiple copies or redactions. This is most likely to be true of both Ibn Ṭuwayr and Ibn Abī Ṭayy's histories, which were each known only to a small number of later authors, especially the latter work. This made the task of conserving salient parts of these histories an archival exigency, in that crafting a record of history and historiography through the evaluation and reuse of rare sources is to guarantee the survival of those narratives and documents for succeeding generations of readers.

Notes

1 Cf. Elshayyal, 'Ibn al-Ṣayrafī, *EI²*.
2 Ibid., 111.
3 *Ta'rīkh al-duwal*, III:163a, ll. 24–5.

4 In *al-Ḍaw ʾ al-lāmi ʿ* (1936), 2:22; *Ḥusn al-muḥāḍara* (1881), 1:239; and *Kashf al-ẓunūn* (1835–58) respectively; also *Ittiʿāẓ*, 1:22.
5 On the changeability of book titles over time, see Ghersetti, 'The book in Fact and Fiction', 1–15, 6; Hirschler, *Medieval Damascus*, 136–7.
6 Lewis, review of *Die Chronik des Ibn ad-Dawādārī*, 430.
7 Little 1998, 420; Robinson 2003, 167.
8 The slight biographical information we have on Ibn al-Ṣayrafī does not mention whether he was an Ismaʿili or not; cf. Mukhlis, *op. cit.*, 106.
9 *Al-Kawākib al-sayyāra fī tartīb al-ziyāra* (Cairo, 1907).
10 By A. F. Sayyid (Beirut, 1992).
11 See Sayyid, *Nuzhat*, 10, following al-Mundhirī (d. 1258), al-Dhahabī (d. 1348) and al-Ṣafadī (d. 1363).
12 Ibid., 11.
13 *Nuzhat*, Sayyid edition, 4; *Taʾrīkh al-duwal*, I:163b, l.24–164b, l.8.
14 Ibn al-Maʾmūn al-Baṭāʾiḥī was another author who personally saw the transition to Ayyubid rule, but his history is also lost, though again, the fragments in later works have been brought together by Sayyid (1983). Ibn al-Furāt does not mention or use this work, though many others did (see Walker, *Exploring an Islamic Empire*, 147; F. Bauden, 'Maqriziana XII. Evaluating the Sources for the Fatimid Period: Ibn al-Ma ʾmūn al-Baṭā ʾiḥī's History and Its Use by al-Maqrīzī (with a Critical Edition of His Resumé for the Years 501–15 AH)', in B. Craig (ed.), *Ismaili and Fatimid Studies in Honor of Paul E. Walker* (Chicago, 2010), 33–85; 7–9). Ibn Ẓāfir (d. 1216 or 1226) is another such figure, whom Ibn al-Furāt uses just once, through Ibn Khallikān.
15 See Elshayyal, 211, following Ahmad in the introduction to his edition of Abu Shāma's *Kitāb al-rawḍatayn*.
16 Lev, *Saladin in Egypt*, 41, following Cahen, 'Quelques chroniques', 17–18.
17 Lev, *loc. cit.*
18 See discussion on II:17b below.
19 I:166a–166b.
20 Cf. *The Chronicle of Ibn al-Athir*, ed. and trans. Richards, 3–6.
21 E. Ashtor, 'Baybars al-Manṣūrī', *EI*[2].
22 Cf. Richards' edition of the *Zubda*, xxvii–xxviii.
23 S. Dadoyan, *The Fatimid Armenians* (Leiden, 1997), 107, 112–13.
24 J. W. Fück, 'Ibn Khallikan', *EI*[2]; Rosenthal, 'Of Making Many Books', 35.
25 J. B. Segal et al., 'Notes and Communications', *BSOAS* 36:1 (1973), 109–18, 113.
26 For the Fatimid section, see Ferré edition.
27 Ferré edition, 10, 92 and *passim*; one passage from al-Quḍāʿī (d. 1062) is on al-Ḥākim's death: 58–9.
28 *Akhbār Miṣr:* this work survives incomplete: the extant parts cover 362–5; 381–7; 439–553 AH.
29 Cf. Sayyid, *Chronique d'Égypte*, هو.
30 The fullest picture of all the known lost historical works from Fatimid times is provided by Sayyid (1977), 1–41.
31 Ẓāfir, *Akhbār al-duwal*, 92.
32 For a discussion of the eight extant MSS, see Abbas' Critical introduction to the *Wafayāt*, 1:15–18.
33 Ibn al-Furāt copied from his sources with great fidelity according to Sayyid, *Nuzhat:* Introduction, 12. His precision in copying from sources can be seen very clearly when his version of accounts by, for example, Ibn al-Athīr or Ibn Khallikān, are juxtaposed with the published versions of these works.

34 *Akhbār al-duwal* survives in two MSS and the *Wafayāt* in eight.
35 *Khiṭaṭ*, ed. Wiet, 4:74.
36 L. Imad, *op. cit.*, 192.
37 It is referred to as both his *ta'rīkh*, and, by al-Nuwayrī, as a *sīra* of his father: P. M. Holt, review of *Passages de la Chronique d'Egypte d'ibn al-Ma'mūn, Prince Gamāl al-Dīn Abū 'Alī Mūsā b. al-Ma'mūn al-Baṭā'iḥī, m. 588 h.* by A. F. Sayyid, *BSOAS* 48:2 (1985), 424.
38 *Nihāyat al-arab*, 28:288–92.
39 Imad, *Fatimid Vizierate*, 191.
40 *Nihāyat al-arab*, 28:292: al-Nuwayrī regards Ibn Muyassar's dating to be correct and Ibn al-Athīr's a mistake, though the majority of subsequent historians follow the latter.
41 *Kanz*, ed. al-Munajjid, 6:493.
42 See Hartmann, 'A Unique Manuscript', 93, for one of few exceptions to this.
43 *Itti'āẓ*, 3:111.
44 In the case of Ibn Taghrībirdī, it is possible that he had access only to an incomplete version of the *Nuzhat*, 31, n. 1.

6

A Micro-Historical Analysis of Ibn al-Furāt's Archive (Part 2): Fatimid Caliphs and Viziers to the Rise of Ṣalāḥ al-Dīn

In the following discussion, the lives and political careers of the following four Fatimid caliphs and fifteen viziers, as treated by Ibn al-Furāt, are analysed in detail:

Fatimid caliphs

al-Ḥāfiẓ	(525–44/1130–49)
al-Ẓāfir	(544–9/1149–54)
al-Fā'iz	(549–56/1154–60)
al-'Āḍid	(556–67/1160–71)

Fatimid viziers

[519–24/1125–9: no viziers]

Hazārmard	(525/1130)
Kutayfāt b. al-Afḍal	(526/1131)
Yānis	(526/1131)
Sulaymān b al-Ḥāfiẓ	(528/1133–4)
Ḥasan b. al-Ḥāfiẓ	(528/1134)
Bahrām	(530–1/1135–6)
Riḍwān	(531–3/1136–8)

[531–44/1136–49: no viziers]

Ibn Maṣāl	(544–5/1149–50)
Ibn al-Sālār	(545–8/1150–3)
'Abbās al-Ṣanhājī	(549/1154)
Ṭalā'i' b. Ruzzīk	(549–57/1154–c. 1161)
Ruzzīk b. Ṭalā'i'	(557-558/1160–2)
Shāwar	(558/1162, 559–64/1163–8)
Dirghām	(558–9/1162–3)
Shirkūh	(564/1168)[1]

The caliphate of al-Āmir and the succession crisis after his death

[sub annis 523/1128–9, 524/1129]

For his account of al-Āmir's life and death, Ibn al-Furāt turns to the following authors and works:

- *Nuzhat al-muqlatayn* by Ibn Ṭuwayr
- *Maʿādin al-dhahab* by Ibn Abī Ṭayy
- *al-Kāmil fī 'l-taʾrīkh* by Ibn al-Athīr, via Baybars
- *Wafayāt al-aʿyān* by Ibn Khallikān
- *Zubdat al-fikra fī taʾrīkh al-hijra* by Baybars al-Dawādār al-Manṣūrī (c. 1247–1325)

The first account cited by Ibn al-Furāt, from the *Wafayāt*, is brief and does not indicate its sources. We must conclude that Ibn Khallikān did not have early material to hand in relation to al-Āmir's death, as he mentions nothing about the succession crisis that ensued after his assassination (which the sources agree was at the hands of Nizaris). One notes, however, that Ibn al-Furāt quotes a longer and more detailed account from the *Wafayāt* than the entry that appears in published versions of the *Wafayāt*, which again suggests that Ibn al-Furāt used a longer recension of the work. A comparison with other sources reveals that Ibn Khallikān's account is notably similar only to Ibn Ẓāfir's, who was probably his source, as he had been for al-Afḍal's life in the *Wafayāt*.[2]

Immediately after Ibn Khallikān's pejorative description of al-Āmir's life and personal characteristics, Ibn al-Furāt appends a short, unattributed account (f. 15b, ll. 3–11) in which the caliph's good qualities, such as his memorization of the Qur'an, are mentioned in the interests, one presumes, of balance. After all, Ibn al-Furāt populates his archive with diverse readings of conduct where possible. This brief report is followed by lines of verse provided by Ibn Ṭuwayr, as evidenced by their acknowledged presence in both al-Maqrīzī's *Ittiʿāẓ* and his *Khiṭaṭ*, though unusually, Ibn al-Furāt does not name Ibn Ṭuwayr at this juncture. The subsequent, longer report on al-Āmir is attributed by Ibn al-Furāt to Ibn Ṭuwayr's *Nuzhat.* After discussing al-Āmir's recovery of wealth embezzled from state taxation by al-Afḍal, and his dealings with those safeguarding it, Ibn Ṭuwayr describes the Nizari plot through which al-Āmir is killed, and the means by which al-Ḥāfiẓ is appointed the new caliph – an event recorded in a *sijill* preserved by al-Qalqashandī and Idrīs ʿImād al-Dīn[3] – including mention of a dream in which al-Āmir foresaw his own death and the birth of a son named al-Ṭayyib, who would succeed him as caliph. Yet Ibn Ṭuwayr mentions nothing about al-Ṭayyib, who was referred to by Ibn Muyassar most probably on the authority of the lost work of the Fatimid author al-Muḥannak (d. 1154),[4] and copied by al-Maqrīzī alone of the later Egyptian and Syrian chroniclers.[5] Ibn Ṭuwayr, who was likely present at the death of al-Āmir, could be regarded as a Ḥāfiẓī historian who would be expected to support the official state position that al-Ṭayyib was not a contender for the throne (and whose fate is not explained in any source). But that presumption is challenged by the fact that Ibn Ṭuwayr's narrative was scripted after the Fatimids fell, when he was employed by the Ayyubids. Added to this is the fact that Ibn Ṭuwayr is not usually given to offering an 'official' line on Fatimid history, and indeed presents rounded views of caliphs and viziers such as al-Afḍal, as discussed earlier; his views must therefore be his own.

Nor indeed does Ibn al-Athīr's *Kāmil*, as transmitted to Ibn al-Furāt in this instance via Baybars' *Zubda*, mention the infant al-Ṭayyib at all. Yet Ibn Abī Ṭayy, who takes up the account next for Ibn al-Furāt, mentions both his birth and that his partisans were active in Damascus after al-Āmir's death. He also indicates that he took this information from informants in San'a, Yemen, where the Tayyibi *da'wa* was initiated soon after al-Āmir's death, and where the birth of al-Ṭayyib had been made known to the Sulayhid queen, a vassal of the Fatimids, by al-Āmir himself.[6]

This reference from Ibn Abī Ṭayy confirms that he preserved for Ibn al-Furāt unique and valuable reports on the Fatimids that circulated outside Fatimid Egypt, and that in Aleppo, he had access to information that authors who lived in Fatimid Egypt were not privy to. This indication is confirmed by the mention of the birth of a son to al-Āmir in three other source types, as follows:

1. A report in the annalistic historiography of Ibn Muyassar (presumed to be quoting the Fatimid chronicler al-Muḥannak) describing public celebrations in Egypt on the birth of al-Ṭayyib. This reference to the birth begs the question of how a public celebration could have been as nearly completely expunged from the public consciousness or the later historiographical record in Egypt as appears to have been the case. Ibn Muyassar's report, if based upon al-Muḥannak's testimony or account, represents an Egyptian, possibly eyewitness strand of information. This problematizes the question of what the 'official' Ḥafiẓī line on al-Ṭayyib's birth was, given that Ibn Muyassar reports it, while Ibn Ṭuwayr does not. Later official decrees obviously tried to 'set the record straight' from an apologetical Ḥāfiẓī point of view, but Ibn Muyassar preserves an earlier reading of events;
2. A passage in the Syrian chronicle *Kitāb al-bustān* (or *Bustān al-jāmi'*) which refers to the birth of a son, whose later fate is unknown, and refers to him as Abū Muḥammad;[7]
3. The mention of a son in a *sijill* (official decree) said to have been sent by al-Āmir to the above-mentioned Yemeni queen, al-Malika al-Sayyida Hurra (or Arwa, d. 1138), on the occasion of this son's birth, preserved in several Isma'ili works. The authors of two of the latter are late twelfth century ('Umāra al-Yamanī, d. 1175, and Hātim b. Ibrāhīm, d. 1199), and a third is a later digest attributed to Idrīs 'Imād al-Dīn (d. 1468) quoting from a number of early Isma'ili sources dating from the tenth century and onwards.[8] Yet another Isma'ili work penned by the Yemeni *dā'ī* al-Khaṭṭāb (d. 1138) provides an eyewitness report of the reaction to news of al-Ṭayyib's birth at the Sulayhid court.[9]

These diverse sources rule out the possibility that al-Ṭayyib's birth was a fiction, and the lack of knowledge of his existence in some – indeed most – of the main historiographical sources dating from both the Fatimid era and later (viz. Ibn

Ṭuwayr, Ibn al-Athīr, Ibn Khallikān and many others) suggests that his concealment by al-Ḥāfiẓ, as some of the sources assert, was a largely successful tactic. At the same time, Ibn Muyassar's report subverts its complete obliteration from the early Egyptian record. Outside Egypt, however, in Syria and the Yemen, the signs of al-Tayyib's birth could not be expunged, and Ibn al-Furāt's preservation of Ibn Abī Ṭayy's slight but revealing report on the issue, which, alongside other accounts, offers a detailed record of this controversy on the basis of the earliest available sources, is thus an important alternative – perhaps corrective – to the view that prevailed among most Egyptian historians writing about the Fatimid era. The archival function of historiography is brought into sharp relief as we consider how replete Ibn al-Furāt's account is with otherwise scarce and precious information about (1) social 'facts'; (2) the vicissitudes of historiography, including the 'travel' of texts through time and across geographical borders in a manner that reveals their inherent plasticity[10] and (3) the epistemic value of inclusivity underlying the work of several historians including Ibn al-Furāt himself, who document a range of accounts and interpretations of a critical moment in late Fatimid imperial history.

The caliphate of al-Ḥāfiẓ and the vizierates of Kutayfāt, Hazārmard, Yānis, Ḥasan b. al-Ḥāfiẓ, Bahrām and Riḍwān

[sub annis 524/1129, 526/1131, 528/1133]

The following series of reports discuss a twenty-year period of fraught political history characterized by internecine hostility and violence between four viziers and the caliph al-Ḥāfiẓ (r. 1130–49). Ibn al-Furāt reuses familiar sources he relied on for the preceding era, augmented by two poems, but varies his strategy by changing author/voice more often, and offers greater detail in the narrative of a complex series of events. Al-Ḥāfiẓ's tenure is covered throughout the second volume of *Ta'rīkh al-duwal* and a few folios into the third. Some thirty-four separate reports under three annals are selected and ordered from the following sources:

- *Nuzhat al-muqlatayn* by Ibn Ṭuwayr
- *Ma'ādin al-dhahab* by Ibn Abī Ṭayy
- *al-Kāmil fi 'l-ta'rīkh* by Ibn al-Athīr, via Baybars
- *Wafayāt al-a'yān* by Ibn Khallikān
- *Zubdat al-fikra* by Baybars al-Manṣūrī

Reports from the five authors whom Ibn al-Furāt relies on for this period are interspersed with some regularity, but Ibn Ṭuwayr, again prioritized as a unique author with 'inside information', provides the bulk of the material and the longest individual reports. Other authors are cited in order to confirm basic information, especially details of identity such as protagonists' names, titles, places of birth, manner of death and so on. The exception to this pattern is reuse of reports from Ibn Abī Ṭayy, who offers useful additional information to fill out the broader historical outline furnished otherwise single-handedly by Ibn Ṭuwayr, and forms a basis of later accounts carried by al-Maqrīzī and Ibn Taghrībirdī.

Ibn Ṭuwayr, newly born at the time of al-Ḥāfiẓ's accession as regent in 1130, was not a witness to this era, but his account is substantial, transmits conversations between several political figures involved, and presents a coherent blow-by-blow account of how caliph and vizier vied with each other and shed blood in the process. Of the thirty-four reports presented for al-Ḥāfiẓ's rule, twelve are from Ibn Ṭuwayr, nine are from Ibn Abī Ṭayy, six from Ibn al-Athīr via Baybars, one from Ibn al-Athīr by himself and one from Ibn Khallikān. Of the rest, two are poetry extracts by al-Iskandarānī and the *qāḍī* al-Rashīd Ibn al-Zubayr, another is attributed to 'several historians' (*baʿḍ ahl al-taʾrīkh*) and the remaining two are unattributed and unidentified. The question of who Ibn Ṭuwayr's informant(s) for this period of Fatimid history were is an intriguing one given the intimate knowledge his reports display. The narrative is remarkable for explaining personal relationships between the protagonists with an eye for detail, and was clearly provided by an eyewitness, though the narrative does not refer to an author or use the first-person pronoun. The account shows knowledge of the personal background of emirs and *mamlūk*s such as Yānis and Hazārmard (each of whom took the vizierate at different stages), and of Bahrām, who came to Egypt from Armenia to become the vizier at al-Ḥāfiẓ's request. The inclusion of details confirmed by an extant decree also reflects Ibn Ṭuwayr's access, as a high-ranking Fatimid official, to state decrees/petitions/legal documents.[11] Yet official documents alone could not provide the full picture transmitted by Ibn Ṭuwayr.

Whatever the provenance of Ibn Ṭuwayr's account which clearly fuses documentary and narrative sources, and possibly oral testimony as well as written, Ibn al-Furāt does not allow this version to hold singular authority on a sombre chapter of Fatimid history from which the caliphate never recovered. He breaks up his narrative at irregular intervals with supplementary reports from authors including Ibn Abī Ṭayy, who back up Ibn Ṭuwayr's description. A report on the fate of vizier Hizabr al-Mulūk that would otherwise run to three folios (III: 18b–20a) is supplemented by a few lines from Ibn Abī Ṭayy to confirm Ibn Ṭuwayr's information that the vizier's head was paraded in Cairo after his death. The additional detail provided by Ibn Abī Ṭayy is exemplified by his description of the honorific titles that Aḥmad b. al-Afḍal (Kutayfāt) adopted while vizier, alluded to briefly by Ibn Ṭuwayr but provided more fully and vividly by Ibn Abī Ṭayy (20a–20b), in which the vizier's hubris is made clear.

Ibn al-Furāt is not the only post-Fatimid annalist to have borrowed these reports from Ibn Ṭuwayr. Al-Maqrīzī and Ibn Taghrībirdī also cite the *Nuzhat* for this period, and in fact, it is through their attributed quotations from the *Nuzhat* that four extracts from that work in this section of *Taʾrīkh al-duwal*, not named as such by Ibn al-Furāt, can be identified as Ibn Ṭuwayr's. These omissions of source name are not habitual for Ibn al-Furāt, and reveal that archival practice in historiography, if meticulous overall, is a fallible human enterprise, and of a piece with the subjectivity and contingency of archives of various kinds noted earlier.[12]

Though an autograph chronicle that did not enjoy the benefits of substantive further copying and wide distribution, *Taʾrīkh al-duwal* transmits and preserves several important pieces in the jigsaw of late Fatimid historiography. For al-Ḥāfiẓ's rule, Ibn Ṭuwayr and Ibn Abī Ṭayy provide the bulk of reports itemized, selected and ordered by Ibn al-Furāt, and for the wider picture of historiographical transmission into later historiography, Ibn Ṭuwayr's contribution ranks alongside Ibn Muyassar's as a substantial source that feeds into several later works, mainly through al-Maqrīzī, as is also the case with Ibn Muyassar's work, which is preserved and transmitted largely by al-Maqrīzī. While we have some notion of Ibn Muyassar's range of sources, however (al-Musabbiḥī up to his death in 1029 and al-Muḥannak, d. 1154, for example), it is less clear whence Ibn Ṭuwayr acquired his information. Direct reports from participants or observers, as noted above, is a distinct possibility in light of Ibn Ṭuwayr's closeness to inner circles of the Fatimid government. On the other hand, the less voluminous accounts transmitted by Ibn Abī Ṭayy, providing some significant details, are not cited in later accounts, even though al-Maqrīzī would have accessed these extracts when he availed himself of Ibn al-Furāt's history. The history of Ibn Abī Ṭayy, as discussed earlier, was reused by few later historians.

The remaining prose sources for al-Ḥāfiẓ's rule in *Ta'rīkh al-duwal* add little original information. Ibn Khallikān's report, the final instalment in a sub-archive of accounts of al-Ḥāfiẓ's rule presented by Ibn al-Furāt, is basic, relies largely on the information provided by Ibn al-Athīr's *Kāmil*, and only adds one colourful snippet regarding al-Ḥāfiẓ's affliction with abdominal pains (*al-qūlanj*), relieved only by the invention of a drum-like instrument presented to him by its creator, a man whose grandson related the story to Ibn Khallikān. This instrument, claims Ibn Khallikān, a lover of idiosyncratic detail, was later found in the treasures left by Ṣalāḥ al-Dīn (d. 1193). Ibn al-Furāt places this report after all others in his arrangement precisely because of its trivial, even levitous nature. The preceding reports are unremittingly dark, describing a sanguinary era of Fatimid history.

On a final note, one of Ibn al-Furāt's two poetic citations for this era is two quatrains on Aḥmad b. al-Afḍal by al-Iskandarānī (d. 1134), an Alexandrian poet who extolled the virtues of many Egyptians personalities in his writings. These are conserved by some authors earlier than Ibn al-Furāt, including Ibn Ẓāfir. The latter's *Akhbār al-duwal* contains the first of these quatrains but not the second. Indeed, the extracts from al-Iskandarānī's *oeuvre* to be found in ʿImād al-Dīn al-Iṣfahānī's *Kharīdat al-qaṣr wa jarīdat al-ʿaṣr* in the volume on the poets of Egypt (*Shuʿarā' miṣr*)[13] do not contain these lines, nor does Ibn Khallikān's *Wafayāt*, which otherwise provides samples of al-Iskandarānī's panegyric poems in its entry on the poet. Some twenty folios later, another Fatimid poet, Qāḍī al-Rashīd b. al-Zubayr (d. 1167), the author of a scintillating versified register of the Fatimids' treasures, on which subject he was a specialist, is quoted for the vizier Riḍwān b. al-Walakhshī from his book of poetry known as *Kitāb al-jinān wa riyāḍ al-adhhān*.[14] This, too, is a little-known work, and the inclusion of extracts from the works of these two poets indicates that Ibn al-Furāt was able to avail himself of early sources that most intervening authorities had no access to, and to extend their life cycles by uniquely preserving extracts from them. This further affirms his intention to itemize and document sources while building a historiographic archive from the bountiful store of material available to him, and to order it into a coherent and trustworthy narrative for the edification of his reader(s). The form is narrative while the function is archival.

The caliphate of al-Ẓāfir and the vizierates of Ibn Maṣāl, Ibn al-Sālār and ʿAbbās al-Ṣanhājī. Usāma b. Munqidh's sojourn in Egypt

[sub annis 544/1149, 548/1153, 555/1160]

The relatively short rule of al-Ẓāfir is covered by Ibn al-Furāt in the first third of volume three of *Ta'rīkh al-duwal*, and is dominated by a series of reports on the murder of the caliph. The narrative is elaborated over more than eleven pages, and appears in at least two main versions that are broadly similar but with several important differences. This section as a whole is related on the authority of four named authors and one unnamed one, namely:

- *Nuzhat al-muqlatayn* by Ibn Ṭuwayr
- *Maʿādin al-dhahab* by Ibn Abī Ṭayy
- *Wafayāt al-aʿyān* by Ibn Khallikān
- An unidentified lengthy account of Usāma b. Munqidh's involvement with members of the Fatimid ruling elite
- Two verse epistles exchanged between Usāma b. Munqidh and his former patron Muʿīn al-Dīn Unar

Some twenty-five pages of *Ta'rīkh al-duwal* are devoted to the events of these six years (1149–54), mostly under the annal for 544/1149 when al-Ẓāfir acceded as caliph, but also under 555/1160, the death year of al-Fā'iz, the subsequent child-caliph whose sovereignty remained nominal. This disaggregated arrangement flags up and mirrors the deep and continuous disruption to caliphal rule caused by the assassination of al-Ẓāfir by ʿAbbās and his son. The raising of children to the caliphate became the modus operandi of the vizier-led Fatimid state after the murder of al-Ẓāfir, as the Palace became a political force that viziers were forced to contend with. Thereafter, Viziers of Sword and Pen attempted to hold the reins of power fully as policy-makers as well as kingmakers, with the help of those army commanders whose loyalties they had secured, though a ceremonial, authority-conferring role was retained for the Fatimid caliphs until 1171. Indeed, the caliphs or their representatives asserted their headship of state by a variety of methods until the last Fatimid vizier, Shāwar, was killed in 1169.[15] Coins, for example, were still minted in the names of young caliphs, on which they continued to be designated 'imams'. The reverberations of ʿAbbās' murder of several members of the ruling family were also to be felt throughout the later caliphate of al-Fā'iz: Ibn al-Furāt describes the five-year-old son of al-Ẓāfir being shown the bodies of his murdered family, and laments that he remained a subdued and passive child after that. The affairs of the state were managed by the vizier Ṭalā'iʿ b. Ruzzīk, who removed ʿAbbās and his son soon after al-Fā'iz's investiture (III: 81a, ll. 14–15).

From the twelfth century itself, four (near) contemporary sources preserve accounts of this six year period, namely works by Ibn Ṭuwayr (1130–1220), Ibn al-Qalānisī (c. 1070–60), Usāma b. Munqidh (1095–1188) and the late twelfth-century *Bustān al-jāmiʿ*. The first of these is reconstituted from later extracts and does not survive in itself. To this we may add a report by Ibn Ẓāfir, which was not, given his year of birth (1171), an eyewitness account, but was likely informed by a direct observer, either orally or through a written work. This is strongly suggested by the detail of Ibn Ẓāfir's account and his closeness in time to the events depicted. Of the four 'primary' sources, only Ibn Ṭuwayr's was reused as a positively identifiable source by more than one later historian in Egypt of those included in this survey, namely Ibn al-Furāt, al-Maqrīzī and Ibn Taghrībirdī. Ibn al-Qalānisī's description is dramatically different from other sources examined here; he is cited solely by Ibn Taghrībirdī. Finally, Usāma's account is not directly used at all, although one unacknowledged passage from his *Kitāb al-iʿtibār* on al-Ẓāfir's lavish gifts to Naṣr, which might have come through an intervening authority, is discernible in al-Maqrīzī's account. Its provenance cannot be doubted because all its details are identical with those in Usāma's eyewitness account.[16] In addition, Sibṭ b. al-Jawzī reports some of the same information as Usāma.[17] As for Ibn Ẓāfir's early account, it was passed through to many later works, often via Ibn Muyassar, and its traces can be found in the works of, inter alia, Ibn al-Athīr, Ibn Khallikān, Ibn Khaldūn, al-Maqrīzī and Ibn Taghrībirdī, with some echoes in Ibn al-Furāt, too.

Ibn al-Furāt opens the narrative of this sobering string of episodes with a brief profile of the new caliph's age, year of accession and years in office via Ibn Abī Ṭayy, whose information is somewhat contradictory (*mutanāqiḍ*), as Ibn al-Furāt notes in typically reflexive fashion (III: 21b, l.3). This is followed by a series of reports describing three episodes of violence, namely the murders by 'Abbās and his son Naṣr firstly of the vizier Ibn al-Salār, then of the caliph al-Ẓāfir and finally of al-Ẓāfir's brothers and nephew. These are presented in a similar (though not identical) way in all but three of the dozen or so known works from the Fatimid and post-Fatimid historiographic archive that describe and/or evaluate this period. A clear pattern in the way moral sympathy for the victims of 'Abbās is evoked becomes apparent in these texts, even when those victims are themselves guilty of violence.

Thus Ibn Maṣāl, al-Ẓāfir's first vizier, is praised for his efficacy in the role, and subsequently portrayed as the victim of Ibn al-Salār's ambition and cruelty. The latter was murdered by Naṣr, at the behest of his father 'Abbās, who had developed a dislike for the man who was his stepfather as well as the vizier; but he was assassinated while sleeping, exhausted after a hard day's fighting, thus killed when he was most vulnerable. 'Abbās stepped up to the vizierate to find that the scandal of his son Naṣr's affair with the caliph al-Ẓāfir was causing commotion that threatened to undermine both caliphal and vizeral authority. Following Usāma b. Munqidh's advice, he persuaded his son Naṣr to kill the caliph and his manservants on a clandestine visit to his house. He then buried the bodies of the caliph and his men in a pit within the house, covering it with stone slabs; a tryst thereby turned into an assassination. Yet word got out that the caliph was last seen at Naṣr's house, which instigated 'Abbās to go to the palace immediately and murder al-Ẓāfir's brothers and nephew (who protested their innocence) in order to deflect blame from himself and Naṣr. Another motive expressed in the sources is 'Abbās desire to remove obstacles from his plan to install al-Ẓāfir's infant son in the caliphate and rule in his name. The young son of al-Ẓāfir, who saw the carnage before he was proclaimed the new caliph by 'Abbās, was traumatized by these events.

Other than Ibn Duqmāq, whose account is brief, all the authors discussed presently use some measure of direct speech to help to convey the intricacies of motive involved, and to bring immediacy to the chain of events depicted. Direct speech is not at all unknown in Arabic historical reports for this period, and Ibn al-Furāt certainly uses it sporadically in *Taʾrīkh al-duwal*, including for the Fatimid period. It is, however, rare to see widespread use of direct speech only for a *particular* set of events, especially where that speech varies somewhat and is not simply a repetition of 'soundbites'. This variety suggests that distinct interpretations and accounts of these events were in circulation from an early point in time, perhaps even at source, and the historiographic archive preserves this range of witnesses and testimonies. The four contemporary or primary works and one early non-primary source that describe these episodes all contain dialogue, though only the versions of Ibn Ṭuwayr and Ibn Ẓāfir finds strong echoes in later tradition.

The main early accounts of the events leading up to al-Ẓāfir's death, and the significant differences of detail to be found in them – with the focus particularly on al-Ẓāfir's murder – are summed up next.

Ibn al-Qalānisī reports that al-Ẓāfir is killed by his two elder brothers, Jibrīl and Yūsuf, and a nephew, Ṣāliḥ b. al-Ḥasan. When 'Abbās learns of this, he goes to them, kills them and proclaims al-Fā'iz the new caliph.

The *Bustān* narrates that al-Ẓāfir visits Naṣr with a manservant as part of his regular '*da'wa*' rounds, because he is suspicious of him (*ittahama bihi*); the caliph's subjects discover and gossip about these visits. 'Abbās tells his son he has brought shame upon their family and urges him to kill the caliph. Naṣr murders both caliph and manservant, and buries them in a pit in his house. 'Abbās goes to the palace to feign a search for the caliph, proclaims him absent and kills the princes' tutors at the palace. Al-Ẓāfir's brothers approach 'Abbās to accuse him of knowing the caliph's whereabouts. 'Abbās orders them to be killed and takes the oath of allegiance for al-Ẓāfir's young son al-Fāiz.

Usāma b. Munqidh reports that after Naṣr's murder of the vizier Ibn al-Salār, carried out in collusion with the caliph al-Ẓāfir, 'Abbās becomes the new vizier, and feels threatened by the growing confidence between the caliph and his son Naṣr. Usāma intercedes for Naṣr in arguments that ensue between father and son. Al-Ẓāfir soon incites Naṣr against his father, bestowing lavish gifts on him and promising him the vizierate. Naṣr confides in Usāma, who urges him not to kill his father. Naṣr tells 'Abbas of al-Ẓāfir's hopes, and 'Abbas persuades Naṣr to murder the caliph instead, along with the caliph's servant; they are buried in a pit under Naṣr's home. 'Abbās pretends ignorance of this, goes to the palace 'seeking' the caliph, announces his absence and blames his two brothers and nephew of al-Ẓāfir's murder. They deny this but 'Abbās kills them and proclaims al-Ẓāfir's son the new caliph.

Ibn Ṭuwayr reports that Usāma b. Munqidh meets 'Abbās when the latter is stationed at Bilbays, in Lower Egypt north-east of Cairo, and feeds his ambition for the vizierate of Egypt, because he knows that the amity between the caliph and Naṣr could be exploited. Naṣr is persuaded to kill the previous vizier Ibn al-Salār with the help of his men, and 'Abbās becomes the new vizier. The Cairenes come to know of these events, which engenders fear and dislike of the caliph, the vizier and the vizier's son. 'Abbās begins to realise the extent of Naṣr's involvement with the caliph, which the previous vizier Ibn al-Salār warned him against, and decides to persuade Naṣr to kill the caliph. 'Abbas goes to the palace ostensibly looking for the caliph, accuses his brothers and nephew of his murder, kills them and proclaims al-Fā'iz the new caliph.

Ibn Ẓāfir reports that Usāma b. Munqidh urges 'Abbās to ask Naṣr to seek the vizierate on his (Abbās') behalf, which he argues will not be refused because of al-Ẓāfir's feelings for Naṣr, and because al-Ẓāfir would prefer to be rid of the sitting vizier, Ibn al-Salār. The latter, known for his despotism, is killed by Naṣr, and the Cairenes are glad of his removal but suspicious of Usāma, whose involvement seeps into public knowledge. Usāma, worried for his own safety, incites 'Abbās against the caliph, emphasising to him that al-Ẓāfir loves his son as if the latter 'were a woman'. 'Abbās is horrified, asks what is to be done, and Usāma advises 'Abbās to dispatch al-Ẓāfir and place someone else in the caliphate. Naṣr kills the caliph and his servants on the instruction of his father and buries them in a pit in his house, which he covers over with slabs. One of al-Ẓāfir's servants, who had hidden in Naṣr's house and escaped the bloodshed, returns to the palace to divulge what he saw. The women of the palace weep in grief. 'Abbās goes to the palace the next morning and finds the caliph absent. He sends for al-Ẓāfir's brothers and asks them about the caliph. They reply: 'Ask your son,' and 'Abbās kills them, while accusing them of the caliph's murder. Al-Ẓāfir is 21 years old at the time of his assassination.

Aside from two undisputed 'facts', namely that 'Abbās killed al-Ẓāfir's two brothers and proclaimed his young son al-Fā'iz the new caliph, there are significant discrepancies in these five sources that could be divided along geographic lines. The first three sources are broadly Damascene. Ibn al-Qalānisī, based in elite Damascus society, served as the head of the chancery and as the city's *ra'īs* or governor, among other roles. 'Imād al-Dīn, if one accepts that the *Bustān* was his work, was originally Persian, and spent time in Baghdad, in lower Iraq and in Damascus, but appears to have built his permanent home in later life opposite the citadel of Damascus, where the collection of North Syrian reports of recent history seems to have preoccupied him in his last years.[18] Usāma b. Munqidh's life as a peripatetic nobleman is well known; his memoirs were finally dictated to a scribe by the ninety-year-old author in Damascus. None of these three accounts implicates Usāma in the murder of al-Ẓāfir. In fact, Usāma presents himself as trying to avert bloodshed within the 'Abbas household and in the palace, while Ibn al-Qalānisī and 'Imād al-Dīn do not mention Usāma at all in their reports of the regicide, which is surprising even in two relatively brief accounts. They died in 1160 and 1188 respectively, while al-Ẓāfir's assassination was in 1154. Could they, writing within a few years of these events, have been unaware of Usāma's sojourn in 'Abbās' house during this period? Indeed, his very presence there at that point in time would have had implications worthy of comment, whether or not he had instigated al-Ẓāfir's assassination.

One can speculate on the reasons for this seemingly regional leaning. The reports on Fatimid Egypt in Ibn al-Qalānisī's *Dhayl*, usually prefaced with the words 'Then news reached us from Egypt that ...' have the quality of 'hot-off-the-press' reports brought to the Damascus court by messenger. In these circumstances, the details of events were perhaps left out when 'headlines' were transmitted. We have even less contextual understanding for the *Bustān*, which was clearly a mere outline of events. The book that the *Bustān* has most in common with in terms of subject matter and interpretation is Ibn Abī Ṭayy's *Ma'ādin al-dhahab*, another Syrian work. However, this chronicle, written a few decades after the *Bustān* (Ibn Abū Ṭayy died in 1233), has no preserved reports recounting the death of al-Ẓāfir. Even Ibn al-Furāt, whose dependence on Ibn Abī Ṭayy for the Fatimids is extensive, preserves accounts from Ibn Ṭuwayr, Ibn Khallikān and a third source whose information yields great detail but is left unattributed, does not appear to supply anything from the Aleppo-based *Ma'ādin* in this instance.

The two early Egyptian accounts above, by Ibn Ṭuwayr and Ibn Ẓāfir, have much more to say about Usāma's role in emboldening 'Abbās's ambition and conniving with him on the murder of Ibn al-Salār, and of the caliph in Ibn Ẓāfir's case. Both texts emphasize Usāma's opportunism – in wanting his patron in Egypt to gather more power for himself – as the chief reason behind the multiple murders that follow, to which the backdrop is Usāma's dependence on 'Abbās after his expulsion from Damascus by his previous patron Mu'īn al-Dīn Unar. Both authors use direct speech and similar wording to depict Usāma's incitement of 'Abbās. In other respects, however, the two versions differ. Ibn Ṭuwayr's earlier, more detailed account was written by an author present in Cairo when the events took place (Ibn Ṭuwayr was born in 1130; al-Ẓāfir was murdered in 1154), and his narrative, which finds some slight verbal echoes in Ibn Ẓāfir's (1171–1216 or 1226) account, was probably seen by the latter or informed an intermediate source that Ibn Ẓāfir was cognizant of. The chief differences between the two are that in Ibn Ẓafir's account, no servant escapes Naṣr's house to apprise the palace of what befell the caliph, and that 'Abbās's motives in his assassination of al-Ẓāfir are, for Ibn Ṭuwayr, not just ambition encouraged in him by Usāma but also his abhorrence of the liaison between his son Naṣr and the caliph.

The attitudes of later sources to these differing interpretations of events is revealing of how Ayyubid and Mamluk historiography approached and secured a record of such controversies. The five reports described above are unevenly distributed in later works, as summarized in the following description (ordered by author death date):

Ibn Abī Ṭāyy: No annal available for this year.

Ibn al-Athīr: The *Kāmil* offers a succinct report, which relies on the Ibn Ẓāfir-Ibn Muyassar version in both outline and wording.

Sibṭ b. al-Jawzī: Presents the same story as Usāma b. Munqidh regarding the latter's role in the affair but adds one detail not found in the early sources: that 'Abbās claims to notables of the palace that al-Ẓāfir drowned while out on a boat that capsized.

Ibn Khallikān: The *Wafayāt* reports al-Ẓāfir's murder in its entries on both al-Ẓāfir and his son al-Fā'iz; the accounts appear to be a re-worded summary of Ibn Ṭuwayr's report in terms of who is deemed responsible for the regicide; but there is no acknowledgement of source, and verbal echoes of Ibn Ṭuwayr appear only intermittently, suggesting that either Ibn Khallikān substantially re-phrased the report from the *Nuzhat*, or used an unknown intermediary source.

Ibn Muyassar: Takes most of his information from Ibn Ẓāfir or a common source. Though his wording has some similarities with Ibn Ẓāfir's, the rest is expressed differently; the outline remains the same.

Al-Nuwayrī: The report in *Nihāyat al-arab* follows the Ibn Ẓāfir-Ibn Muyassar line, with no attribution, though the wording is closer to Ibn Muyassar's account than Ibn Ẓāfir's.

Al-Ḍhahabī: The report from *Ta'rīkh al-Islām* first re-writes what appears to be a fusion of Ibn Ṭuwayr's and Ibn Ẓāfir's reports, followed by an attributed quotation from Ibn al-Athīr's *Kāmil*.

Ibn al-Furāt: In addition to lengthy accounts taken from an unattributed source and from Ibn Ṭuwayr, Ibn al-Furāt cites Ibn Khallikān and, uniquely, provides extracts from two verse epistles exchanged between Usāma and his previous patron Mu'īn al Dīn Unar (of which the part by Usāma can be found in his published *Dīwān*, but Mu'īn al-Dīn's reply is apparently preserved solely by Ibn al-Furāt);[19] the point of the exchange is to establish Usāma's good character, and to underline that he is at the mercy of his patrons. However, the unattributed report in *Ta'rīkh al-duwal*, and to a lesser extent the account by Ibn Ṭuwayr, implicate Usāma deeply in the murders that follow.

Ibn Khaldūn: The report in *Kitāb al-'ibar* displays confusion as to how Ibn al-Salār met his end, and again appears to conflate aspects of the lives of the two viziers prior to 'Abbās. (Ibn Duqmāq and Ibn Khaldūn were contemporaries of Ibn al-Furāt, who clearly has fuller and more wide-ranging material available to him.) For the assassinations of Ibn al-Salār and al-Ẓāfir, Ibn Khaldūn relies on Ibn Ṭuwayr's report, of which he offers a summarized version.

Ibn Duqmāq: His very brief annals in *al-Jawhar al-thamīn* are inaccurate in omitting Ibn al-Salār from the list of al-Ẓāfir's viziers, and stating that Ibn Maṣāl was killed to allow 'Abbās to become the new vizier (a conflation of aspects from the stories of Ibn Maṣāl and Ibn al-Salār); the death of al-Ẓāfir takes the shape of Ibn Ṭuwayr's description.[20]

Al-Maqrīzī: The *Itti'āẓ* has one report on this event, taken mostly from the Ibn Ẓāfir-Ibn Muyassar version (though closer to the latter's precise wording), with some additional lines similar to those in Ibn Khallikān's entry on al-Ẓāfir.

Ibn Taghrībirdī: Alongside Ibn al-Furāt, Ibn Taghrībirdī presents the most broad-ranging discussion of the episode of al-Ẓāfir's assassination. He relates the event through citations from: Sibṭ b. al-Jawzī, Ibn Khallikān, Ibn al-Qalānisī, Ibn Muyassar (presumably through al-Maqrīzī, a chief conduit for Ibn Muyassar's use in later Egyptian historiography) and Ibn Ṭuwayr. He also twice comments that Ibn al-Qalānisī departs from the consensus of the historians (*jumhūr al-mu'arrikhīn*) in

> his belief that al-Ẓāfir was murdered by his brothers. Of the many reports itemised and cited by Ibn Taghrībirdī, he decides in a process of hierarchisation that the most illuminating account is the one originating with Ibn Muyassar, though Ibn Taghrībirdī only names him as 'one of [the historians]'. He quotes a passage from his chronicle, then mentions that the subsequent account proceeds along the same lines as those by Sibṭ and Ibn Khallikān. Ibn Taghrībirdī begins with Ibn Muyassar evidently because the latter describes Usāma as setting these events in motion, whereas Sibṭ and Ibn Khallikān (the latter following Ibn Ṭuwayr) do not hold Usāma responsible for planting the idea of al-Ẓāfir's assassination.

In the dissemination of early material elaborated here, it is clear that the strands of information and interpretation that are most reused and conserved are those by Egyptian authors: Ibn Ṭuwayr, Ibn Ẓāfir and Ibn Muyassar. The last had access to Fatimid-era sources that are now entirely lost, possibly even an official or semi-official Fatimid chronicle, and his account is thus likely to be an amalgam of the reports by Ibn Ẓāfir and some other unnamed early source(s). Ibn al-Qalānisī's version is picked up by no one but Ibn Taghrībirdī, who mentions its radical departure from the outlines present in other accounts of al-Ẓāfir's murder. The question of Usāma's involvement in that event remains open because one early source (Ibn Ẓāfir) implicates him; another (Ibn Ṭuwayr) exonerates him from regicide, while portraying him as instigating Ibn al-Salār's murder; meanwhile, Ibn al-Qalānisī says nothing about him at all. Needless to say, Usāma does not implicate himself, either, but rather presents himself as a peace broker in the whole affair.

One may see here that the identification of the person(s) responsible for the regicide, and the drawing out of its connection with the assassinations of the caliph's former vizier and members of his immediate family, as well as the motives behind these, were subjects that both earlier and later historiography were justifiably preoccupied with. The multiplicity of versions of these events is keenly reflected in Ibn al-Furāt's history, which archives the controversy in its historical, historiographical and epistemological dimensions: in his explanation of the subject, he juxtaposes several sources which conflict with one another in respect of several crucial details, but overall properly reflect the complexity of views that, in both Fatimid history and historiography, often emerged at the point of origin.

Ibn al-Furāt accomplishes this multifaceted interpretation through several steps. First he sets up Usāma's character by quoting his aggrieved verse epistle to his former master and the latter's reply, on which Ibn al-Furāt comments that it was Unar's duty to protect Usāma after his long service to him, and that once he came to Egypt, Usāma found a generous patron in 'Abbās.[21] Ibn al-Furāt comments, with his usual epistemic self-awareness, that he reproduces these poems in full despite their length because they demonstrate the difference between exemplary conduct (Usāma's) and its opposite (Mu'īn al-Dīn's).

Following this, Ibn al-Furāt turns to a long report by Ibn Ṭuwayr on Ibn al-Salār's murder, in which Usāma's involvement is instrumental, but the vizier is presented as being as cruel and barbaric in his previous conduct as those who then kill him. After some perfunctory detail adduced from Ibn Khallikān on al-Ẓāfir's character, Ibn al-Furāt turns to an unattributed account that further complicates the reading of these events. This account, not obviously traceable to the generally known accounts of the period, has echoes of Ibn Muyassar's report but otherwise presents its own version, in which Naṣr is confronted by Usāma with the rumours that the caliph is having an affair with him, and that Naṣr and the caliph have conspired to bring down 'Abbās. Naṣr is furious, denies the accusations and takes Usāma's advice to kill the caliph surreptitiously, since, as Ibn al-Furāt wryly comments, 'Fire is preferable to disgrace; misfortune to censure.'[22]

The rest follows the outline of Ibn Muyassar's account but adds more detail, though not from Ibn Ṭuwayr, who differs in his description of Usāma's role in the regicide. Ibn al-Furāt was either informed by a fuller recension of Ibn Muyassar's work, or by an unnamed earlier work providing a more complete picture than other later reports, especially those of his contemporaries Ibn Khaldūn and Ibn Duqmāq, who evidently had few sources at their disposal to describe these events. Ibn al-Furāt thus assembles, sifts, itemizes and arranges the earliest available historical accounts of this series of events. Notably, and in contrast with Ibn al-Athīr or al-Maqrīzī before and after him, Ibn al-Furāt does not paper over cracks in the narrative but rather discusses differences in the reportage, as Ibn Taghrībirdī (his successor via al-Maqrīzī) does some sixty years later. In this regard, Ibn al-Furāt's sophisticated archival methodology entails the collation and juxtaposition of accounts, yet he does not yoke his material to a predetermined position on Fatimid legitimacy, or indeed on the legitimacy of individual caliphs and viziers. As a keen and meticulous archivist, Ibn al-Furāt forces us to reconsider Paula Sanders' verdict that

> Mamluk authors preserved elements of stories from different stages of Fatimid historiography that represent different political commitments and rhetorical strategies. They transmitted these versions uncritically in narratives that both de-contextualized and de-politicized highly charged issues, apparently untroubled by the contradictory nature of the claims that each of them made.[23]

The first part of this statement is adequately borne out by the sources, early and late. The context, the politics and the contradictions referred to by Sanders, however, as reflected in the chronicles of Ibn al-Furāt and Ibn Taghrībirdī (in this instance), remain clearly visible in the Mamluk record. Ibn al-Furāt recounts these events with the aid of five sources, each representative of an independent, distinctive narrative tradition; three of them, four if Ibn Ṭuwayr is counted among them, are unique in the Arabic historiographical tradition. This shows that Mamluk authors drew on a wide basin of original sources for the Fatimid era if they were resourceful enough, and intermittently offered reflexive commentary on these sources. It also demonstrates that the presence of these sources in later chronicles ensured that early controversies, far from being ossified under intermediate layers of flattening narrative, remained 'live' issues that later historians, such as Ibn al-Furāt and Ibn Taghrībirdī, were committed to analysing and archiving, for present and future audiences, as fully as possible. Text reuse in this sense conveyed the socio-political, historiographical and epistemological meanings of critical historical events to present and future audiences via the double reflexivity evinced by the more ingenious Mamluk chroniclers.

The caliphate of al-Fā'iz and the vizierates of Ṭalā'i' b. Ruzzīk and al-'Ādil Ruzzīk. The rise of the vizier Shāwar

[sub annis 556/1160–1, 558/1162]

Ibn al-Furāt covers the al-Fā'iz/Ṭalā'i' era and the subsequent eighteen-month tenure of Ruzzīk over almost thirty pages, through four as yet unidentified reports and another five on the authority of the following:

- *Nuzhat al-muqlatayn* by Ibn Ṭuwayr
- *al-Muntaẓam fī ta'rīkh al-umam* by Ibn al-Jawzī (1114-1201)
- *Ma'ādin al-dhahab* by Ibn Abī Ṭayy
- *Wafayāt al-a'yān* by Ibn Khallikān

The number and range of Fatimid-era reports available for the Ṭalā'i'-Ruzzīk stage of Fatimid history are comparable to those available for the assassinations of al-Ẓāfir and his family, but for the newer phase, the sources do not differ except in relatively inconsequential details. Unlike the spectrum of early views on al-Ẓāfir's death dispersed through the later sources, which sustain and perpetuate the controversy as Ibn al-Furāt and Ibn Taghrībirdī elaborate, for *this* troubled period of Fatimid political history, some consensus emerges in the early sources, even in those at variance with one another on preceding events of Fatimid history. Several questions arise from this: to what extent do the sources agree on the outline for this eight-year period of Fatimid history, and how and why did the consensus, such as it is, materialize in the earliest contemporary sources?

To establish this relative consensus, one may observe the similarity of detail to be found in the following early sources on the issue of how Ṭalā'i' came to Cairo during the 'Abbās vizierate and the resulting departure, capture and death of 'Abbās and Naṣr: Ibn Ṭuwayr (1130–1220), Usāma b. Munqidh (1095–1188), the late twelfth-century *Bustān al-jāmi'*, Ibn Ẓāfir (1171–1216 or 1226) and Ibn Muyassar (d. 1287), who preserves extracts from earlier Fatimid-era historiography to take us to two years before the death of al-Fā'iz in 1160.[24] All mention that Ṭalā'i' came to Cairo from Upper Egypt to answer pleas for help from the Fatimid house against 'Abbās, murderer of the caliph al-Ẓāfir. Each describes the defeat of Abbās at the hands of Ṭalā'i'. Most accounts also allude to his discovery of the former caliph's body, interred under the house of Naṣr, and his arrangement of a state funeral and burial for him, all using similar wording. The main discernible exception to this agreement of reportage is that Usāma, writing his experiences many decades after they took place, recalls a battle between Ṭalā'i' and 'Abbās outside Cairo before the latter flees.[25] Yet the other sources, including the book of Ibn Ṭuwayr, who was in Cairo at this juncture and offers the temporally closest account, describe a bloodless coup.[26] The disparity between reports by Usāma and Ibn Ṭuwayr is easily explained: the tendency towards hyperbole in Usāma's memoirs, as he tries to magnify and embellish the rectitude or heroism of both himself and those whom his allegiance – and therefore narrative – favours, is self-evident. On the other hand, Ibn Ṭuwayr, though a Ḥafiẓī author, appears a more reliable narrator with an unsentimental style of both observation and presentation, whose account was written well after the Fatimids fell. One might expect Usāma's account to be 'emotion recollected in tranquillity', and Ibn Ṭuwayr's to be the 'spontaneous overflow' of a more recent narrative from memory, but it is the latter whose version is reused and conserved by later historians for its quality of seeming lack of partiality, up to the rule of Ṭalā'i', where the extant narrative of events by Ibn Ṭuwayr ends.[27]

Further into this political phase, there are other areas of unanimity manifested in later works. These include the means by which Ṭalā'i' is persuaded to answer the palace's request for help: namely the locks of hair of women of the royal house, cut off by them in grief at the murders of al-Ẓāfir and his family members, and sent to him in envelopes of black. There is also wide agreement on the fact that Ṭalā'i' was an accomplished policy-maker who restored stability, if short-lived, to the state, though exceptions to a laudatory view can also be observed, such as Ibn Ẓāfir's umbrage at Ṭalā'i''s partisanship towards fellow Imami Shi'a.[28] All but the briefest sources also mention his love of literature, poetry and theology.

The portrayal of Ṭalā'i's manner of death sees some variation on the issue of the mastermind behind his assassination. One view is that an aunt of the newly throned caliph, al-'Āḍid (r. 1160–71), persuaded her nephew to remove Ṭalā'i', while other sources suggest that the caliph acted alone, motivated by resentment of his vizier.[29]

On the other hand, the sources agree on the benign rule of Ṭalā'i''s son Ruzzīk, his cautious management of policy, his popularity and his eventual death at the hands of Ṭayy b. Shāwar, whose father took the vizierate after Ruzzīk. Most longer sources also recount a story about Ṭalā'i''s *waṣiyya* or deathbed advice to Ruzzīk, in which he laments three actions of his lifetime, one of which is his appointment of Shāwar over Upper Egypt. This has the familiar hallmarks of a literary trope designed to alert the reader to the machinations of a future 'villain', which is precisely what Shāwar becomes in the subsequent series of reports describing his unfolding career. The origin of the vignette is hard to determine, however, given that some early sources, or those that preserve them, chiefly Ibn Ṭuwayr, Ibn al-Qalānisī and Ibn Muyassar, have dried up by this point; it must thus be treated as a literary device rather than an eyewitness report, even if based in some unreachable kernel of 'fact'. The best proximity to the germinal account(s) is Ibn Ẓāfir's statement, just before he recounts that incident, that he had seen it depicted in 'several histories'.[30] This suggests that by his time (he was born in the final Fatimid year of 1171, and died in either 1216 or 1226, while the event in question took place in 1160), more than one source had heard and reported this information, quite possibly from one or more eyewitnesses, but whom we cannot identify. This reveals an important clue about the earliest sources of information for late Fatimid history: that several sources transmitted news or reports from the point of origin is useful in explaining the proliferation of views that often comes to characterize later accounts. Moreover, the verisimilitude of such narrations increases commensurately with the earliness of the reportage: where an account has stabilized and solidified within the historiographic tradition as early as Ibn Ẓafir's time, it may be concluded that there was something of substance in the early agreement of account, even if the point cannot be proven definitively. As for the issue of why a consensus was reached, the story likely comes from first-hand witness, with little or no recasting. As Lena Salaymeh recently observed, the 'myriad political and theological debates that animated late antique [medieval] Muslim societies suggest that moments of consensus among Muslim historians are unlikely to be mere fabrications.'[31] In such instances of textual accord, 'rhetorical strategies' as termed by Paula Sanders are conspicuous by their absence, and an agreement of accounts emerges from primordial text witnesses. Moreover, later tradition in its hierarchization of accounts appears to respect this consensus and to reify it within the historiographic archive. This is in sharp contrast to the previous clusters of reports on al-Ẓāfir's murder, where the availability of non-Egyptian (Syrian) sources (Ibn al-Qalānisī, 'Imād al-Dīn) throws doubt on the 'Egyptian consensus', and in which differences of reporting could be ascribed to both geographical vantage point and to political difference.

The pattern of dispersal of these early narratives is as follows: the earliest sources include Ibn Ṭuwayr, a chief original voice. While not directly known to many later compilers, he is the likely source of information for contemporary accounts that later tradition has not clearly identified. These are integrated into sources of the thirteenth century: Ibn al-Athīr, Ibn Khallikān and Ibn Muyassar among others, who conserve a number of named and unnamed earlier reports, though more of the latter. These in turn inform the later digests of authors from al-Nuwayrī to Ibn Khaldūn to al-Maqrīzī to Ibn Taghrībirdī, who cannot, by and large, disaggregate the earlier sources since they receive them as seamless synthesized accounts. Ibn al-Furāt is no exception, and in this part of his work, unidentified reports outweigh those with clear ascriptions in terms of volume of pages covered; for actual numbers of reports, the named and unnamed ones are evenly matched. To this rather opaque process of transmission, in which his archival practice is at risk of being partially compromised, Ibn al-Furāt nonetheless adds a valuable dimension in the shape of unique and attributed reports from an otherwise unknown eyewitness (to be presently elaborated), alongside a rhetorical anecdote that creatively rather than dogmatically casts Ṭalā'i' in a positive light, in which Ibn al-Furāt is followed by al-Maqrīzī.

To offer some context for Ibn al-Furāt's literary shaping of the narrative of Ṭalā'i''s rule, one may observe that the parts of *Ta'rīkh al-duwal* devoted to it are disorganized in sequence. Ṭalā'i''s rule is inserted under titular sections on both al-Fā'iz (r. 1154–60) and al-'Āḍid (r. 1160–71), even though the latter's caliphate did not coincide greatly with Ṭalā'i''s vizierate. In fact, Ibn Ẓāfir shows the same arrangement in his history (of which there are unacknowledged echoes in Ibn al-Furāt's for this section), though it is the case that Ṭalā'i' died after al-'Āḍid had taken his place as caliph.[32] One explanation for this protraction of narration is that by the times of al-Fā'iz and al-'Āḍid, the caliph's role had diminished to the extent that the historiographical sources have much less to say about them than about the viziers. Ibn al-Furāt's history, following Ibn Ẓāfir in this aspect, reflects that dislocation. After introducing the subject of al-'Āḍid's caliphate with a heading, Ibn al-Furāt immediately goes on to focus exclusively on the Fatimid viziers until the end of this volume of his history, thus archiving for posterity a key socio-political phenomenon of the late Fatimid era: the replacement of civilian by military government.

The named sources that Ibn al-Furāt uses in his itemization and retrieval of source material include three that recur often in *Ta'rīkh al-duwal*: Ibn Ṭuwayr, Ibn Khallikān and Ibn Abī Ṭayy. The first two provide influential reports that inform later tradition in clear and identifiable ways; the last furnishes unique information from participants. Added to this is an early source, Ibn al-Jawzī's *Muntaẓam*, which yields only a brief statement confirming the fact of Ṭalāʾiʿ's management of the state on behalf of al-Fāʾiz. This is likely included by Ibn al-Furāt for the authority that a figure of Ibn al-Jawzī's stature confers upon his chronicle.[33] The unnamed source(s) drawn upon by Ibn al-Furāt, an amalgam of disparate materials (the 'several authors' he mentions twice in this section by way of attribution), largely discuss the same details as other works covering this period with the exception of Ibn Abī Ṭayy; there are few distinguishing marks to allow a positive identification.[34] There is some shared material with Ibn Khallikān but this in itself provides few leads since the *Wafayāt* uses a broad array of earlier sources and was widely copied by historians after his time. For this portion of Fatimid history, Ibn al-Furāt represents an important stage of archiving in his collection, hierarchization, ordering and transmission of sources, unlike his peers Ibn Khaldūn and Ibn Duqmāq, who could offer little that was either new or even comprehensive. In line with his penchant for seeking out and conserving unusual sources to offer alternative angles on events, Ibn al-Furāt brings passages with extra detail to add to the narrative that are later taken up by al-Maqrīzī, Ibn Taghrībirdī and others[35] (though the slim possibility remains that they could have taken their own extracts from earlier or original accounts; there is no way to eliminate all doubt because of the lack of attribution).

Within these reports, unique elements provided by Ibn al-Furāt include a '*qiṣṣa ʿajība*' (strange tale, which can be taken to indicate a topos or tropological feature), taken from 'some histories', in which Ṭalāʾiʿ as a Twelver Shiʿi makes a youthful pilgrimage to Najaf to visit the shrine of the caliph ʿAlī (r. 656–61), and where the imam Ibn Maʿṣūm dreams that Ṭalāʾiʿ will be appointed over Egypt by ʿAlī himself.[36] The story, followed by an account of Ṭalāʾiʿ's learning and a description of his written contributions to Imami theology, is not to be found in the other political histories of the period, and presumably comes from Ibn Abī Ṭayy, known for his contributions to various branches of Shiʿi literature and learning, including hagiography.[37] The story is picked up by al-Maqrīzī not in the *Ittiʿāẓ* but in the *Khiṭaṭ*, under his entry on Ṭalāʾiʿ's mosque, in wording similar to that of Ibn al-Furāt (or his source), though al-Maqrīzī contracts the account.[38] The inclusion of this anecdote is typical of Ibn al-Furāt, who is less tied to a sectarian view of Fatimid caliphs and viziers than he is to keeping his archivalia diverse and comprehensive. Though the tale is as far-fetched as such rhetorical elements in the 'Cairo narrative style' tend to be,[39] it provides a contextual justification for one of the endowments that Ṭalāʾiʿ later makes as vizier, namely a handsome *waqf* settled upon Ibn Maʿṣūm, the Najaf imam. This practical detail justifies its incorporation by Ibn al-Furāt into his archive of reports.

For a second unique angle provided by Ibn al-Furāt, he is again indebted to Ibn Abī Ṭayy, though this time the report is attributed. The account describes the experience of an Aleppo-born *faqīh* (jurisconsult), Khalīl b. Khumārtakīn, sent out with a group of his compatriots to Egypt by Nūr al-Dīn Zengī, where they are warmly received by Ṭalāʾiʿ; the *faqīh* eventually settles in Egypt thanks to Ṭalāʾiʿ's generosity. The element of eulogy is not absent in this short report, but the *faqīh*'s direct quotation is significant eyewitness testimony. The wider context here is still the enumeration of Ṭalāʾiʿ's merits as vizier, yet Ibn al-Furāt procures, itemizes and coordinates a breadth of sources to present his case, including material from the poets ʿUmāra and ʿArqala (who were of course employed to write panegyrics) and unidentified sources that recount his contributions to poetry, his pious endowments, his commitment to seeing off the incursions of the Franks and his architectural commissions.[40] In the process of hierarchization, the question of what to include, of the different genres and authors available, is an intricate one for Ibn al-Furāt, who comments reflexively that while he has included selections from Ṭalā'i''s own verses, he has decided against reusing the court poet 'Umāra's eulogy on the Ruzzīk family tombstone at length in his archive because of 'the multiple presence of 'Umāra's poetic *ouevre* in the public domain' [*lam adhkurhā li kathrati wujūdi dīwāni 'Umāra bi aydi 'l-nās*], giving us a vital clue as to his strategy in this instance: the key archival concerns of prioritizing valuable material for posterity and managing epistemic space.[41]

Following this treatment, Ibn al-Furāt counterbalances the panegyrics with alternative angles: the firm hand with which Ṭalā'i' ruled, the mistakes of policy that contributed to his downfall and the suffering of emirs at Ṭalā'i''s hands. Indeed, the coverage of these aspects of Ṭalā'i''s rule is as systematic as the documentation of sources setting out his praiseworthy qualities. It is tempting to speculate that these anti-Ṭalā'i' narratives were put into circulation by members of the caliphal family whose power had been considerably curtailed by him, though the sources of our sources, Ibn Khallikān in particular, have not been identified. One might conclude that where Ibn al-Furāt could no longer rely on the narrative of Ibn Ṭuwayr, which cuts off at this point in all the later works that use it, his recourse to Ibn Abī Ṭayy is all the more salient, and this choice, along with the eyewitness informants it draws on, adds a valuable dimension to the documentation of historiography. It also confirms the supposition that *Ta'rīkh al-duwal* evinces a dynamic rather than static outlook, incorporating a play of divergent texts and perspectives, and varies in method as Ibn al-Furāt's sources change in strength or availability. The overall strategy, as he outlines in his preface, is consistent, and, notwithstanding the element of *jouissance* in bringing together an opportune range of sources, follows a typical rubric of the universal Arabic chronicle. His archive of sources, however, elucidates in both historiographical (specific and literary) and epistemological (on wider issues of knowledge transmission) terms the choices made by an individual historian, as commented on by the author himself from time to time, and the breadth of the stock from which he made his selections. The reports of this sub-era of Fatimid history are interconfessional, transregional and expertly balanced between differing views of protagonists, as reflected in Ibn al-Furāt's intelligent range of archivalia.

The vizierates of Shāwar and Ḍirghām. The arrival of Shīrkūh and the Syrian army in Egypt. Ṣalāḥ al-Dīn's acquisition of Bilbays and the siege of Alexandria

[sub annis 559/1163, 560/1164, 562/1166]

For the five years he devotes to this period of Fatimid history in *Ta'rīkh al-duwal*, Ibn al-Furāt cites the following named sources:

- *Wafayāt al-aʿyān* by Ibn Khallikān
- *al-Taʾrīkh al-Manṣūrī* by Ibn Naẓīf al-Ḥamawī (d. 1240)
- al-Sharīf al-Idrīsī (via Ibn Abī Ṭayy?)
- Fakhr al-Dīn b. Shams al-Khilāfa (via Ibn Abī Ṭayy?)
- *Naẓm al-sulūk fī taʾrīkh al-khulafāʾ wa ʾl-mulūk* by Nāṣir al-Dīn Shāfiʿ b. ʿAlī (1251–1330)
- *Mufarrij al-kurūb fī akhbār Banī Ayyūb* by Ibn Wāṣil (1208-1298)
- *Akhbār al-dawla al-Miṣriyya wa mā jarā bayn al-mulūk wa ʾl-khulafāʾ min al-fitan wa ʾl-ḥurūb min ayyām al-Āmir ilā ayyām Shīrkūh* (author unknown)

Between them, these seven sources provide Ibn al-Furāt with twenty separate extracts. Another fifteen or so reports are unattributed and are either a fusion of different sources or, more likely, come from Ibn Abī Ṭayy as they contain the testimony of the Alexandrian al-Idrīsī, who is named elsewhere in this third volume of *Taʾrīkh al-duwal* and is only known via Ibn Abī Ṭayy in later Arabic tradition. Ibn al-Furāt and Abū Shāma provide the best archive for Ibn Abī Ṭayy's *Maʿādin al-dhahab*. Given that Ibn al-Furāt usually indicates when he is about to conflate accounts with the words 'several historians said …', the unidentified extracts are less likely to be a synthesis of other sources. Another eyewitness account by an emir named Fakhr al-Dīn b. Shams al-Khilāfa, whose father participated in the events narrated by Ibn al-Furāt, was very likely also transmitted via Ibn Abī Ṭayy, who – as evidenced in previously mentioned quotations from fellow Aleppan and eyewitness informant Khalīl b. Khumārtakīn – collected and incorporated first-hand descriptions.

Overall, the historiography of the final years of Fatimid rule in Egypt is characterized by several distinct if related phenomena that are omnipresent in chronicles and biographical works from the Ayyubid and Mamluk eras but are particularly well-crystallized in Ibn al-Furāt's source-specifying history. The first of these is the involvement of Ṣalāḥ al-Dīn in Shāwar's campaign to reinstate himself as vizier of Egypt for a second time in 559/1163, which ensures that a much greater variety of sources can be adduced by authors like Ibn al-Furāt to document the history and historiography of the closing years of Fatimid rule.[42] This sub-era is no longer promulgated in historiography by the Egyptian sources used for preceding years, for example Ibn Ṭuwayr (1130–1220) or Ibn Muyassar (1231–78). Rather, they come, in the main, from the pens of ʿImād al-Dīn (1125–1201), Ibn ʿAsākir (1106–75), Abū Shāma (1203–68), Ibn Wāṣil (1208–98) and other early and late Ayyubid-era non-Egyptian works, some of which inform Ibn al-Furāt's chronicle directly or indirectly. The exceptions to this general observation are the treatise known as *Akhbār al-dawla al-Miṣriyya*, which clearly presents an Egyptian account of history, the testimony of the Alexandrian emir al-Idrīsī transmitted by the Aleppan Ibn Abī Ṭayy and the reports provided by the Cairo-based early Mamluk historian Shāfiʿ b. ʿAlī.[43]

A second feature arising from the first is that the events of a very few years (558–62/1162–6 in the case of the last portion of *Taʾrīkh al-duwal*'s third volume) are covered in great detail. For the Shāwar-Ḍirghām era, five years are covered in circa fifty pages, while the previous forty years after the death of al-Afḍal were documented in only thirty.

Finally, there is, with a few exceptions, greater agreement between the wide reservoir of sources available for this period on how events unfolded, attributable in part to the fact that several men who accompanied Ṣalāḥ al-Dīn on one or more of his military campaigns either wrote about their experiences or passed on first-hand information to those who did, as Ibn Wāṣil's *Mufarrij* and accounts by al-Idrīsī, discussed presently, demonstrate. Whether or not these sources constitute a consistent interpretation of the general career of Ṣalāḥ al-Dīn, they certainly recount a similar trajectory of his rise to prominence, from accompanying his uncle Shīrkūh on the latter's first expedition to Egypt, to proving himself a capable individual on whom Shīrkūh and then the Fatimid caliph al-ʿĀḍid came to rely for the perpetuation of their respective roles.

A further corollary of Ibn al-Furat's greater reliance on quasi-courtly historiography for the final era of Fatimid rule, that is to say the narratives of men formally commissioned or informally expected to write the histories of the powerful men they served, is that it gives the archive a hegemonic leaning.[44] This is not a new phenomenon, as earlier historians, such Ibn al-Ṣayrafī and Ibn al-Athīr, also wrote, in varying degrees, under the influence of ruling families. Indeed, Middle Period historiography as a whole, as discussed earlier, is in one aspect an elitist discourse, written by and for members of the literate strata of society, for whom the 'ability to take part in the literary communication of the educated class was an important signal of distinction and proof that one belonged to the elite'.[45] On the other side of this proposition, however, are indications that 'literary communication' as a broad category reached into many levels of medieval Islamic urban society, for example, Hirschler's depiction of expanding participation in reading activities via widespread investment in elementary education and in local libraries, Shoshan's examination of popular text-dissemination in accessible spheres and the limited space for non-elite agency discernible in biographical dictionaries, as discussed by Petry.[46] In this latter form of historiography, while 'notable' individuals inhabit its pages, the qualities involved in being 'noteworthy' are multi-layered and, crucially, often precarious or dynamic. Social mobility, after all, gave the biographical dictionaries added dramatic impetus, as they delineated the trajectories of individuals as much as their status in society. Overall, a broader ethnographic study of the intersectional nature of historiography's roles in medieval Islamic communities awaits scholarly attention. As Hirschler's 2012 study of reading practices reveals, such a project could well be supported by a variety of extant source types, which might yield a range of context-specific insights. The fraught issues of putative elitism and the hegemonic aspects of the chronicle are touched upon further in the next and final chapter. For Ibn al-Furāt's chronicle, however, one key implication of the shift in his source material towards some of Ṣalāḥ al-Dīn's chroniclers is that while Ibn al-Furāt looks out widely in his historiographic frame of reference, the chronicle as an archive is inherently subjective, and limited in this instance by Ibn al-Furāt's personal epistemic and textual contingencies.

Overall, Ibn al-Furāt exploits four new sources for this era, in addition to Ibn Wāṣil, that are not cited for earlier periods of Fatimid history. The only familiar informant is Ibn Khallikān, whose three named quotations in this section are paraphrased by Ibn al-Furāt rather than cited verbatim as per his habit in earlier parts of *Ta'rīkh al-duwal*. In other words, Ibn al-Furāt archives a fresh body of sources for this period. Of these, three are broadly Egyptian in origin (al-Idrīsī's reports, the anonymous *Akhbār al-dawla al-Miṣriyya* and Shāfiʿ b. ʿAlī)[47] and are unique in the historiographical record, while two (Ibn Naẓīf al-Ḥamawī and Shāfiʿ b. ʿAlī) are quoted very rarely. Indeed, the second of these, *Naẓm al-sulūk fī taʾrīkh al-khulafāʾ wa 'l-mulūk*, may also be one of a kind as it is not extant and appears to be unattested in other later works.[48] Shāfiʿ b. ʿAlī was known to transmit material collected by his uncle Ibn ʿAbd al-Ẓāhir, including rare excerpts from the Fatimid official al-Quḍāʿī. Although the provenance of reports from Shāfiʿ b. ʿAlī cited by Ibn al-Furāt for the years 1163–7 of Shāwar's vizierate in Egypt is unknown, it would be reasonable to surmise that he is informed by the native Egyptian tradition in which his uncle wrote.

From the foregoing pattern of selection, itemization and arrangement, several questions arise: what do these rare or unique sources add to the historiographical record of late Fatimid rule, and how do Ibn al-Furāt's archival strategies of compilation alter or augment the record as he received it, and influence later digests?

The main outline of these years in terms of background knowledge is provided to Ibn al-Furāt by Ibn al-Athīr, Ibn Khallikān, Ibn Wāṣil and al-Nuwayrī among others.[49] Though these accounts vary in length – al-Nuwayrī's is the most detailed and Ibn al-Athīr's the most succinct – with little identification of source from any of these authors, the contours of the story remain stable. Two authors, the contemporaries Ibn Khallikān and Ibn Wāṣil, feature explicitly in Ibn al-Furāt's compilation for this period: they set the scene by introducing and outlining the main theme, namely Shāwar's use of the Syrian army to regain the vizierate of Egypt, an event recorded in documentary format by al-Qalqashandī.[50] For events of the preceding two years surrounding the ousting of Ruzzīk from the vizierate, the narrative does not name informant(s), though Ibn al-Furāt appears to compile one main narrative thread to which he adds extra clarification, alternative dates and other detail from complementary (also often unnamed) sources, signalled by '*wa qīla*' ['and it is said'] before returning to the principal account.[51] The detail and immediacy of the narrative imply an eyewitness source at the heart of the flow of information, and on 166a, we get an explicit clue that the author might be Ibn Abī Ṭayy: a first person aside by a notable called Fakhr al-Dīn b. Shams al-Khilāfa, who provides a description of the piety of a protagonist named Sayf al-Dīn Ḥusayn b. Abi 'l-Hayjāʾ, the brother-in-law of the vizier Ruzzīk and his most conciliatory adviser, in which his love for the Prophetic descendants in Madina is set out. This appears to be vintage Ibn Abī Ṭayy: a first-hand anecdote on the Shiʿi-favoured theme of love of *ahl al-bayt* or the Prophetic family. Another informant called 'al-Ṭuwayr' also appears on 167a, with details about Ruzzīk's taxation policy; this, too, comes across as one component of the patchwork of personal informants whose testimonies are woven into Ibn Abī Ṭayy's narrative. Ibn Abī Ṭayy, it is worth repeating, has pride of place in Ibn al-Furāt's account of the Fatimids, alongside Ibn Ṭuwayr.

The subsequent report, however, is clearly identified by its title: *Akhbār al-dawla al-Miṣriyya wa mā jarā bayn al-mulūk wa 'l-khulafāʾ min al-fitan wa 'l-ḥurūb min ayyām al-Āmir ilā ayyām Shīrkūh* [*Account of the Egyptian dynasty, and the tribulations and wars that afflicted monarchs and caliphs, from the era of al-Āmir to the era of Shīrkūh*]. This unique account of the years 1101–74 is extant only via its conservation by Ibn al-Furāt, who received it without its author's name and presents a sizeable (ten-page) extract.[52] The narrative recounts a series of incidents culminating in Ḍirghām's removal from the vizierate, political isolation and finally murder, and is saturated with often poignant detail that could only have come from first-hand witness. Of other historians of the Fatimids, only Ibn Muyassar and al-Maqrīzī (in the *Khiṭaṭ*)[53] – who can be as diligent in their archiving of Fatimid-era sources as Ibn al-Furāt – are aware of its contents. However, al-Maqrīzī, who certainly exploited it only via Ibn al-Furāt's chronicle, as his citation is circumscribed by the very boundaries of Ibn al-Furāt's extract, summarizes only parts of it.

That treatise is followed by reports from both common sources (Ibn Khallikān) and uncommon ones (Shāfiʿ b. ʿAlī, Ibn Naẓīf al-Ḥamawī and al-Idrīsī). The criteria for selection in this compilation seem designed to keep the reader reassured: familiar and unusual sources are alternated so as to sustain an equilibrium between known history and the unfamiliar explication provided by rare or original extracts. That Ibn al-Furāt deliberately orchestrates his sources in this way, following the archival model of selection-itemization-hierarchization-ordering, is evident: the change of 'voice' is frequent, and Ibn Khallikān is inserted between many newer sources with noticeable regularity, though the information he provides is usually set out already by other sources, or merely sets the scene for greater elaboration on their part.

This greater elaboration encompasses several facets of historiography. The anonymous fragment alluded to above, from the Fatimid work entitled *Akhbār al-dawla al-Miṣriyya*, fills the outline provided by other sources with a minutely-observed narration and local colour, as it charts the progress of Shāwar's loyalists as well as his enemies. For instance, the account provides a myriad of detail on the stages of Ḍirghām's elimination from the vizierate, including the names of historical actors and some direct speech not quoted by other sources recounting these years, notably the fuller narratives of Ibn Taghrībirdī's *Nujum, sub anno* 556 and the third volume of al-Maqrīzī's *Ittiʿāẓ*. The five short excerpts taken from Shāfiʿ b. ʿAlī's lost history, however, offer interjections to merely confirm or underline aspects of the picture drawn by other sources, while Ibn Naẓīf al-Ḥamawī is retrieved twice to briefly offer a Syrian angle on Shīrkūh's standing and career, since his reports clearly evince a Syrian point of view. In the same vein, the *pièces de résistance* of Ibn al-Furāt's final cluster of reports on Fatimid history in the third volume of *Taʾrīkh al-duwal* are seven eyewitness reports from al-Idrīsī, an Aleppo-born emir who accompanied Shīrkūh on his expeditions to Egypt. Al-Idrīsī was present in both Damascus and Alexandria when Shāwar and Shīrkūh made their negotiations there, which he, as the Alexandrian envoy to Shīrkūh, was party to: he witnessed the truce between Franks, Egyptians and Syrians (under Ṣalāḥ al-Dīn) with which Ibn al-Furāt's third volume ends. Such first-hand reports came to be less novel in later Ayyubid works devoted to Ṣalāḥ al-Dīn's career (see, for instance, Ibn Wāṣil's preservation of testimonies from men whose grandfathers had served with Ṣalāḥ al-Dīn). Al-Idrīsī, however, was one of the first, and certainly unique in describing the turmoil in Alexandria during the last years of Fatimid rule in Egypt from the perspective of a diplomat and outside observer.[54]

Ibn al-Furāt is not the only author to have procured and adduced accounts by al-Idrīsī: Ibn Abī Ṭayy cites him, and Ibn al-Furāt's access is possibly through Ibn Abī

Ṭayy (as Abu Shāma's is in the *Rawḍatayn*).[55] Certainly, the unattributed reports in this last Fatimid-related section of *Ta'rīkh al-duwal* provide information paraphrased by al-Maqrīzī and Ibn Taghrībirdī (both of whom knew *Ta'rīkh al-duwal* independently, as their distinct citations and paraphrase of it show), just as al-Maqrīzī summarizes the information in the anonymous Fatimid fragment referred to earlier in his *Khiṭaṭ*. To summarize, Ibn al-Furāt's reuse and extending the life cycles of obscure but revealing sources for Fatimid history exemplifies the archival ingenuity of the Mamluk record of late Fatimid history. He brings to the genre of the chronicle a narrative inventory of invaluable compositional and structural clarity, which in turn allows al-Maqrīzī and Ibn Taghrībirdī after him to write critical and widely dispersed later digests of Fatimid history, with all the wealth of information and range of perspective that they provide. Ibn al-Furāt's review and analysis of the closing sub-eras of Fatimid history offer a substantive laboratory of observation for the chronicle's function as an archive of knowledge and knowledge-making practice.

The present-day reader may wonder what was at stake for a Sunni chronicler who took pains to record the history of the Fatimids with the erudition, and in the multivalent modes, elaborated in this chapter, in writing about a dynasty of a different confessional character than his own, and whose history preceded his own era by some two centuries. However, just as Fatimid libraries in Cairo or late Ayyubid/early Mamluk libraries in Damascus had contained books expressing a range of confessional as well as 'disciplinary' orientations,[56] so too was the chronicle often an archive of heterogeneous and contradictory 'information', interpretation and type of textual contribution. How was this plurality so deeply inscribed in textual culture? The answer to this conundrum is not recondite but disarmingly transparent. Historical knowledge, in an 'omnivorous' medieval Islamic intellectual sphere, in which the love of written materials verged on 'pathological',[57] was highly desired in itself. It was worth investing in, exploring, disagreeing over, committing to paper and sharing, because this was the developed, normative practice of the Mamluk bibliosphere. Archivality was but its key *modus operandi*.

Notes

1 I am indebted to Leila Imad's *The Fatimid Vizierate* (Berlin, 1990), 168–70 for several of the vizieral dates presented here.
2 Ibn Ẓāfir, *Akhbār al-duwal*, 87.
3 Stern, 'Succession', 17; Idrīs, *'Uyūn*, 253.
4 Daftary, *The Isma'ilis*, 246.
5 *Itti'āẓ*, 3:128.
6 II:17b, ll. 12–13.
7 *Bustān*, ed. Cahen, 121.
8 Stern, 'Succession', 196–202. Idrīs, *loc. cit.*
9 Daftary, 'Sayyida Hurra: The Isma'ili Sulayhid Queen of Yemen', in G. R. G. Hambly (ed.), *Women in the Medieval Islamic World: Power, Patronage and Piety*, reprinted in *The New Middle Ages* 6 (New York, 1998), 117–30.
10 Pfeiffer and Kropp, *Theoretical Approaches*, 9–11.

11 *Nuzhat*, 31.
12 McSheffrey, 'Detective Fiction', 67.
13 *Kharīdat*, 2:1 for the entry on al-Iskandarānī.
14 Entitled *Kitāb al-dhakhā'ir wa 'l-tuḥaf* (1959).
15 M. C. Lyons and D. E. P. Jackson, *Saladin: Politics of the Holy War* (Cambridge, 1982), 24–5, 33–5.
16 Both *Itti'āẓ* and *Khiṭaṭ* lack evidence that al-Maqrīzī used Usāma's autobiography; al-Maqrīzī names his authorities much less consistently in the *Itti'āẓ* than in the *Khiṭaṭ*.
17 On the use of Usāma's memoirs by later authors writing Fatimid history, Abū Shāma's direct quotation from them in his *Rawḍatayn* (1:245) stands out, but few others used the work in this way.
18 For 'Imād's movements and appointments, see D. S. Richards, 'Imād al-Dīn al-Iṣfahānī: Administrator, Littérateur and Historian', in M. Shatzmiller (ed.), *Crusaders and Muslims in Twelfth-Century Syria* (Leiden, 1993), 133–46, esp. 138, 146. If 'Imād turns out not to be author of the *Bustān*, that the text presents a Syrian angle on history is not in doubt (cf. Tadmuri and Cahen editions).
19 Usāma, *Diwān*, 40–1, 146–8; *Ta'rīkh al-duwal*, III:24b–25b.
20 *Al-Jawhar al-thamīn*, I:263–4.
21 *Ta'rīkh al-duwal*, III:24b, 25b, 26a.
22 *Ta'rīkh al-duwal*, III:78a.
23 Sanders, 'Claiming the Past', 82.
24 Ibn al-Qalānisī (c. 1070–1160), an important counter-source to the main ensemble of views on al-Ẓāfir's death examined in the previous section, wrote until 1159, the year before his death, and does not appear to cover the Ṭalā'i' era.
25 *Memoirs*, 48.
26 *Nuzhat*, 72.
27 To borrow the English poet William Wordsworth's phraseology: Preface to *Lyrical Ballads*, 266.
28 Ibn Ẓāfir, *Akhbār al-duwal*, 111.
29 'Imād al-Dīn, 133; Ibn al-Furāt, III:151b–152a for the former view; Ibn Ẓāfir, 112 for the latter.
30 Ibn Ẓāfir, *Akhbār al-duwal*, 112.
31 Salaymeh, *Beginnings*, 33.
32 See for instance the similar wording used for Ṭalā'i''s murder: *Ta'rīkh al-duwal*, III:151a; Ibn Ẓāfir, *Akhbār al-duwal*, 112.
33 For Ibn al-Furāt's use of Ibn al-Jawzī for the other regions he covers, and for obituaries, see Elshayyal, 205, where he states that Ibn al-Furāt quotes from the *Muntaẓam* more than 200 times in the second volume of *Ta'rīkh al-duwal* alone, making him the most-cited source for that volume.
34 *Ta'rīkh al-duwal*, III:148b, 152a.
35 Cf. *Ta'rīkh al-duwal*, III:82a and *Itti'āẓ*, III:216, for example, or *Ta'rīkh al-duwal*, III:149b–150a and *al-Nujūm al-ẓāhira* V: 314.
36 *Ta'rīkh al-duwal*, III:148b–149a.
37 Lev, *Saladin in Egypt*, 41.
38 *Khiṭaṭ*, IV:85.
39 Cf. Guo, *Early Mamluk Syrian Historiography*, 95–6.
40 *Ta'rīkh al-duwal*, 150b–151b. Ṭalā'i''s (d. 1162) contributions to Shi'i poetry are well-attested by *inter alia* Ibn Khallikān (d. 1283), al-Nuwayrī (d. 1333), Ibn al-Dawādārī

(d. after 1337) and Ibn al-Furāt (d. 1406); several copies were evidently made and circulated; see his *Dīwān*, ed. A. A. Badawī (Cairo, 1958).

41 *Ta'rīkh al-duwal*, III:153a.

42 NB: the third volume of *Ta'rīkh al-duwal* takes us to 562/1166; the death of al-ʿĀḍid in 1171 and Ṣalāḥ al-Dīn's assumption of absolute sovereignty as sultan in 1174 are covered in the fourth volume.

43 Little, 'Historiography of the Ayyubid and Mamluk epochs', 422.

44 See, for this historiography, Richards, 'A Consideration', 46–65.

45 Bauer, 'Mamluk Literature', 14.

46 K. Hirschler, *The Written Word in the Medieval Arabic Lands: A Social and Cultural History of Reading Practices* (Edinburgh, 2011), chapters three and five; Petry, 'Scholastic Stasis'.

47 Abū Shāma does use a few similar extracts from al-Idrīsī in the *Rawḍatayn*, vols 1–2; despite echoes of the latter in Ibn al-Furāt's account of the years 560–2/1164–6, clearly, Ibn al-Furāt has independent access to Ibn Abī Ṭayy's work: his extracts are largely different from those in the *Rawḍatayn*; when similar (in two or three instances), they are longer than Abū Shāma's. The pattern is that Ibn al-Furāt follows Abū Shāma not for the narrative itself but in his choice of sources (cf. Ashtor, 'Some Unpublished Sources', 18, 22).

48 For more on Nāṣir al-Dīn Shāfiʿ b. ʿAlī, see Cahen, 'Quelques chroniques', 25.

49 There are no direct quotations from al-Nuwayrī's *Nihāyat al-arab* in the first three volumes of *Ta'rīkh al-duwal*, but Ashtor, *loc. cit.*, has noted that Ibn al-Furāt used it 'mainly in the choice of sources', and that Ibn al-Furāt generally transmits his sources more faithfully than other authors who use the same material.

50 Cf. Richards: Shāwar, *EI*^{2}.

51 *Ta'rīkh al-duwal*, III:163b–170b.

52 Cahen, 'Un récit inédit de vizirat de Dirgham', edited the extract but his transcript has many reading and orthographical errors probably due to his having had access only to an unclear copy on paper or microfilm; a new diplomatic edition is offered in Appendix B (*Ta'rīkh al-duwal*, III:185a–190a).

53 Cahen, 'Un récit', 27–8. See *Ittiʿāẓ*, 3:267 for more echoes of the treatise.

54 The *Mufarrij* has many such accounts that are also picked up by Mamluk compilers such as Ibn Taghrībirdī (*al-Nujūm*, 5:324).

55 Cf. D. S. Richards, 'The Early History of Saladin', *IQ* 17 (1973), 140–59, 150.

56 Bora, 'Salah al-Din'; Hirschler, *Medieval Damascus*.

57 Muhanna, *World in a Book*, 8, 14; Ghersetti, 'The Book in Fact and Fiction', 1.

7

Concluding Remarks: The Value of Chronicles as Archives

To return to the unicum chronicle of Ibn al-Furāt, with its patchy survival in two autograph series and no further complete copies: the book improbably – though fortuitously – withstood more than six centuries of historical disruptions better than the sultan-endowed al-Muʿizziyya madrasa where its author worked. The image evoked by this circumstance, of textual endurance juxtaposed with institutional-cum-edificial loss, is specific and not generalizable to many authors and institutions. Yet it is eloquent in articulating a fundamental facet of the medieval Islamic episteme: the will-to-survival of intellectual assets in a system where books including chronicles were to be invested with sufficient pedagogic or recreational value as to survive wholly as discrete copies, or partially as components within the chain of text witnesses contributing to newer archival texts, as manifested in the configuration of *Taʾrīkh al-duwal wa ʾl-mulūk* and the plethora of works like it itemized by Little.[1] A potential misconception engendered by survival bias – in urban settings where many great institutions of the Mamluk empire still stand architecturally if not functionally – is that institutions of both material and socio-cultural solidity did not easily yield to physical effacement. This al-Maqrīzī's *Khiṭaṭ* reveals to be far from the truth: like his topographic predecessors al-Quḍāʿī and Ibn ʿAbd al-Ẓāhir, he indexes buildings no longer standing in his lifetime.[2] At the same time, chronicles in their function as archives ensure the longevity and productive afterlives of historical narratives that transcend the lifespans of dynasties and eras, as well as political change in a longer view. That Mamluk texts inscribed on low quality paper outlived Mamluk buildings constructed in expensive materials should not surprise the modern observer, for it is an outcome of medieval Islamic archivality.

This archivality, which encompassed both 'different types of archival sensibilities and different cultures of documentation', to borrow from a recent study of early modern Islamicate archives, seems to favour the preservation of books (i.e. codices) over statutory document collections, and helps to answer the puzzle, long pondered by Islamicists, of why the documents meticulously transcribed into chronicles, legal texts and administrative manuals are largely not independently extant. The expectation that non-European administrative archives should follow the patterns of social meaning and survival of European archives is erroneous, as several recent works point out.[3] Concomitantly, medieval Islamicate archivalities attached different kinds and degrees of importance to different genres of texts: administrative documents – one category of which has been described by Rustow as ephemeral, performative and ultimately transient in socio-political function except inasmuch as reuse of its paper extended its life cycle – can be contrasted with the much greater attention given to the copying, re-copying and preservation of books. To coin a typology drawing from both Rustow and Bauden, the medieval Islamic chronicle, Ibn al-Furāt's in particular, aids our understanding of a particular balance between 'ephemerality' and 'eternality' in the textual culture of the Mamluk era,[4] and offers a heuristic key to why books like his, and those of Ibn al-Ṣayrafi before him or al-Qalqashandi after him, preserve administrative documents subsequently lost to later historians as particular specimens of a much wider corpus.

Thus the archival dimension of Ibn al-Furāt's universal history offers valuable insights into the multi-layered ontology of the chronicle as a narrative, documentary and archival text, and demands that we ask again: what were chronicles for? Among other functions, they built capacity for, and iterated, socio-political memory as a key facet of identity, in this case the memory of the Mamluks' political forbears, the Fatimids. This memorialization was in a bookish world of epistemic abundance and yet evanescence, where texts were chosen, excised and recontextualized to fit the rubrics of new works. The ingress and egress of archivalia were ingrained in this process, as the historiographic archive was simultaneously fixed and fluid in key senses. Discrete works captured the epistemic moment of the author's current project, while in the larger flow of collective memory-capture, the formulation of new books of history remained a necessity as fresh lines of enquiry, in response to particular social or cultural exigencies, and/or the opportunity or motivation of the author, were pursued within historiography. Ibn al-Furāt's archivally rich account of the Fatimids, which draws on the broad range of previously under-appreciated original and intermediary narrative and documentary sources for the Fatimids itemized in Chapter 3, shows that the history and historiography of the Isma'ili polity remained relevant, and a key theme of scholarly attention in the work of Mamluk savants.

This scholarly attention was not always laudatory, as discussed in the preceding two chapters. Yet Ibn al-Furāt in *Ta'rīkh al-duwal* and al-Maqrīzī in the *Khiṭaṭ* (which is less prone to conflating sources without attribution than his *Itti'āẓ*) write Fatimid history in ways that clearly privilege epistemic and archival concerns over confessional ones, and, in recapturing developments of the Fatimid era, bypass the identity politics and sectarian tensions assumed of Mamluk authors. Such assumptions are not altogether surprising in view of the voluble denunciations of the Isma'ili creed offered by al-Ghazālī (d. 1111), the ambivalences of al-Suyūṭī and Ibn Taghrībirḍi alluded to in Chapters 1 and 6, and the strident terms of Ibn Ḥajar's disapproval of Ibn Khaldūn's and al-Maqrīzī's failure to critique Isma'ili genealogical claims.[5] Regardless, in the late fourteenth century and well into the fifteenth, major Arabophone historians could and did represent the Fatimids non-confessionally, as one highly productive dynasty in a line of several to rule over Egypt and based in 'Cairo the Protected', as the city was so often styled. In Ibn al-Furāt's case, this feature is manifested in his frequent and appreciative use of the historian Ibn Abī Ṭayy, his rounded view of the vizier Ṭalā'i' b. Ruzzīk (both Twelver Shi'ites) and his attribution of both caliphate and imamate to the Fatimids, his own background as Sunni hadith scholar notwithstanding. This can be fruitfully compared with his contemporary Ibn Khaldūn's characterization of the

Fatimids as a legitimately 'Alid dynasty comparable to their arch-rivals, the 'Abbasids.[6] Further, this meta-confessional aspect can be usefully viewed alongside recent studies of medieval Islamic libraries, which reveal – separately but synchronously – that inter-sectarian strife and asset-stripping are often medieval and/or modern assumptions if not tropes in relation to the medieval Islamicate, and fall apart on closer examination.[7]

The preservation of Fatimid works was of key epistemic importance given their limited investment in historiography as discussed in Chapter 3, including to post-Fatimid chroniclers, a point noted by al-Maqrīzī in the *Itti'āẓ*.[8] As the dynasty that built the madrasa-rich city of Cairo in which Ibn al-Furāt, al-Maqrīzī and others like them lived, followed their vocations and composed their works, the Fatimids' achievements and weaknesses in the face of a variety of existential threats are presented with an ultimately unsurprising degree of sympathy in major historiographical treatments, or at the very least with as much neutrality of tone as is mustered for Sunni polities and elites.

The *Ta'rīkh al-duwal* is certainly more focused on preserving a range of perspectives on history than on yoking its archivalia to a tendentious reading of historical events. Ibn al-Furāt clearly wishes to make sense not simply of 'what happened' but, as an interpretive substrate, to understand the moral and social conduct of the protagonists of history. His concern, expressed in his preface to the first volume of AA, is to understand how appointees to social, political or religious roles succeeded or failed; these were issues of heightened relevance in Mamluk political administration as much as they had been in the Fatimid era, as demonstrated in detail through Massoud's study of pivotal moments in Mamluk political history.[9] Thus Ibn al-Furāt's engagement with the past via the archiving and reproduction of its historiographical sources is also a grappling with the complex human struggles of the present, no matter whether his ostensible narrative-documentary theme is 'Fatimid' or 'Mamluk' history.

In this quest to explicate the present via the past, the preservation of both narrative and documentary assets is a key exigency that lay behind the structural and sequential arrangement of *Ta'rīkh al-duwal*, as demonstrated in detail in Chapters 5 and 6. In the process of archive building within historiography – against the spectre of documentary and narrative loss, which should be regarded as both a medieval and a modern anxiety given the 'conspicuous consumption' of paper and texts in the medieval Islamicate – conservation is paramount.[10] While Ibn al-Furāt's account of the late Fatimids demonstrates what might be anachronistically termed a pre-modern and pre-digital hypertextuality of intense referencing and occasional cross-referencing, his aim is also one of epistemic recovery: securing the survival of books via use of their extracts, and underlining their authority and value, as instantiated by his use of full honorific titles for authors as expressive of their social scholarly prestige. Al-Sakhāwī in the Burji Mamluk period and Little in the modern era certainly refer to works that are no longer extant, and yet others that exist solely or mainly as citations in later works, such as al-Yūsufī's (d. 1358).[11] The desire to preserve is less a corollary of concern about wholesale book destruction as a result of military conflict and violent dynastic change, a notion debunked in a recent study,[12] than a creative act of hermeneutical agency. That said, the natural vicissitudes of urban socio-cultural life – in which, despite the preponderance of libraries and teaching institutions, a vast, seemingly panoptic archive of texts could succumb to upheavals including famine and subsequent book-looting, the dissolution of libraries and teaching institutions, the dispersal of personal book collections and so on – might indeed lead to focused efforts to secure the longevity of historical works. Even where long-elapsed history was concerned, such as that of the Fatimids, the documentary aspect of historiography, as manifested not simply in the incorporation of documents per se but evidenced in the archival mindset of the historian, resulted in historical texts that functioned less as *exampla* and more as 'social documents' in which the controversies of the day, whether of the Fatimid, Ayyubid or Mamluk eras, would be recorded with the aid of multiple written testimonies, and functioned as archives of textual inheritance *and* legacy.[13]

In this respect, the notion that the chronicle might be read as in some sense documentary in itself while also retaining characteristic literary and narrative qualities, as exemplified by the archival practices of collating, sifting, extracting and incorporating source materials, brings to the fore a problematic aspect of over-rigid generic divides for a culture suffused with multivalent, often multi-generic historiographical texts. Salaymeh has recently pointed out the crucial importance – in a medieval Islamic legal context but with pointed relevance to historiography – of not fetishizing documents or approaching them with 'false trust', and avoiding a 'false dichotomy' between narrative and documentary sources given that there are 'slippages and ambiguities in all historical sources', which can nonetheless be 'productive sites of historical enquiry'.[14]

The dichotomy between narratives and documents arises in part from the distinctions between 'pragmatic' and 'literary' textual modes,[15] and between witting and unwitting evidence: specifically, the performative and witting utterance of storytelling versus the 'unwitting', pragmatic testimony of documents. Ibn al-Furāt's chronicle obfuscates this taxonomy, including the putative lack of authority of the former and the widely assumed authority of the latter, by demonstrating that narrative and documentary sources are co-essential building blocks in his edifice of historiography, which treats both types of material as appropriate archivalia chosen for their value in the task of piecing together an intelligible and socially meaningful record of history. In pragmatic terms, the 'second life' of a document, as explained by Bauer, often boiled down to its inclusion in a longer, later book.[16] For the Mamluk record of Fatimid rule, Ibn al-Furāt's inclusion of documents and narratives emerging from the late Fatimid political milieu reveals the ultimate derivation of that historiography from a cluster of native sources less-represented in later tradition.

In this respect, it is worth reiterating that the notion of the historiographical archive is more than a metaphor. With due acknowledgement of a recent trend in the study of culture in which the '"archive" has a capital "A," is figurative, and leads elsewhere', and 'may represent neither material site nor a set of documents' but rather serves 'as a strong metaphor for any corpus of selective forgettings and collections',[17] the medieval Islamic chronicle expresses its archivality in two principal ways: as a repository of texts (the tangible spatial archive) and as a set of methods (archival practices) applied to the ordering of knowledge in the concentric epistemic circles of book (*Ta'rīkh al-duwal*), atelier (al-Mu'izziyya), city (Cairo-Fustat) and cultural setting (Mamluk Cairo) of the medieval Islamicate. Ibn al-Furāt's chronicle provides, moreover, unambiguous evidence of the double reflexivity of historiographical works that draw attention both subtly and explicitly to their own mechanics, and the epistemic values to which they respond, including the use of multiple sources, in which Ibn al-Furāt 'evinces a conscious attempt to give a comprehensive, considered view of an event by combining data from various authors';[18] a privileging of testimonies that are early and local; analytical engagement with causality, and the efficiencies of not citing material already well-attested in popular works. Taken together, the intention of archivality here could scarcely be doubted.

In the Mamluk episteme, the archival practices of the historian were less a choice than a necessity in an urban culture of book management in which the appetite for collecting and repackaging epistemic resources was insatiable.[19] Madrasas, elementary schools, mosques, private homes of men and women of the educated classes, sites of legal activity, palaces and stately homes of the upwardly mobile wealthy, hospitals, hostels and Sufi lodges: the urban, not necessarily elite, venues hosting the 'consumption' of knowledge in various forms – whether scholarly, popular or in a growing space in-between – is long and varied.[20] The embrace of archivalism as a key methodology can be regarded as a parallel, though not fully coterminous, development to those of textualization, increased manuscript production and a general expansion in the numbers of readers of scholarly and popular texts as documented in a recent study. In the latter, al-Qalqashandī is cited as an author whose compendium was designed to 'facilitate the quick retrieval of information', via a set of textual strategies that are notably archival, as discussed earlier in Chapter 2: the use of headlines, rubrication, punctilious space management and so on.[21] While typical authors of multi-volume works, al-Qalqashandī and Ibn al-Furāt among them, produced works that the contemporary reader might be conditioned by modern reading norms to regard as prolix (indeed, the full extent of Ibn al-Furāt's two autograph series is a hundred volumes), these works were nonetheless relatively efficient summaries and reformulations of a variable but usually substantial number of previous works. This circumstance signals that the archival instinct was both a practical imperative and a particularly profitable set of mechanisms for both the writers and readers of these works. But for Ibn al-Furāt's incorporation of now almost-perished works penned by Ibn al-Ṣayrafī, Ibn Ṭuwayr, Ibn Abī Ṭayy and eyewitness treatises whose authors' names were effaced from the historiographic record by his own time, the Mamluk-era reader of his chronicle might have had little or no access to them, or simply lacked opportunity to read multiple detailed accounts of late Fatimid history, especially those that subsisted in single or rare copies.

The archival prism for understanding the Mamluk chronicle also brings clarity to notions of 'transmission', 'narrative choice', 'bias' and so on, that are well understood to underpin historiographical activity but remain in some senses imprecise, and when named as 'archival practices' can be more fully contextualized as paradigmatic strategies devised for efficient and fruitful handling of copious epistemic textual capital. The materialistic metaphor here is apposite: chronicles as archives were inscribed interpretations of historical and contemporary developments, set down by hand on physical media that were bound into corporeal quires and thence codices. Ibn al-Furāt's autograph chronicle divulges the connections between an archive's material and semantic features as discussed earlier in Chapter 2, which helpfully augments his disclosures about which sources he selects, by what criteria and to what end, to seal the interrelatedness of the twin phenomena of knowledge-gathering (encyclopaedism) and knowledge-arranging (archivalism) discussed in Chapter 1 as cognate activities, each necessary for and facilitating the other. In other words, archivality is written into both the materiality and the subject matter of this chronicle. Arguably, enough as has been said to underline the bookishness of medieval Islamic cultures, and in this sense, the conventional wisdom on the transmission of historical and other forms of knowledge does not need updating. But its mechanics could indeed be better understood, which is where the archival model is especially illuminating.

One of the less-discussed aspects of medieval Islamic book culture in general and historiography in particular is the thorny issue, alluded to in Chapters 3 and 4, of the 'canon' as hegemonic, as reflecting and serving the interests of elites. Indeed, if the archive is analogous to the canon, then a critique of its power is well-placed. The conventional social archive, after all, originally functioned as 'the locus of legal authority and regulation',[22] and state and other institutional archives were often a physical manifestation of social and communal hierarchies and power relations.[23] Yet a recent collection of essays on global archivalities reveals that the identification of archives with polities largely makes sense in early modern European contexts but not in other eras and cultural spheres.[24] Another study of early modern Islamicate archivalities reveals the detrimental limitations of assuming that archives of various kinds are instruments of domination, and at the same time, minority communities often kept their own archives as a resource against political or legal developments that sought to regulate and often reduce their rights or agencies.[25] Indeed, the medieval Islamic chronicle as archive does not fit a hegemonic conceptualization, because it is constituted from range of contributory materials of variable provenance, and sits in the interstitial intellectual space that is not fully identifiable with either governments or reading publics.[26] What, however, is its character, and is Ibn al-Furāt's chronicle representative of the genre?

Ibn al-Furāt's account of late Fatimid history throws light on the agency of the historian in shoring up or resisting social or confessional hierarchies. Ibn al-Furāt's informants and resulting archivalia take a range of views on the legitimacy or probity of late Fatimid protagonists and antagonists, as discussed in depth in Chapters 5 and 6. For the history of the Mamluk era in his later volumes, Ibn al-Furāt shows no qualms in criticizing sultanic or elite behaviour, as discussed in Chapter 2. In these aspects, it is clear that his chronicle is not hegemonic, even if it cannot be called *subaltern* either, as textual agency in a largely (not wholly) post-oral intellectual culture was the sole privilege of the literate. The archival approach to building chronicles from a myriad of first-, second- or third-hand text witnesses undercuts the notion that chronicles were canonical in the manner of advice literature, theological tracts or even, to some extent, biographical dictionaries. Ibn al-Furāt's chronicle is neither a state archive or, strictly-speaking, a people's archive, but might be said to tacitly address the author's scholarly peers[27] and is thus somewhere between an elite discourse and a popular one, as reflected in its polyglossic register in the 'Cairo narrative style'. As an archive, the chronicle is certainly outward-facing rather than personal, as its features of enhancing accessibility, ease of retrieval, clarity of structure, and so on, have a wider audience of readers in mind.[28] Moreover the archival analytical prism brings historiographic practice out from 'behind the scenes' and into the foreground, and in this sense, Ibn al-Furāt's chronicle is representative of a ubiquitous methodology, but unusual in displaying that methodology so clearly and reflexively.

The ultimate value of reading chronicles as archives is that it answers a set of pressing research priorities set out by Marilyn Waldman three decades ago, where she decried a tendency to treat historical narratives virtually exclusively as 'unstructured, uninterpretive mines of factual information' of which the internal dynamics have been neglected, as has the 'interaction of the author's mind' with the material presented in historical works. She advocated instead the use of more systematic methods and categories of analysis that deeply interrogate premodern Muslim authors' aims and methodologies.[29] The archival dimension of Ibn al-Furāt's *Ta'rīkh al-duwal* is deeply fulfilling of these goals, and enables a far-reaching elucidation of the refined form, multivalent function and rich content of the medieval Islamic chronicle. If the archive, understood in its different senses, makes a society readable to itself and legible to its members, the chronicle must be placed at the centre of any conceptualization of medieval Islamic intellectual culture and its well-established archival sensibility.

Notes

1 Little, 'Historiography of the Ayyubid and Mamluk epochs'.
2 Bora, 'An Historiographical Study', 11.
3 Friedrich, 'Epilogue: Archives and Archiving', 421–5.
4 Rustow, 'Fatimid State', Friedrich, 'Epilogue: Archives and Archiving', 436, citing F. Bauden, 'Du destin des archives en Islam. Analyse des données et éléments de réponse', in D. Aigle and S. Péquignot (eds), *La correspondance entre souverains, princes et cités-États. Approches croisées entre l'Orient musulman, l'Occident latin et Byzance (XIIIe–début XVIe siecle)* (Turnhout, 2013), 27–49; 34.
5 F. Mitha, *Al-Ghazali and the Ismailis: A Debate on Reason and Authority in Medieval Islam* (London, 2001); Ibn Ḥajar, *Inbā' al-ghumr bi abnā' al-'umr*, 3 vols (Cairo, 1969–72), 5:331.
6 A. al-Azmeh, *Ibn Khaldun: A Reinterpretation* (London, 2012), 23.
7 Bora, 'Salah al-Din'; Hirschler, *Medieval Damascus*.
8 *Itti'āẓ*, 3:346.
9 Massoud, *Chronicles*.
10 Rustow, 'Fatimid State'.
11 *I'lān*, section 15a, 478–99, Little, 'Historiography of the Ayyubid and Mamluk epochs', 420–44; cf. idem, 'An Analysis of the Relationship between Four Mamluk Chronicles for 737–45', *JSS* 19:2 (1974), 252–68, 253; Van Steenbergen, *Order Out of Chaos*, 11–12.
12 Muhanna, *The World in a Book*, 16–19.
13 M. Tillier in M. van Berkel et al., eds, *Legal Documents*, 3.
14 Salaymeh, *Beginnings*, 33–4.
15 Bauer, 'Mamluk Literature', 24.
16 Ibid., 25; cf. Haji, *Inside the Immaculate Portal.*

17 A. Stoler, 'Colonial Archives and the Arts of Governance', *Archival Science* 2 (2002), 87–109, 94.
18 Little, *Introduction*, 74.
19 Rich documentation of this appetite is offered throughout Hirschler, *The Written Word* and Musawi, *The Medieval Islamic Republic of Letters*.
20 For reading practices and knowledge 'consumption' in schools, libraries and 'popular' settings between the eleventh and fifteenth centuries, see Hirschler, *The Written Word*, chapters 2–5.
21 Hirschler, *The Written Word*, 17–18.
22 Harriet Bradley, 'The Seductions of the Archive: Voices Lost and Found', *History of the Human Sciences* 12:2 (1999), 107–22, 109.
23 El-Leithy, 'Living Documents'.
24 Friedrich, 'Epilogue: Archives and Archiving', 421–5.
25 Sartori, 'Seeing Like a Khanate', 231–5; el-Leithy, *passim*.
26 Petry's 'Scholastic Stasis' still offers one of the most detailed discussions of the space between the ruling elite and the Mamluk academy. For comparison with an early modern Islamicate counterpart to this debate, see Sartori, 'Seeing Like a Khanate', 233 ff., where he discusses the successes and failures of the state in attempting to shape 'the production of knowledge affecting the public sphere and the control of historicity'.
27 Bauer, 'Mamluk Literature', 26.
28 This is in contrast with the origins of al-Nuwayrī's encyclopedia as a personal archive, a 'storehouse for the author's treasured clippings': Muhanna, *The World in a Book*, 24.
29 Waldman, *Toward a Theory*, 3–4.

Appendix A: Ibn al-Furāt's Use of Reports for Late Fatimid Egypt (1094–1166)

References to published extracts, where available, are indicated in the central column, under the author's name.

Vol./folio/line	Subject	Author cited	Work cited	Quote ends
VOL. I				
163(a), l. 23	Al-Afḍal's life and death [515/1121]	Ibn al-Ṣayrafī (Mukhlis edition, 54)	*Kitāb al-wuzarā' li 'l-dawla al-Fāṭimiyya bi 'l-Qāhira al-Mu'izziyya*	163 (b), l. 22
163 (b), l. 22	Al-Afḍal's life and death [515/1121]	[Ibn Ṭuwayr – identified by work not name] (Sayyid edition, 3–9)	*Nuzhat al-muqlatayn fī akhbār al-dawlatayn*	165 (a), l. 5
165 (a), l. 6		Ibn al-Athīr (Daqqaq edition, 9:208–9	*al-Kāmil fī 'l-ta'rīkh*	165 (b), l. 12
165 (b), l. 13	Al-Afḍal's life and death [515/1121]	Yaḥyā b. Abī Ṭayy	*Ma'ādin al-dhahab fī ta'rīkh al-mulūk wa 'l-khulafā' wa dhawi 'l-rutab* [not named]	166 (b), l.3
166 (b), l.4		Ibn Khallikān (no. 286; Abbas edition: 450–1)	*Wafayāt al-a'yān* [not named]	167 (a), l. 4
167 (a), l. 7	Al-Afḍal's life and death [515/1121]	Yaḥyā b. Abī Ṭayy	*Ma'ādin al-dhahab fī ta'rīkh al-mulūk wa 'l-khulafā' wa dhawi 'l-rutab* [not named]	167 (a), l. 11
167 (a), l. 12	Al-Afḍal's life and death [515/1121]	[Ibn Ṭuwayr – identified by work not name] (10–11)	*Nuzhat al-muqlatayn fī akhbār al-dawlatayn*	167 (a), l. 27
206 (a), l. 16	The vizierate of al-Baṭā'iḥī [fuller acc.][519/1125, 519/1125]	Ibn al-Athīr (9:234)	*al-Kāmil* [not named]	206 (b), l. 10
206 (b), l. 10	The vizierate of al-Baṭā'iḥī [fuller acc.][519/1125, 519/1125]	Yaḥyā b. Abī Ṭayy	*Ma'ādin al-dhahab fī ta'rīkh al-mulūk wa 'l-khulafā' wa dhawi 'l-rutab* [not named]	207 (a), l. 4
207 (a), l. 4	The vizierate of al-Baṭā'iḥī [fuller acc.][519/1125, 519/1125]	[Ibn Ṭuwayr – identified by work not name] (11–16)	*Nuzhat al-muqlatayn fī akhbār al-dawlatayn*	208 (b) l. 12
208 (b), l. 12	The vizierate of al-Baṭā'iḥī [fuller acc.][519/1125, 519/1125]	Ibn Khallikān (299)	*Wafayāt al-a'yān* [not named]	208 (b), l. 22

VOL. II

14 (b), l. 27	The caliphate of al-Āmir and his assassination [523/1128-9, 524/1129]	Ibn Khallikān (no. 743; 299–300)	*Wafayāt al-aʿyān* [not named]	15 (b), l. 19
15 (b), l. 19	The caliphate of al-Āmir and his assassination [523/1128-9, 524/1129]	[Ibn Ṭuwayr – identified by work not name] (19–26)	*Nuzhat al-muqlatayn fī akhbār al-dawlatayn*	17 (a), l. 9
17 (a), l. 9	The caliphate of al-Āmir and his assassination [523/1128-9, 524/1129]	Ibn Khallikān (301)	*Wafayāt al-aʿyān* [not named]	17 (a), l. 23
17 (a), l. 23	The caliphate of al-Āmir and his assassination [523/1128-9, 524/1129]	Ibn al-Athīr and Baybars (*al-Kāmil*, 9:255)	*al-Kāmil* and *Zubdat al-fikra* [not named]	17 (b), l. 2
17 (b), l. 2	The caliphate of al-Āmir and his assassination [523/1128-9, 524/1129]	Yaḥyā b. Abī Ṭayy	*Maʿādin al-dhahab fī taʾrīkh al-mulūk wa ʾl-khulafāʾ wa dhawi ʾl-rutab* [not named]	17 (b), l. 13
17 (b), l. 14	The caliphate of al-Ḥāfiẓ [524/1129]	Yaḥyā b. Abī Ṭayy		17 (b), l. 19
17 (b), l. 20	The caliphate of al-Ḥāfiẓ [524/1129]	Ibn al-Athīr (9:255)	*al-Kāmil* [not named]	18 (a), l. 15
18 (a), l. 15	The caliphate of al-Ḥāfiẓ [524/1129]	[Ibn Ṭuwayr – identified by work not name] (26–7)	*Nuzhat al-muqlatayn fī akhbār al-dawlatayn*	18 (a), l. 23
18 (a), l. 23	The caliphate of al-Ḥāfiẓ [524/1129]	Ibn al-Athīr and Baybars (*al-Kāmil*, 9:255)	*al-Kāmil* and *Zubdat al-fikra* [not named]	18 (b), l. 1
18 (b), l. 1	The caliphate of al-Ḥāfiẓ [524/1129]	Yaḥyā b. Abī Ṭayy	*Maʿādin al-dhahab fī taʾrīkh al-mulūk wa ʾl-khulafāʾ wa dhawi ʾl-rutab* [not named]	18 (b), l. 12

(*Continued*)

Vol./folio/line	Subject	Author cited	Work cited	Quote ends
18 (b), l. 13	The [brief] vizierate of Hizabr al-Mulūk [Hazārmard] and the vizierate of Aḥmad b. al-Afḍal [524/1129]	[Ibn Ṭuwayr – unidentified by work or name] (27–30)	*Nuzhat al-muqlatayn fī akhbār al-dawlatayn*	19 (b), l. 10
19 (b), l. 10	The [brief] vizierate of Hizabr al-Mulūk [Hazārmard] and the vizierate of Aḥmad b. al-Afḍal [524/1129]	Yaḥyā b. Abī Ṭayy	*Maʿādin al-dhahab fī taʾrīkh al-mulūk wa ʾl-khulafāʾ wa dhawi ʾl-rutab* [not named]	19 (b), l. 13
19 (b), l. 13	The [brief] vizierate of Hizabr al-Mulūk [Hazārmard] and the vizierate of Aḥmad b. al-Afḍal [524/1129]	[Ibn Ṭuwayr – unidentified by work or name] (30–3)	*Nuzhat al-muqlatayn fī akhbār al-dawlatayn*	20 (a), l.18
20 (a), l. 18	The vizierate of Aḥmad b. al-Afḍal [526/1131]	Ibn al-Athīr and Baybars (*al-Kāmil*, 9:255)	*al-Kāmil* and *Zubdat al-fikra* [not named]	20 (a), l. 24
20 (a), l. 24	The vizierate of Aḥmad b. al-Afḍal [526/1131]	Yaḥyā b. Abī Ṭayy	*Maʿādin al-dhahab fī taʾrīkh al-mulūk wa ʾl-khulafāʾ wa dhawi ʾl-rutab* [not named]	20 (b), l. 20
20 (b), l. 21	The vizierate of Aḥmad b. al-Afḍal [526/1131]	'several men of history'		20 (b), l. 26
41 (b), l. 10	More detailed account of Aḥmad b. al-Afḍal's vizierate [526/1131]	?	?	41 (b), l. 19
41 (b), l. 19	Poem about Aḥmad b. al-Afḍal	al-Iskandarānī [?]		41 (b), l. 39
42 (a), l.1	More on Aḥmad b. al-Afḍal [526/1131]	Ibn al-Athīr and Baybars (*al-Kāmil*, 9:261–2)	*al-Kāmil* and *Zubdat al-fikra* [not named]	42 (a), l. 17

42 (a), l. 18	More on Aḥmad b. al-Afḍal [526/1131]	Yaḥyā b. Abī Ṭayy	*Maʿādin al-dhahab fī taʾrīkh al-mulūk wa ʾl-khulafāʾ wa dhawi ʾl-rutab* [not named]	42 (a), l. 23
42 (a), l. 23	More on Aḥmad b. al-Afḍal [526/1131]	[Ibn Ṭuwayr – identified by work not name] (33)	*Nuzhat al-muqlatayn*	42 (b), l. 7
42 (b), l. 12	Consolidation of the rule of al-Ḥāfiẓ over Egypt [526/1131]	Ibn al-Athīr and Baybars (*al-Kāmil*, 9:261–2)	*al-Kāmil* and *Zubdat al-fikra* [not named]	42 (b), l. 16
42 (b), l.17	Consolidation of the rule of al-Ḥāfiẓ over Egypt [526/1131]	Yaḥyā b. Abī Ṭayy	*Maʿādin al-dhahab fī taʾrīkh al-mulūk wa ʾl-khulafāʾ wa dhawi ʾl-rutab* [not named]	42 (b), l. 20
42 (b), l. 21	The vizierate of Yānis and his death [526/1131]	[Ibn Ṭuwayr – unidentified by work or name] (35–6)	*Nuzhat al-muqlatayn fī akhbār al-dawlatayn*	43 (b), l. 2
43 (b), l. 3	The vizierate of Yānis and his death [526/1131]	Yaḥyā b. Abī Ṭayy	*Maʿādin al-dhahab fī taʾrīkh al-mulūk wa ʾl-khulafāʾ wa dhawi ʾl-rutab* [not named]	43 (b), l. 15
43 (b), l. 16	The vizierate of Ḥasan b. al-Ḥāfiẓ [526/1131]	Yaḥyā b. Abī Ṭayy		43 (b), l. 26
43 (b), l. 26	The vizierate of Ḥasan b. al-Ḥāfiẓ [526/1131]	Ibn al-Athīr and Baybars(*al-Kāmil*, 9:261–2)	*al-Kāmil* and *Zubdat al-fikra* [not named]	43 (b), l. 28
44 (a), l.1	The vizierate of Ḥasan b. al-Ḥāfiẓ [526/1131]	[Ibn Ṭuwayr – identified by work not name] (37)	*Nuzhat al-muqlatayn fī akhbār al-dawlatayn*	44 (a), l. 14
58 (a), l.17	Ḥasan b. al-Ḥāfiẓ's rebellion against his father [528/1133]	[Ibn Ṭuwayr – identified by work not name] (37)	*Nuzhat al-muqlatayn fī akhbār al-dawlatayn*	59 (a), l. 14
59 (a), l. 14	Ḥasan b. al-Ḥāfiẓ's rebellion against his father [528/1133]	Yaḥyā b. Abī Ṭayy	*Maʿādin al-dhahab fī taʾrīkh al-mulūk wa ʾl-khulafāʾ wa dhawi ʾl-rutab* [not named]	59 (a), l. 28

(Continued)

Vol./folio/line	Subject	Author cited	Work cited	Quote ends
59 (a), l. 28	Ḥasan b. al-Ḥāfiẓ's rebellion, and the vizierate of Bahrām [528/1133]	[Ibn Ṭuwayr – unidentified by work or name] (40–3)	[Ibn Ṭuwayr – identified by work not name]	60 (b), l. 17
60 (b), l. 17	Ḥasan b. al-Ḥāfiẓ's rebellion, and the vizierate of Bahrām [528/1133]	Yaḥyā b. Abī Ṭayy	*Ma'ādin al-dhahab fī ta'rīkh al-mulūk wa 'l-khulafā' wa dhawi 'l-rutab* [not named]	61 (a), l. 14
61 (a), l. 15	Bahrām and Riḍwān's struggle for the vizierate [528/1133]	[Ibn Ṭuwayr - unidentified by work or name] (44–8)	*Nuzhat al-muqlatayn fī akhbār al-dawlatayn*	62 (a), l. 27
62 (a), l. 27	Bahrām and Riḍwān's struggle for the vizierate [528/1133]	Ibn al-Athīr and Baybars (?)	*al-Kāmil* and *Zubdat al-fikra* [not named]	62 (b), l. 4
62 (b), l. 4	" [poem]	al-Rashīd b. al-Zubayr	*Kitāb al-jinān*	62 (b), l. 13
62 (b), l.14		[Ibn Ṭuwayr – unidentified by work or name] (49–50)	*Nuzhat al-muqlatayn fī akhbār al-dawlatayn*	63 (a), l.14
63 (a), l. 15	" [poem]	Attributed to Ibn al-Athīr and Baybars; quote is actually from Ibn Ṭuwayr (50)	*Nuzhat al-muqlatayn fī akhbār al-dawlatayn*, and is not in the *Kāmil*	63 (a), l. 27
VOL. III				
2o(a), l. 5	The life and death of the caliph al-Ḥāfiẓ [544/1149]	Ibn Khallikān (no. 407; 235-7)	*Wafayāt al-a'yān* [not named]	21 (a), l. 5
21 (a), l. 5	The life and death of the caliph al-Ḥāfiẓ [544/1149]	Yaḥyā b. Abī Ṭayy	*Ma'ādin al-dhahab fī ta'rīkh al-mulūk wa 'l-khulafā' wa dhawi 'l-rutab* [not named]	21 (a), l. 9
21 (a), l. 9	The life and death of the caliph al-Ḥāfiẓ [544/1149]	[Ibn Ṭuwayr – identified by work not name] (51)	*Nuzhat al-muqlatayn fī akhbār al-dawlatayn*	21 (a), l. 13

21 (a), l. 13	The rule of al-Ẓāfir [544/1149]	Yaḥyā b. Abī Ṭayy	*Maʿādin al-dhahab fī taʾrīkh al-mulūk wa ʾl-khulafāʾ wa dhawi ʾl-rutab* [not named]	21 (b), l. 6
21 (b), l. 6	The vizierate of Ibn Maṣāl [544/1149]	[Ibn Ṭuwayr – unidentified by work or name] (55–7)	*Nuzhat al-muqlatayn fī akhbār al-dawlatayn*	22 (a), l. 19
21 (b), l. 6	The vizierate of Ibn Maṣāl [544/1149]	Yaḥyā b. Abī Ṭayy	*Maʿādin al-dhahab fī taʾrīkh al-mulūk wa ʾl-khulafāʾ wa dhawi ʾl-rutab* [not named]	22 (b), l. 12
22 (b), l. 13	Reports on the vizierate of Ibn al-Salār [544/1149]	[Ibn Ṭuwayr – unidentified by work or name] (57–9)	*Nuzhat al-muqlatayn fī akhbār al-dawlatayn*	23 (b), l. 19
23 (b), l. 19	Reports on the vizierate of Ibn al-Salār [544/1149]	Ibn Khallikān (416–17)	*Wafayāt al-aʿyān* [not named]	24 (a), l. 25
24 (b), l. 1	Usāma b. Munqidh's visit to Egypt [incl. two long poems] [544/1149]	?	?	26 (a), l. 9
64 (a), l. 3	The murder of Ibn al-Salār and the vizierate of ʿAbbās al-Ṣanhājī [548/1153]	[Ibn Ṭuwayr – unidentified by work or name] (59–66)	*Nuzhat al-muqlatayn fī akhbār al-dawlatayn*	67 (a), l. 11
77 (b), l. 1	The death of al-Ẓāfir; & Usāma b. Munqidh's visit [548/1153, 555/1160]	?	?	79 (a), l. 9
79 (a), l. 10	The death of al-Ẓāfir; the rule of al-Fāʾiz [555–6/1160–1]	?	?	79 (b), l. 22
79 (b), l. 22	The death of al-Ẓāfir; the rule of al-Fāʾiz [555–6/1160–1]	? [Ibn Ṭuwayr – identified by work not name] (67–68)	*Nuzhat al-muqlatayn fī akhbār al-dawlatayn*	80 (b), l. 13
80 (b), l. 18	The death of al-Ẓāfir; the rule of al-Fāʾiz [555–6/1160–1]	"(69–70)	*Nuzhat al-muqlatayn fī akhbār al-dawlatayn*	81 (a), l.9

(*Continued*)

Vol./folio/line	Subject	Author cited	Work cited	Quote ends
81 (a), l. 21	The death of al-Ẓāfir; reports about Ṭalā'i' b. Ruzzīk [555-6/1160–1, 558/1162]	[Ibn Ṭuwayr – unidentified by work or name] (70–2, 82, 73)	*Nuzhat al-muqlatayn fī akhbār al-dawlatayn*	83 (b), l.24
140 (a), l. 11	The death of al-Fā'iz [555/1160]	al-Ḥāfiẓ b. al-Jawzī (*sub anno* 555/1160)	*al-Muntaẓam*	140 (a), l. 24
140 (a), l. 25	The rule of al-ʿĀḍid [556/1160–1, 558/1162]	?		142 (a), l. 3
148 (b), l.1	The vizierate of al-Ṣāliḥ b. al-Ruzzīk [556/1160–1, 558/1162]	'several authors'	?	150 (a), l. 18
150 (a), l. 18	The vizierate of al-Ṣāliḥ b. al-Ruzzīk [556/1160–1, 558/1162]	Yaḥyā b. Abī Tayy	*Maʿādin al-dhahab fī taʾrīkh al-mulūk wa 'l-khulafā' wa dhawi 'l-rutab* [not named]	150 (b), l. 1
150 (b), l. 2	" [incl. lots of poetry]	Ibn Khallikān (no. 311; 527–8)	*Wafayāt al-aʿyān* [not named]	152 (a), l. 25
152 (a), l. 25	" [incl. lots of poetry]	'someone else' [i.e. another historian]	?	153 (a), l. 22
153 (a), l. 23	The vizierate of Ruzzīk b. al-Ṭalā'iʿ [556/1160–1, 558/1162]	?	?	153 (b), l. 22
163 (b), l. 12	The struggle for power betw. Ruzzīk and Shāwar [558/1162]	several authors	?	170 (b), l. 18
184 (a), l. 1	Shāwar and his army come to Egypt from Syria; Sh. kills Dirghām 559/1163]	Ibn Khallikān (444)	*Wafayāt al-aʿyān* [not named]	184 (a), l. 19
184 (a), l.20	Shāwar and his army come to Egypt from Syria; Sh. kills Dirghām 559/1163]	?	?	184 (a), l.21

184 (a), l.22	Shāwar and his army come to Egypt from Syria; Sh. kills Dirghām 559/1163]	Ibn Wāṣil (al-Shayyal edition, 1:138)	*Mufarrij al-kurūb fī akhbār Banī Ayyūb*	184 (a), l.29
184 (a), l.29	Shāwar and his army come to Egypt from Syria; Sh. kills Dirghām 559/1163]	?	?	184 (b), l.11
184 (b), l.11	Shāwar and his army come to Egypt from Syria; Sh. kills Dirghām 559/1163]	?	?	185 (a), l.6
185 (a), l.7	Shāwar and his army come to Egypt from Syria; Sh. kills Dirghām 559/1163]	?	*Akhbār al-dawla al-Miṣriyya wa mā jarā bayn al-mulūk wa 'l-khulafā' min al-fitan wa 'l-ḥurūb min ayyām al-Āmir ilā ayyām Shīrkūh*	190 (a), l.20
190 (a), l.20	Shāwar and his army come to Egypt from Syria; Sh. kills Dirghām 559/1163]	?	?	190 (a), l.26
190 (a), l. 27	Shāwar and his army come to Egypt from Syria; Sh. kills Dirghām 559/1163]	Shāfi' b. 'Alī	*Naẓm al-sulūk fī ta'rīkh al-khulafā' wa 'l-mulūk*	190 (b), l. 31
190 (b), l. 31	Shāwar returns to the vizierate in Cairo [559/1163]	?	?	191 (a), l. 14
191 (a) , l. 14	Shāwar returns to the vizierate in Cairo [559/1163]	poem by 'Umāra b. 'Alī al-Yamanī	?	191 (a), l. 17
191 (a), l. 17	Shāwar returns to the vizierate in Cairo [559/1163]	?	?	192 (b), l. 26
192 (b), l. 26	The Franks enter Egypt while Shāwar is there [559/1163]	?	?	193 (a), l. 30

(*Continued*)

Vol./folio/line	Subject	Author cited	Work cited	Quote ends
193 (a), l. 30	The Franks enter Egypt while Shāwar is there [559/1163]	Ibn Khallikān (?)	*Wafayāt al-aʿyān* [not named]	193 (b), l. 20
193 (b), l. 20	The Franks enter Egypt while Shāwar is there [559/1163]	Ibn Naẓīf al-Ghassānī al-Ḥamawī (Moscow facsimile edition, 84a)	*al-Taʾrīkh al-Manṣūrī* [not named]	193 (b), l. 31
196 (a), l. 3	A pact is made betw. Shīrkūh, the Franks and the Egyptians [incl. poem on ff. 196(b)–197(a)] [559/1163]	?	?	196 (b), l. 6
196 (b), l. 17	The seige of Shīrkūh at Bilbays [559/1163]	Ibn Wāṣil [quoting ʿUmāra al-Yamanī] (1:141–3)	*Mufarrij al-kurūb fī akhbār Banī Ayyūb*	197(a), l.14
200 (b), l.1	Shīrkūh goes from Egypt to Damascus [560/1164]	?	?	201 (a), l. 4
201 (a), l. 4	[includes another poem by ʿUmāra al-Yamanī]	Ibn Khallikān (?)	*Wafayāt al-aʿyān* [not named]	201 (a), l. 17
201 (a), l. 17	ʿWhat happens to Shāwar after the departure of Shīrkūh' [incl. news from outside Egypt] [560/1164]	still Ibn Khallikān? al-Idrīsī in parts (after l. 23)	?	203 (b), l. 4
203 (b), l. 4	Brief note on the movements of Shīrkūh [560/1164]	Ibn Naẓīf al-Ghassānī al-Ḥamawī (84b)	*al-Taʾrīkh al-Manṣūrī*	203 (b), l. 7
211 (a), l.1	Shīrkūh returns to Egypt [562/1166]	? [includes poem by ʿArqala al-Dimashqī]	?	212 (a), l. 7
212 (a), l. 7	Shīrkūh returns to Egypt [562/1166]	Shāfiʿ b. ʿAlī and other ʿpeople of history'	*Naẓm al-sulūk fī taʾrīkh al-khulafāʾ wa ʾl-mulūk* [not named]	212 (a), l. 15

212 (a), l. 15	Shīrkūh returns to Egypt [562/1166]	'someone else'	?	212 (b), l. 7
212 (b), l. 8	More on Shīrkūh [562/1166]	'several historians'	?	212 (b), l.14
212 (b), l.14	More on Shīrkūh [562/1166]	al-Idrīsī		213 (b), l. 11
213 (b), l. 11	More on Shīrkūh [562/1166]	Shāfiʿ b. ʿAlī and other 'people of history'	*Naẓm al-sulūk fī taʾrīkh al-khulafāʾ wa 'l-mulūk* [not named]	213 (b), l. 16
213 (b), l. 16	More on Shīrkūh [562/1166]	Ibn Khallikān	*Wafayāt al-aʿyān* [not named]	214 (b), l. 2
214 (b), l. 2	Shīrkūh takes over Alexandria [562/1166]	?	?	214 (b), l. 16
214 (b), l. 16	Shīrkūh takes over Alexandria [562/1166]	Ibn Khallikān and others (?)	*Wafayāt al-aʿyān* [not named] and ?	214 (b), l. 24
214 (b), l. 24	About the Egyptian and Frankish armies [562/1166]	?	?	215 (a), l. 5
215 (a), l. 5	About the Egyptian and Frankish armies [562/1166]	Shāfiʿ b. ʿAlī	*Naẓm al-sulūk fī taʾrīkh al-khulafāʾ wa 'l-mulūk* [not named]	215 (a), l. 16
215 (a), l. 16	The pact betw. Shīrkūh, Egyptians and Franks [562/1166]	?	?	215 (a), l.28
215 (a), l.28	The pact betw. Shīrkūh, Egyptians and Franks [562/1166]	al-Idrīsī		215 (b), l. 16
215 (b), l. 16	The pact betw. Shīrkūh, Egyptians and Franks [562/1166]	Ibn Khallikān and others	*Wafayāt al-aʿyān* [not named] and ?	216 (a), l. 20
216 (a), l. 20	Nūr al-Dīn enters Frankish territory [562/1166]	?	?	217 (a), l. 6

Appendix B: Diplomatic Edition of Selected Extracts from Ibn al-Furāt's *Taʾrīkh al-duwal*: Arabic Text

Methodology of text edition and translation

The extracts from Ibn al-Furāt's *Taʾrīkh al-duwal* reproduced here are prose passages from the first three volumes of the Vienna series of codices that describe late Fatimid rule in Egypt, and appear not to be found elsewhere in the published material on the subject. Comparison with reports available in published sources, for example Ibn al-Furāt's quotations from Ibn al-Athīr or Ibn Khallikān, reveals that he quotes from earlier sources faithfully. For this reason, only unique material has been edited and translated. The presentation of unique prose extracts from *Taʾrīkh al-duwal* serves the purpose of isolating those areas in which Ibn al-Furāt potentially offers new material to augment current knowledge of the sources for late Fatimid history.

These extracts represent significant new material on the late Fatimids, but do not constitute the whole of Ibn al-Furāt's contribution to the Mamluk record of Fatimid rule: of the two most useful single authors whose work Ibn al-Furāt preserves, the Egyptian Ibn Ṭuwayr (d. 1220) and the Aleppan Ibn Abī Ṭayy (d. 1233), only the latter's reports on the Fatimids are offered here, as Ibn Ṭuwayr's reports have been collected from various later chronicles and published in a separate volume by Sayyid (1992); his efforts have not been duplicated.

On the question of how much editorial 'interpretation' is justified in the presentation of extracts from Ibn al-Furāt's history, which is a relatively unusual example of a well-known Mamluk-era autograph chronicle of which no further copies were produced, the editorial principles expounded in detail in al-Qāḍī (2007) served as a guide. Put simply, this recommends that an editor find ways to make a difficult text accessible to modern readers while simultaneously remaining true to the manuscript *as it appears*, finding a middle path between her/his roles as the passive preserver and the cautious reconstructor of an original text. The potentially contradictory impulses innate in these requirements were overcome by the provision of an English translation of Ibn al-Furāt's extracts in which I have aimed for fidelity to the Arabic as it appears rather than literary panache, to which punctuation and full paragraphing are added so as to increase readability, and where readings of faded or orthographically unclear words are provided, albeit in square brackets. The Arabic text, on the other hand, a unique holograph for which comparable readings are seemingly not available for the reports offered here, and in which a great many reports are perforated by damage to the codex, is presented with very few textual emendations, which are noted underneath. These deal with doubtful readings, indicated in square brackets, or water-damaged/worm-eaten areas, denoted by curly brackets, with footnotes added for explanation. Some minimal paragraphing is added to the Arabic text chiefly to break up the longer reports. The identification of some places and the figures mentioned in the text occurs in footnotes to the English translation.

For the identification of place names within Egypt, the city of Cairo and the Levant, Yāqūt's *Muʿjam al-buldān*, al-Maqrīzī's *Khiṭaṭ* and his *Ittiʿāẓ* served as useful resources, the latter through both the text itself and the editor's footnotes. Where a source is not indicated, plates 29–31 of Kennedy (2002) and pp. 119–29 of Nicolle (2004) were relied on.

As the work is an autograph, orthographical difficulties obviously originate with the author's hand rather than later scribal errors. Two types of emendation have been made to the text – the addition of points on many letters, and correcting the spellings of words in which the *hamza* is used in a non-standard way, chiefly by the omission of medial and final *hamza*s; this is done without indication except where the reading might give rise to doubts. For the rest, the Arabic text and all its idiosyncrasies, which is 'ungrammatical and unclassical' in places in keeping with its author's adherence to the so-called Cairo narrative style, are left in place. The subject headings that Ibn al-Furāt wrote in red ink are marked out in both Arabic text and translation with bold letters, as are those words that Ibn al-Furāt made prominent in the body of the text by using red ink, which often indicate a change of 'voice'/source or topic. The change of manuscript page is similarly signalled in square brackets within the text, with 'a' denoting recto and 'b' denoting verso. The text below opens with accounts of the life of the vizier al-Afḍal (1094–1121) and ends with a truce between Fatimids, Syrians and Franks (c. 1167).

[Vol. I: 165b, l.12]
وقال الشيخ يحيى بن ابي طي حميد النجار الغساني الحلبي في تأليفه ما صيغته كانت طريقة الافضل جميلة من العلم والعدل والفضل والكرم وحسن الاحدوثة وكان ذا ادب جم وله شعرٌ حسن منه قوله وقد اهدى اليه مسعود الدولة قطائفاً فكتب **اليه** ... [l.17]

[l.27] **وكان** قد استولي على الامور بمصر وحصل من الاموال ما خرج عن حد الاحصاء وكان شديد التحرز على نفسه لا يكاد يسير الى مكان الا ومعه جماعة ويثق بهم ويحفظونه فبينما هو يوما راكب في السوق إذ وثب عليه رجل فاشتغل به عبيده فوثب عليه آخر من الزحمة فضربه بسكين فقتله

وقيل ان قتله كان بترتيب الآمر وكان السبب في ذلك ان الافضل كان [166a] قد ضيق على الآمرومنعه التصرف في نفسه وماله وكان الآمر عول على الايقاع به اذا دخل عليه للسلام او في ايام لاعياد فقبح ذلك عليه وقيل فيه شناعة عظيمة لان هذا الرجل هو وابوه تربيا في هذا البيت وخدماه منذ خمسين سنة ومتى اعتمدتَ ذلك في حقه سائت السمعة و نفر الناس عن هذا البيت الصواب ان ترتّب له مَن يغتاله فرضي بذلك وجري الامر على ما ذكرناه

وقيل انه ركب من داره بمصر وقصد خزانة السلاح بالقاهرة وركب بين يديه عدد كبير من الفرسان ومشى بين يديه عالم من الرجال فارتفع عليه وهجُ عظيمُ من الغبار تاذي به الافضل فامر الناس ان يبعدوا عنه ليقلّ الغبار ففعلوا ذلك وانفرد من العسكر وحده وبين يديه ركابيان فوثب عليه ثلاثة انفس من الباطنية فجرحوه بسوق الصياقلة عدة جراحات سقط منها عن فرسه ورجع اصحاب فقتلوا الباطنية وحملوه الى داره وبه رمق وركب اليه صاحب مصر من القصر عائداً له وقال له قدكنت حذرتك من هؤلاء القوم ولكن "لكل اجل كتاب" ولكل حي اعقاب ثم قال له أين اموال بيت مال المسلمين فقال اما الظاهر منها فهذا الشيخ واومأ الى بعض الكُتّاب واما الباطن منها فهذا القائم واشار الى شخص في المجلس فقال لهما صاحب مصر ما تقولان فقالا الامر كما زعم الوزيروعيننا القيام بأدائها واوصى الافضل لصاحب مصر باولاده ومأمن يومه وكان مقتله عند كرسي الجسر عند الصياقلة قال الشيخ يحيى وكان مقتله في سنة اربع عشرة وخمسمائة **قال** وقيل انه قتل في سلخ شهر رمضان سنة خمس عشرة وخمسمائة وكان عمره يوم قتل سبعة وخمسون سنة

وكان **مولده** بعكّا في سنة ثمان وخمسين واربعمائة وكانت وزارته ثماني وعشرون سنة وستة اشهر واياماً **ووُجدت** في خزانته خمسة آلاف الف ومائتا الف دينارا ذهبا عينا سوى الفضة والآنية المضروبة من الذهب والفضة واحد وعشرون الف ثوبا من الاطلس وغيره من الحرير وخمسة آلاف قطعة آنية من الذهب والفضة وعشرين [166b] الف قطعة من المحكم والصيني والاجناس الغريبة وعلى مرابطة عشرة آلاف فرس ومن خشب المراكب ما قيمته مائة الف دينار ومن السلاح والسروج المذهبة ما قيمته خمسمائة الف دينار

وقال قاضي القضاة شمس الدين احمد بن خلكان ومن خطه نقلت ما صيغته كان ابو القاسم شاهنشاه الملقب الافضل بن امير الجيوش بدر الجمالي حسن التدبير فحل الرأي وهو الذي اقام الآمر بن المستعلي موضع ابيه في المملكة بعد وفاته ودبر دولته وحجر عليه ومنعه من ارتكاب الشهوات فانه كان كثير اللعب فحمله ذلك على ان عمل على قتله وكان يسكن بمصر في دار الملك التي على بحر النيل المبارك وهي اليوم دار الوكالة فلما ركب من داره المذكورة وتقدم الى ساحل البحر وثب عليه رجلان فضرباه بالسكاكين فجرحاه وجاء ثالث من ورائه فضربه بسكين في خاصرته فسقط عن دابة ورجع اصحابه فقتلوا الثلاثة وحملوه الى داره وبه رمق فركب الآمرالخليفة اليه وتوجع له وسأله عن الاموال فقال اما الظاهر منها فابو الحسن بن ابي اسامة الكاتب يعرفه واما الباطنة فابن البطائحي يعرفه وقتل في سلخ شهر رمضان سنة خمس عشرة وخمسمائة وكانت ولايته بعد ابيه ثمانيا وعشرين سنة وكان حسن السيرة عادلا

حُكِي انه لما قتل الافضل وظهر الظلم بعده اجتمع جماعة واستغاثوا الى الخليفة وكان من جملة قولهم انهم لعنوا الافضل فسُئلوا عن سبب لعنهم اياه فقالوا لانه عدل واحسن السيرة ففارقنا بلادنا واوطاننا وقصدنا بلده لعدله فقد اصابنا بعده هذا الظلم فهو كان سبب ظلمنا فاحسن الخليفة اليهم وامر بالاحسان الى الناس **وقيل** وقف ابو عبد الله محمد بن بركات اللغوي النحوي للافضل متظلما من توقف جارية **وانشد** ... [l.27]

[29 .l] فقال له يا شيخ قد حملنا عنك الوقوف وامر ان يحمل اليه جاريته قال ابن خلكان وخلف الافضل من الاموال ما لم يسمع بمثله قط قال صاحب الدول المنقطعة خلف ستمائة الف الف دينار عينا [167a] ومائتين وخمسين اردباً دراهم نقد مصر وخمسة وسبعين الف ثوب ديباج اطلس ودواة ذهب فيها جوهر قيمته اثنى عشر الف دينار وخلف خارجا عن ذلك من البقر والجواميس والغنم ما يستحيي من ذكر عدده وبلغ ضمان البانها في سنة وفاته ثلاثين الف دينار والله اعلم [l.5]

[206b, l.12]
وقال الشيخ يحيي بن ابي طي حميد ا لنجار الغساني الحلبي ما صيغته **وفي** سنة تسع عشرة عزل المأمون وزير مصر واخوه المؤتمن وقتلا وكانا اللذان صنعا في قتل الافضل وصلب ابن البطائحي برأس الطابية وانفرد الآمر بالتدبير الى ان مات قال وكان السبب في قتل البطائحي والقبض عليه انه وشى الى الآمر انه يريد ان يبايع لبعض اهل بيته فقبض عليه وعلى اخيه وعلى داعي الدعاة وعلى ذلك المشار اليه من اهل بيته واعتقلهم في القصر وخرج الآمر الى بعض متنزهاته وكان عادته اذا خرج الى مكان ان تخرج الامراء وتُضْرَب خيمها حول المكان الذي ينزله فمن كان من الامراء يشرب الخمر ارسل اليه خمرا وطعاما ومن لم يشرب ارسل اليه طعاما وحلواء وكان في جملة الامراء امير ارمني يقال له زريق وكان داهية شجاعا فاتكا وله نكاية عظيمة في الفرنج حتي ان الفرنج كانت تتعوذ منه وان اخذهم كان اذا ورد الماء ليسقي فرسه ويمتنع من الشرب يقول اشرب فما زريق في الماء وكان هذا زريق بينه وبين ابن البطائحي الوزير معاداة فاتفق ان خرج مع الآمر الى هذه النزهة فارسل اليه الآمر بطعام وحلواء فوجده الفراشون وعليه لأمة جوخة وهو يبكي وانهوا ذلك الى الآمر فاحضره وسأله عن سبب [207a] بكائه فقال وكيف لا ابكي ومولانا في هذا المكان وفي القصر في الاعتقال خليفة ووزير وداعي فقام الآمر من وقتهودخل القصر وقتل ابن البطائحي وصلبه وقتل الداعي والمشار اليه بالبيعة **انتهي** كلامه [207a, l.4]

[Vol 2: 17b, l.2]
وقال الشيخ يحيى بن ابي طي حميد النجار الغساني الحلبي ما صيغته **وفي** يوم ثلاثا ثالث عشر ذي القعدة سنة اربع وعشرين وخمسمائة **قُتل** [الآمر] في زقاق من ازقّة الجزيرة وقيل عند كرسي الجسر وقد عدا اليها وثب عليه سبعة نفر من الاسماعيلية من فُرن هناك كانوا اختفوا فيه وحُمل الى قصره وبه رمق في زورق ودخل على خليج القاهرة وحُمل الى قصره في شليل من اشلة الخيل ومات من ليلته وعمره اربع وثلاثون سنة ومدة ايامه تسع وعشرون سنة ولم يعقب وهو العاشر من وُلْد عبد الله الناجم القائم بسجلماسة **وقيل** ان اهل صنعا يروون ان له ولد اسمه الطيّب وهم آمرية المذهب وبالشام جماعة من الآمرية والله اعلم اي ذلك كان [17b, l.13]

[18b, l.1]
وقال شيخ يحيى بن ابي طي حميد النجار الغساني الحلبي ما صيغته لما قُتل الآمر قام بعده ابو الميمون عبد المجيد بن الامير ابي القاسم بن المستنصر وكانت ولايته بوصيّة من الآمر لانه كان خلف عدة من النساء حبالى فامره بحفظ ما في بطونهن وتكفل ان ولدن ولدا ذكرا حفظه وسلم اليه الامر **ولما** ولي عبد المجيد المذكور الامر لُقب بالحافظ لان الآمر كفله ما في بطون نسائه كما قدمنا شرحه **وكان** سن الحافظ يوم ولي احدى وستون سنة ولم يلي منهم من ليس ابوه خليفة عندهم غيره وغير العاضد كما سنذكره ان شاء الله تعالى **وكان** الحافظ رَبعَة ديد الأدَمَة جاحظ العينين حسن الخط جيد المعرفة ظاهر العقل والله اعلم [18b, l.12]

[19b, l.10]
وقال الشيخ يحيى بن ابي طي حميد النجار الغساني الحلبي ما صيغته لما بويع الحافظ استوزر هزار المعروف بالعادل جوامرد وهو مملوك فولي بعض يوم وقتل وطيف برأسه في القاهرة والله اعلم [19b, l.13]

[20a, l.24]
وقال الشيخ يحيى بن ابي طي حميد النجار الغساني الحلبي ما صيغته **ولي** بعد هزبر الملوك ابن الافضل بن امير الجيوش امير علي كتيفات وكان سبب ولايته ان غلمان ابيه الافضل وغلمان المظفر اخيه قاموا في مصر وطلبوا ولايته فاجيبوا الى ذلك واُخلع عليه وقام بالوزارة وكشف عن الناس المظالم واعاد اليهم ما كان قد اُخذ منهم على جهة الظلم والغصب واحسن [20b] السيرة ولما استوسق امره وانتظم عقد وزارته اظهر مذهبه وكان

إماميا وجمع من بمصر من الإمامية وقال قد عوّلتُ ان اعطل خطبة الحافظ واخطب للامام المنتظر صاحب الزمان ابن الحسن فما تقولون فمنهم من اجابه الى ذلك ومنهم من قال الصواب ترْك ذلك واشتغال سيدنا بامر نفسه واصلاح شأنه فلم يقبل واعتقل الحافظ وضيق عليه وخطب للامام القائم المنتظر واسقط ذكر المصريين من الخطبة وامر المؤذنين ان يسقطوا من الاذان "محمد و علي خير البشر" وابقاء "على خير العمل" وعقد بمصر والقاهرة وجميع الولاية صلاة الجمعة على رأي الإمامية وقنت في الصلاة قنوتين في الركعتين وجمع بين صلاتي الظهر والعصر وامر ان يُدعى له على المنابر **بنعوت منها** وهو السيد الافضل سيد ممالك ارباب الدول الحامي عن حوزة الدين ناشر جناح العدل على الابعدين والاقربين ناصر إمام الحق في حالتي غيبته وحضوره والقائم في نصره بماضي سيفه وصائب رأيه وتدبيره امين الله على عباده وهادي القضاة الى اتباع شرع الحق واعتماده ومرشد دعاة المؤمنين بواضح بيانه وارشاده مولى النعم ورافع الجور عن الأمم وما لك فضيلتي السيف والقلم ابو على احمد بن السيد الافضل ابي القاسم شاهنشاه ابن امير الجيوش بدر الجمالي من غير تعرّض لذكر الحافظ اصلا والله اعلم [20b, 1.20]

[41b, l.10]

ذكر بعض خبر الوزير الافضل وزير الديار المصرية وقتله

هو احمد بن الافضل شاهنشاه بن امير الجيوش بدر **الجمالي يكنى** ابا على **وينعت** الافضل كوالده **قد** قدمنا سبب وزارة الافضل احمد المذكور وبعض خبره فاغنى عن اعادته ها هنا ولكن نذكر بعض ما قاله اهل التاريخ **وكان** الوزير الافضل احمد المذكور جوادا بالمال كثير العطاء له غزير العلم له كتاب سماه "البيان في اثبات بقاء صاحب الزمان" جمع له الفقهاء وناظر فيه لكافة العلماء لجميع المذاهب وجمعهم على تصحيحه وكان يحب الشعر ويُثيب عليه وفيه يقول ابو المنصور ظافر بن القاسم الجزري الحداد الاسكندراني ... [41b, l.20]

[42a, l.18]

وقال الشيخ يحيى بن ابي طي حميد النجار الغساني الحلبي ما صيغته **وفي هذه السنة قُتل** ابو علي وزير الحافظ بمصر بالميدان بتدبير دبّر عليه وقد وقف متفرجا وخلى مكانه من اصحابه فوثب عليه قوم من الاجناد فقتلوه فلما خرّ صريعا قطعوا رأسه بسيفه وكان سيفه سيف الحسين بن علي بن ابي طالب رضي الله عنهما [l.23]

[42b, l.17]

وقال الشيخ يحيى بن ابي طي حميد النجار الغساني الحلبي ما صيغته لما قتل ابو علي الافضل اعيد الدعاء في الخطبة للحافظ وسُلم عليه بإمرة المؤمنين وبويع له بيعة ثانية وكان ما سنذكره ان شاء الله **تعالى** [42b, l.20]

[43b, l.3]

وقال الشيخ يحيى بن ابي طي حميد النجار الغساني الحلبي ما صيغته **استوزر** الحافظ يانس ونعت بامير الجيوش سيف الاسلام فاقام مدة واراد الحافظ قتله فاشار الى طبيب عنده بان يدبر في قتله وخاف الطبيب عاقبة ذلك فامتنع وقال يا امير المؤمنين لا يجوز لمن يدخل على الملوك ان يتظاهر عندهم بهذا السبب **واتفق** ان يانس اصابه زحير فعالجه طبيبه فلما اراد ان يبرأ احضر الحافظ طبيبه وخاطبه في قتله فقال يا مولانا ان هذا المرض دواءه التودّع فان كان في نفس مولانا ان يعمل شيئا فليمضِ اليه يزوره فان حركته بسبب زيارة مولانا تكون سبب هلاكه ففعل الحافظ ذلك فكان سبب موته في ذي الحجّة مَن هذه السنة والله اعلم اي ذلك كان [43b, l.15]

[59a, l.14]

وذكر الشيخ يحيى بن ابي طي حميد النجار الغساني الحلبي في حوادث سنة تسع وعشرين وخمسمائة ما صيغته **قام** حسن بن الحافظ على ابيه الحافظ واعتقله واستخدم رجلا يقال له عبدالله الاحناوي وقدمه على السودان فعظم امره وبدع في الاجناد وصادرهم ونهبهم واستولي على القاهرة فانضاف الاجناد الى والي المحلّة تاج الدولة بهرام وكان ارمنيا على دينه واستنصروه فركب معهم وانضوى اليهم بنو [حدروج] وكانوا في عدة عظيمة يسكنون بالريف وقصدوا القاهرة وحاصروها واحرقوا باب زويلة وباب القنطرة وباب الخوخة وباب

سعادة وباب البرقية وبذّلوا السيف في السودان وهرب حسن بن الحافظ الى ابيه واستتر عنده وطلبه الاجناد فمنعه منهم فعزموا على لتخريب القصر وقتله الحافظ فيقال ان الحافظ سقاه سمّا فقتله واراهم اياه وهو ميت فسكتوا **انتهي كلامه** [59a, l.28]

[60b, l.117]

وذكر الشيخ يحيى بن ابي طي حميد النجار ما صيغته **وزر** بهرام للحافظ وكان بهرام ارمنيا من المقيمين بقلعة الروم التي بالشام الاسفل التي يقوم بها خلفاء الارمن وكان يدعي انه من اولاد داوود – على سيدنا ونبينا محمد رسول الله وعليه افضل الصلاة والسلام – وهم اهل بيت من يدعون ذلك وفيهم علامة وهو ان الرجل منهم اذا وقف ومدّ يده وصلت الى ركبته واذا ادارهما الى خلف ظهره اجتمعتا وكان سبب قدوم بهرام مصر ان خليفة الارمن مات وسلم الامر الى غيره وكان بهرام احق الناس به فابعد عن المكان فصار الى [القاهرة] فتقبل بها احسن تقبل واذن له في استقدام اهله فصار منهم جماعة بمصر[61a] يقال ان عددهم يزيد على ثلاثين الف بيت نقل اكثرهم من بلد حلب وبلد تل باشر ولما ولي بهرام الوزارة ولي اخاه مدينة قوص بالصعيد الاعلى فبسط يده في الظلم والعسف وعمر الكنائس المتهدمة بمصر جميعها [وقيل] لما ثبت بهرام في الوزارة سأل الحافظ ان يسمح له باحضار اخيه واهله واذن له في ذلك فاحضرهم من تل باشر ونهر الجور الى ان احضر من اهله وغيرهم ما مقداره ثلاثين الف انسان فاستطالوا ولحق المسلمين منهم جور عظيم وكان قد ولي اخاه المعروف [بالباساك] قوص واعمالها فجار فيها جورا عظيما واستباح اموال الناس وظلمهم وبنت الارمن كنائس واديرة حتى كل رئيس منهم بني له كنيسة وخاف اهل مصر منهم ان يغيروا المِلّة الاسلامية وكثرت الشكاية من بهرام ومن اخيه [الباساك] فعظم ذلك على أمراء المصريين وكاتبوا رضوان بن ولخشي والي الغربيّة وكان ما سنذكره ان شاء الله تعالى [l.14]

[Vol. 3: 21a, l.5]

وقال الشيخ يحيى بن أبي طي توفي [الحافظ] يوم الخميس في سنة أربع وأربعين وخمسمائة وسنه يوم مات إحدى وثمانون سنة **وخلف** من الولد حيدرة وابا علي حسن ويوسف وجبريل واسماعيل [21a, l.8]

[21a, l.13]

ذكر ولاية الظافر بأمرالله العبيدي الديار المصرية

بويع ابو المنصور إسماعيل بن الحافظ أبي الميمون عبد المجيد بن محمد بن المستنصر **العبيدي** يوم وفاة والده على ما فيه من الاختلاف بوصيته من ابيه وهو أصغر أولاد أبيه سناً **ولُقب** الظافر بأمرالله **قال** الشيخ يحيى بن ابي طي حميد النجار الغساني الحلبي ما صيغته **بويع** بعد الحافظ ولده أبو المنصور إسماعيل وهو اصغر اولاده ولُقب بالظافر بأمرالله وعمره خمسة عشر سنة في اليوم الخامس من جمادى الآخرة من سنة ثلاث وأربعين وقيل سنة أربع وأربعين وهو [21b] الصحيح فدام الى أن قتله الأمير ناصرالدين بن عباس ليلة الخميس سلخ محرم سنة تسع وأربعين وخمسمائة وايامه اربع سنين وثمانية اشهر وعمره خمسة وعشرين سنة وكلامه متناقض في مبلغ عمره كما ترى **ولما** بويع الظافر بأمرالله جلس في منظرة باب الذهب وفرّق الأموال في الناس والله اعلم [21b, l.5]

[22a, l.19]

وقال الشيخ يحيى بن ابي طي حميد النجار الغساني الحلبي **لما** قرب [ابن السلار] من القاهرة امر الظافر ابن مصال ان يعدي الى الصعيد فاذا حصل فيه جمع وقصد ابن السلار فلم يفعل ذلك وخرج اليه بمن في القاهرة من العساكر فكسره ابن السلار وقتله **والصحيح** [22b] انه خرج الى الصعيد ودخل ابن السلار الى القاهرة واستولى على الوزارة وتكرر كسر العساكر بين ابن السلار وابن مصال فخرج الامير عباس وفارس المسلمين طلائع ابن رزيك وجميع من اطاع ابن السلار واجتمع الجمعان على طُنبُدى وكانت الحرب وكان اكثر عسكر ابن مصال غائبين يوم المصاف ولم يكن معه سوى بدر بن رافع وبعض اصحابه وراجل يسير من السودان فكان اول النهار لعساكر ابن مصال واخره لعساكر ابن السلار فقُتل بدر بن رافع يقنطر به فرسه **وقُتل** ابن مصال لم يعرف قاتله وقُتل من الراجل ما لا يحصى كثرة وذلك بعد ولاية ابن السلار بستة اشهر والله أعلم أي ذلك كان [22b, l.12]

[23b, l.8]

وقيل لم يرض الظافر بأمرالله بوزارة ابن السلار وعوّل على قتله فخافه وكان لا يدخل عليه مُسَلِّما الا من باب يقال له باب العيد وهذا الباب كان يدخل منه الى ساحة عظيمة ويدخل معه جماعة من غلمانه واصحابه ويجلس له الظافر في شباك يشرف عليها يدخل العادل ويُسَلِّم عليه من وراء ذلك لشباك وكان الذين يدخلون معه قوم سمّاهم بصبيان الزرد وكانوا ينيفون على الف انسان **وكان** اذا دخل لا يدخل الا في وسطهم وكان ابن السلار المذكور ذا سيرة جائرة وسطوة قاهرة [23b, l.17]

[24a, l.23]

فلما مات أُمر به فصلب على باب زويلة لا اله الا الله ما اعظم هذه القسوة **وتقدم** الامير عباس حين وزر ابن السلار ونبغ نبوغا عظيما [24b] **وفي هذه السنة** ورد الى مصر مؤيد الدولة اسامة ابن منقذ من دمشق مغاضباً للأمير معين الدين صاحب ولايتها واتصل بالأمير عباس الصنحاجي ونفق عليه وكان مؤيد الدولة اسامة قد خلف نسائه واثقاله بدمشق فسلمهم الأمير معين الدين انر الى الفرنج فكتب اليه ابن منقذ المذكور القصيدة التي **اولها** ... [24b, l.6]

[25b, l.9]

وانما ذكرنا هذه القصيدة بجملتها لما فيها من الفضل الذي نحبّ ان يقتدي به الافاضل والسياسة التي نحبّ ان يعلمها الاماثل وقبيح فعلة الامير معين الدين مع مؤيد الدولة اسامة بعد طول الخدمة وواجب الحرمة فلما وصلت هذه القصيدة الى الامير معين الدين [طلب] الامير محمود بن سنان الشيرزي النحوي بجامع دمشق يومئذ ان يجيبه فاجابه بالقصيدة التي **اولها** ... [25b, l.15]

[26a, l.7]

والقصيدة طويلة ولما حصل اسامة بن منقذ عند الامير عباس نفق عليه وخصّ لديه حتى صار احد سُمّاره في الحلوة وخاصّته في الخلوة والله اعلم [26a, l.9]

[77b, l.13]

وكان ابن منقذ اشار على عباس المذكور بقتل الوزير ابن السلار كما قدمنا شرحه فظهرت فعلة ابن عباس وظهر انها كانت بمشورة ابن منقذ وبلغ ذلك ابن منقذ فخاف على نفسه ووقع العتب له من جماعة اهل السنة بمصر ومن كان يهوى هوى الوزير [ابن السلار] ويعتقد اعتقاده وتحدث جماعة مع الظافر في امر ابن منقذ واقدامه بما اشار به وقالوا هذا رجل غريب من دولة أخرى غير خالص الدِخلة لهذا الدولة ولا لاهلها وربما ان تُرِك وقع منه امر لا يمكن تداركه وبلغ اسامة ابن منقذ ذلك فاشتد خوفه وخشي ان يُفاجِأ بما لا يمكنه الخلاص منه والاحتراز من وقوعه فاخذ في التدبير لنفسه

[78a] **واتفق** ان الامير ناصر الدين نصر بن الوزير عباس[كان] عند الظافر واقام عنده مدة ايام بلياليها و[وصله] في [احدى] تلك الليالي بمائة الف دينار مصرية فوقعت الشناعات في ذلك وتحدث الناس به وقالوا ان الظافر يستمْرِد ناصر الدين ابن عباس وبلغت هذه المقالة للوزير عباس فاحضر اسامة بن منقذ وقال له ما الحيلة فيما يقول الناس فانفتح لاسامة بِن منقذ باب القول وتهيأ له اعمال الحيلة على الظافر فحمل نفسه على التغرير وركوب الخطر واعمال احدى الكُبَر فقال للوزير عباس يا مولانا انني ولي نعمتك وغرس صنيعتك وعذيّ احسانك وربيب فضلك ويجب عليّ لك المناصحة وقول الحق وهذا امرٌ قد شاع وانتشر ووضح للناس خبئه وظهر وفيه وضع الشرف وهدم المنزلة وهو شيء لا يبقى معه رتبة عالية ولا امرة سامية والعرب تقول النار ولا العار والمصيبة ولا المعيبة فقال الوزير عباس فمن يقدرْ يواجِه ناصر الدين بما يقول الناس مع جبريته وعظمته وجرائه فقال له اسامة [اني] القاه بذلك وان كان فيه هلاك نفسي

ثم امر أن يُحضَرَ فاحضره عباس واخلى مجلسه فقال له اسامة بعد ان اخذ عليه العهود ان الناس قد اكثروا في امرك وخاضوا في شأنك وانت اليوم عين هذه البلاد وابن رئيس العباد الذي يرى جميع الناس فضيلته ويعرفون قَدْرَ مرتبته فان كنت راضيا بذلك رأى ابوك رأيه في مقامه على الذّلة او رحيله بالحسرة فاغتاظ ناصر الدين وعظم

ذلك عليه وانكره وحلف الأيمان المُغلّظة في نزاهته عنه [78b]] [...] هذا لا يفيد مع ما قد سار وذاع ولا حيلة [...] وهذا الرجل يظهر للناس انك برئ مما رَمَوك به وقزفوا عِرضك بسببه فقال وكيف اقدر على ذلك والاجناد له كثيرة والاموال غزيرة عنده وله مثل هذه المعاقل فقال ليس قتله بالمناصبة والمصالبة والمكاثرة والمغالبة انما الستر بينك وبينه قد خُرق والحجاب قد رُفع فتتلطف حينئذ في خدمته وتخرق حجاب حرمته وتقول اذا رأيته وقد مال اليك يا مولاي اشتهي ان تُشرفني بالحضور في داري والاكل من طعامي فاذا اجابك إلى ذلك تقول له اشتهي ان يكون ذلك ليلا في خف من اصحابك وخدامك لتتمّ لذّتي وتكمل مسرّتي فاذا حضر عندك نظرت في سبب قتله وتدميسه ثم ان اباك يقيم من اهل بيته عوضه ويذهب كما ذهب امس الدابر فوقر ذلك في سمع الامير ناصر الدين بن عباس واعدّ مكانا للذي يريده واجتمع بالظافر وسأله زيارته فاجابه الى ذلك لشدة ميله اليه

وخرج اليه مختفيا من اعين الناس وكانت دار عباس وهي دار ابن المأمون البطائحي قريبة من القصير في السيوفيين بالقاهرة ودخل اليه من باب سر لداره في سرب الى مجلس قد اعدّه له وكان معه عدة يسيرة من الخدم فلما حصل عنده ادخله بيتا ثم وثب عليه فقتله وقتل من كان معه من الخَدَم وافلتَ خادم صغير ووقف في بعض ملَفّات ابواب الدار واخذ ابن عباس الظافر والخدم الذين قتلهم معه والقاهم في جُبّ في وسط الدار ووضع عليه رُخامة من رخام الدار وغسل آثار الدم وبسط بُسُطه [79a] وفرشه وذلك كله بعين الخادم وجلس [...] يصنع شيئا واجتمع الامير ناصر الدين بن عباس بابيه من ليلته وعرّفه ما صنع بالظافر وكان ما سنذكره ان شاء الله تعالى وُلد الظافر يوم الاحد منتصف شهر ربيع الآخر سنة سبع وعشرين وخمسمائة وقُتل ليلة الخميس سلخ شهر الله المحرم من سنة تسع واربعين وخمسمائة هذه السنة **وقيل** قُتل ليلة النصف من المحرم الشهر المذكور وعمره خمسة وعشرين سنة وايامه اربع سنين وثمانية اشهر والله اعلم

ذكر ولاية الفائز العبيدي بالديار المصرية

لما كان يوم الخميس وقيل يوم الاثنين صبيحة ليلة قُتل فيها الظافر العبيدي صاحب الديار المصرية وهو احد اليومين اللذين يدخل على الخليفة العبيدي فيهما للسلام حضر الوزير عباس الصنهاجي الى القصر على جاري عادته في الخدمة واظهر عدم الاطّلاع على قضية الظافر ومعه وجوه الامراء والاجناد ووقف على باب القصر واستدعى خادما وقال له أجَلس مولانا فقال لا فقال اذهب وخذ اليه طريقا واعْلِمْه اجتماع الناس للسلام فدخل الخادم الى القصر ولم يكن أهل القصر علموا بقتله بعدُ لانه كان قد خرج من عندهم في خفية وما اعلم احد[اً] بخروجه فلما دخل الخادم الى القصر دخل معه الخدم ليستأذنوا للوزير عباس فلم يجدوه فدخلوا الى قاعة الحرم وفتّشوا عليه عند [79b] [...] نسائه وجلوسه وخلوته وجميع مَظانّه في القصر فقيل لهم انه لم يبتْ هاهنا فخرج الخادم الى الوزير وقال له مولانا له عذر وليس الى الوصول اليه سبيل فقال لا يمكن ان امضي حتى اراه فانه قد حدث امر مهمّ اريد مشاورته فيه فرجع الخادم الى القصر وسأل النساء والخدم ثانيا فما قدر احد له على خبر ولا وقف له على اثر فتحققوا حينئذ عدمه وقال جماعة من الخدم وقالوا البارحة خرج الى دار ناصر الدين ابن عباس وما عاد فترجل عباس وهجم ودخل القصر الى ان صار في قاعة باب البحر وهي احدى القاعات التي جرت عادة الخليفة العبيدي ان يكون جالسا فيها وقال ما صنع مولانا واين هو؟ فقالوا البارحة خرج الى دار ولدك والى الساعة ما عاد ووجد ذلك الخادم المختفى في دار ابن عباس فرصة فخرج وجاء الى القصر واعلمهم بما شاهد من قتل الظافر فتماسك القوم وقالوا حتى نكشف الحال واراد النساء النوح [فمنعهن] اخوة الظافر وقال عباس اخْرِجوا اخوة الظافر فخرج اليه جبريل و يوسف وابن اخيهما ابا التقي صالح بن حسن فسألهم عن الظافر فقالوا له اسأل ولدك عنه فانه اعلم به منّا فامر بهم فضربت رقابهم بعد ان قال لهم أنتم قتلتموه **وقيل** انهم قالوا له لما خرجوا اليه أمهلنا حتى ننقب عنه ونسأل عن خبره فقال قتلتموه وتقولون نسأل عنه [79b, l.22]

[80b, l.13]
وقيل اخرج الوزير عباس اخوي الظافر وقال لهما انتما قتلتما امامنا وما نعرف حاله الا منكما فأصرّا على الأنكار بانهما لم يقتلاه وكانا صادقين في انكارهما فقتلهما في الوقت لينفي عن نفسه وابنه التهمة واخذ أهل القصر في النوح والبكاء على الظافر واخوته [80b, l.18]

[81a, l.10]
وقيل لما قتل الوزير عباس اخوي الظافر وابن عمّهما قال لزمامِ القصر اين ابن مولانا قال حاضر فقال قُدّامي الى مكانه فدخل بنفسه الخلوة وكان عند جدته لأمه فحمله على كَتِفه واخرجه للناس قبل رفع المقتولين وبايع له بالخلافة فرأى القتلى فتفزّع واضطرب ودام مدة خلافته لا يطيبِ له عيش
[81a, l.15]

[81a, l.21]
ذكر استنصار اهل مصر بطلائع بن رزيك على الوزير عباس وهروب عباس وولده وقتلهما

قد قدمنا ما قيل في قتل الظافر [العبيدي] وولاية ولده الفائز العبيدي بالديار المصرية [81b] [وقيام] الوزير عباس بالتصرّف في الدولة ثم تعاود الاجناد [الوزير] العباس وانكروا قتله للظافر ولاخوته وقاموا عليه واستظهر عليهم وقهرهم وعاد الى امره وكان ذلك في عاشر صفر من هذه السنة وفيه تقرر امر الفائز واستحلف الناس واستقل عباس بالامور ولم يبقَ على يده يد

[82a, l.15]
وقيل لما بلغ الوزير عباس خبر طلائع بن رزيك سيّر اليه حسين بن حمديه وهو يومئذ زوج ابنة الصالح فمضى اليه موبّنا له وصارفا له عمّا عزم عليه فلما خلا به فقال له بمن تقاتل عباسا وله اليوم خمسة آلاف مملوك فقال له الصالح ما تعلم بمن اقاتله اقاتله بنفسي ونفسك فقال حسين اما الان فنعم وكان حسين هذا فارسا مذكورا بالشجاعة موصوفا بالشدة في الديار المصرية مرهوبا في تلك العساكر وسارا جميعا وقد لبس الامير طلائع وجميع عسكره [82b] [ثيابا سوداء] [...] على [رؤوس] الاعلام حتى قارب جيزة [...واجتمع] الاجناد الذين بالقاهرة وبمصر على عباس فهرب [هو وولده] واهله واحتقب اموالا كثيرة جعلها على [او]ساط غلمانه وخرج معه اسامة بن منقذ وخرج الى الشام على طريق ايلة وخرج من بالقاهرة من الاجناد والسودان الى فارس المسلمين ابي الغارات طلائع بن رزيك هذا ما كان من هؤلاء [82b, l.7]

[82b, l.26]
وقيل كان دخول الصالح الى القاهرة في يوم الاحد [83a] ثالث عشري شهر ربيع الاول ولما دفن الصالح بن رزيك الظافر اخذ في اصلاح الامور واستحلاف الناس للفائز وله من بعده وبذل الاموال واصطنع الرجال وكان رئيسا في نفسه عظيما في ابناء جنسه وافر العقل بصيرا بالتجارب عالما بايام الناس مداخلا في جميع الامور لا سيما علم الكلام والادب فانه كان فيهما الفارس الشجاع والمقدم الهُمام واخذ اهل الدولة بإظهار الفضل والدين وانكار الفساد والظلم والغشم فاحبه الناس ومالوا اليه بكليتهم **هذا** ما كان من امر الصالح ابن رزيك ومن بمصر [83a, l.9]

[83a, l.18]
وقيل إن أخت الظافر كاتبت الفرنج وقد كانوا ملكوا عسقلان وضمنت لهم إن هم قتلوا عباسا أو ولده أو قبضوا عليهما أن تعطيهم بمائة ألف دينار فخرج الفرنج وعارضوهم مكمنين لهم فظفروا بهم في المزّة وأم كعب وهو احد المناهل وقيل في المويلح وقيل في زرع فاوقعوا به وقتلوا ولده حسام الملك واخذوا ولده نصرا أسيرا وسبوا اولاده الصغار واهله وانهزم بعض اصحابه الى الشام فسلموا وفيهم اسامة بن منقذ وحصل الفرنج على ما كان صحبته من المال وارسل من في القصر [83b] [المعـ]روف بالتوزري في سادس عشري شهر ربيع [الاول] [...] المال فسلّمه الى الفرنج وتسلّم منهم نصر بن [عباس] وجعله في قَفَص حديدٍ وقدم به القاهرة وخرج الناس [...] وسبّوه ولعنوه وبصقوا عليه حتى ادخل الى [القصر] فيقال إن الجواري قَتَلْنَهُ نخسا بالمسال الحديدة وقيل صفعا بالوطيات وقيل انهن قطعن لحمه واطعمنه اياه حتى مات ثم أُخرج وصُلب على باب زويلة احد أبواب القاهرة المحروسة واحرق بعد ذلك هذه خلاصة الواقعة وان كان فيها طُول **وطلب** الصالح بن رزيك الذين اعانوا نصر بن عباس على قتل الظافر العبيدي فظفر منهم بقيماز وفتوح الاخرس وابن غالب فقتلهم بين يديه صبرا وقتل جماعة كثيرة بهذا السبب واستقرت امور الصالح ونعت نفسه بفارس المسلمين نصير الدين الصالح ومدحه الشعرا بذلك [83b, l.14]

[148b, l.9]
وفيها ورد محمد بن حسين بن نزار بن المستنصر من الغرب ومعه عساكر كثيرة وجنود عظيمة فلما قارب بلاد مصر تلقب بالمستنصر فخدعه الامير حسام بن فضة من بني رزيك ووعده انه يبذل نفسه في خدمته وتلطف معه الحال الى ان حصل معه في خيمته ثم قبض عليه وحمله الى مصر وسلمه الى الصالح بن رزيك وزير الديار المصرية والله اعلم

ذكر بعض خبر الصالح بن رزيك وزير الديار المصرية وقتله

هو طلائع بن رزيك الارمني يكنى ابا المعارف **وينعت** بالصالح **كان** الصالح بن رزيك شجاعا كريما سمحا جوّادا فاضلا محبا لاهل الفضل جيد الشعر **ورأيت في** بعض التواريخ ما **صوّرته** كان الصالح طلائع بن رزيك رجلا بليغا فصيحا شاعرا ذا سطوة وشجاعة وجرت له قصة عجيبة **وهي** ان الصالح في اول امره قدم من المغرب صحبة فقراء قصدوا زيارة النجف الذي دُفن فيه امير المؤمنين علي بن ابي طالب رضي الله عنه فلما وصلوا الى النجف وكان عدتهم اربعين انسانا وكان طلائع رجلا متواليا بحب آل محمد صلى الله عليه وسلم فلما زاروا وباتوا تلك الليلة في النجف وكان امام النجف السيد بن معصوم **فرأي** الامام في نومه امير المؤمنين علي بن ابي طالب رضي الله عنه وهو يقول له إنه قد ورد عليك الليلة اربعون فقيرا ومن جملتهم رجل يقال له طلائع بن رزيك من اكبر محبّينا قل له رُح فقد وليناك مصرًا فلما اصبح الامام ابن معصوم وصلّي الصبح امر المؤذن ان ينادى من فيكم طلائع بن رزيك فليقم الى السيد ابن معصوم فلما نادى المؤذن بذلك نهض طلائع بن رزيك وسلّم على الامام فقال له رأيت الامام [149a] علي بن ابي طالب رضي الله عنه وقال لي كذا وكذا وقد ولاك مصر

فنهض طلائع بن رزيك وتوجه الى الديار المصرية فترقّي الى ان يتولي نيابة الوجه القبلي بمنية بني خصيب ثم حكي ما قدمنا شرحه ان اهل مصر كاتبوه وسألوه الانتصار لهم والخروج على الوزير عباس وانه توجه الى القاهرة ومعه جمع عظيم وهرب منه عباس الى الشام ودخل الصالح ابن رزيك القاهرة بغير قتال وتولي الوزارة بالديار المصرية للفائز العبيدي كما قدمنا شرحه الى ان توفي وتولي العاضد العبيدي واستقر الامر للعاضد المذكور اسما وللصالح ابن رزيك جسما وزادت حرمته وسار في ايام العاضد سيرة مذمومة فانه احتكر الغلات فارتفع سعرها وقتل امراء الدولة كما قدمنا شرحه وتزوج العاضد بابنة الصالح فاغترّ بالسلامة وكان ما سنذكره ان شاء الله تعالى **وقال** بعض اهل التاريخ كان الصالح بن رزيك رجل وقته فضلا وعقلا وسياسة وتدبيرا وكان مهيبا في شكله عظيما في سطوته وجمع اموالا عظيمة وحصل من الاقمشة والثياب والاثاث اشياء كثيرة وكان محافظا على الصلوات فرائضها ونوافلها وكان عظيم التشَيُّع وقد صنّف كتابا سماه الاعتماد في الرد على اهل العناد جمع له الفقهاء الجمهور وناظرهم عليه وفي تصحيح امامة امير المؤمنين علي بن ابي طالب رضي الله عنه انتزعه من صحيح البخاري ومسلم والترمذي وغيرها من كتب اهل السنة وتكلم فيه على متون الاحاديث وانتزع منها الاستدلال على تصحيح الامامة وله اشعار حسان في كل فن منها ما أبان به عن عقيدته **قوله** ....[149a, l.24]

[149a, l.29]
وله قصيدة سمّاها الجوهرية في الرد على القدريةِ وبني [149b] الجامع الذي بظاهر بابي زويلة المعروف بجامع الصالح وبني جامع القرافة الكبيرة **ووقف** ثُلثَي بلبيس على السادة الاشراف وسبع قراريط على مدينة سيدنا ونبينا محمد رسول الله صلى الله عليه وسلم وعلى بني معصوم امام النجف قيراط [149b, l.4]

[150a, l.18]
وقال الشيخ يحيى بن ابي طي حميد النجار بن ظافر بن علي الغساني الحلبي صاحب كتاب معادن الذهب في تاريخ الملوك والخلفاء وذوي الرتب **كان** الصالح بن رزيك كريما ممدحا يرى حق من قصده **حدثني** الفقيه خليل بن خمارتكين الحلبي **وكان** اخرجه الملك العادل نور الدين محمود بن الملك المنصور عماد الدين اتابك زنكي في جملة من اخرج من الحلبيين انه صار الى الصالح بن رزيك فاكرمه واحسن تقبله فلما اراد الخروج عن مصر اعطاه الف دينار من ماله وفرض له على الامراء بالديار المصرية الف دينار اخرى فعاش بها مدة حياته واغنى مُخلفيه بعد وفاته وكان الفقيه ابن اسعد العراقي يمدحه في كل سنة بقصيدة وينفدها اليه فيرسل اليه اجارة خمسمائة دينار ومن قصائده التي مدحه بها القصيدة **التي اولها** [150b] ...

[150b, l.20]
وكان الصالح بن رزيك مدة ولايته لا يترك غزو الفرنج وكان يغزوهم سنة في البر وسنة في البحر وربما غزاهم في البر والبحر وقد حكي ذلك الشعراء في اشعارهم **وكان** يحمل في كل سنة الى الحرمين الشريفين مكة والمدينة جميع ما يحتاجه الاشراف من الكسى وآلات النساء والرجال حتى كان يحمل اليهم الواح الصبيان واقلام الكتابة ومداد الدوى وكذالك كان يحمل الى علويين المشاهد وكان يفد عليه من العلماء والفضلاء من سائر البلاد الجم الغفير فلا يرجع منهم احد الا بما امله ومن شعر الصالح طلائع بن رزيك **قوله** [151a] ...

[151b, l.1]
حكي ان الصالح بن رزيك قال في الليلة التي قتل في صبيحتها في مثل هذه الليلة ضُرب امير المؤمنين علي بن ابي طالب رضي [الله] عنه وامر ان يقرأ عليه مَقتل علي رضي الله عنه واغتسل في تلك الليله وصلى على رأي الامامية مائة وعشرين ركعة **ويقال** ان الصالح بن رزيك خرج في اليوم الذي قُتل فيه ليركب فعثر فسقطت عمامته عن رأسه وتشوّشت فقعد في دهليز دار الوزارة وامر باحضار ابن الصنف وكان يتعمّم الخلفاء بمصر والوزراء وله على ذلك الجامكية السنية فلما احضر امره باصلاح العمامة فتقدم اليه رجل يقال له ابن بيان وقال له يعيذ الله مولانا ويكفيه عن الكمال وهذا الذي جرى امر يتطيّر منه فان رأي ان يؤخر الركوب فعل فقال الطيرة من الشيطان ليس الى تأخر الركوب سبيل وركب فكان ما سنذكره من قتله ان شاء الله تعالى **واختلف في** سبب قتله [151b, l.14]

[151b, l.26]
وقيل عمل على الصالح بن رزيك عمة العاضد لتقتله وانفدت الاموال الى الامراء وبلغه ذلك فاستعاد جميع المال واحتاط على عمة العاضد احسن الحياط واوثقه وقتل جماعة من الامراء ونكبهم وتمكن من [152a] الدولة وبلغ فيها مبلغا عظيما وعادت عمة العاضد وتمّمت الحيلة عليه وبذلت لقوم من السودان مالا عظيما حتى اوقعوا به الفعل كما سنذكره وكانوا يعرفون ببني الراعي و[جلسوا] له في بيت في دهاليز القصر مختفين فيه واتفق ان الصالح خرج فقاموا ليخرجوا اليه فاراد احدهم ان يفتح غلق الباب الذي كانوا وراءه فغلقه ولم يعلم وفاتهم الامر تلك الليلة **فلما** كان يوم تاسع عشر شهر رمضان من شهور هذه السنة دخل الصالح وسلم على العاضد وخرج من عنده فخرجوا عليه ووقعت الصيحة فعثر الصالح باذياله فتخلل الجماعة رجل يقال له ابن الراعي فطعنه بالسيف في ظاهر رقبته فقطع احد عمودَي الرقبة وحمل الى باب القصر وركب الى داره واصيب ولده رزيك في كتفه واسرعا الى دار الوزارة **وبقي** حسين بن ابي الهيجاء في دار الخلافة يقاتل السودان حتى يقال انه قتل منهم خمسين رجلا [152a, l.14]

[152b, l.18]
وقيل لما حصل الصالح بن رزيك في داره احضر ولده رزيكا وقال له بعد ان اوصاه بما يعتمده وما ندمتُ على شيء كندمي على ثلاثة اشياء فعلتُها **بنائي** الجامع على باب زويلة فانه مَضرّة على القاهرة **وتوليتي** شاور الصعيد الاعلى وخروجي بالعساكر الى بلبيس وتأخيري ارسالهم الى بلاد الفرنج **وكان** الصالح انفق في هذه العساكر مائتي الف دينار **وقال** له يا ولدي اوصيك بشاور لا تزلزله من ولايته فانه اسلم لك ولملكك **وقيل** ان الصالح لما حضر به الوفاة اوصى ولده رزيك بوصايا من جملتها انك لا تغير [153a] على شاور فانني انا اقوي منك وقد ندمتُ على استعماله ولم يمكنني عزله فلا تغيروا ما به فيكون لكم ما تكرهون ويقال انه انشد ابياتا **منها** ...

[l.7] **ومات** الصالح بعد ساعة من يوم خرج **يوم الاثنين** تاسع عشر شهر رمضان سنة ست وخمسين وخمسمائة هذه السنة **ودُفن** بالقاهرة ثم نقله ولده العادل رزيك الى تربته التي بالقرافة الكبرى فعمل في ذلك الفقيه عمارة اليمني قصيدة طويلة اجاد فيها ومن جملتها قوله في صفة **التابوت** ...

[l.14] **وقد** رثي الفقيه عمارة اليمني الشاعر المشهور الوزير الصالح بن رزيك المذكور بمرات كثيرة لم اذكرها لكثرة وجود ديوان عمارة بايدي الناس **ورثي** حسان الدمشقي المعروف بالعرقلة الصالح بن رزيك فقال من **قصيدة** ...

[l.20] **رزيك** بضم الراء المهملة وتشديد الزاي المعجمة المكسورة وسكون الياء المثناة من تحتها وبعدها كاف **والله اعلم**

ذكر وزارة العادل رزيك بن الصالح طلائع ابن رزيك بالديار المصرية

كان الصالح طلائع ابن رزيك اوصى الى ولده العادل رزيك وجعل صهره سيف الدين حسين بن ابي الهيجاء الكردي مدبرًا لامر ولده وكان حسين احد الابدال في العبادة والدين والزهادة واحد الافراد في العلم والشجاعة وكان مهيبا معظما في الديار المصرية **ولما** دُفن الصالح طلائع بن رزيك ارسل العاضد العبيدي صاحب الديار المصرية خلع [153b] الوزارة الى رزيك بن صالح وولاه الوزارة مكان والده ولقبه مجد الاسلام الملك العادل امير الجيوش وركب الناس الى الهناء له ولزم سيرة حميدة من اظهار العدل والاحسان وتفقد احوال العامة بنفسه ودبر امور الدولة واستقام امره وكاتبه الاطراف بالطاعة ولما استقرت احوال العادل رزيك ارسل الى عمة العاضد وخنقها بمنديل الى ان ماتت وكانت لما رأت الصالح بن رزيك وقد حمل من القصر وركب ولَوَلَت وقالت هلكنا وكان الصالح بن رزيك لما سقط ابرقت عظامه والقي ابن الشريف نفسه عليه يقيه من السيوف فخلص بذلك [153b, l.11]

[163b, l.12]

ذكر الفتنة الواقعة بين العادل رزيك وزير الديار المصرية وبين شاور السعدي والي قوص والصعيد الأعلى وانتزاع العادل من الوزارة وولاية شاور الوزارة بالديار المصرية وقتل العادل رزيك

كان الصالح طلائع بن رزيك وزير الديار المصرية في مدة وزارته اخذ من الغلمان والمماليك من قويت نفسه بهم واراد ان يبدّل بهم جميع الامراء والاجناد وولاهم الولايات الكبار مع كثرة اهله واقاربه واصهاره الذين كانوا عدة كثيرة لا يحصون وكان قد ولاهم ايضا اعيان الولايات مثل الغربية وولى اخوه بدر الشرقية وشرع يضعّف الجند ويقوّي غلمانه واقاربه فلما امن ودانت له الدنيا ولم يعلم ان الخوف قريب الامن وآخر العافية السقم وطالت وزارته وثقلت وطأته على الجند **وقال** فيه وفي اقاربه القائل ... [1.24]

[1.27] وكان لطلائع غلام يسمى ورد له مائتا مملوك وغلام اسمه يانس له اكثر من ذلك وكان اخوه سلطان مثله وسعادة الاسود وبختيار قريب من ذلك فاستعبدوا الناس وفتكوا فيهم واضعفوهم وكسروا شوكة [164a] الخاص والعام ولم يزل الناس في الضرر والشدة والشر مما يحلّ بهم من غلمان طلائع واقاربه فلما قُتل طلائع وولي ولده العادل رزيك الوزارة كما قدمنا شرحه قوي امر غلمان ابيه مثل ورد ويانس وسعادة الاسود وبختيار وجسروا في ايام رزيك ما لم يجسروا في ايام والده طلائع لان رزيك كان صبيا وطلائع شيخ وقويت شوكتهم وحصل لهم الولايات السنية ومدوا ايديهم الى ظلم الناس واخذ الاموال واغتصابها وضجّ الناس الى الله سبحانه وتعالى ويصل الامر الى العادل رزيك فلا يقدر على دفعه

وكان الصالح طلائع نقل كل ما كان في القصر من الاموال المُدّخرة من تقادم السنين الى داره فلما مات ورث ولده العادل كنوز الارض والاموال لا توصف فما كان يطلب شيئا من المال لان الذي عنده وورثه من ابيه لا يكاد ان ينفد وكان يقنع بما يحمل اليه من خراج الدولة وينسب الى جاري الوزارة والى كلف الدولة ويترك الغلمان يفعلوا ما ارادوا ولا يتعرض اليهم وولي ابن عمه عز الدين حسام الأشمونين فسار سيرة ذميمة وكان رديء الطباع فاجتمع هو وبقية اولاد عمة العادل رزيك اليه واشاروا عليه بعزل الامير شاور السعدي عن قوص والصعيد الاعلى وان يستبدل به غيره او يستعمل بعضهم مكانه وخوّفوه منه ان اقره على عمله وجرت في ذلك امور في اوقات عديدة ثم اطاعهم في عزله فاشار عليه الامير سيف الدين حسين بن ابي الهيجاء الكردي بابقائه فقال رزيك ما انا ابي ولا لي طمع فيما اخذه منه واريده يطأ بساطي فقيل له ما يدخل ابدا فما قبل المشورة وكتب الى شاور كتابا يستدعيه [164b] الى الحضرة فلما وقف الامير شاور على كتاب العادل رزيك اوجس في نفسه خيفة وعزم على خلع الطاعة ثم تماسك وكتب جواب الكتاب كتابا اظهر فيه الرِقّة والاستعطاف ومن بسابق خدمته وقال بعد ذلك ان كان الغرض ان يلي الموضع احدكم فليسير اليه ويتسلمه مني وانا اسير الى القاهرة ما خلا حسام وان كان الغرض تولية غيركم من امراء مصر فانا احق به من جميع الناس وقد سمعتم وصية ابيكم الصالح في حقي وكفى بها واعظاً

فلما وصل الكتاب الى العادل رزيك احضر اولاد عمته واوقفهم على الكتاب فقالوا له ان تركته بعد هذا طمع فيك فلما رآهم مجمعين على ذلك عزم على عزله وكان شاور يسّير الهدايا والحمول الى رزيك ويريد ان يبقى على ولايته وكان الامير سيف الدين حسين بن ابي الهيجاء صهر رزيك يقول له لا تعترض شاور وأقره في ولايته ما دام يظهر لك الطاعة ويسارع الى ما تأمر به من حمل الاموال فكان تارة يرجع الى قوله وتارة يغريه ابن عمته

عز الدين حسام وثلج في معاداة شاور وبلغه عنه القبيح الى ان احضر العادل رزيك الامير نصير الدين بن شيخ الدولة وقيل امير يعرف بابن العسقلاني وقيل امير يقال له ابن الرفعة احد الامراء بالقاهرة واخلع عليه وولاه قوص وكتب على يده كتابا الى الامير شاور بتسليم البلاد اليه وحضوره الى القاهرة

فلما توجه الامير نصير [الدين] ووصل الى إخميم تخوف جانب الامير شاور وقال اكتب اليه كتابا وانظر ما عنده فكتب الى شاور كتابا وارسل طية كتاب العادل رزيك فلما بلغ الامير شاور عزله اضطرب لصرفه فلما وصل اليه كتاب الامير نصير الدين ووقف على كتابه سير اليه يقول ارجع من حيث جئت ولا تعرض نفسك فقد وهبتُك [165a] دمك فرجع ذلك الامير الى القاهرة

واستفسد شاور بعض جند قوص ومن قدر عليه من العربان وجمع غلمانه ومن نهض من امراء المتعينين في قوص واخذ معه ابن ناصر الدولة ياقوت المعروف بفارس الشام وكان قد ظهر له في ديار مصر اسم كبير وصيت عظيم وخرج من قوص بما انضم اليه من العرب حتى وصل البهنساء فبلغ ذلك العادل رزيك فجمع اهله واعلمهم بذلك وقال لابن عمته الامير عز الدين حسام هذا الذي اردتم فخرج حسام لتلقّيه فتوفق العربان جميعها عن شاور وقالوا انّا لا نفسد السلطان ولا نقدم معك وقد جوّزناك ارضنا ولا نقدر على اكثر من ذلك وتفرقوا فعلم الامير شاور انه لا يقدر على تملّك ديار مصر بالذين معه ولا بقي يمكنه الرجوع الى قوص فدخل في جماعة قليلة الى طريق واحات

ولما سمع العادل رزيك بذلك جهّز ورد ويانس وكبار غلمان ابيه فتوجهوا الى البهنساء وعادوا وعليهم كآبة والاخبار تتواتر بوصول شاور ومن معه الى واحات وانه متأهّب للعود وبدأ الزمع يأخذ العادل رزيك وغلمانه وغلمان طلائع والعلم عند الله هذا مع ما كان القوم يعتقدونه ان ملوك الارض لا طاقة لهم بهم وكان الناس يظنون ذلك لما يرونه من شدة بأسهم وقوة شوكتهم وما عندهم من السلاح والغلمان والآلات والكراع والاموال وانضم اليهم ايضا من الناس الذين يختارونهم ويبتغون مسالمتهم وكل منهم يعتقد انه قد يمكّن من الارض ولم يزالوا كذلك الى ان صحّ لهم ان الامير شاور قد توجه في الوجه الغربي على الواحات وعلى القراح في البريّة واخترق تلك البراري الى ان خرج عند تروجة بالقرب من ثغر الاسكندرية فعندها سيّر رزيك العادل عمّه بدر المعروف بفارس المسلمين وكان ذلك نعت لا فِعْل ولقد قيل عنه انه لما خرج من القاهرة الى الخيم التي ضربت له ببركة الحبش لحقه درب من الخوف وعدى بمن معه من الاجناد والعساكر الى برّ الجيزة ونزل في الاعمال الجيزية [165b]

فوصل الخبر ان شاور وصل الى بيوت ابن فريج السنبسي فوجد زوجته [خبيئة] في البيوت وابن فريج غائب وكانت تجير من استجار بها فأجارته فلما وصل ابن فريج ووجده فتحيّر في امره لا تمكنه مشاققة السلطان ولا ان يحقر ذمة زوجته ولما رأته زوجته متحيرًا زجرته وقالت يابا فريج ما لي أراك متحيرًا قال قد وقعت في امر عظيم ان أجرت هذا الرجل ما لي بمشاققة السلطان قدرة ولم ارد افساد جواري فقالت تموت انت واهلك وبنو عمك ولا تفسد الجوار ويقال بين العرب انك افسدتَ حسبك وسلمت جارك هذا ما لا يكون قبائل العرب تُحدث به ابدًا وشجعته فانذر بني عمه [ابن سنبسي] وجمعهم

وكانت سمعة عظيمة في ديار مصر ان فارس الشام بين يدي شاور ولما بلغ بدر فارس المسلمين عم العادل رزيك ذلك ارتعدت فرائصه واضطربت أحشاؤه وعلم انه لا طاقة له به فتأخّر وتقدم شاور بمن معه الى جهة القاهرة وكان أمراء القاهرة قد كاتبوا شاور لاحن في صدورهم على آل رزيك وحسد لما صاروا اليه من الملك فلما قرب شاور من القاهرة خرج اليه الأمراء وبلغ هذا الخبر للعادل رزيك وادركه ما ادرك عمه من الخوف فلما علم الجند بذلك سارع جماعة للتلقي لشاور منهم اولاد الحاجب ومُلهَم وضرغام وهمام وحسام وكانت لهم السمعة العظيمة بالشجاعة والفروسية ورجع كل من كان يلتهب على الخروج وحلّوا عن الخيل ولما خرج العسكر وضرغام لم يتعدّ احد كوم الفضول ولم يزالوا يتردّدون من باب الى باب ثم جمع العادل رزيك امواله وجعلها على اوساط غلمانه في الهمايين وقال لهم اركبوا طريق الشام [165b, l.24]

[166a, l.11]
وسار الى الحوف واستجار بطريف بن مكنون احد امراء العرب فاجاره وحمله في البحر الى مدينة سيدنا ونبينا محمد رسول الله صلى الله عليه وسلم فأقام بها حكي الامير فخر الدين بن شمس الخلافة قال مرض الامير سيف الدين حسين بن ابي الهيجاء مرة بالمدينة على ساكنها افضل الصلاة والسلام فظن انه ميّت فأحضر العلويين

وفرق عليهم جميع ما كان له حتى لم يبق شيئا ثم تعافا فاحتاج الى ان كتب الى مصر الى عند والدي يستجذيه شيئا فارسل اليه بمال وكان الامير سيف الدين حسين لما اراد ان يخرج الى المدينة المشرفة اودع امواله كما قدمنا شرحه وكانت كثيرة ثم حملت اليه لما استقر بالمدينة فانفقها جميعها على اهل المدينة ولم يزل مقيما بالمدينة الى ان توفي ودفن بالبقيع رحمه الله تعالى هذا ما كان من الامير سيف الدين حسين بن ابي الهيجاء

واما العادل رزيك فانه سأل عن الامير سيف الدين بن ابي الهيجاء فقالوا خرج فانقطع قلبه وخرج اقاربه مستترين وخرج هو في اثر اهله متوجها نحو الوجه الشرقي تحت الليل فضّل الطريق فوقع عند اطفيح في بيوت رجل من العرب يعرف بسليمان [166b] ابن النيص اللخمي فقام اليه اهل البيوت وكانوا يصطلون نارا فقبضوا عليه

ودخل الامير شاور القاهرة ومعه خلق كثير ونزل بدار السعيد السعداء التي هي الآن خانقاه برحبة باب العيد هو واولاده طي وشجاع والطاري وقيل ان العادل وقع على عربان يصطلون نارا فقاموا اليه فانهزم الى الجبل الاحمر واخذت العربان غلمانه وما كان معهم من الاموال والجواهر وسمى العرب تلك السنة سنة الخليط لانهم خلطوا الذهب بالجوهر وقيل ان الدنانير كان فيها رباعيات فسموها الخليط بذلك وانفرد العادل رزيك في الجبل الاحمر ولم يدر كيف يتوجه فرأى نارًا فقصدها فوجد عندها جماعة من الرعاة فاستخبرهم عن الطريق فاسترابوا به وشمّوا منه رائحة الطيب فتعلقوا به ورموه عن دابته واخذوا ما كان بقي معه من الجوهر وكان معه من الجوهر ما يزيد قيمته على الف الف دينارا وآل امره معهم الى ان جذبوا خفافه وهو يسحب على الارض عريانا فتقطع ظهره ثم حملوه الى مقدمهم سليمان بن النيص اللخمي **وقيل** ان العادل خرج من القاهرة مع جماعة من غلمانه ومعه عدة بغال موسقة من المال والجواهر والثياب الخاص وما درى كيف يروح فوقع بظاهر اطفيح عند مقدم امير العرب الذي يقال له ابن النيص فأخذو[ا] كل ما معه **وكان** الامير شاور لما خرج العادل رزيك من القاهرة دخلها وتسلمها واخرجت له خلع الوزارة من جهة العاضد صاحب الديار المصرية ولقب بامير الجند واستحلف الامراء لنفسه وجلس للهناء فانشده علم الملك ابن النحاس.... [166b, l.24]

[166b, l.30]
ولما حصل الامير شاور بالقاهرة واستقر امره في الوزارة [167a] استخرج اموال ابن رزيك وودائعه جميعها من الناس [...] ابن النيص اللخمي العادل رزيك وكان يعرفه ويعرف اباه [...] شاور بالقاهرة فلما حصل عنده اكرمه واقام عليه الوظا[ئف] وكان سبب اكرامه له ان شاور طلب من الوزير طلائع بن رزيك تولية قوص في اول امره فامتنع لما يعلم من شاور وقوة نفسه فسأل شاور رزيكا فشفع الى ابيه في امره ولم يزل به حتى ولاه قوص فرأى له شاور ذلك ويقال ان الصالح بن رزيك قال لولده رزيك قد قبلت قولك في شاور واني اعلم انه هو الذي يخرج الامر عنك فكان الامر كما قال واحضر الوزير سليمان بن النيص اللخمي الذي حمل اليه رزيكا وقال له يا ويلك كيف استجزتَ ان تحمل ولد الصالح اليّ وله ولأبيه عليك من الايادي والانعام ما لا يحصر كثرةً ما اظن الصالح فعل بك ذلك وخبأك لولده الاّ مضرّة وانا لا شك انني اخبأك ايضا ذخيرة لولدي ثم امر به فصُلب ونودي عليه هذا جزاء من لا يرعي الجميل وصُلب علي كوم الفضول [167a, l.16]

[167a, l.20]
وقال الطوير اتى واقام العادل رزيك وزيرا سنة وكسرا فما رأى الناس احسن من حاله معهم وسامح الناس بما عليهم من البواقي الثابتة في الدواوين ولم يسبق الى ذلك ولما انهزم من شاور ودخل شاور القاهرة في سنة ثمان وخمسين وخمسمائة وكتب للاجناد والعرب وحواشي القصر من الرواتب والزيادات نظير مالهم عشر مرات وهو غير ظاهر للناس والابواب مغلقة عليه خيفة [l.28]

[167b, l.5]
وقيل لما ولي الامير شاور الوزارة بالديار المصرية واشتدت ولايته وعظمت ومكن اولاده واخوته من الناس وكان له ثلاثة اولاد طي والكامل وسليمان فبسطوا على الناس وتعاظموا عليهم فمجّتهم الانفس وكان الكامل اشدهم فانه استهان جانب الدولة وبسط يده في الاموال وجاوز المقدار في التجبّر والتكبّر وحدّث نفسه بالاستيلاء على الامر وكان الامير مُلهَم واخوه الامير ضرغام من صنائع الصالح بن رزيك فلما شاهدا ميل الناس عن الوزير شاور بسبب اولاده أخذا في مراسلة العادل رزيك بن الصالح طلائع وهو في السجن والعمل في اعادته الى الوزارة واتصل ذلك بولد شاور طي فدخل على ابيه شاور وقال له انت غافل وملهم وضرغام يفسدان امرك

وينقضان ولايتك وقد شرعا في امر رزيك واستحلفا له جماعة من الامراء ولا يمكن تلافي حالك الا بقتل رزيك فقال له شاور يا بني لا تلتفت الي ما قيل وتمهل في امرك ولا تكشف سرّك الى احد فقال له لا بد من قتل رزيك فاذا قتلته امنت فقال له شاور ان والد هذا رزيك أولاني جميلا وبسببه حللت هذا المحلّ فتركه ولده ودخل على رزيك فقتله في سجنه وسمع ابوه ذلك فقامت قيامته وكان ما سنذكره ان شاء الله تعالى وقيل ان ذلك جميعه كان في سنة سبع وخمسين السنة الماضية [168a] والاظهر ان ذلك كان في سنة ثمان وخمسين هذه السنة كما قدمنا شرحه والله اعلم

ذكر اتفاق الامراء بالديار المصرية على محاربة الوزير شاور وهروبه الى الشام ووزارة ضرغام بالديار المصرية

كان الوزير الصالح طلائع بن رزيك وزير الديار المصرية أنشأ امراء يقال لهم البرقية يقال لمقدمهم ضرغام وكان فارسا كاتبا فلما نمى اليه خبر قتل العادل رزيك بن الصالح طلائع بن رزيك جمع رفقته واخيه ملهم ومن استحلفاه من الامراء وزحفا بالعساكر الى الوزير شاور **وقيل** ان سبب قيام الامراء على شاور ما كان يعتمده اولاده في حقهم وما كان يظهر من امر الكامل **وقيل** كان سبب ذلك ان شاور لما ولي الوزارة نقص ارزاق الجند وعسفهم فتعاهدوا على قتله **ويقال** ان الكامل بن الوزير شاور عمل له مظلة كانت تحمل على رأسه كما تحمل للخلفاء وكتب بذلك الى ابيه شاور فلم يصنع شيئا فقامت الامراء عليه

وقيل كان ضرغام في إبتداء امره احد حجّاب امير الجيوش الوزير شاور وكان له عصبة واهل وكان يسكن بالبرقية وفيها جماعة من الاجناد وكانوا يعظموه ويطيعوه وكان ذا حظّ وافر من العقل مع جودة الخط وحسن العبارة وكان يحب العلم والادب ويميل الى الشعر ويحب الشعراء وبسببه حصل التقدم للقاضي الفاضل فلما اراد ان يثور بالوزير شاور جمع جموعا كثيرة ونازع شاور في الوزارة في شهر رمضان من شهور سنة ثمان وخمسين هذه السنة وظهر امره وانهزم الوزير شاور منه الى الشام ولما هرب شاور وخرج من باب القاهرة وتبعه اولاده ادركهم العساكر فقتلوا طيا ابن شاور وكان الذي لحقه وقتله غنيم غلام العادل رزيك ولم يهنأ طي بالحياة بعد قتل رزيك وقتلوا [168b] اخاه سليمان بن شاور واسروا الكامل بن شاور فأخذه ملهم واعتقله عنده ومنع اخاه ضرغاما من قتله وجعله عنده في داره وحفظ له جميلا كان قد فعله معه ولما انهزم شاور وقصد الشام وقُتل من قُتل من اولاده وأُسر من أُسر تولي الامير ضرغام الوزارة واخلع عليه العاضد صاحب الديار المصرية ولقّبه بالملك المنصور واستحلف له الاجناد وكانت وزارة شاور هذه سبعة اشهر

وقال القاضي ناصر الدين شافع بن علي سبط القاضي محي الدين بن عبد الظاهر في تأليفه نظم السلوك في تواريخ الخلفاء والملوك وبعض اهل التاريخ ما صيغته سار شاور وزير العاضد صاحب مصر الى دمشق لست مضين من شهر ربيع الاول سنة ثمان وخمسين وخمسمائة واجتمع بالملك العادل نور الدين صاحب الشام ووصف له الديار المصرية وضُعف اهلها وضمن له ان بعث معه عسكرا اخذها له والاظهر القول الاول **وكان** الوزير شاور بعد هزيمته من مصر واستيلاء ضرغام عليها وتحقق شاور قتل ولديه سار قاصدا الى الشام الى خدمة الملك العادل نور الدين محمود بن الملك المنصور عماد الدين اتابك زنكي صاحب الشام ملتجئا اليه ومستجيرا به فلما وصل الى بُصرى بلغ خبره الى الملك العادل نور الدين فندب جماعة الى تلقّيه وانزله في جوسق الميدان الاخضر واحسن في ضيافته واكرامه ولم يخرج الملك العادل نور الدين الى لقائه فلما كان بعد سابعة من تقدم شاور الى دمشق احضر الملك العادل نور الدين ابن الصوفي وجماعة من وجوه الدمشقيين وقال لهم اخرجوا الى هذا الرجل وسلموا عليه وعرّفوه اعذارنا في التقصير في حقه وأسألوه فيما قدم وما غرضه وحاجته فان كان ورد علينا مختارا للاقامة افردنا له من جهاتنا ما يكفيه ونقوم بأربه ونكون عونا له على زمانه ونعينه على التوفر على الجهاد في سبيل الله تعالى وان كان ورد لغير ذلك فيفصح عن حاجته وغرضه لنبلغه منها امنيته

فخرج الجماعة اليه بالرسالة فشكر احسان الملك [169a] العادل نور الدين الواصل اليه واثنى علي جميله المنثال عليه وسكت عن ما وراء ذلك فسأله القوم الجواب فقال اذا لم تثبت المرامى [...] فعاد القوم الى الملك العادل نور الدين وعرفوه ما وعوه منه ورووه عنه فامرهم بالعود اليه من غد ذلك اليوم وسماع ما يقول لهم فعادوا اليه وطلبوا الجواب فسكت ايضا وأطال ثم قال ان رأى نور الدين أطال الله بقاءه الاجتماع بي فله عُلُوا الرأي فعادوا الى الملك العادل نور الدين وعرفوه مقالته فأجاب نور الدين الى ان يكون الاجتماع بالميدان على ظهر

الدواب وركب الملك العادل نور الدين من الغد في وجوه دولته وخواص مملكته في احسن زي واكمل شارة فلما دخل الميدان ركب شاور من الجوسق والتقيا في وسط الميدان بالتحية فقط ولم يترجل احد منهما لصاحبه ثم سارا من موضع اجتماعهما وهو نصف الميدان الى آخره ثم انفصلا من هناك فكان مقدار اجتماعهما مقدار سيرهما في نصف الميدان ولم يُعلم ما جرى بينهما وعاد الملك العادل نور الدين الى القلعة وأخذ من وقته ذلك في جمع العساكر واختيار الأبطال وجمع السلاح واعطاء الاجناد وكان اسد الدين شيركوه بن شاذي بن مروان عمّ السلطان صلاح الدين يوسف بن والد الملوك نجم الدين ابي الشكر ايوب بن شاذي بن مرو[ا]ن في الرحبة وكانت له فارسل الملك العادل نور الدين واستدعاه منها وكان قد تيمّن باسد الدين وتبرك بيمن نفسه لانه لم يرسله في امر الا نجح ولم يولجه في مضيق الا تفتح وامره ان [169b] يستصحب ما يحتاجه للسفر فانه لا مقام له فورد عليه اسد الدين شيركوه بجميع ما يحتاجه للسفر وكان ما نذكره ان شاء الله تعالى [169b, l.3]

[170a, l.4]

وقال غيره بلغ ضرغام ان جماعة من الأمراء قد حسدوه واستصغروه وكاتبوا شاور وهو في الشام يستدعونه فأخذ في اعمال الحيلة عليهم واحضرهم الى دار الوزارة ليلاً وهم الخلواص واسد العاري واولاد منير الدولة وابو اصبع وعلي بن الزيد وعين الزمان بن عين الزمان وكمن لهم في خزائن الدار الرجال بالسلاح وكان كلما دخل عليه أمير قال اذهبوا به الى الخزانة واخلعوا عليه فيذهبوا به ويقتلوه وارسل خلف قوم آخرين كانوا غيابا عن القاهرة فقتلهم جميعا ولم يعرض لأموال الذين قتلهم ولا لمنازلهم

وقال صاحب نظم السلوك في تواريخ الخلفاء والملوك قتل الضرغام من الأمراء الذين كانوا مع شاور ما يزيد عن سبعين أميرا سوى اتباعهم **وقال غيره** يقال انه قتل منهم تسعين أميرا **ويقال** انه جعلهم في توابيت وكتب اسم كل واحد على تابوته وامر ان يسلّم كل واحد الى اهله وكان في جملة من قتل ثلاثة اخوة من اكابر الأمراء وان أمّهم وقفت له وقالت يا ضرغام قتلت اولادي ايتم الله اولادك فقال لها يا حرمة ما فرحتُ بما فعلت بهم اليوم لهم وغدا لنا فكان ذلك اكبر الاسباب في هلاكه لانه اضعف عسكر مصر بقتل الأمراء ثم ان ضرغاما كتب كتابا الى الملك العادل نور الدين صاحب الشام على يد علم الدين بن النحاس يظهر فيه الطاعة ويعرض لخذلان شاور فاظهر الملك العادل [170b] نور الدين لعلم الدين ابن النحاس القبول في الظاهر وهو مع شاور في الباطن وأجاب عن الكتاب وانفصل علم الدين ابن النحاس عن دمشق فلما حصل بظاهر الكرك أخذه فليب بن الرفيق الفرنجي وحصل على جميع ما كان معه وانهزم علم الدين ابن النحاس بنفسه وتوجه الى الساحل وسار الى مصر والله اعلم [l.6]

[184a, l.1]

ذكر مسير الوزير شاور وعساكر الشام الى الديار المصرية وقتل الوزير ضرغام واستقرار شاور بوزارة الديار المصرية وغدره بالعساكر الشامية

كنا ذكرنا ان الملك العادل نور الدين محمود صاحب الشام امر بتجهيز عساكر لتسيير صحبة الوزير شاور الى الديار المصرية وانه استدعي الأمير اسد الدين شيركوه من الرحبة وفي يوم وروده عليه وجد العسكر مزاج العلل مبررا للسفر فدخل الى الملك العادل نور الدين واجتمع به خلوة وافضى اليه باشياء في أمر مصر فكان هوي اسد الدين شيركوه في ذلك وعنده من اشجاعه وقوة النفس ما لا يبالي مخافة **وكان** شاور اطمع الملك العادل نور الدين صاحب الشام في اموال مصر ورغّبه في ملكها وان يكون من قِبَله فيها ولما بلغ شاور استتمام امر العساكر سأل عن المقدم عليه فقيل له الأمير اسد الدين شيركوه فلم يطب له ذلك لانه ظن ان تكون التقدمة له فيحكم في العساكر بمراده فلما زوحم بهذا العود سقط في يده وفت في عضده ولم يجد بدا من المسير وسارا جميعا بالعسكر في جمادى الأولى من شهور سنة تسع وخمسين وخمسمائة هذه السنة **قاله** قاضي القضاة شمس الدين احمد بن خلكان **وقال غيره** كان ذلك عشرين جمادى الآخرة من هذه السنة **وقيل** في سنة ثمان وخمسين

وسار معهما الملك العادل نور الدين الى طرف بلاد الاسلام مما يلي بلاد الفرنج في بقية عسكر دمشق ليشغل الفرنج عن التعرض للأمير اسد الدين شيركوه فكان قصارى الفرنج حفظ بلادهم من الملك العادل نور الدين ثم فارق اسد الدين الملك العادل نور الدين وسار بمن معه الى الديار المصرية وكانت الطريق اذ ذاك شرقي الكرك والشوبك الى عقبة ايلا ثم الى صدر وسويس ثم الى البركة التي على باب القاهرة المحروسة **وقيل** لما وصلت العساكر الى اطراف البلاد المصرية نزلوا على تل في الجوف قريب من بلبيس يعرف بتل بسطة

وبلغ الملك المنصور[184b] ضرغام وزير الديار المصرية خبر وصول شاور والأمير اسد الدين شيركوه بالعساكر الشامية فجمع الأمراء واستشارهم فاشار شمس الخلافة محمد بن مختار ان يجتمع العساكر ويخرج جريدة ويلقى العساكر الشامية بصدر وهو على يومين من القاهرة فانهم لا يبيتون لان القوم يخرجوا من البرية ضعفا لمكان قِلة الماء عليهم لانهم يحملون الماء من الايلة مسيرة ثلاثة ايام فلم يروا ذلك ومالوا الى ان يلقوهم على بلبيس **فامر** الوزير ضرغام الأمراء بالخروج فخرجوا في احسن زي واكمل عدة وجائوا حتى احاطوا بالتل الذي كان الامير اسد الدين شيركوه نازلا عليه ولما عاين اسد الدين شيركوه كثرة العساكر المصرية وانهم قد ملكوا عليه الجهات وسدوا منافذ الطرقات قال للوزير شاور يا هذا لقد اوهقتَنا وغررتَنا وقلت انه ليس بمصر عساكر فجئنا في هذه [الشرذمة] فقال لا يهولنَّك ما تشاهد من كثرة الجموع فاكثرها الحاكة والفلاحون الذين يجمعهم الطبل وتفرقهم العصا فما ظنك بهم اذا حمى الوطيس وكلبت الحرب واما الأمراء فان كتبهم عندي وعهودهم معي ويستظهر لك ذلك اذا لقيناهم ثم قال اريد ان تأمر العساكر بالاستعداد والركوب فنادى اسد الدين بالركوب فثارت العساكر الى السلاح وركبوا وترتبوا للحرب فنهاهم شاور عن القتال واصطفت عساكر مصر للحرب ايضا

وحمي النهار فالتهب الحديد على اجساد الرجال وانتظر اهل مصر ان العساكر الشامي تخرج الى القتال فلم تخرج منهم احد فأمر اكثرهم اصحابهم بضرب الخيم الصغار والصواوين ونزلوا عن الخيول وجلسوا في الظل وخلع اكثرهم السلاح **ولما** عاين ذلك الوزير شاور امر الناس بالحملة وشنّ الغارة عليهم وكان اسعد الأمراء من ركب فرسه الجواد واطلق عنانه منهزما وتركوا خيمهم واموالهم ليس لها حافظ فاحتوي عليها اصحاب الامير اسد الدين شيركوه وغنموا جميع ما تركوه وساق اسد الدين وشاور [185a] في اثرهم قاصدان القاهرة **وكان** في قلب عسكر المصِريين ناصر الدين اخو ضرغام وفي الميمنة شمس الخلافة محمد بن مختار وفي الميسرة فارس المسلمين فأُسر شمس الخلافة وجماعة من المصريين ولما قاربوا القاهرة هرب جميع من كان معهم في الاسر لان الوزير شاور لم يمكن من تقييدهم ولم يحيط عليهم ونزلوا على القاهرة اواخر جمادى الآخرة **وقيل** في اواخر جمادى الاولى من هذه السنة

ورأيت في جزء لطيف سمّاه مؤلفه "اخبار الدولة المصرية وما جرى بين الملوك والخلفاء من الفتن والحروب من ايام الآمر الى ايام شيركوه" ولم يُذكر اسم مؤلفه فنقلتُ منه ان الصالح بن رزيك وزير الديار المصرية كان قد قرر للفرنج مالا يحمل اليهم في كل سنة من جواري المستخدمين ومن ولايات الأمراء وغيرهم وكان مقداره ثلاثة وثلاثين الف دينار في كل سنة فلما مات طلائع وولي الوزارة بعده ولده العادل رزيك ونزعه شاور من الوزارة وتمكن منها حِمل من الاموال التي كانت لطلائع ابن رزيك ولولده ما يزيد عن الخمسمائة الف دينار وحصل لاولاده وهم طَي [و]الكامل مال عظيم وآلات وكراع وسلاح والطاري كان في المنزلة عظيما وكان له ايضا مال عظيم وحصل لهم في ولايتهم من الاموال ما لم يحصل لاحد قبلهم وكان شاور كلما يحصل له في ايام ولايته من المال لا يترك في داره منه الدرهم الفرد بل يودعه عند العربان ويقضى حوائجهم ويدبر امورهم وكانت العربان قد كثرت اموالها حتى قيل عنهم انهم كانوا يكيلوه بالقَدَح ويتحدثون ان فلان له قدحين وفلان له ثلاثة اقداح وفلان له كذا وكذا [185b] وكان العربان في وزارته لا يفارقون باب الفتوح وباب النصر

وولي احد اخوته الشرقية والاخر الغربية واستقر له الملك ودانت له الدنيا واستولى العربان في تلك السنة على غلة الحوف ونهبوها وطمعوا في المقطعين فلم ينكر عليهم الوزير شاور لانه كان في نفسه ان يجعلهم له ردًا وعدّة كما جعلهم الوزير رضوان قبله وكان شاور من جملة أمراء الوزير رضوان فحفظ تلك الصورة التي كان رضوان يفعلها وتواصلت رسل الفرنج يطلبون العادة من الوزير شاور فلما كان شهر رمضان من سنة ثمان وخمسين وخمسمائة وقد مضى من وزارته ثمان شهور وايام اغرى شاور ولده طي بالعادل رزيك بن الصالح طلائع وكان شيء اوقعه الله في قلوبهم من الخوف وشنعوا ان رزيك برد القيد واراد الهروب وان اخاه غمز عليه فدخل طي الى رزيك فقتله ووقع في قلب شاور الخوف من ضرغام اخو ملهم صاحب بابه وتكاشفوا في ذلك الى ان استحلف شاور ضرغام انه لا يغدره ولا يخون ولا يمالئ وكان شاور هم ان يقبض على ضرغام

فبات في دار السلطان فلما اصبح ركب الى داره وجمع غلمانه وارسل الى ابن شاهنشاه واسد العاري وعين الزمان وكان قد وصل من الحجاز بعد قتل طلائع والخلواص واجتمعوا هم واصحابهم وصبيان البرقية فصاروا في عسكر كبير وضرغام معهم فخيل شاور وحقق ظنه ولم يشك انهم جائوا للقبض عليه فلم يكذب خبر حتى

خرج من باب النصر كأنه كان متاهبا لذلك ومعه ولداه الكامل والطاري وحمل معه ما قدر عليه من المال ثم قتل ولده [186a] الكامل طي بين القصرين واقامت جثته يومين ملقاةً وكذلك ابن اخيه ورجل يسمى حسان كان عنده بمنزلة الولد فقتل ايضا ونهبت دار شاور ودور اولاده ودور اصهاره وانسلّ من الملك كأنه لم يكن وذهب جميع ما حصل لهم من آل رزيك وسار شاور فوصل الى الاعمال الفاقوسية فاقام عند بني منظور وغيرهم ولم يرسل اليه ضرغام احد وكانت وزارته حينئذ تسع شهور

ووزر ضرغام واخلع عليه وثبتت قاعدته فلم يشعر الا والفرنج قد توجهوا الى ديار مصر وبلغه انهم قد وصلوا السدير فاخرج اخاه همام وكان شجاعا ووصل الى الفرنج والتقي معهم وصبر وهزمهم وقتل خلقا من الفرنج وزحف الملاعين الى حصن بلبيس وملكوا بعض السور فردّهم عنه همام وبنوا كنانة واما العسكر فان اكثره طلب الحوف بحكم ان العربان كانت تحول بينهم وبين القاهرة وكل من ظفروا به قالوا منهزم فقتلوه وأخذوا ما معه والذي طلب الحوف من العسكر حل بهم من فلاحين البلاد اشد مما حصل من العرب وقُتل خلق كثير وعاد العسكر خاسرين بهذ السبب وعاد الفرنج الى الشام وكان شاور فيما بين بلبيس والقاهرة من الشرق بالعرب الذين كانوا معه لم يكن مع العسكر ولا مع الفرنج بل انه ربما كان مع المسلمين ونفعهم

وكان خبره قد وصل الى الفرنج بان السلطان يحول بينكم وبين القاهرة ورحل الفرنج عن بلبيس وعادوا الى الشام بمن اسروه من المسلمين وفيهم احد الامراء [186b] وهو القطورى وكان من اكابر الدولة ولما عاد همام اخي الوزير ضرغام الى القاهرة بعد رحيل الفرنج كان هو واخوه ضرغام متفقان كأنهما شركا في الوزارة كل منهما يُوَقِّع ويقطع ويوصل ومهما فعله هذا امضاه هذا ولم يحصل بضرغام في وزارته من المال شيء لان المال الذي كان يحصل للوزراء يهب ويتلف ويؤخذ فجعل هو كل ما يحصل له يتلفه ويوهبه وينعم به ولا يذخر منه شيء ويصانع به الامراء عن نفسه لانه كان لا يطمع بالوزارة فكان يستجلب قلوب الناس اليه بكل ممكن

وكان قد **وُلي** مرتفع الخلواص ثغر الاسكندرية وكان قد اشمأزت نفسه منه ومن رفقته ابن شاهنشاه وكان اكبرهم واجلهم وعين الزمان وأسد العاري وابن الزيد وذكر انه دبر من يقفز على الخلواص في الاسكندرية وان مرتفع الخلواص ظفر بالقوم الذين بعثهم ضرغام وقررهم واقرّوا وكان في نفس كل واحد من هؤلاء الأمراء المذكورين انه احق بالوزارة من ضرغام لانه كان اقلّهم لم يذكر قط كما ذكروا فحسنت لمرتفع الخلواص نفسه ان جمع غلمانه ومن معه من القبائل وكان مرتفع الخلواص قد احسّ ان اهل الاسكندرية عقيب ما كان جرى بينهم وبين وال كان عندهم يعرف بابن الحاجب وقيامهم عليه وقتل غلمانه وكاتبه ونهب داره وجميع ما كان معه لما عاملهم بالسيرة القبيحة وسار الامير مرتفع الخلواص وخرج من الاسكندرية ووصلت الاخبار بذلك الى الوزير ضرغام فما تكلم حتى قبض على اسد العاري وابن شاهنشاه وابن عين الزمان ثم سيّر اخوه الامير همام بالعسكر ليلقوا مرتفع الخلواص

وبعد خروج العسكر من القاهرة بطش الوزير ضرغام باسد العاري وابن شاهنشاه وابن عين الزمان وقتلهم [187a] ورمى جثثهم خارج الطريق فلما اصبح الناس ورأوا القتلى اشاعوا ذلك وسارت به الاخبار ووصل خبرهم الى الامير مرتفع الخلواص فبطلت مضاربه لانه كان بلا شك وعدوه الجماعة قبل خروجه من الاسكندرية بالنصرة فسبقهم الوزير ضرغام وقتلهم وقبل وصول العسكر وهمام الى البحيرة والتعدية تفلل جمع الامير مرتفع الخلواص لما بلغهم قتل الامراء وخروج العسكر الى الامير مرتفع الخلواص ولما رأى العربان تفلل اصحاب الامير مرتفع الخلواص وصار في طائفة يسيرة طمعوا فيه وقبضوا عليه من سنبس وتنصّحوا به الى الامير همام بعد ان قبض همام على قوم كانوا معه في العسكر منهم ابن الزيد وعاد الامير همام بالعسكر وقد ظفر بالامير مرتفع الخلواص معه اسير فلما وصل الى القاهرة فرح اخوه الوزير ضرغام وبادر بمرتفع الخلواص وضرب رقبته خارج باب زويلة وصلبه

واقام الوزير ضرغام واخوته على ما ذكرنا ورسل الفرنج يتردد في طلب مال الهدنة وهو يدافع عنها ويعيق الرسل وتارة يقول لهم ما عندي الا السيف ولا اهادن وتارة يقول اهادن حتى وقعت طيور طيرها اخوه الامير حسام من بلبيس وكان والي الشرقية وكان يظلم الامة قبل وزارة اخيه ضرغام وفي حال الوزارة اشد وكان بقية اخوته اصلح منه في ذلك فلما قرأ الوزير ضرغام ما في بطائق الطيور وجدها تتضمن وصول الوزير شاور

والامير اسد الدين شيركوه التركي الى الكرائم ومعهما من الاتراك خلق كثير فانزعج الوزير ضرغام وتأهب لتسيير العساكر[187b] واصبح الناس يوم التاسع والعشرين من جمادى الاولى سنة تسع وخمسين هذه السنة وقد شاع ذلك بينهم فخافت انفسهم وابتدوا ينتقلوا من مكان الى مكان على عادتهم ويحصلوا الماء الحلو والاقوات والاحطاب ووقع على الناس الخوف

وتوجه الامير همام بالعساكر في اول جمادى الاخرة سنة تسع وخمسين هذه السنة وخرج معه من العساكر مقدار ستة آلاف فارس واكثر بالخيول المسوّمة والدروع المثمّنة والسلاح الذي يعجز عنه سائر الدول ورأي الناس ذلك العسكر ومسارعتهم وخروجهم بصدور مسترحة وآمال منفسحة فظنوا انهم منصورين لانهم رأوا عسكرا لم يُرَ مثله ووصل العسكر الى بلبيس يوم الاحد ثاني جمادى الآخرة المذكور ووصل الوزير شاور والامير شيركوه بالعساكر الشامية يوم الاثنين ثالث جمادى الآخرة المذكور والتقوا يوم الثلاثاء رابع جمادى الآخرة المذكور

فسمع بعض الترك من عسكر الشام يقول والله لقد أيسنا من الحياة لما رأينا من كثرة العساكر قوم ركاب ونحن رجالة وقوم لبس ونحن عراة ومستريحين ونحن تعبانين وجياع وعطاش قد وقف اكثرنا وماتت خيولنا وفينا من مات برذونه وفينا من ورمت رجليه ونحن على حال مقاربة ولقد لمنا شاور وقلنا له يا رجل انت تقول ان سلطانك ارسل اليك يستدعيك وان جند مصر ما يقابلوك وهم راضون بك وبوصولك ورميتّنا في هذه المصيبة التي فعلت بنا فقال اثبتوا فالنصر من عند الله وكذا كان فلما رجعوا الينا طلعنا على ربوة واشرفنا منهم على خوف عظيم لكثرتهم

فلما التقى الفريقان حمل الامير ناصرالدين همام والامير فخر الدين حسام اخوي الوزير ضرغام في عسكر الامير شيركوه والوزير شاور وخرج الامير همام من الجانب بعد ان لحقه جراح من السهام والتفت [188a] يطلب معه احد من العسكر فلم يجده وسبب ذلك ان ميسرة عسكر الامير همام كان فيها العرب فلما رأوا النشّاب انهزموا وانهزم العسكر بهزيمتهم وعاد جميعه الى بلبيس وعسكر شاور في اعقابهم ودخلوا جميعهم من باب الشام والترك في اثرهم فاسروا منهم جماعة واخذوا جميع ما معهم من الزمول والخيول والسلاح والالات والعدد ولم يفلت منهم الا الامير همام فانه وصل الى القاهرة سحر يوم الاربعاء خامس جمادى الاخرة المذكور مجروح ومعه سهام لم تخرج وهو على انحس قضية

واما اخوه الامير فخر الدين حسام فانه اختفي في بلبيس في مكان دل عليه بعض الكنانة لما كانوا يلقون من ظلمه فهذه عاقبة الظلم فأُسر وقيد وحمل مع الوزير شاور وثم شاور وشيركوه ووصلوا الى القاهرة بكرة يوم الخميس السادس من جمادى الآخرة المذكور ونزلوا عند التاج بظاهر القاهرة المحروسة وكان شاور قد ارسل بعض الترك الى منية الشيرج لحفظ من بها من الجند لا يؤذوهم وكان العسكر قد انبثّ في الاملاك والمنية يريدوا ما يأكلوا ويعلفوا خيلهم وكان الوزير ضرغام قد كاتب سائر الاعمال يستنفرهم ويستدعيهم ويخبرهم الخبر وكان الناس قد خافوا من الترك خوفا عظيما وقالوا غربا[ء] لا نأمن ان يحدثوا حوادثا لا نعرفها ولا لاحد باخلاقهم طاقة فلما وصل الوزير شاور بمن معه من العساكر ونزل على الخرقانية وما يليها ضم الوزير ضرغام جميع الراجل والريحانية والجيوشية وغيرهم الى داخل القاهرة فلما نزل شاور بمن معه من الجيوش على التاج بظاهر القاهرة اقام اياما حتى استراح من كان معه وان كانوا قد استراحوا وحصل لهم من وقعة بلبيس من الخيول والالات والاسلحة [188b] ما استغنوا به وطمعوا وتعلقت آمالهم فجمعهم الوزير شاور واستحلفهم واخذ عليهم العهود والمواثيق انهم لا يغدروه ولا يسلموه ولا ينهزموا الا عن غلبة وان يكونوا عونا له ونصرة

وكانت طوالعه ابداً من العربان تطارد عسكر الوزير ضرغام في ارض الطبّالة فلما وقع الطراد ظن اهل المنية ان عسكر القاهرة فيهم قوة ولهم نصرة فعطفوا على عسكر شاور وقتلوا الترك فامر الوزير شاور بنهب منية الشيرج فنهبت وحلّ باهلها اشد النكال واقام شاور بمن معه في ناحية الخرقانية وشبرا ودمنهور اياما وكان بعض من معه من العربان يطارد بعض عسكر ضرغام في ارض الطبّالة ويخرج العسكر فلا يتعدا كوم الفضول **وتوجه** الوزير شاور بمن معه الى القاهرة من ناحية المقسم فخرج اليهم عسكر الوزير ضرغام وحملوا عليهم حملة واحدة فهزموهم هزيمة عظيمة ففرح الوزير ضرغام بذلك فرحا عظيما واحضر قاضي القضاة وقال له تحمل جميع ما في المودع من الاموال فقال يا مولانا هذه اموال الايتام وكيف يُحمَل فقال الامر اشد من ذلك فحملها فلما علم الناس ان ضرغام اخذ اموال الايتام علموا ضعفه وعلموا انه هالك من عدة وجوه اولها اخذ اموال الايتام والثاني قتل من لم يذنب والثالث الايمان الحانثة

ثم ان الوزير شاور رحل وطلب بركة الحبش وتقدم الى مسجد سعد الدولة ثم قصد الرصد وما يليه وملك مصر واقام بها اياما ولم يكن للوزير ضرغام ولا لمن معه منعة تردّه وجعل يركب في مصر ويطمن اهلها ويمنع الاتراك عن اذيتهم وكان ضرغام والعسكر قد تواعدوا اهل مصر وقالوا ان ظفرنا بشاور لنحرقنّ مصر بما فيها لانكم [189a] مكنتموه من دخولها وبايعتموه وشاريتموه فقالوا لهم انتم ارباب السيف وفيكم الخليفة والسلطان والعساكر لو منعتموه ما وصل الينا لما عجزتم عنه استولي على البلد واستعانوا الى الله تعالى وسألوه كفاية شرهم ثم ان شاور اقام بعد ذلك اياما ونزل الى اللوق وطارد خيل الوزير ضرغام وخلت المنصورة والهلالية وتقدم الى الانسية فمسك عنهم رعاية للفقيه رسلان وعثمان وقاتل الناس قتالا خفيفا ثم تقدم هو والامير شيركوه الى باب سعادة وباب القنطرة ودار الامير جبريل واوقعوا النار في دار ابن دلال ووصلت النار الى اللؤلؤة وكانت وقعة عظيمة مشهورة بين الفريقين قتل من العسكرين خلق لا يعلم عددهم الا الله عز وجل وجرحوا فلما كان الليل اجتمع المقدمون من رجالة الريحانية وقالوا نحن نقاتل دون عسكر مصر يلقون بنا ولا يخرجون فان كانت الغلبة لنا أي شيء جرا عليهم وان كانت علينا كانوا سالمين وقد فنى منا رجال كثير وتقرر ان يخرجوا الى شاور ويستأمنوا معه وقد قيل ان الوزير شاور كان يرسل اليهم كل ليلة ويعدهم ويستفسدهم

وقيل ان الخليفة لما رأى الوزير ضرغام وقد ولّت عنه السعادة وعلم انه لا يفلح وقوي عليه الترك ارسل الى الرماة وقال لا يرمى احد منكم بسهم واحد ولما اصبح خرج الراجل الى الوزير شاور وسلموا انفسهم اليه فاكرمهم وفرح وقويت نفسه ووقعت على اهل القاهرة خمدة وبردت نيّاتهم ورجع كل من كان يلتهب على الخروج وحلّوا عن الخيل وخرج العسكر والوزير ضرغام ولم يتعدا احد كوم الفضول ولم يزالوا يترددون من باب الى باب وكان فيهم فرسان مشهورين بالحرب مثل ابن ملهم اخو الوزير وابن فرج الله وحازم بن ابي الخليل وجماعة وكانوا يطاردون من يطاردهم وكان ضرغام لما كتب يستنفر الناس لم يصل اليه من سائر النواحي [189b] سوى طلحة وجعفر وصلوا في ثلثمائة فارس وكانوا يصطلوا [؟] الطراد والحرب فاهلكهم الترك اصحاب شاور بالنشاب وعادوا الى اهاليهم خاسرين

ولما رأى الوزير ضرغام هذا الامر وشدّته امر بضرب البوقات والطبول على الاسوار لاجتماع الناس فلم يخرج احد ولم يجتمع احد وتفلل الناس وكان يظن ان الجند عند اخيه فبعث ينظر من عنده فلم يجد سوى اربعين فارسا من الاهل والامراء كلهم قد جلسوا في دورهم فعاد الوزير ضرغام الى باب الذهب وحوله خمسمائة فارس فوقف تحت الطاق وطلب الخليفة ان يفتح الطاق على جاري عادته ويكلمه ويشير اليه بما يفعل وكانت هذه عادة خليفة مصر يامر وينهى من الطاق ويعد بالنصر او يمنع من القتال ففي الحال بلغ شاور ذلك فامر ولده سليمان الطاري ان يدخل من باب القنطرة ولا يتعدا خطوة واحدة بل يملك الباب ويقف فلما طال على الوزير ضرغام الامر نادي اريد امير المؤمنين يكلمني لاسأله عن ما افعل فلم يجبه احد فصاح يا مولانا كلمني يا مولانا ارني وجهك الكريم يا مولانا بحرمة اجدادك على الله وهو يبكي فلم يجبه احد

فقويت الشمس وتنقّل الى ناحية الظل حتى انقضى من النهار خمس ساعات [اومأ] الى احد غلمانه وقال له اركض في القصبة وصح ما كانت إلا مكيدة على شاور وقد قتل الريحانية جماعة من الترك اصحاب شاور فلما سمع الناس ذلك اخذوا خيلهم وعادوا الى القاهرة وكانت الخيل والرجالة يهرعون من كل جانب من الحارات والازقّة مثل السيل العظيم فلما وصلوا ورأوا الوزير ضرغام على تلك الحالة والطاق لم تفتح والخليفة لم يكلمه [190a] بكلمة واحدة عاد كل من اسرع كالحين يقولون ارجعوا فهي كذّابة والغلبة لشاور فبقي الوزير ضرغام على حاله الى التاسعة من النهار ولم يبق معه سوى ثلاثين فارسا فأيس من الحياة

وراسل الوزير شاور العاضد بالله في اصلاح الحال وان يأذن له في الدخول الى القاهرة فأذن له فارسل شاور الى ولده ان يدخل القاهرة فدخل وسمع الوزير ضرغام صوت بوق عجيب لم يسمع مثله من ابواق الترك اصحاب ولد شاور فإذا به من ناحية التبّانين فسأل فقالوا له الطاري ابن شاور قد زحف اليك فذهب على وجهه منهزما وطلب باب زويلة وتحقق الناس هزيمته فتخطفوا ممن كان معه بعض العدد وعطعطوا عليه ولأجل هذا سُمُوا المنافقين يفرحون بالمصائب ويشمتون ويحسدون على النعم وتارة يدعون للامير بغير سبب وتارة يدعون عليه واخوان من دامت له النعم

ولما خرج ضرغام من باب زويلة والعامة تلعنه وتصيح عليه فالتحقه رجل من اهل الشام فقال له ضرغام اوصلني الى الامير اسد الدين شيركوه ولك مناك فلم يقبل منه وحمل عليه فطعنه فارداه ونزل اليه **فاحتزّ رأسه** عند مشهد السيدة نفيسة بنت الحسن بن زيد بن الحسن بن علي بن ابي طالب رضي الله عنهم في سلخ جمادى الآخرة **وقيل** في سلخ جمادى الاولى من هذه السنة **وقيل** قُتل ضرغام عند ركن بستان عباس قبالة الجامع الطولوني **قتله** ابن عرب ومضى برأسه الى شاور فامر ان يطاف به القاهرة ونعوذ بالله من تحوّل الحال الى الشر **وقيل** خرج ضرغام من القاهرة بعد غلق ابواب القصر في وجهه حتى وصل الى الجسر الاعظم فقُتل هناك قتله غلام طي بن شاور

وقال القاضي ناصر الدين شافع في تأليفه نظم السلوك [190b] في تأريخ الخلفاء والملوك ان الامير شيركوه لما وصل الى مصر وشاور في خدمته علم الضرغام انه قد احيط به فاتى قصر الخلافة ونادي يا مولانا فلم يجب ووردت اليه رقعة مكتوبة فيها خذ لنفسك وانج بها فخرج هاربا فادركوه غلمان شاور فقتلوه وقتلوا معه اخوته **وقيل** ان ملهم تم هاربا الى مسجد التبن فقُتل عنده قتله بعض الترك واخذ سلاحه من عليه فوجده بعض الناس مطروحا قتيلا فقطع رأسه واتى به الى شاور فامر بها فجعلت على رمح وطافوا بها **وقيل** قُتل ناصر الدين اخا ضرغام عند بركة الفيل وقُتل ايضا فارس المسلمين **وقيل** لما حمل الشامي رأس الوزير ضرغام الى الامير اسد الدين شيركوه واعلمه بما جرى بينه وبين ضرغام فصعب عليه فعله واوجعه ضربا واراد قتله فشفع فيه الوزير شاور وبقي جسد ضرغام مُلقى يومين ثم حُمل فدفن بالقرافة فانظر ايها الحاضر القلب هذه الاعمال التي يشبه بعضها بعضا قُتل ابن شاور يوم الجمعة الحادي والعشرين من شهر رمضان سنة ثمان وخمسين وخمسمائة فقتل هو يوم الجمعة الثامن والعشرين من شهر رمضان الشهر المذكور وقُتل معه حسان بن عمه وقتل الوزير ضرغام ابن شاهنشاه وابن عين الزمان واسد العاري

فيقال ان ام عين الزمان خرجت وقالت يا ضرغام احرقت قلبي على ابني لا اماتني الله او تذيق امك ما اذقتني ويبرد قلبي وتحرق قلبها وكذا كان قتلوه واخوه يوم الجمعة واحرق الله قلب امهما وكان لما خرج شاور من القاهرة وتوجه الى دمشق عاد ولده شجاع المنعوت بالكامل واصهار شاور واخوه وطلبوا امان من ضرغام على يدي همام وكانت وزارة شاور الاولى تسع شهور ووزا[ر]ة ضرغام تسع شهور محررة **وكان** ضرغام من اعيان الامراء واجلاء الفرسان وكان يجيد اللعب بالكرة ورمى السهام والرماح ويكتب كتابة ابن مقلة وينظم موشحات جيدة

ذكر دخول شاور القاهرة واعادته الى الوزارة [191a] وما وقع بين شاور وشيركوه من الخلاف واستيلاء صلاح الدين يوسف على بلبيس

دخل الوزير شاور القاهرة واخلع عليه العاضد صاحب الديار المصرية خلع الوزارة في مستهل شهر رجب الفرد من شهور هذه السنة واعاده الى الوزارة بالديار المصرية ومكنه منها ولما حصل الوزير شاور بالقاهرة خرج ابنه الكامل من دار ملهم اخو ضرغام وكان معتقلا فيها وخرج معه القاضي الفاضل وكان ايضا معتقلا معه فيها وكان قد تأكد بينهما مودة واتفاق فادخله الى ابيه الوزير شاور ومدحه واثنى على فضله فسمي من ذلك الوقت القاضي الفاضل ويساق خبره وما صار اليه امره وكان القاضي الفاضل قبل هذا الوقت يعرف بالقاضي الاسعد **وفي عود** الوزارة الى شاور بعد عزله منها يقول عمارة بن علي اليمني يمدحه من **قصيدة** ... [l.15]

[l.19] **وقيل** ان الوزير شاور والامير شيركوه لما قتل الوزير ضرغام اقاما في مخيّمهما بظاهر القاهرة من ناحية المقسم يوم السبت ويوم الاحد ودخل شاور يوم الاثنين الى القاهرة وحضر بين يدي الخليفة العاضد في باب الملك بالايوان وهنأه بالسلامة والنصر وهو فرح مستبشر وخرج من باب زويلة وعاد من باب القنطرة ونزل في دار الوزارة **وركب** الامير شيركوه الى مصر وتفرج بها وقصد الفقهاء وسلم عليهم مثل ابن الكيزاني وابن الحطية وابن مرزوق وعاد الى [191b] خيمه

وقُرئ سجل شاور بالوزارة في الرابع من شهر رجب من هذه السنة وبقي الامير شيركوه في الخيم واستمر خروج الضيافة في كل يوم وليلة عشرون طبقا من سائر الاطعمة ومائتا قنطار خبز وثمانين اردب شعير وكان كلما وصل اليه احد بتلك الضيافة يدعوا للخليفة ويكثر الشكر والدعاء وكان الخليفة قد اعدّ له ملبوسا وسريرا كان الآمر قد وضعه لبعض غلمانه مرصعا بالجوهر له قيمة عظيمة وكان الخليفة قد امره بالدخول ليخلع عليه ويكسيه من الملابس التي اعدها له على جاري العادة فامتنع وكان اولئك القوم الذي يأتونه بالضيافة قد جاءوا

بها فلم يكترث بها ولم يقبلها منهم لانه اقام في العسكر خارج القاهرة على المقسم ينتظر امر الوزير شاور في ما كان ضمن للملك العادل نور الدين محمود من البلاد المصرية وله ايضا فغدر بهما وعاد عمّا كان قرره لهما وراسل الامير اسد الدين شيركوه شاور يقول له قد طال مقامنا في الخيم وقد ضجر العسكر من الحر والغبار فارسل اليه شاور ثلثين الف دينار وقال ترحل الآن في أمن الله ودعته فلما سمع الامير اسد الدين شيركوه ذلك ارسل اليه يقول ان الملك العادل نور الدين اوصاني عند انفصالي عنه وقال اذا ملك شاور تكون مقيما عنده ويكون لك ثلث مغل البلاد والثلث الآخر لشاور والعسكر والثلث الثالث لصاحب القصر يصرفه في مصالحه فقال شاور انا ما قررتُ شيئا مما تقول انا طلبتُ نجدة من الملك العادل نور الدين فاذا انقضى شغلي عادوا الى الشام وقد سيّرتُ اليكم نفقة فخذوها وانصرفوا وانا افتصل مع نور الدين فقال الامير اسد الدين لا يمكنني مخالفة نور الدين ولا اقدر على الانصراف الا بامضاء امره

فلما سمع الوزير شاور ذلك اخذ في الاستعداد والحصار وقتال اسد الدين واستعدّ ايضا الامير اسد الدين شيركوه وسيّر الامير صلاح الدين يوسف بن اخيه نجم الدين ايوب بن شادي بن مروان الايوبي [192a] في قطعة من الجيش الى بلبيس وامره بجمع الغلال الحولية والاتبان وما تدعوا الحاجة اليه وان يجعل جميع ما يحصله معدًّا في بلبيس ليكون ذخيرة ان دعته الحاجة اليه واخذ في قتال اهل القاهرة فغلق شاور ابواب القاهرة وسار صلاح الدين وتغلّب على الحوف وملكه باجمعه وبثّ خيله وامر بجباية الغلال والاموال فاخذها ثم امتدّ طمعه فتقدم الى جزيرة قويسنا واراد اصحابه نهب منية زفتى

فلما بلغ الخليفة العاضد بالله ذلك ارسل ثلاثة من الاستاذين المحنّكين فاستنفر الناس من الصعيد وكان بجزيرة قويسنا والٍ يقال له ابن شاس فاجتمعت كلمة الناس وقاتلوا الترك وقاتلوهم فهزموهم ورموا باقيهم الى البحر وغرق اكثرهم ولو كان اهل مصر متّفقي الكلمة مطيعين لله ولولاة الامر لم يدخل عليهم عارض وعادت العساكر والجيوش الى اماكنهم وبقي الامير اسد الدين شيركوه مجبرا لم يحصل له مقصود ولم يمكنه الرجوع الى بلاده وامر شاور باخراج العساكر والجنود وجميع الحشود والمقدمين ونصبها مما يلي البستان الكبير وعاد الامير اسد الدين شيركوه الى ضواحي القاهرة فزحف ولقيه الوزير شاور واستجرّ من عسكره طائفة الى ان صاروا في قبضة كمين من كمناء الوزير ونصر عليهم وانهزم بعض من كان مع شيركوه فعند ذلك عطف عسكر شيركوه جميعه على عسكر شاور فهزموهم حتى وصلوا الى ابواب القاهرة ووصل الامير اسد الدين شيركوه الى القاهرة فاغلقت واقام الى آخر النهار ولما كان الليل احرق الامير شيركوه من باب سعادة الى ناحية الخليج مثل المرة الاولى وتفاقم الامر [192b] وصار كلما خرج اليه من عسكر مصر احد اباده وقتله

وخرج الوزير شاور ثم عاد فازدحم الناس على السور ينظروا ما يكون فوقعت شُرّافة على رأس شاور لم يحط رأسه فتألّم لها وغُشي عليه ودخلوا به الى الكافوري وقد أيسوا منه فاحضر اليه رئيس الاطباء فعصر في انفه حصرما فأفاق فاحضر اليه شراب من عند الخليفة فشربه وركب ونزل داره وقد حصل له ورمٌ في وجهه ثم ان الامير اسد الدين شيركوه صلب القتال على باب القنطرة واحرق وجه الخليج جميعه كلما رأى شاور فعله فعل مثله واحترقت الدور التي بحارة زويلة وساعده بنو كنانة وقوم كثير من عسكر المصريين ثم ان اصحابه رجعوا الى الحارة الريحانية وصلب القتال عليها وفتحوا ثغرة ووقع القتال القوي الى الظهر **وجلس** الخليفة العاضد بالله عند باب الذهب وامر الناس بالخروج وتسارع صبيان الركاب وغيرهم الى الثغرة قصدوهم ولم يزالوا يقاتلون الترك والكنانية واصحاب الامير شيركوه الى ان اوصلوهم الى مضاربهم وسدّوا الثغرة **وقد كان** الوزير ضرغام قبل قتله عند قدوم الوزير شاور والامير شيركوه ومن معهما من عسكر الشام وارسل الى الفرنج وطلب منهم التوجه الى مصر لنصرة الخليفة على هذا العدو الثقيل الذي وصل الى بلبيس وشرط ان يزاد لهم في القطيعة التي لهم فامتنع ملك الفرنج ان يفعل ذلك حتى يأتي امر الخليفة واما من الوزراء فلا يقبل لان الوزراء لا يثبت امرهم وفي كل وقت يقتل وزير ويقوم وزير وكان ما سنذكره ان شاء الله تعالى

ذكر استدعاء الوزير شاور الفرنج ووصولهم الى الديار المصرية ومحاصرتهم اسد الدين شيركوه ببلبيس

قيل لما تحقق الوزير شاور انه لا قِبَل له بقتال الامير اسد الدين شيركوه كتب الى مري ملك [193a] الفرنج بالساحل يستنجده ويقول له ان اسد الدين شيركوه كان قد طلع نجدة لي فلما حصلوا في البلاد طمعوا فيها ومتى ملكوها اخرجوك من بلادك وفعلوا بك كما فعلوا بي وقرر له في كل مرحلة يرحلها اليه الى مصر الف دينار وقرر شيئا [لقضيم] دوابّه وشيئا لاستاذيته وكان الفرنج قد ايقنوا بالهلاك ان تمّ ملك الملك العادل نور الدين

[صاحب] الشام للديار المصرية فلما ارسل اليهم الوزير شاور فطلب منهم ان يساعدوه على اخراج الامير اسد الدين شيركوه من البلاد جائهم فرج لم يحتسبوه وسارعوا الى تلبية دعوته ونصرته وطمعوا في ملك الديار المصرية فتجهّزوا وساروا

وخرج مري ملك الفرنج من عسقلان في جموعه الى قابوس في سبع وعشرين مرحلة وقبض عنها سبعة وعشرين الف دينار **وقيل** لما سمع الفرنج بتوجه عساكر نور الدين الى الديار المصرية خافوا خوفا شديدا وايقنوا بالهلاك وان بلادهم ستستأصل فلما وصلتهم رسل شاور يدعوهم الى مساعدته سرّوا بذلك وبادروا اليه وساروا الى تلبيته وطمعوا في الديار المصرية وتجهّزوا بعد وقوع الاتفاق بينهم وبين شاور على مال كثير يحمله اليهم ان رحل عسكر الملك العادل نور الدين عن البلاد **ولما** تحقق الامير اسد الدين شيركوه قرب الفرنج من القاهرة انتقل عنها الى بلبيس ونزلها فوجد الامير صلاح الدين يوسف بن نجم الدين ايوب قد احسن الاستعداد فدخل الى بلبيس وانضاف اليه من اهلها الكنانية وخرج الوزير شاور في عساكر مصر واجتمع بالفرنج وجاء حتى خيم على بلبيس واحاط بها محاصرا لاسد الدين يباكر الحرب ويراوحها واقاموا على ذلك ثمانية اشهر وانقطعت اخبار مصر ومن بها عن الملك العادل نور الدين صاحب الشام وبلغه ان العسكر الفرنجي سار الى مصر فتحقق غدر شاور وأخذ في جمع العساكر [193a, l.29]

[193b, l.20]
وقال الشيخ محمد بن علي بن عبد العزيز بن نظيف الغساني الحموي كاتب الملك الحافظ ارسلان شاه بن الملك العادل سيف الدين ابي بكر بن ايوب **في** سنة تسع وخمسين وخمسمائة توجه المولى اسد الدين شيركوه الى مصر مع شاور بعساكر الشام والسلطان للبلاد يومئذ الملك العادل نور الدين محمود ابن زنكي وكان اسد الدين من اكابر أمرائه وخواصّ دولته والمشار اليه فملك مصر وقتلوا ضرغام ثم غدر شاور باسد الدين شيركوه وخافه فكاتب الفرنج فاتاه ملك الفرنج بخلق عظيم فخرج اسد الدين الى بلبيس فحاصرته الفرنج عليها ستة اشهر وكان ما سنذكره ان شاء الله تعالى [193b, l.30]

[196a, l.3]
ذكر وقوع الصلح بين الامير اسد الدين شيركوه والمصريين والفرنج

لما فتح الملك العادل نور الدين محمد بن الملك المنصور عماد الدين زنكي صاحب الشام بانياس اخذ في ادخال الوهن على الفرنج فاستدعي نجّابا يقال له فضل الفيضي وجمع اعلام الفرنج وشعافهم وجعلها في عبئه وسلمها اليه وقال اريد ان تجد السير ليلا ونهارا وتعمل الحيلة في الدخول الى بلبيس فاذا دخلت اليها تسلم على اسد الدين وتخبره بما فتح الله على المسلمين ويعطيه هذه الاعلام والشعاف وتامره بنشرها على اسوار بلبيس فان ذلك مما يفتّ في اعضاد الكفار ويدخل الرعب في قلوبهم ففعل ذلك **ولما** رأي الفرنج الاعلام وشاهدوها قلقوا لذلك وخافوا على بلادهم وسألوا شاور الاذن لهم في الانفصال فانزعج شاور لذلك وخاف من اسد الدين شيركوه وسألهم المهل عليه اياما وجمع الامراء للمشورة فاشاروا عليه بالصلح وتكفل اتمامه له الامير شمس الخلافة محمد بن مختار فندبه شاور رسولا الى اسد الدين فدخل اليه وتم الصلح على يده

وحكي ان شاور ارسل الى الامير اسد الدين شيركوه وهو محصور ببلبيس يقول له اعلم انني ابقيت عليك ولم امكن الفرنج من اخذك لانهم كانوا قادرين على اخذك في ايسر مدة وانما فعلت ذلك لامرين احدهما انني ما اشتهي اكسر جاه المسلمين واقوي الفرنج عليهم والثاني انني خشيت ان الفرنج اذا فتحوا بلبيس طمعوا فيها وقالوا هذه لنا لاننا فتحناها بسيوفنا وما من يوم كان يمضى الا وارسل الى اكابر الفرنج الجملة من المال واسألهم ان يكسروا همة الملك عن الزحف متى عزم عليه واشياء من هذا الباب قدمها وطلب الصلح منه على ان يحمل اليه ثلاثين الف ديناراً أخرى فاجاب الامير اسد الدين شيركوه الى الصلح **وقيل** ان الامير اسد الدين شيركوه ضعف ببلبيس وخاف على نفسه لانه قتل من اصحابه جماعة وضاقت عليه المير وكان [196b] يظن ان الملك العادل نور الدين ينجده بعسكر فلم ينجده باحد فكاتب ملك الفرنج مري وخطب منه الصلح فاتى ذلك الوزير شاور فكتب اسد الدين الى ابن الرفيق احد ملوك الفرنج والهنفري وغيرهما من الاعيان فقرر الصلح ولم يلتفت الى الوزير شاور وخرج الامير اسد الدين شيركوه من بلبيس في ذي الحجة من شهور هذه السنة وكان قتل من اصحابه جماعة منهم سيف الدين محمد بن بران صاحب صرخد اصابه سهم فانشد وهو يجود **بنفسه** ...
[196b, l.9]

[196b, l.12]
وقيل معه من الكنانية من اهل بلبيس عالم عظيم وحصل للفرنج من الوزير شاور اموال عظيمة فانه كان يعطيهم في كل يوم الف دينار واقام الامير شيركوه بظاهر بلبيس ثلاثة ايام وكان ما سنذكره ان شاء الله تعالى **وفي حصار** بلبيس والانتصار على اسد الدين شيركوه يقول الشيخ عمارة بن علي اليمني من قصيدة يمدح بها العاضد خليفة مصر ووزيره شاور **اولها** ...[l.18]

[200b, l.19]
ذكر ما اتفق للامير اسد الدين شيركوه في طريقة حين توجه من مصر ووصوله دمشق سالما

لما توجه الامير اسد الدين شيركوه من مصر سار في البرية وسار الفرنج على الساحل **واتفق** ان اللعين البرنس ارناط صاحب الكرك والشوبك وكان طاغية تاوّل بيمينه وتفقّه في حلفه وقال لعنه الله تعالى انا حلفتُ انني ما الحق اسد الدين شيركوه ولا عسكره في البر وانا اريد الحقه في البحر وركب لعنه الله في البحر وسار الى عسقلان في يوم واحد وخرج منها الى الكرك والشوبك وجمع عسكره المقيم هناك وقعد مرتقبا خروج اسد الدين شيركوه من البرية ليوقع به **وعلم** الامير اسد الدين شيركوه رحمه الله تعالى بمكيدة ملك الفرنج بالحدس والتخمين فجاء [201a] الى موضع يعرف بالمزة وام كعب وشق الى الغور وخرج من البلقاء فكأنه جاء من خلف المكان الذي كان فيه ارناط لنعه الله تعالى وخلص ولم يعلم به ارناط وسلمه الله تعالى من كيده ... [l.4]

[l.10] **ووصل** الامير اسد الدين شيركوه الى دمشق سالما في اول هذه السنة واجتمع بالملك العادل نور الدين صاحب الشام واخبره بما جرى عليه من شاور وكيف غدر به واخبره بضعف بلاد مصر ورغبه فيها وكان الامير اسد الدين شيركوه بعد عوده من مصر لا يزال تحدث بها ويحرص على قصدها حتى كان ما سنذكره ان شاء الله تعالى

ذكر ما اتفق من الوزير شاور بعد مسير الامير اسد الدين شيركوه من الديار المصرية

قيل لما فارق الامير اسد الدين شيركوه الديار المصرية وعاد الوزير شاور الى القاهرة لم يكن له همة الا تتبع من علم ان بينه وبين الامير اسد الدين شيركوه معرفة أو صحبة وكان شاور استفسد جماعة من عسكر اسد الدين شيركوه منهم خشترين الكردي واقطعه شطنوف **حدث** الادريسي قال اشتد الوزير شاور في طلب خالي الشريف المحنك لانه كان من اصحاب ضرغام وهو الذي ارسله ضرغام رسولا الى الملك العادل نور الدين صاحب الشام في صرف رأيه عن نجدة الوزير شاور ولما وصل الى نور الدين اكرمه وكان بينه وبين نور الدين انسة لان [201b] الوزير الصالح بن رزيك كان ارسله اليه عدة دفعات وكانت الفرنج عارضته في الطريق وأخذوه وأخذوا غلمانه وحملوه الى عسقلان فاتفق انه هرب منهم وصار الى الملك العادل نور الدين وحضر عنده وأدى الرسالة في امر الوزير شاور **وكان** الملك العادل نور الدين قد مال الى الوزير شاور لأمور **منها** انه مت اليه بالمذهب وانه تكره الفاطميين **ومنها** انه وعده بملك مصر **ومنها** انه ضمن له اموالا كثيرة وكذلك جماعة الامراء **وعلم** الوزير شاور ان الشريف المحنك قد بالغ في امره بحضرة الملك العادل نور الدين فحقدها عليه

وحدث الادريسي قال اقترح الوزير شاور على الملك العادل نور الدين ان يجمع بينه وبين خالي الشريف المحنك فارسله اليه قال وكنتُ معه فدخلنا اليه الى جوسق الميدان الاخضر بدمشق فقام لخالي الشريف المحنك واكرمه وأخذ في عتابه وقال له في جملة قوله انت ايها الشريف تعلم ان سبب قيامي على آل رزيك انما كان لاجل ضرغام واخوته ولاجل جماعة من الامراء منهم المفضّل شاهنشاه وعين الزمان واسد العاري وغيرهم من الامراء البرقية واتّبعت غرضهم في ما نقموه على ابن الصالح رزيك ولما حصلتُ بالقاهرة رفعتُ من اقدارهم وزدتُ في ارزاقهم وحقّقتُ ظنونهم فيّ وبلغتُ بهم أمانيهم ثم لم يكن لهم همّ بعد فعلي بهم ما فعلتُ الا إزالتي عن موضعي ثم لم يقنعهم ذلك حتى قتلوا اولادي ونهبوا اموالي وشتّوا جماعتي وبذلوا السيف في خاصّتي وغلماني فهل تعلم لي ذنبا اليهم فقال له خالي الشريف المحنك انت تعلم ايها الامير ان ابنك طيّا كان قد تعدى طوره وجاوز حدّه حتى تعاظم عليك ونفذ امره دون امرك وانه بعد ان قتل رزيك بن الصالح اطلق لسانه في الامراء ومدّ يده الى اموالهم ونسائهم وبهتهم في المجالس وصاح عليهم في المواكب حتى حقدوا عليه ذلك وشكوه اليك فلم تشكهم واستغاثوا من افعاله فلم [202a] تَقْلَهم وعامل اصحابك وغلمانك الناس بكل قبيح فمالت عنك قلوب الخاصة والعامة وتوجه لهم ما فعلوه بك ثم انشده في غضون **قوله** ...[l.2] [l.4] **فلما** سمع ذلك الوزير شاور سكت وقمنا فخرجنا عنه فكان هذا في نفس شاور على خالي الشريف المحنك فلما عاد الى القاهرة لم يكن همّه الا طلبه فانهزم الشريف المحنك الى الاشراف الجعفريّين حدث الادريسي قال وكنتُ معه فصرنا الى الاشمونين وكان معظّم بالخالي الشريف بها فحصل ما قدر عليه وسار مع العرب الى الشام واقام عند الملك العادل نور الدين صاحب الشام واما اولاده الرضى والمرتضى فركبا في البحر الى مكة المشرّفة وخرجا منها الى الجران ثم صارا الى ابيهما الى دمشق [l.12]

[203b, l.4]
وقال محمد بن علي بن نظيف الغساني الحموي الكاتب في التأريخ الصغير الذي الّفه ما صيغته **في** سنة ستين وخمسمائة طلع اسد الدين شيركوه طلعة ثانية الى مصر وكاد يفتحها ورجع **انتهي** كلامه والاظهر ان عوده الى مصر المرة الثانية كان في سنة اثنين وستين كما سنذكره ان شاء الله تعالى [l.9]

[211a, l.11]
ذكر مسير الامير اسد الدين شيركوه الى الديار المصرية

لما عاد الامير اسد الدين شيركوه من مصر وحصل بدمشق قوي طمع الملك العادل نور الدين محمود بن الملك المنصور عماد الدين اتابك زنكي صاحب الشام في الديار المصرية وفي ملكها لان الامير اسد الدين شيركوه لم يزل يحدث بها ويحرض على قصدها فلما كان في هذه السنة امر الملك العادل نور الدين الامير اسد الدين شيركوه بتجنيد العساكر لقصدها فجهّزها وتوجه في جيش قوي وسيّر معه الملك العادل نور الدين صاحب الشام جماعة من الامراء وكان كارها لذلك ولكن لما رأى جدّ اسد الدين في المسير لم يمكنه الا ان يسيّر معه جماعة خوفا من حادث يتجدد عليهم فيضعف الاسلام **ورحل** الامير اسد الدين شيركوه عن دمشق في شهر ربيع الاول وقيل في شهر ربيع الآخر من شهور هذه السنة وسار معه الملك العادل نور الدين الى اطراف البلاد خوفا من معرة الفرنج فكان صلاح الدين ابو المظفّر يوسف بن نجم الدين ايوب بن شاذي بن مروان الايوبي مع عمّه الامير اسد الدين شيركوه في هذه السفرة وفي ذلك يقول عرقلة الدمشقي يمدح [211b] الامير صلاح الدين ... [l.1]

[l.7] **ثم سار** اسد الدين شيركوه الى الديار المصرية وترك بلاد الفرنج عن يمينه فوصل الديار المصرية فما راع الوزير شاور بالديار المصرية الا ورود كتاب مري ملك الفرنج يعرفه فيه ان الامير اسد الدين شيركوه قد فصل عن دمشق بعساكره قاصدا مصر فاعاد عليه شاور الإجابه بالاحماد وطلب منه اعادة الانجاد في عساكره الامجاد وان المقرر له من المال يصل اليه على ما كان يصل اليه في العام الماضي فسار مري في عسكر الفرنج قاصدا نجدة شاور وطمعا في ملك مصر وخوفا ان يملكها الامير اسد الدين فلا يبقى لهم في بلادهم مقام معه ومع الملك العادل نور الدين وسار مري في عساكره الى مصر على جانب البحر وكان الامير اسد الدين شيركوه سائرا في البرّ وسبق الفرنج ونزلوا على ظاهر بلبيس وخرج العسكر المصري وفيهم شاور الوزير بالديار المصرية واجتمع بملك الفرنج وقعدوا جميعا في انتظار اسد الدين وعلم الامير اسد الدين بحصول الفرنج مع شاور وكونهم على بلبيس فنكب عن طريقهم وامّم الجبل وترك الفرنج على ميمنة وخرج الى اطفيح وهي في الجنوب من مصر وشنّ الغارة هناك واتصل بالوزير شاور خبره فسار في اثره هو والفرنج وبلغ ذلك الامير اسد الدين شيركوه فاندفع بين ايديهم حتى بلغ بشرونة من صعيد مصر وتحيّل في جمع مراكب ركبها وعدّى الى البرّ الغربي

وقيل ان رجلا يقال له [212a] رضوان من غلمان الشريف المحنّك دلّه على مخاض عبرا منه ولما استكمل تعديته ادرك الوزير شاور بعض ساقته ومنقطعي عسكريته فاوقع بهم واحضر شاور مراكبا وقطع النيل في اثر الامير اسد الدين شيركوه بجميع جيوشه وجيوش الفرنج وسار الامير اسد الدين شيركوه الى الجيزة مقابل مصر المحروسة وخيّم بها مقدار خمسين يوما

وقال القاضي ناصر الدين شافع سبط القاضي محي الدين بن عبد الظاهر وبعض اهل التأريخ ما صيغته **في سنة** اثنين وستين كان مسير اسد الدين ثانية الى مصر بجيش كثيف من العساكر النوريّة وكان اعلم نور الدين باحوال مصر وضعف عسكرها فجهّزه مرة ثانية في عدة من العساكر وذلك في شهر ربيع الاول فسار الى مصر ونزل بالجيزة واقام محاصرا لها سبعا وخمسين يوما ومعه ابن اخيه صلاح الدين يوسف واستنجد

شاور بالفرنج فقدموا طالبين مصر لنجدة شاور **وقال غيره** اقام نيفا وخمسين يوما وكان الامير اسد الدين شيركوه لما حصل بالجيزة ارسل الرضى ابا عبد الله الحسيني بن المحنّك الى الاشراف [الجعفريّين] والطّلحيّين القرشيّين واستدعاهم وكان الوزير شاور قد اساء اليهم فصاروا الى خدمته مسرعين **ويقال** ان الامير اسد الدين شيركوه لما حضر الوزير شاور بعساكر الفرنج بالجانب الغربي ارسل اليه يقول له انا احلف لك بالله ومغلّظة الايمان انني لا اقيم ببلاد مصر ولا يؤذيك احد من اصحابي ونجمع انا وانت على اعداء الله الملاعين الفرنج وننتهز فيهم فرصة قد امكنت وغنيمة قد حصلت وما اظن انه يعود يتّفق للاسلام مثلها ابدا فلما صار الرسول الى الوزير شاور وأدى اليه الرسالة امر به فقتل وقال ما هؤلاء الفرنج هؤلاء الفرج

ولما بلغ ذلك الامير اسد [212b] الدين اكل يديه ندما على مخالفة الوزير شاور له في هذا الرأي وقال لعنه الله لو اطاعني لم يبق بالشام احد من الفرنج بعدها وحاصر مصر نيفا وخمسين يوما والتجأ الى دَلْجَة ونزل الوزير شاور في اللّوق والمقسم وامر بعمل الجسر بين الجيزة والجزيرة وامر بالمراكب فشُحنت بالرجال وامرهم ان يأتون من خلف عسكر الامير اسد الدين شيركوه وكان ما سنذكره ان شاء الله تعالى

ذكر وقعة البابين قال بعض اهل التأريخ كتب الامير اسد الدين شيركوه الى اهل ثغر الاسكندرية يستنجدهم على الوزير شاور لاجل نصره الفرنج وتضييعه اموال المسلمين فيهم فقاموا معه وامروا عليهم نجم الدين ابن مصال وهو احد اولاد وزراء المصريّين وكان لجأ الى الاسكندرية مستخفيا فظهر في هذه الفتنة **حدث** الادريسي قال كنت بالاسكندرية يومئذ فكتب معي ابن مصال كتابا الى الامير اسد الدين وقال لي قل له ان احضرك ان السلاح والحديد واصل وكان ارسل الى اسد الدين خزانة من السلاح قال فسبقتُهما بيومين وحضرتُ بين يدي اسد الدين واعطيتُه الكتب وشافهتُه برسالة نجم الدين ابن مصال في معنى السلاح والآلات ثم وصلت بعد يومين مع ابن اخت الفقيه ابن عوف

قال وبقينا على الجيزة يومين فوصل الينا رسول ابن مدافع يخبر الامير اسد الدين بقرب الوزير شاور منه ويأمره بالنجاة فترك الامير اسد الدين الخيام والمطابخ وما يثقل حمله وسار سيرا حثيثا حتى قارب دلجة فأمر الامير اسد الدين بنهبها فنهبت وأخذ العسكر منها شيئا كثيرا ونزل الناس لتعشية الدوابّ فلم يتمّ عليقها حتى امر الامير اسد الدين الناس بالرحيل واوقدت المشاعل ليلا وسرنا فاذا الجاووش [213a] ينادي في الناس بالرجوع وسبب ذلك ان الوزير شاور لم يأخذ هو والفرنج بالجزم لانهم انفردوا من الساحل [...] يطلبون الامير اسد الدين وعاد اسد الدين الى دلجة فنزل عليها ونزل الوزير شاور على الاشمونين وامر اسد الدين الناس ان [يقفوا] على تعبئة وذلك قبل و[صول] الصباح واخبرهم ان شاور والفرنج قد لحقوا بهم ولم [يبق] الا مصافهم ومجاهدتهم واصبح الناس على تعبئة قال [فنظرتُ] فاذا عسكر الفرنج كأنهم اسنان المشط في رمل دهاس وقدم شاور بعض رجاله فحملوا على الناس [فانهزم] عز الدين الجاولي فلم يرده شيء الا اسكندرية و [امـ...] على المصري فوصل الى اسيوط منهزما

واما الامير اسد الدين فانه اول من تنحّا عن موضعه وفرّ لما رأى من كسل اصحابه حتى اتى ابن تليل وكان في القلب واما صاحب قيسارية فانه توكّل بالمنهزمين يطردهم على [خيول] رازحة وقف اكثرها وقتل من اصحاب الامير اسد الدين جماعة كبيرة ولا سيّما من اهل الاسكندرية وكان السبب في ذلك ان الامير اسد الدين شيركوه فرّق اصحابه فرقتين فرقة معه وفرقة مع صلاح الدين يوسف ابن اخيه نجم الدين ايوب فلما كان وقت الظهر تجمع اصحاب الامير اسد الدين بعضهم الى بعض وقالوا اعلموا انكم طعمة لهؤلاء ولا منجا لكم الا الموت وطلب الشهادة بايدي الكفّار فوطّنوا انفسهم على الصبر وتحاموا وحملوا على شاور ومن معه من العساكر المصرية والفرنجية ووافي صلاح الدين يوسف في عساكره فقتلوا منهم مقتلة عظيمة وكان صاحب هذه الحرب صلاح الدين يوسف فانه كشف عن رأسه وحمل من الميمنة فرد الصّفوف وفرّق شمل تلك الجيوش وكان جعل وكده [213b] وقصده طائفة الفرنج لعلمه انهم همّ الذين قد ابلوا جهدهم وانكوا في العساكر الاسلامية فبذل فيهم السيوف حتى ردهم على اعقابهم ورأى ذلك اسد الدين وكان شاور هو والفرنج قد كسروا القلب فعاد من الميمنة وبذل نفسه واعمل سيفه حتى اجنّ الفريقين الليل فولّت طوائف الفرنج والمصريين الادبار واتبعوا الفرار وعاد باقي الفرنج الذين كانوا خلف المنهزمين من اصحاب الامير اسد الدين فوجدوا عساكرهم وقد انقضت وجيوشهم وقد انهزمت ووجدوا اصحاب الامير اسد الدين في انتظارهم فما كان لهم ملجأ غير الهزيمة وكاد ملك الفرنج المخذول يؤسر في ذلك اليوم لولا اصحابه

وقال القاضي ناصر الدين شافع سبط القاضي محي الدين ابن عبد الظاهر صاحب نظم السلوك في تراجم الخلفاء والملوك وغيره **لما** علم اسد الدين شيركوه بمجيء الفرنج رحل الى موضع يعرف بالبابين فعبّى أصحابه والتقي الفرنج وجرت حروب انتصر فيها اسد الدين على الفرنج وقتل منهم خلقا وأسر سبعين فارسا ... [213b, l.17]

[214b, l.2]
ذكر استيلاء اسد الدين شيركوه على ثغر الاسكندرية

لما انتصر الامير اسد الدين شيركوه واصحابه على الوزير شاور ومن معه من عساكر مصر والفرنج وهزمهم كما قدمنا شرحه سار الامير اسد الدين شيركوه الى الاسكندرية على الفيّوم ولما انتهي الى البحيرة امر العسكر بنهبها فذهبوا بغلال الناس ومواشيهم وسار حتى دخل الاسكندرية ونزل القصر وجعل فيه محبس الفرنج الذين أسرهم وكان بها ابن الزبير متوليا ديوانها يحمل اليه الاموال وقوّاه بالسلاح وخاف الامير اسد الدين ان يقصده الوزير شاور والفرنج ويحصروه فربما تأذّي بالحصار فترك الامير صلاح الدين يوسف بن اخيه عند اهل الاسكندرية لانهم قاموا معه لاجل المذهب وبغضا للوزير شاور وللمصريّين وجرّد الاقوياء من عسكره وخرج قاصدا الصعيد الاعلى ... [l.15]

[l.23]
ذكر محاصرة عساكر مصر والفرنج الامير صلاح الدين يوسف بثغر الاسكندرية

لما انكسر الوزير شاور ومن معه من عساكر مصر والفرنج من الامير اسد الدين شيركوه واصحابه كما قدمنا شرحه عاد عسكر مصر والفرنج منهزمين الى القاهرة المحروسه واصلحوا حالهم وتجهّزوا [215a] وتجمّعوا وساروا الى ثغر الاسكندرية فحصروا الامير صلاح الدين بها واشتد الحصار وقلّ الطعام بها [فصبر] اهلها على ذلك **وقيل** وصل الوزير شاور والفرنج و[نزلوا على] الاسكندرية وحاصروا صلاح الدين فيها مدة [...] اشهر **وقال** القاضي ناصر الدين شافع صاحب نظم الـ[سلوك] وغيره حاصروها اربعة اشهر وكان اهل الا[سكندرية] كارهين الدولة المصرية **واما** الامير اسد الدين [شيركوه] لما حصل بالصعيد استولي عليها وعلى ما فيها من ما[ل] وغلال وجبى الخراج وحصل ما قدر عليه ولم يزل مقيـ[ما] هناك حتى صام شهر رمضان من شهور هذه [السنة] و[عيّد] هناك واتصل به اشتداد الامر على اهل الاسكندر[ية] فوصل من قوص الى جهتها واتصل ذلك بشاور فرحل هو والفرنج طالبين القاهرة لانهم بلغهم ان الامير اسد الدين حاصر مصر وكانت بينهما وقعة وكان ما سنذكره ان شاء الله تعالى

ذكر ما وقع بين اسد الدين والمصريّين والفرنج من الصلح

ارسل الامير اسد الدين شيركوه الى الامير صلاح الدين يوسف بن اخيه يأمره بتقرير الصلح فارسل الامير صلاح الدين يوسف الى ملك الفرنج وخطب منه الصلح فاجابه الى ذلك وتقرّر ان الوزير شاور يحمل الى الامير اسد الدين جميع ما غرمه في هذه الخرجة ويعطي الفرنج ثلاثين الف دينارا ويعود كل منهم الى بلاده وجرت على ذلك الايمان **وارسل** الامير صلاح الدين الى ملك الفرنج يقول له ان لي اصحابا منهم القوي ومنهم الضعيف فأما القوي فيتبعنا في البرّ وأما الضعيف فنريد له مراكب يحمله فيها فارسل له الملك عدّة مراكب فخرج فيها اصحابه **حدث** الادريسي قال كنتُ في جملة من خرج في المراكب [215b] [مع] الامير صلاح الدين من الاسكندرية واجتمع [با]لامير اسد الدين شيركوه وارسل الوزير [شا]ور وقبض على كل مصري كان مع الامير صلاح [الدين] يوسف منهم نجم الدين ابن مصال وبلغ ذلك للامير [صلاح] الدين فاجتمع بملك الفرنج وقال له ان شاور [نقض] الايمان قال وكيف ذلك قال لانه قبض على من [...] الينا فقال ليس له ذلك وارسل الى شاور وانكره [عليه] فعله واستحلفه على جميع من لجأ الى الامير صلاح [الدين] والامير اسد الدين وامتنع الناس من الاقامة [في] مصر ورحلوا الى الشام فخرج الوزير شاور نفسه وجمع وجوه من كان عزم على الرحلة من الديار المصرية وحلف لهم الاحسان اليهم واضعاف اموالهم فمنهم من سكن الى ايمانه واقام ومنهم من لم يسكن ورحل عنها الى الشام **واما** اصحاب المراكب فانهم وصلوا الى عكّا فأخذوا واعتقلوا في معصرة القصب الى ان وصل ملك الفرنج واطلقهم ... [215b, l.16]

Appendix C: English Translation of Selected Extracts from *Ta'rīkh al-duwal*

[Vol. I: 165b, l.12] *sub anno 515/1121*

Shaykh Yaḥyā b. Abī Ṭayy Ḥamīd al-Najjār al-Ghassānī of Aleppo **said** the following in his book: The way of al-Afḍal **was** beautiful in its knowledge, justice, virtue, grace and good conversation. He was a person of superior breeding, and wrote excellent poetry, among which were the words he wrote to Mas'ūd al-Dawla when he had presented some doughnuts to him .... [l.17]

[l.27] **He had** taken over the affairs of Egypt, acquired more wealth than could be measured and was extremely wary in regard to himself; he hardly ever went anywhere except with a group he could rely on, who protected him.

One day, while riding in the market among [his men], a man pounced on him, and his retainers were distracted by [dealing with] this; [meanwhile] another [individual] from the crowd pounced on him, stabbed him with a knife and killed him.

It is said that his murder was arranged by al-Āmir. The reason for this was that al-Afḍal had [166a] restricted al-Āmir, and prevented him from acting freely in relation to his affairs and his wealth, so al-Āmir decided to assault him when he came to him for the greeting or on the festival days. [But] this [course of action] was deemed disgraceful for him, and it was said [to him] that 'There is great ignominy in it, as this man and his father were raised in [the Fatimid] House and both served it for fifty years. If you act thus towards him, your reputation will be ruined, and people will turn away from this House. The right course is for you to arrange for someone to assassinate him,' and [al-Āmir] was happy with this. Then the affair took place in the way we mentioned.

It is said that [al-Afḍal] rode out from his house in Egypt heading for the weapons store of Cairo, with a large number of horsemen riding before him and a crowd of people proceeding [on foot]. Then a great cloud of dust rose up to [the party], which troubled al-Afḍal, and he ordered the people to move away from him, to diminish the dust. They did this, and he became separated from the troops [except for] his two grooms. Thereupon, three Bāṭinī men pounced on him by the Polishers' Market and wounded him so many times that he fell from his horse. His men then returned and killed the Bāṭinīs, and carried him to his house while he had the last spark of life.

The ruler of Egypt rode to him from the palace to pay him a sick-visit and said to him 'I warned you against these people, but "Every term is decreed,"[1] and every person has [his] deserts.' Then he asked him: 'Where is the treasury of Muslim public wealth?'

and [al-Afḍal] replied: 'As for the known portion of it, this old man [knows about it],' and gestured towards one of the scribes; 'and as for the hidden part of it, this man standing [knows],' and he pointed to a person in the assembly. Then the ruler of Egypt asked them both: 'What do you two say?' They replied: 'The matter is as the vizier states, and we've determined to undertake to deliver it.' Then al-Afḍal entrusted his children and his secure future to the ruler of Egypt.

His assassination took place at Kursī al-Jisr by the Polishers' [Market]. Shaykh Yaḥyā **said** his assassination was in the year 514, and he **said** it was also mentioned that he was killed at the end of the month of Ramaḍān of the year 515, and that his age at the time of his death was 57 years.

His **was born** in Acre in the year 458, and his vizierate had lasted 28 years, six months and a few days. In his treasury, 5,200,000 gold *dīnār*s in cash were **found**, in addition to silver [bullion]; drinking vessels struck in gold and silver; 21,000 satin robes and others of silk; 5,000 utensils of gold and silver; 20,000 [166b] items [like] bridle-rings and porcelain [objects] and other exotic items; and there were 10,000 horses at the tethering posts; there was also saddle wood with a value of 100,000 *dīnār*s and gilded weapons and saddles valued at 500,000 *dīnār*s.

The Chief Qāḍī Shams al-Dīn Aḥmad b. Khallikān **said** in his manuscript, from which I copied my version: Abu'l Qāsim Shāhanshāh, who was called al-Afḍal b. Amīr al-Juyūsh Badr al-Jamālī, was very good at planning and a master of sound judgement. It was he who raised al-Āmir b. al-Mustaʿlī to the place of his father [as caliph] in the realm after his death, and managed his state, restrained him and stopped him from [merely] pursuing his desires. For [al-Āmir] was much given to frivolity, and this led him to pursuing [al-Afḍal's] assassination. [The latter] lived in Egypt in the royal palace on the banks of the blessed Nile, which is the Commerce Centre today. When he rode from the aforementioned house and approached the river harbour, two men pounced on him and struck him with their swords and injured him. Then a third came up from behind and struck him in the waist with his sword. He then fell from his mount, and his men returned to him and killed the three [assassins]. They carried him to his house while he had the last spark of life, and the caliph al-Āmir rode to him and felt pity for him. He asked him about the wealth and he replied: 'The accessible part of it is known to Abu'l Ḥasan b. Abī Usāma the scribe, and the hidden part of it is known to Ibn al-Baṭā'iḥī.'

He was **killed** at the end of the month of Ramaḍān of year 515, and his rule, after his father, lasted 28 years. His conduct was excellent and he was just.

It is **related** that after al-Afḍal had been killed, oppression came to the fore, and a group of people gathered to seek the help of the caliph. Among the things they said, they cursed al-Afḍal. On being asked their reason for cursing him, they said: 'It is because he [stood for] justice and good conduct. We left our countries and homelands and made for this land because of his just [rule]. Yet now, after his [passing], we are afflicted by this oppression, and he is the cause of our oppression [through his death].' Then the caliph was good to them and ordered the people to be treated well.

It is **said** that Abū 'Abd Allāh Muḥammad b. Barakāt, the linguist and grammarian, appeared before al-Afḍal, complaining of the cessation of an allowance, and **he recited in verse** . . . . [1.27] [l.29] So [al-Afḍal] said to him: 'O shaykh! We have lifted from you [the need for] a personal appearance.' And he ordered [Ibn Barakāt's] salary to be paid to him. Ibn Khallikān said that al-Afḍal left behind [an amount of] wealth the like of which had never been heard of, and the author of *[Akhbār] al-duwal al-munqaṭi'a* said that he left behind 600 million *dīnārs* in cash [167a] and 250 *ardabbs* [dry measures] of *dirhams* of Egyptian coinage; 75,000 robes of satin brocade; and a gold inkwell containing a jewel worth 18,000 *dīnārs*. And apart from this, he left behind cows, buffaloes and sheep whose number cannot be reckoned; and their milk fetched taxes of 3,000 *dīnārs* in the year of his death alone. And God knows best.

[206b, l.12] *sub anno 519/1125*

Shaykh Yaḥyā b. Abī Ṭayy Ḥamīd al-Najjār al-Ghassānī of Aleppo **said** the following in his book: **In** the year [5]19, al-Ma'mūn the vizier of Egypt and his brother al-Mu'tamin were deposed and killed; they were the ones who had planned the assassination of al-Afḍal, and Ibn al-Baṭā'iḥī was crucified by Ra's al-Ṭābiya.[2] Al-Āmir then ruled single-handedly [without a vizier] until he died.

[Yaḥyā b. Abī Ṭayy] **said**: The reason for the arrest and killing of Ibn al-Baṭā'iḥī[3] was that information was given to al-Āmir that he had wanted to pledge his allegiance to someone [else] from his family, so he was seized, along with his brother, with the Chief Dā'ī and the aforementioned family member. They were detained in the palace. Al-Āmir went out to some of his parks. It was his habit, when visiting places, to take some of his emirs with him, and their tents would be pitched around the place where he dismounted. Then he sent wine and food to the wine-drinkers among his emirs, and food and sweets to those who didn't drink.

Among the group of emirs there was an Armenian called Zurayq, who was clever, brave and murderous. He harboured a great grievance against the Franks, such that they sought refuge from being captured by him. When [a Frank] arrived at a watering hole to water his horse and the horse refused to drink, he would say: 'Drink! You will not find Zurayq in the water!' Between this Zurayq and the vizier Ibn al-Baṭā'iḥī there was enmity.

It so happened that [the latter] had gone out with al-Āmir to this garden, and when al-Āmir ordered food and sweetmeats to be sent to him, the errand-boys found [Zurayq] with a broadcloth jerkin on him, and he was crying. They apprised al-Āmir of this, who summoned him and asked the reason for his crying. He replied: 'How should I not cry when my master is here in this place while a caliph, the vizier and the [Chief] Dā'ī are in detention in the palace?' So al-Āmir stood up immediately, entered the palace and killed Ibn al-Baṭā'iḥī by crucifying him, and then killed the [Chief] Dā'ī, and the one mentioned [to whom] the oath of allegiance [was alleged to have been made]. Here **ends** his report. [207a, l.4]

[Vol. II: 17b, l.2] *sub anno 524/1129*

Shaykh Yaḥyā b. Abī Ṭayy Ḥamīd al-Najjār al-Ghassānī of Aleppo **said** the following in his book: **On** Tuesday the 13th of Dhu'l-Qa'da of year 524, [al-Āmir] **was killed** in one of the alleys of the Jazīra,[4] and it is [also] said near Kursī al-Jisr.[5] [When] he had crossed over to it, seven Isma'ilis pounced on him from the bakery there, where they had been hiding. He was carried to his palace in a boat while he still had the last signs of life. He entered [through] the canal of Cairo, and was carried in a horse-blanket, and he died that night. His was 34 years old, his rule had lasted 29 years and he left no heir. He was the 10th son of 'Abd Allāh al-Nājim al-Qā'im of Sijilmasa. **It said** that the people of San'a [Yemen] transmit [a report] that he had a son named al-Ṭayyib, and they were Āmiriyya in creed, and a group of Āmiriyya were [also] in Syria. God knows best if this was case. [17b, l.13]

[18b, l.1] Shaykh Yaḥyā b. Abī Ṭayy Ḥamīd al-Najjār al-Ghassānī of Aleppo **said** the following in his book: **When** al-Āmir was killed, Abu 'l-Maymūn 'Abd al-Majīd b. al-Āmir Abi 'l-Qāsim b. al-Mustanṣir rose [to power] after him, and his [assumption of] rule was by the testament of al-Āmir, because [al-Āmir] had [died] leaving a number of his women pregnant. He ordered ['Abd al-Majīd] to protect [the babies] in their wombs, and to undertake the protection of a male child child if they gave birth to one. He entrusted him with affairs. **When** the aforementioned 'Abd al-Majīd took the reins of power, he was given the honorific al-Ḥāfiẓ, because al-Āmir had entrusted what was in the wombs of his women to him, as we have mentioned. The age of al-Ḥāfiẓ when he took over **was** 61 years, and none among [the Fatimids] had succeeded [the caliphate] without his father being the caliph except [al-Ḥāfiẓ] and al-'Āḍid, as we shall report, God-willing. Al-Ḥāfiẓ **was** medium-sized, very dark, with protruding eyes, excellent at penmanship, and he was knowledgeable and obviously intelligent. And God knows best. [18b, l.12]

[19b, l.10] Shaykh Yaḥyā b. Abī Ṭayy Ḥamīd al-Najjār al-Ghassānī of Aleppo **said** the following in his book: When the oath of allegiance was given to al-Ḥāfiẓ, he appointed Hazār, known as al-'Ādil Jawāmard, a *mamlūk*, as his vizier, who held office for part of a day. He was [then] killed, and his head was paraded around Cairo. And God knows best.

[20a, l.24] Shaykh Yaḥyā b. Abī Ṭayy Ḥamīd al-Najjār al-Ghassānī of Aleppo **said** the following in his book: After Hizabr al-Mulūk, a son of al-Afḍal b. emir al-Juyūsh, the emir 'Alī Kutayfāt, **ruled**, and the reason for his accession was that his father al-Afḍal's *mamlūk*s, and those of his brother Muẓaffar, rose up in Egypt [in rebellion], seeking his succession. They were granted this, so it was bestowed on him and he took the vizierate. He removed injustices [afflicting] people, and returned to them what had been taken from them due to the injustice and extortion [of former leaders]. He ruled well [20b]. When his rule became settled, and his position as vizier well-organised, he manifested his creed. He was an Imāmī. Then he gathered together all the Imāmīs of Egypt and said, 'I intend to suspend the *khuṭba* for al-Ḥāfiẓ, and to make the *khuṭba* [in the name of] the Awaited Imām, the Master of the Ages, the son of al-Ḥasan, so what do you all say?' Some of them accepted this, and [others] said, 'It would be better to leave that [course of action]. Our master [should] be busied with his rule, and the improvement of his own state of affairs.'

But [the vizier] did not accept this, and arrested al-Ḥāfiẓ and kept him under close supervision. He made the *khuṭba* [in the name of] the Awaited Imām al-Qā'im. He removed the mention of the Egyptians [Fatimid caliphs] from the *khuṭba*, and ordered the muezzins to drop 'Muḥammad and 'Alī are the best of men', but to retain '[Hasten] to the best of works.' He instituted the Friday prayer according to the Imāmī rite in Egypt, Cairo and all the areas under his rule, and ordered that there should be two *qunūts* in the two cycles of prayer. And he joined together the prayers of *al-ẓuhr* and *al-ʿaṣr*.

He ordered himself to be **addressed with titles from** the pulpit, such as 'And he is the most virtuous Master, the Chief of the Realms of the Leaders of the Dynasties; the Protector of the Territories of the Religion; the Spreader of the Wings of Justice for those who are Far or Near; Helper of the Imām of Truth in his two states of Occultation and Presence; and Steadfast in helping him with the sharpness of his sword and the correctness of his opinion and his planning; God's Trustee over His servants; Guide to the judges in following the True Law, and its Support; the Supreme Guide of the Missionaries of the Believers by dint of the clearness of his speech and his instruction; the Benefactor, and Lifter of Injustice against the Nations; the Owner of the two Virtues of the Sword and the Pen; Abū ʿAlī Aḥmad b. al-Sayyid al-Afḍal Abu 'l-Qāsim Shāhanshāh, the son of Amīr al-Juyūsh Badr al-Jamālī' – without a hint of the mention of al-Ḥāfiẓ whatsoever. And God knows best. [20b, l.20]

[41b, l.10] *sub anno 526/1131*

Account of some reports about the vizier al-Afḍal, the vizier of Egypt, and his assassination

He was Aḥmad b. al-Afḍal Shāhanshāh b. Amīr al-Juyūsh Badr **al-Jamālī, known by his *kunya*** Abū ʿAlī, **styled** al-Afḍal like his father. We **have** already presented the reasons for the vizierate of the aforementioned al-Afḍal Aḥmad and some reports about him, and dispense with their repetition here. Rather, we will report some of what has been said by historians.

The aforementioned vizier al-Afḍal Aḥmad **was** generous with his wealth, abundant in his gift-giving and learned. He wrote a book named *An Explanation of the Authentication of the Continued Existence of the Master of the Age*, in which he synthesised the [views of] jurists, and debated [this position] with all the scholars from all the religious schools, and brought them to an agreement to authenticate it. He was a lover of poetry, and gave rewards for it, and on this Abu'l Manṣūr Ẓāfir b. al-Qāsim al-Jazarī al-Ḥaddād al-Iskandarānī said in his **poem** .... [l.20]

[42a, l.18] Shaykh Yaḥyā b. Abī Ṭayy Ḥamīd al-Najjār al-Ghassānī of Aleppo **said** the following: **In this year** Abū ʿAlī the vizier of al-Ḥāfiẓ was killed in Egypt at the Maydān [Hippodrome], by a plot devised against him.

He had stopped to look about, become separated [from his group] at that spot and was deprived of his men. Then a group of soldiers set upon him and killed him. When he fell to the ground, they cut off his head with his [own] sword, which had been the sword of al-Ḥusayn b. ʿAlī ibn Abī Ṭālib, may God be pleased with them both. [l.23]

[42b, l.17] Shaykh Yaḥyā b. Abī Ṭayy Ḥamīd al-Najjār al-Ghassānī of Aleppo **said** the following: **When** Abū ʿAlī al-Afḍal was killed, the prayers for al-Ḥāfiẓ in the Friday sermon were brought back, and he was greeted as 'Amīr al-Mu'minīn'. The oath of allegiance to him was made for a second time, and then, God wiling, what we will narrate took place. [1.20]

[43b, l.3] Shaykh Yaḥyā b. Abī Ṭayy Ḥamīd al-Najjār al-Ghassānī of Aleppo **said** the following: al-Ḥāfiẓ **appointed** Yānis **as his vizier**, and styled him Commander of the Armies and the Sword of Islam. He stayed [in office] for a while, and then al-Ḥāfiẓ desired to kill him, so he suggested to his physician that he contrive his murder. The physician was afraid of the consequences of this and refused, saying, 'O Commander of the Believers, it is not permitted for one who enters upon monarchs to work towards this purpose openly.' **And it so happened** that Yānis was afflicted by dysentery, and this physician treated him. Then when he wanted to acquit himself, al-Ḥāfiẓ fetched his doctor and talked to him about [how to carry out] the murder. [The doctor] said: 'O my Master, the remedy for this illness is repose. If my Master intends to do anything himself, then proceed to visit him. His being upset by our lord's visit will be the cause of his demise.' So al-Ḥāfiẓ did this, and he brought about [Yānis'] death in Dhu 'l-Ḥijja of this year. God knows best how much of this took place. [l.15]

[59a, l.14] *sub anno 528/1133*
Shaykh Yaḥyā b. Abī Ṭayy Ḥamīd al-Najjār al-Ghassānī of Aleppo **related**, in the [account of the] events of the year 529, the following: Ḥasan b. al-Ḥāfiẓ **rose up** against his father al-Ḥāfiẓ, and arrested him. He employed a man called 'Abd Allāh al-Ikhnāwī, and appointed him over the black soldiery.

[Ḥasan's] rule grew strong, and he introduced new arrangements for the soldiers, oppressed them, robbed them and took over the rule of Cairo. So the army joined with the deputy over al-Maḥalla,[6] Tāj al-Dawla Bahrām, who was of the Armenian religion, and sought his help. He rode with them, and joined the Banū Ḥadrūj, who were a great number [of men] living in Lower Egypt, to [that party].

They made for Cairo, surrounded it, burned down the Gates of Zuwayla, al-Qanṭara, al-Khūkha, Sa'āda and al-Barqiyya,[7] and they wielded the sword over the black soldiery. Ḥasan b. al-Ḥāfiẓ then fled to his father, hid with him, and the armies sought him. But [al-Ḥāfiẓ] kept him from them, so [the armies] decided to destroy the palace. Then al-Ḥāfiẓ killed [Ḥasan]. It said that al-Ḥāfiẓ gave [Ḥasan] poison to drink, killed him, and then showed him to them, so they were silenced, **and there ends his report.** [l.28]

[60b, l.17] Shaykh Yaḥyā b. Abī Ṭayy Ḥamīd al-Najjār al-Ghassānī of Aleppo **related** the following: Bahrām became the vizier for al-Ḥāfiẓ, and he was one of the Armenians residing at the Byzantine fortress in Lower Syria, which the Armenian deputies looked after. [Bahrām] made *da'wa* [claiming] that he was one of the progeny of David – the choicest salutations and peace be upon both our Master the Messenger of God and upon him – and they were the Armenian family who made *da'wa* on this [claim]. They had a distinguishing characteristic, which was that if one of them stood and stretched out his hand, it would reach his knee, and if he circled [his hands] around his waist, they would meet.

The reason for Bahrām's arrival in Egypt was that the Armenian deputy died, and his power was handed over to someone else, and Bahrām was the fittest for it. Then he left that place to come to [Cairo], and was met there with a great reception. He was permitted to send for his people, so a group of them travelled to Egypt [61a]. It said that they numbered more than 30,000 families, most of them coming from Aleppo and Tall Bāshir.[8]

When Bahrām took over the vizierate, his brother was appointed over the city of Qūṣ in Upper Egypt, [but] he spread his hand in injustice and tyranny and rebuilt the ruined churches throughout Egypt. It is said that when Bahrām was established in the vizierate, he asked al-Ḥāfiẓ to permit him to fetch his brother and his family [to Egypt], and he was granted this [permission]. So they were brought from Tall Bāshir and Nahr al-Jawr,[9] until his family and the others who were brought to him numbered 30,000 individuals. They became overbearing, and the Muslims were afflicted by great oppression at their hands. [Bahrām] had appointed his brother, known as al-Bāsāk [Basil], over Qūṣ and its districts, and he oppressed [the people] there greatly, confiscated their wealth and was unjust towards them.

The Armenians built [so many] churches and monasteries that each of their chiefs had a church built for him[self]. The people of Egypt feared that they would change the Islamic religion, and complaints against Bahrām and his brother al-Bāsāk multiplied. This pained the emirs of Egypt, so they wrote to Riḍwān b. Walakhshī, the governor of al-Gharbiyya.[10] Then what we shall relate, God-willing, came about. **[l.14]**

[Vol. III: 21a, l.5] *sub anno 544/1149*

Shaykh Yaḥyā b. Abī Ṭayy **said**: [al-Ḥāfiẓ] died on a Thursday in the year 544, and he was 81 years old on the day he died. He **left behind** his sons Ḥaydara, Abū ʿAlī Ḥasan, Yūsuf, Jibrīl and Ismāʿīl. [l.8]

[21a, l.13] Account of the Rule of al-Ẓāfir bi-Amrillāh al-ʿUbaydī Over Egypt

Abu'l-Manṣūr Ismāʿīl b. al-Ḥāfiẓ Abu 'l-Maymūn ʿAbd al-Majīd b. Muḥammad b. al-Mustanṣir **al-ʿUbaydī received the oath of allegiance** on the day of his father's death, in spite of disagreement about the testament for him from his father, and his being the youngest in years of his father sons. **He was given the title** al-Ẓāfir bi-Amrillāh.

Shaykh Yaḥyā b. Abī Ṭayy Ḥamīd al-Najjār al-Ghassānī of Aleppo **said** the following: After al-Ḥāfiẓ, **the oath of allegiance was made to** his son Abu'l-Manṣūr Ismāʿīl, the youngest of his sons, and he was titled al-Ẓāfir bi-Amrillāh when he was fifteen, on the Thursday of Jumāda 'l-Ākhir of year [5]43, or it said year [5]44, and that is [21b] correct. He lasted [as caliph] until he was killed by the emir Nāṣir al-Dīn b. ʿAbbās, on a night of Thursday at the end of Muḥarram of the year 549. His rule lasted four years and eight months, and his age [at death] was 25 years. The narrative about him is contradictory on the age he had reached, as you see.

When al-Ẓāfir bi-Amrillāh took the oath of allegiance, he sat in the belvedere of the al-Dhahab Gate and distributed wealth among the people. And God knows best. [l.5]

[22a, l.19] Shaykh Yaḥyā b. Abī Ṭayy Ḥamīd al-Najjār al-Ghassānī of Aleppo **said**: **When** Ibn al-Salār neared Cairo, al-Ẓāfir ordered Ibn Maṣāl to cross into Upper Egypt, gather [troops] and pursue Ibn al-Salār when he got there. But [Ibn Maṣāl] did not do this and went out to [confront] him with the troops who were in Cairo. Ibn al-Salār then defeated and killed him.

[But] the correct [account] is [22b] that [Ibn Maṣāl] did go out to Upper Egypt, and Ibn al-Salār entered Cairo and took possession of the vizierate. The defeat of the army [in the battle] between Ibn al-Salār and Ibn Maṣāl was repeated. Then the emir ʿAbbās, and the 'Hero of the Muslims' Ṭalāʾiʿ b. Ruzzīk, and all those who followed Ibn al-Salār, went out [in battle]. The two groups met in Tunbudā,[11] where the battle took place. Most of Ibn Maṣāl's troops were absent on the day of the battle, and he had none with him but Badr b. Rāfiʿ and some of his men, and a small band of infantry from the black soldiery.

The first part of the day [of the battle] [saw victory] for the troops of Ibn Maṣāl, but the end [of it] [saw victory] for the troops of Ibn al-Salār. Then Badr b. Rāfiʿ was killed as his horse fell under him. Ibn Maṣāl **was killed** by an unknown killer, as were innumerable foot-soldiers; this was after six months of Ibn al-Salār's rule. God knows best how much of this [really] took place. [l.12]

[23b, l.8] **It is said** that al-Ẓāfir bi-Amrillāh was not pleased with the vizierate of Ibn al-Salār, and decided upon his murder, and [the vizier] feared him. He did not enter [his company] to make salutations to him except through the door known as the Gate of ʿĪd, and this was the door through which one entered a great courtyard. A group of his *mamlūks* and companions would enter with him, and al-Ẓāfir would sit for him by a window, which looked down on them. Al-ʿĀdil [Ibn al-Salār] would enter and salute him from behind this window. There entered with [Ibn al-Salār] a group he called the Youths of Chain Mail, and they numbered nearly a thousand men. When he entered, he would only do so surrounded by them. And this Ibn al-Salār **was** despotic in his conduct, and had overpowering authority. [l.17]

[24a, l.23] When Ibn al-Salār died, his corpse was ordered to be exhibited on the Zuwayla Gate – there is no deity but God – and how cruel this was!

The emir ʿAbbās **advanced** while Ibn al-Salār was vizier, and greatly distinguished himself by his brilliance.

[24b] **In this year** [544], Muʾayyad al-Dawla Usāma b. Munqidh arrived in Egypt from Damascus, on bad terms with the emir Muʿīn al-Dīn [Unur],[12] its ruler. He then joined the emir ʿAbbās al-Ṣanhājī and became a favourite with him. Muʾayyad al-Dawla Usāma had left his wives and his possessions in Damascus, and the emir Muʿīn al-Dīn Unur had surrendered them to the Franks, so Ibn Munqidh wrote him a poem which **begins** … . [l.6]

[25b, l.9] **We have only** related this poem in its entirety because of the merits it contains, which we would love learned men to be guided by, and because of its politics, which we would love to acquaint them with. Also, [we want to show] the vile conduct of the emir Muʿīn al-Dīn towards Usāma after a long [period of] service, [in disregard of] the duty of inviolability [towards him].

When this poem reached the emir Muʿīn al-Dīn, he requested the emir Maḥmūd b. Sinān al-Shayradhī al-Naḥawī, in the Mosque of Damascus, to reply to [Usāma] that day, so he replied with a poem which **begins**. … . [l.15]

[26a, l.7] **The poem** is lengthy. When Usāma b. Munqidh got to the emir ʿAbbās, he made a great impression on him and became close to him until he became one of his nightly companions in pleasant [conversation], and his special friend in private moments. And God knows best. [l.9]

[77b, l.13] *sub anno 549/1144*
Ibn Munqidh **had** urged the aforementioned 'Abbās [al-Ṣanḥājī, the vizier's nephew] to kill the vizier Ibn al-Salār, as we previously explained. Then this act [of killing] came to be known, and also that it was on the advice of Ibn Munqidh. [News of] this reached Ibn Munqidh, who feared for himself. Then the censure of all the *ahl al-sunna* of Egypt came down on him, as well as that of all those who loved what Ibn al-Salār loved, and followed his creed. A group of those with al-Ẓāfir discussed the matter of Ibn Munqidh with him, and his audacity in what he had suggested [to 'Abbās], and they said: 'This man is a stranger from another realm, who is not inwardly sincere towards this dynasty or its people. Perhaps if left [to his own devices], he might bring about an event not possible to repair.' [News of] this [discussion] reached Usāma b. Munqidh, and his fear increased, and he dreaded being surprised by something not possible to be saved from, and which he could not take precautions against. So he set about planning for himself.

[78a] **Then it so happened** that the *emir* Nāṣir al-Dīn Naṣr, son of the vizier 'Abbās, was present with al-Ẓāfir and stayed with him for a few days and during the nights. On one of those nights, [al-Ẓāfir] gifted him 100,000 Egyptian *dīnār*s. Harsh condemnation of this followed, and people spoke about it. They said: 'Al-Ẓāfir seeks the rebellion of Nāṣir al-Dīn b. 'Abbās [against his own father 'Abbās].' This talk reached the vizier 'Abbās, who sent for Usāma b. Munqidh and said to him: 'What's to be done about what the people are discussing?' So an open opportunity was provided for Usāma b. Munqidh to make suggestions, and [Usāma] prepared for him the execution of a strategy against al-Ẓāfir. [Usāma] thus took himself towards delusion, the riding of danger and carrying out one of the enormities [i.e., murder].

He said to the vizier 'Abbās: 'My lord! I am your client, the sapling of your favour, the fruit of your beneficence and the child of your kindness. I am obliged to give you good counsel and speak the truth. This matter has become known and spread, and its secret has been brought out and made manifest to people. There is a fall from honour in it, and the destruction of rank, and it is something by which one can no longer retain a lofty standing or high authority.' **The Arabs** say 'The fire, rather than disgrace; misfortune, rather than being blamed.' The vizier 'Abbās said: 'Who can oppose Nāṣir al-Dīn in what people say about him, despite his power, his greatness and his boldness?' Usāma said to him: 'I will meet him in this, even if I perish through it.'

So it was ordered that [Nāṣir al-Dīn] be sent for, and 'Abbās sent for him and cleared his salon. Then Usāma said to him, after he had extracted oaths from him: 'Truly, the people have praised you greatly, and are deeply concerned with you, for you are the leading man of this land. You are the son of the leader of all the subjects, whose good qualities all people see and whose power of rank they recognise. If you are happy with all of this, [know that] your father will decide himself about staying in humiliation or leaving regretfully.'

Nāṣir al-Dīn was furious, for this was painful for him, so he denied it, and swore binding oaths regarding his blamelessness in relation to [al-Ẓāfir]. [78b] {...} 'this does not benefit, and nothing can be done about what has happened and spread around {…} and this man, to make manifest to people that you are innocent of what they accused you of, because of which they stripped away your honour.'

So he said: 'How am I able to do this, while [al-Ẓāfir's] troop are so many, his wealth is plentiful and he has the equivalent of these strongholds?' [Usāma] replied: 'His killing will not be by hostility, hardness, by outnumbering him or by fighting; it is only that the curtain between you and him has been torn, and the veil lifted. So be tender in your service to him at that time, tear the veil of his inviolability and say, when you see him inclined towards you, 'O my lord, I crave that you honour me with your presence at my house and eat my food.' Then when he acquiesces in this, say to him, 'I desire that this should be at night, with [you leading] a small number of your men and servants, to complete my happiness and perfect my joy.' Then when he is present with you, look to the means of his murder and burial. Thereupon, your father will set up a replacement for him from among his family, and [al-Ẓāfir] will pass away as if vanished into thin air.' This made an impression on the emir Nāṣir al-Dīn b. 'Abbās, and he prepared a place for what he had in mind. Then he met with al-Ẓāfir, asked him for a visit, and [the caliph] assented to this, because of the strength of his affection for him.

He went out to [Nāṣir al-Dīn] hidden from the view of people. The house of 'Abbās – which had been the house of Ibn al-Ma'mūn al-Baṭā'iḥī – was near the small palace in the Swordsmiths' Quarter of Cairo. He entered [Nāṣir's house] through a secret door in an underground passage, to the sitting room he had prepared for him. [The caliph] had a small number of manservants with him, and when he arrived, [Nāṣir al-Dīn] took him into a room, pounced on him, killed him, and killed the servants who were with him. One young servant escaped and stood still inside one of the coverings of the doors of the house. Then [Nāṣir al-Dīn] Ibn 'Abbās took [the bodies of] al-Ẓāfir and the servants whom he had killed along with him, dropped them into a pit in the middle of the house, and put down some of the house's marble slabs over it. He washed away the traces of blood and spread out carpets [79a] and rugs [over the area]. All this was in view of the servant [who had escaped]; he sat down and [wanted to do something.] The emir Nāṣir al-Dīn b. 'Abbās met with his father that night and informed him of what had been done to al-Ẓāfir. We shall relate the sequel, God-willing.

Al-Ẓāfir was **born** on a Sunday in the middle of the month of Rabī' al-Ākhir of the year 527, and he was killed on the eve of Thursday at the end of God's month of al-Muḥarram in the year 549. **And it is said** that he was killed on the 15th of al-Muḥarram, the aforementioned month, aged 25 years, and that his rule had lasted four years and eight months. And God knows best.

Account of the rule of al-Fā'iz al-'Ubaydī over Egypt

On that Thursday, and some say it was a Monday, the morning after the night in which al-Ẓāfir al-'Ubaydī the ruler of Egypt was killed, which was one of the two days on which one could enter the [presence of the] 'Ubaydī caliph to offer salutations, the vizier 'Abbās al-Ṣanhājī came to the palace according to his habit, to pay his respects, feigning a lack of intelligence about the fate of al-Ẓāfir. With him were leading emirs and troops. He stopped at the door of the palace and summoned a servant. [The vizier] said to him: 'Is our lord in session?' He replied: 'No.' So he said: 'Go, take yourself to him and let him know of the gathering of people for salutation.' The servant entered the palace – and the people of the palace did not yet know of [the caliph's] murder, because he had left them in secret, and not told anyone of his departure. When the servant entered the palace, [other] servants entered with him, to ask permission for the vizier 'Abbās [to enter]. They did not find [the caliph], so they went into the chamber of the private quarters and searched for him there among his womenfolk, [79b] [the area of] his sitting [rooms] and secluded quarters, and all the places where he was likely to be in the palace. It was said to [the servants] that he had not spent the night there. So the servant went out to the vizier and said to him: 'My master has some excuse [for his absence], and there is no way to reach him.'

'Abbās said: 'It is not possible for me leave until I've seen him because an important matter has occurred on which I want to consult him.' The servant returned to the palace and asked the womenfolk and the servants once again, but none could give him news or acquaint him with any clues. They became convinced at this point that the caliph was missing. The group of servants spoke up and said: 'Yesterday, he went to the house of Nāṣir al-Dīn b. 'Abbās, and did not return.' 'Abbās dismounted and forced his way to enter the palace, [proceeding] until he got to the hall of the al-Baḥr Gate, which was one of the chambers where the 'Ubaydī caliph habitually sat, and said: 'What has my master done, and where is he?' [The people of the palace] said: 'Yesterday he went to your son's house and until this very hour has not returned.' Then the servant who had hidden in the house of Ibn 'Abbās found his opportunity and came out to the palace and informed them of what he had witnessed of the murder of al-Ẓāfir. The people [of the palace] stayed calm and said: '[Let us wait] until the situation is uncovered', and the women wanted to weep [but] were prevented [from weeping] by the brothers of al-Ẓāfir.

Then 'Abbās said: 'Bring out the brothers of al-Ẓāfir.' So Jibrīl, Yūsuf and their nephew Abu 'l-Taqī Ṣāliḥ b. Ḥasan came out to him, and he asked them about al-Ẓāfir. They replied: 'Ask your son about him – he knows more than we do.' Then he gave the command [for their execution], and they were decapitated, after he had said to them: 'You murdered him.'

It is said that they said to him, when they came out to him: 'Give us some time to look for him and ask for news of him,' [but] he said 'You killed him, and [yet] you say "Let us ask about him."' [l.22]

[80b, l.13] **It is said** that the vizier 'Abbās brought out the brothers of al-Ẓāfir and said to the two of them: 'You have killed our Imam, and we do not know anything about his condition except from you two.' And they persisted in denying that they had murdered him, and were truthful in their denial, [yet] he killed them there and then, to preclude himself and his son from suspicion. Then the people of the palace took to weeping and crying for al-Ẓāfir and his brothers. [l.8]

[81a, l.10] **It is said** that when the vizier 'Abbās killed the brothers and nephew of al-Ẓāfir, he said to the controller of the palace: 'Where is the son of our master?' He replied: 'He's here.' Then he said: 'Lead me to where he is.' Then he entered the secluded chamber where [the caliph's son] was with his maternal grandmother, carried him on his shoulder, and took him out to the people before the murder victims were removed, and made the oath of allegiance to him as caliph. [The young caliph] saw those who had been killed, and was frightened and disturbed; for the duration of his caliphate, he remained without any enjoyment of life. [l.15]

[l.21] Account of the Egyptians' seeking the aid of Ṭalā'i' b. Ruzzīk against the vizier 'Abbās and his son; the flight and murder of 'Abbās and his son

We have already set out what was said about the murder of al-Ẓāfir [81b] [al-'Ubaydī] … and the accession of his son al-Fā'iz al-'Ubaydī in Egypt, with the vizier 'Abbās continuing to rule actively for the dynasty. Thereafter the armies reacted [with hostility towards] al-'Abbas, and disapproved of his killing of al-Ẓāfir and his brothers. They revolted against him, and he got the better of them and overcame them, then returned to his rule. This was on the tenth of Ṣafar of that year [549], and in [that year], the rule of al-Fā'iz was settled, and he received the oath of allegiance from people; 'Abbās became sole ruler, and no hand remained over his hand. [l.7]

[82a, l.15] **It is said** that when news about Ṭalā'i' b. Ruzzīk reached the vizier 'Abbās, he sent Ḥusayn b. Ḥamdiyya out to him, who was at the time the son-in-law of al-Ṣāliḥ [Ṭalā'i' b. Ruzzīk]. [Ḥusayn] went to him, rebuking him, to persuade him from what he had [previously] decided upon. When he was alone with him, [Ḥusayn] asked him: 'With whom will you fight 'Abbās, when he has 5,000 *mamlūk*s at this time?' Al-Ṣāliḥ replied: 'You do not know whom I shall kill him with. I shall fight him by myself and with you.' Then Ḥusayn said: 'As of this moment, yes.'

This Ḥusayn was a celebrated horseman, courageous, known all over Egypt for [his] vigour, and dreaded by the army [of 'Abbās]. So the two [Ḥusayn and Ṭalā'i'] set off together. The emir Ṭalā'i' and all his men had donned [82b] black garments {…} on the tops of their banners, until they neared Gīza, and the armies that were in Cairo and [all of] Egypt [came together] against 'Abbās. So he [and his son] fled, along with his family. He had made up packages of great amounts of wealth, [and] fixed them {…} to the waists of his servants. Usāma b. Munqidh [also] left with him, and they went out to Syria along the road to Ayla.[13] Then the troops and the black soldiery who were in Egypt went out to [greet] the [chief] "Horseman of the Muslims", Abu 'l-Ghārāt Ṭalā'i' b. Ruzzīk. This is [what we know] of their story. [l.7]

[82b, l.26] **It is said** that al-Ṣāliḥ's entry to Cairo was on Sunday [83a] the thirteenth of the month of Rabī' al-Awwal. When al-Ṣāliḥ b. Ruzzīk had buried al-Ẓāfir, he turned his hand to improving the affairs [of the state], and sought the people's oath of allegiance to al-Fā'iz, and to himself after him. He spent money freely, and attracted men [to be his retainers]. He was a leader in himself, and great among the scions of his race [the Armenians]; he had great intelligence, had seen a great deal, was knowledgeable about the histories of mankind, and he engaged all subjects, especially scholastic theology and literature. In these two [subjects] he was a courageous adventurer, and the foremost of heroes. He won over the followers of the dynasty by grace, religious piety and the repudiation of immorality, oppression and injustice. The people in their entirety loved him, and were well-disposed towards him. **This** is what [we have heard] of the affairs of al-Ṣāliḥ the son of Ruzzīk, and of those who were [then] in Egypt. [l.9]

[83a, l.18] **It is said** that the sister of al-Ẓāfir had corresponded with the Franks, who had taken possession of Ascalon, and guaranteed to give them 100,000 *dīnārs* if they killed ʿAbbās or his son, or captured them. So the Franks set out and lay in wait in ambush, and then seized them in Mizza, or Umm Kaʿb, which was one of the watering holes, or it said in Muwaylij, or [perhaps] in Zarʿ. They then assaulted [ʿAbbās], killed his son Husām al-Mulk, took his son Naṣr as a prisoner and his small children and family as captives. A number of his men fled to Syria and so escaped, among them Usāma b. Munqidh. The Franks thereby came into possession of the wealth that accompanied him.

They sent away whoever was in the palace [83b] {…} [known as] al-Tawzarī on the sixteenth of the month of Rabīʿ [al-Awwal] {…} the wealth. He then surrendered him to the Franks, and obtained Naṣr b. [ʿAbbās] from them {…} and he put him in an iron cage and went ahead with him to Cairo. The people came out {…} [to him] … and insulted him, cursed him and spat on him, until he was brought into [the palace]. {…} And it is said that the servant girls killed him by prodding him with needles made of iron, or it is said by slapping him with their clogs, or it said that they cut off his flesh and fed it to him until he died. Then he was brought out and crucified at the Gate of Zuwayla, one of the Gates of Cairo the Protected, and after that he was burnt. This is only a summary of what happened, even though it is rather long [an account].

Al-Ṣāliḥ b. Ruzzīk **pursued** those who had helped Naṣr b. ʿAbbās in murdering al-Ẓāfir al-ʿUbaydī, of whom he seized Qaymāz, Futūḥ al-Akhras and Ibn Ghālib, and killed them in cold blood. He also killed [another] large group for that same reason. The situation of al-Ṣāliḥ then stabilised, and he styled himself the "Horseman of the Muslims, Helper of the Religion, al-Ṣāliḥ", and the poets eulogised him thus … . [l.14]

[148b, l.9] *sub anno 556/1160-1*
In [this year], Muḥammad b. Ḥusayn b. Niẓār b. al-Mustanṣir appeared from Morocco, along with many soldiers and a great army. When he approached Egyptian territory, he took the surname al-Mustanṣir. The emir Ḥusām b. Fiḍḍa, of the Banū Ruzzīk, deceived [Muḥammad] and promised him that he would sacrifice himself in his service. He played along with [Muḥammad], until he got him into his tent. Then [Ḥusām] seized him, brought him to Egypt and surrendered him to al-Ṣāliḥ b. Ruzzīk, the vizier of Egypt. And God knows best.

Account of some reports about al-Ṣāliḥ b. Ruzzīk, the vizier of Egypt, and his assassination

He was Ṭalāʾiʿ b. Ruzzīk the Armenian, with the agnomen Abu ʾl-Maʿārif, **known as** al-Ṣāliḥ. Al-Ṣāliḥ b. Ruzzīk was brave, gracious, generous, magnanimous, learned, fond of cultured people and an excellent poet. **I have seen** in some histories that al-Ṣāliḥ Ṭalāʾiʿ b. Ruzzīk **was portrayed** as an eloquent man, fluent, a poet, possessed of authority and courage. And a strange tale is circulated about him, **which is** that in his early years, al-Ṣāliḥ advanced from Morocco in the company of dervishes, intending to visit Najaf, where the Commander of the Faithful ʿAlī b. Abī Ṭālib, may God be pleased with him, is buried. When they arrived in Najaf, [the party] numbered forty men. Ṭalā'i' was a man who was constant in his love for the family of Muḥammad, God's salutations and peace be upon him. So when they made their visit, they spent that night in Najaf, where the *imām* was al-Sayyid Ibn Ma'ṣūm. This *imām* **saw** the Commander of the Faithful 'Alī b. Abī Ṭālib, may God be pleased with him, in a dream, and he said to him, 'Some forty dervishes have reached you this night, and among their group is a man named Ṭalā'i' b. Ruzzīk, one of the greatest in love for us. Say to him: Be at ease! For we have appointed you over Egypt.' Then when Ibn Ma'ṣūm rose in the morning and had performed the morning prayer, he ordered the muezzin to call out, 'Whoever among you is Ṭalā'i' b. Ruzzīk, [he should] take himself to al-Sayyid Ibn Ma'ṣūm.' When the muezzin made this announcement, Ṭalā'i' b. Ruzzīk rose and greeted the the *imām*. [The *imām*] said to him: 'I saw the Imām [149a] 'Alī b. Abī Ṭālib, may God be pleased with him, and he said such and such to me, and he has appointed you over Egypt.'

So Ṭalā'i' b. Ruzzīk got up and set off for Egypt, and he progressed [in his career] until he took over as deputy of Upper Egypt in Minya Banū Khaṣīb.[14] Then what we said before is related: that the people of Egypt wrote to him to ask him to help them, to rebel against the vizier 'Abbās and to set off for Cairo with a large group. 'Abbās fled from [Ṭalā'i'] to Syria. Then al-Ṣāliḥ b. Ruzzīk entered Cairo without opposition and took up the vizierate of Egypt on behalf of al-Fā'iz al-'Ubaydī, as we have set out, until [the caliph] died and al-'Āḍid al-'Ubaydī took over. Nominal power was established for the aforementioned al-'Āḍid, and for al-Ṣāliḥ b. Ruzzīk in practice, and [the latter's] untouchability increased, as he proceeded, during the rule of al-'Āḍid, with blameworthy conduct. He monopolised the crops so their prices rose, and killed emirs of the state, as we have set out. Al-'Āḍid married the daughter of al-Ṣāliḥ, and was [thus] deceived into a false sense of security, and then there came about what we shall relate, God-willing.

One of the historians **said** that al-Ṣāliḥ b. Ruzzīk was the man of his time for learning, intelligence, good policy and good management. He was awe-inspiring in his appearance, great in his authority, and he amassed great wealth. He had acquired countless items of clothing, robes and furnishings. He was observant of ritual prayers, both the obligatory and voluntary ones, and was great in his partisanship [towards the Imāmī creed]. He had compiled a book entitled *The Reliance in the Refutation of the People of Obduracy*, in which he had gathered [views of] the majority of jurists, [and] debated [the Imāmī creed] with them, [writing] about the validity of the imāmate of the Commander of the Faithful 'Alī b. Abī Ṭālib, may God be pleased with him, and he extracted [his material] from *Ṣaḥīḥ al-Bukhārī*, *Muslim*, *al-Tirmidhī* and other books of the ahl al-sunna. He discussed [the subject] on the [authority of] texts of *ḥadīth*, and extracted proofs of the legitimacy of the imāmate from them. He also wrote exquisite poetry in every genre, among which is some that makes clear his creed, where **he says....** [1.24]

[1.29] **He wrote** a poem entitled 'The Essence in the Refutation of the Qadariyya'.[15] He built [149b] the mosque that is outside the Gate of Zuwayla, known as the Mosque of al-Ṣāliḥ, and he built the Mosque of the Great Cemetry.[16] **He endowed** the chiefs of the noble Prophetic descendants with two thirds of [the revenues of] Bilbays,[17] [gave] seven *qirāṭ*s [measures] to the City of our leader and prophet Muḥammad, God's salutations and peace be upon him, and one *qirāṭ* to the sons of Ibn Maʿṣūm, the *imām* of al-Najaf. [l.4]

[150a, l.18] Shaykh Yaḥyā b. Abī Ṭayy Ḥamīd al-Najjār b. Ẓāfir b. ʿAlī al-Ghassānī of Aleppo, author of the book *Goldmines of the History of Kings, Caliphs and Those of High Standing*, **said**: al-Ṣāliḥ b. Ruzzīk **was** distinguished, praised and saw the worth of those who sought him out. The *faqīh* Khalīl b. Khumārtakīn al-Ḥalabi[18] **who had been** sent out by al-Malik al-ʿĀdil Nūr al-Dīn Maḥmūd b. al-Malik al-Manṣūr ʿImād al-Dīn Atabeg Zengī with a group of Aleppans he had dispatched, **related to me** that he went to al-Ṣāliḥ b. Ruzzīk, and [al-Ṣāliḥ] was generous towards him and his reception [of them] was excellent. Then when [the *faqīh*] wanted to leave Egypt, he bestowed a thousand *dīnār*s of his [own] wealth on him, and assigned to him, at the expense of the noblemen of Egypt, another thousand *dīnār*s. So he [stayed and] lived in Egypt all his life, and [al-Ṣāliḥ] enriched his descendants after his death. The *faqīh* Ibn Asʿad al-ʿIrāqī **used to** praise him in a poem each year, and dispatch it to him, so [al-Ṣāliḥ] would send him a reward of 500 *dīnār*s. Among the poems in which [al-ʿIrāqī] eulogised [al-Ṣāliḥ] is the one which begins… [150b]

[150b, l.20] During his rule, al-Ṣāliḥ b. Ruzzīk **did** not stop his raids against the Franks, and he would fight them on land one year, and by sea another year, and sometimes both on land and by sea, as has been related by the poets in their verses. Every year, he **would** convey to the noble sanctuaries of Makka and Madina all that the noble [Prophetic] descendants needed of garments and utensils for the women and men, to the point where he even sent them childrens' writing tablets, pens for writing and inkwells of ink. In the same way he supplied the ʿAlids of the shrines. A great crowd of scholars and notables would visit him from all the lands, and not one of them would return except with what he had hoped for. **And among** the poetry of al-Ṣāliḥ Ṭalāʾiʿ b. Ruzzīk is **his saying** … [151a]

[151b, l.1] **It is related** that al-Ṣāliḥ b. Ruzzīk said, the night before the morning of his murder, 'The Commander of the Faithful ʿAlī b. Abī Ṭālib, may God be pleased with him, was struck down on a night like this one,' and he ordered the [story of the] murder of ʿAlī, may God be pleased with him, to be read out to him. He took a ritual bath on this night and prayed 120 *rakʿa* according to the Imāmī rite.

And it is said that al-Ṣāliḥ b. Ruzzīk went out riding on the day in which he was killed, and he tripped. His turban fell from his head and became disarranged. He sat in the hallway of the Chamber of the Vizierate, and summoned Ibn al-Ṣanaf, who was the one who tied the turbans of the caliphs and viziers of Egypt, for which he had a splendid salary. When he was summoned, [al-Ṣāliḥ] ordered him to fix his turban, and then a man known as Ibn Bayān came forward him and said, "May God protect our master and suffice him in the completion [of his days], for the matter that has come to pass has an evil omen emanating from it,' and could [the vizier] perhaps decide to postpone his ride? [Al-Ṣāliḥ] said, "Evil omens are from the devil, and there is no way to postpone the ride," and then he rode. Then there came about what we shall relate regarding his murder, God-willing. And [the historians] **differ** on the reasons for his murder. … [l.14]

[151b, l.26] **It is said** that the paternal aunt of al-ʿĀḍid worked against al-Ṣāliḥ b. Ruzzīk in aid of his murder, and spent [great] wealth on the emirs. [News of] this reached him, and he retrieved all of that wealth, and took the best and most secure precautions against her. Then he killed a group of emirs, [thus] removing them, took control of [152a] the state and attained a high rank within it.

Then the aunt of al-ʿĀḍid returned, and carried through her strategy against him. She offered a huge amount of wealth to a group of black soldiers, until they came down upon him with the deed [of murder], as we shall shall relate. They were known as the Banū al-Rāʿī, and they sat [waiting] for [him] in a room in the ante-chambers of the palace, concealed there. It so happened that al-Ṣāliḥ came out, and so they stood up to go to him; one of them intended to unlock the door that they were behind, [but] he locked it unwittingly, and the task [of his murder] eluded them that night.

Then on the 19th day of the month of Ramaḍān of that year, al-Ṣāliḥ entered upon al-ʿĀḍid, greeted him and left his presence. The [black soldiers] went out to him, a huge outcry arose and al-Ṣāliḥ tripped over his robes. A man named Ibn al-Rāʿī had mingled with the crowd, and he pierced [al-Ṣāliḥ] with a sword at the back of his neck and cut one of the two supporting ligaments in his neck. Then [al-Ṣāliḥ] was carried to the Gate of the palace. [The assassin] rode to [al-Ṣāliḥ's] house and his son Ruzzīk was struck on the shoulder, and then they both raced to the vizieral palace. [Meanwhile] Ḥusayn b. Abi 'l-Hayjā' **had remained** in the caliphal palace fighting the black soldiers until, it is said, he had killed 50 of them. [l.14]

[152b, l.18] **It is said** that when al-Ṣāliḥ arrived at his house, he sent for his son Ruzzīk, and said to him, after recommending what steps he should take, 'I do not regret anything the way I regret three things that I did: **my building of** the mosque at the Gate of Zuwayla, since this became a disadvantage for Cairo; **my appointment of** Shāwar over Upper Egypt; **and my going out** with the army to Bilbays and delaying sending [the troops] to Frankish territory.' Al-Ṣāliḥ **had** spent 200,000 *dīnār*s on this army. **And he said** to him: 'O my son, I assign Shāwar to you. Do not upset him in his governorship, for [his staying there] is safer for you and for your rule.'

It is said that when death was present near al-Ṣāliḥ, he gave advice to his son, including: 'Do not change [153a] towards Shāwar, for truly, I am stronger than you, and I have regretted appointing him to office, and his removal was not possible for me. So do not change his situation or he will become that which you all dislike.' And it is said that he recited some verses **among which were**. ...

[l.7] Al-Ṣāliḥ **died** soon after, on the day he rode out, **Monday** the 19th of the month of Ramaḍān of the year 556, and was buried in Cairo. His son al-ʿĀdil Ruzzīk transported him to his tomb, which was in the great cemetery. The jurist ʿUmāra al-Yamanī produced, for this [occasion], a long poem, excelling therein. Part of it are his words on the description of the **sarcophagus**....

[l.14] The jurist ʿUmāra al-Yamanī, the famous poet, **had** eulogised the aforementioned vizier al-Ṣāliḥ b. Ruzzīk in poetry on many occasions; I do not relate them because of the multiple presence of ʿUmāra's poetic archive in the public domain. And Ḥassan al-Dimashqī, known as al-ʿArqala, **celebrated** al-Ṣāliḥ b. Ruzzīk in poetry, and he said in his **poem**....

[l.20] Ruzzīk: with a *ḍamma* over the unpointed *rā'*, and a *tashdīd* on the pointed *zāy* with a *kasra* under it, a *sukūn* on the *yā'* with two points beneath it, and after that a *kāf*. **And God knows best.**

Account of the vizierate of al-ʿĀdil Ruzzīk b. al-Ṣāliḥ Ṭalāʾiʿ Ibn Ruzzīk over Egypt

Al-Ṣāliḥ Ṭalāʾiʿ b. Ruzzīk **had** bequeathed [his position] to his son al-ʿĀdil Ruzzīk, and made his brother-in-law Sayf al-Dīn Ḥusayn b. Abi ʾl-Hayjāʾ al-Kurdī the manager of his son's affairs. Ḥusayn was one of the foremost mystics in worship, religious piety and abstinence, one of a kind in his knowledge and courage, and he was awe-inspiring and revered in Egypt. **When** al-Ṣāliḥ Ṭalāʾiʿ b. Ruzzīk was buried, al-ʿĀḍid al-ʿUbaydī, the ruler of Egypt, ordered the conferral [153b] of the vizierate upon Ruzzīk b. Salih and appointed him to the post in place of his father. [The caliph] gave him the title Majd al-Islām al-Malik al-ʿĀdil, Commander of the Armies, and the elite proceeded to congratulate him.

[The new vizier] kept to praiseworthy conduct by showing fairness and goodness, and looking into the situation of the public himself. He managed the affairs of the state, and his rule was sound. He corresponded with [those in the outer] regions, gaining their allegiance. When his situation solidified, al-ʿĀdil Ruzzīk sent for the aunt of al-ʿĀḍid and strangled her with a scarf until she was dead. When she had seen al-Ṣāliḥ b. Ruzzīk, as he was carried from the palace, and rode away, she had howled and cried 'Woe is me!' **When** al-Ṣāliḥ b. Ruzzīk fell, his nobles were thunderstruck, and Ibn al-Sharīf threw himself on him to protect him from the swords [of the black soldiers] and he saved [the vizier] by this [deed]. [l.11]

[163b, l.12] *sub anno 558/1162*

Account of the conflict between al-ʿĀdil Ruzzīk, the vizier of Egypt, and Shāwar al-Saʿadī, the governor of Qūṣ and Upper Egypt; the removal of al-ʿĀdil from the vizierate; the rule of Shāwar over Egypt; and the murder of al-ʿĀdil Ruzzīk

For the duration of his vizierate, al-Ṣāliḥ Ṭalāʾiʿ b. Ruzzīk, the vizier of Egypt, **used to** take as servants and *mamlūks* those through whom he could strengthen his own position. He intended to replace all of the emirs and troops with them, and appoint them to high positions, along with much of his family, his relatives and in-laws, who were numerous, too many to count. He had appointed them to many important posts already, such as al-Gharbiyya, and his brother Badr over al-Sharqiyya.[19] He began to weaken the army and strengthen his own [fighting] men and relatives. Then he felt safe, and the world yielded to him, and he did not realise that fear follows close behind security, and that the end-point of wellbeing is sickness. His vizierate was lengthy, and his violence weighed upon the army. Someone **said**, about him and his relatives.... **[l.24]**

[l.27] Ṭalāʾiʿ had a man named Warad, who owned two hundred *mamlūks*, another named Yānis, who had even more than that, and his brother Sulṭān had the same. Saʿāda the Black and Bakhtiyār had close to that [number of *mamlūks*]. They enslaved people, murdered them, weakened them and broke the resistance [164a] of both the ordinary people and the elite. The people continued to be in distress, [with] adversity and injustice visited upon them them by Ṭalāʾiʿ's men and relatives. Then when Ṭalāʾiʿ was killed and his son al-ʿĀdil Ruzzīk appointed to the vizierate, as we have set out, the power of his father's men, like Warad, Yānis, Saʿāda the Black and Bakhtiyār, strengthened, and they grew audacious during Ruzzīk's rule in a way they had not dared during the tenure of his father Ṭalāʾiʿ. This is because Ruzzīk was young while Ṭalāʾiʿ had been mature. Their power increased and they took hold of high positions, and stretched their hands in oppressing people. They appropriated the [nation's] assets and extorted [money]. [Then] the people raised a shout to God most glorious and exalted, and the matter came to al-ʿĀdil Ruzzīk, [but] he was not able to deflect it.

Al-Ṣāliḥ Ṭalāʾiʿ had transported all the wealth stored away over the course of the years from the palace to his house. When he died, his son al-ʿĀdil inherited the treasures of the land and indescribable wealth, and did not want any of the [public] wealth since he had [so much] of it [already]: the wealth from his father could scarcely be spent. He was satisfied with the land-taxes of the state that were brought to him, and he was suited to the running of the vizierate, and to the ceremonial of the dynasty. He left the men [who had served his father] to do whatever they wanted, did not hinder them and appointed his nephew ʿIzz al-Dīn Ḥusām over al-Ushmūnīn.[20] [The latter] conducted himself badly and was ill-natured. [Ḥusām] met with the remaining nephews of al-ʿĀdil Ruzzīk and they urged [al-ʿĀdil] to remove the emir Shāwar al-Saʿadī from [the governorship of] Qūṣ and Upper Egypt, and to replace him with someone else, or to make use of one of them in his place. They made [al-ʿĀdil] afraid of [Shāwar], if he kept him confirmed in his office, and they carried on [like this] in the matter on many occasions. So [al-ʿĀdil] submitted to them in [planning to] remove him. But the emir Sayf al-Dīn Ḥusayn b. Abi 'l-Hayjāʾ al-Kurdī[21] suggested retaining [Shāwar], and Ruzzīk said: 'I am not my father, and I have no avidity for what [Shāwar] has taken from him. I [merely] want him to recognise my authority.' It was then said to him [by the emir] that [Shāwar] would never enter [Cairo, if summoned]. But [the vizier] did not accept this counsel and wrote to Shāwar summoning [164b] his presence. When the emir Shāwar read the letter of al-ʿĀdil Ruzzīk, he felt fear in himself, and resolved to throw off obedience [to al-ʿĀdil]. He then collected himself and wrote a reply to the letter, in which he manifested grace and affection, and something of his previous service to him. He said, after this [in the letter]: 'If the objective is to appoint one of you to this position then, with the exception of Ḥusām, let him approach it and obtain it from me, and I will travel to Cairo. But if the aim is to appoint someone other than yourselves, from among the noblemen of Egypt, then I am more entitled to it than all other people. You have all heard the last instruction of your father al-Ṣāliḥ regarding my claim; let this suffice as a warning.'

When this letter reached al-ʿĀdil Ruzzīk, he summoned his nephews and apprised them of its contents, and they said to him: 'If you leave him after this, he will be ambitious for [your position].' When [al-ʿĀdil] saw that they were united in this, he resolved upon [Shāwar's] removal. Shāwar had sent gifts and loaded camels to Ruzzīk, and wanted to remain in his governorship. The emir Sayf al-Dīn Ḥusayn b. Abi 'l-Hayjāʾ, the brother-in-law of Ruzzīk, said to him: 'Do not stand against Shāwar, and keep him in his position for as long as he shows obedience, and hastens towards what you command from him in the supply of revenues.'

[Al-ʿĀdil] at times resorted to [the emir's] advice, while at other times his nephew ʿIzz al-Dīn Ḥusām incited him [to enmity with Shāwar]. [Ḥusām] took pleasure in the hostilities of Shāwar and informed [al-ʿĀdil] of vile things against [Shāwar], until al-ʿĀdil Ruzzīk summoned the emir Nāṣir al-Dīn b. Shaykh al-Dawla, or it said an emir known as Ibn al-ʿAsqalānī, or it said an emir called Ibn al-Rifʿa, one of the notables of Cairo, and awarded him [Shāwar's position by] appointing him over Qūṣ. He wrote a letter to the emir Shāwar in his own hand [informing him of] the subjugation of the land to [the new appointee] and [requesting] his presence in Cairo.

When the emir Nāṣir al-Dīn set out and reached Ikhmīm,[22] he became fearful of the emir Shāwar, and he said [to one of his men]: 'Write him a letter, and look to what he's up to.' So he wrote a letter to Shāwar, and secretly sent him the letter of al-ʿĀdil Ruzzīk. When [news of] his removal reached Shāwar, he became disturbed at his dismissal. When the letter of the emir Nāṣir al-Dīn arrived, he perused it, and approached him, saying 'Return to where you came from! Do not show yourself, for I have spared [165a] your life.' The emir then returned to Cairo.

Shāwar then sought to corrupt some of the army of Qūṣ and those of the Bedouin who had power. He gathered his men and those who had taken up [his cause] among the emirs he had appointed in Qūṣ, and he took Ibn Nāṣir al-Dawla Yāqūt[23] with him, who was known as the Horseman of Syria, and had earned great public name and high renown in Egypt. So he set off from Qūṣ with those Bedouin who had joined him, until they reached al-Bahnasā.[24]

[News of] this reached al-ʿĀdil Ruzzīk, who gathered his kinsfolk and informed them of it. He said to his nephew, emir ʿIzz al-Dīn Ḥusām: 'This is what [all of] you wanted.' So Ḥusām went out to confront [Shāwar]. Then all of the Bedouin turned against Shāwar and said to him: 'We cannot ruin the sultan, and we will not go forward with you. We have allowed you to pass over our lands, but we cannot do more than that.' Then they dispersed, and Shāwar knew that he did not have the ability to seize power in Egypt with those with him, and no longer had the possibility of returning to Qūṣ. So he entered [the region around Cairo] leading a small group along a route of oases.

When al-ʿĀdil Ruzzīk heard about this, he prepared Ward, Yānis and his father's leading men, and they set out for al-Bahnasā, but returned dejected, [while] the reports kept circulating about the arrival of Shāwar and those with him at the oases, and that they were well-prepared for the return [to Cairo]. The beginnings of apprehension then took hold of al-ʿĀdil Ruzzīk, his men and the men of Ṭalāʾiʿ.

God [alone] has knowledge of this, but in addition, people believed firmly that they, the rulers of the land, had no power against [Shāwar's party]. They thought this because of what they had observed of the firmness of [Shāwar's men's] courage, and the strength of their power, and the weapons, manpower, instruments, pack-horses and wealth they possessed. So those people who preferred [Shāwar's party] and sought to make peace with them also joined them, and each one of them believed that [Shāwar] would be handed power in the land. They continued in this [belief] until it became clear to them that the emir Shāwar had set out in a westerly direction, by way of the oases and the plantation in open country. [Shāwar's men] traversed these steppes until they emerged near Tarūja,[25] close to the port of Alexandria, and there, Ruzzīk al-ʿĀdil [had] sent his uncle Badr, known as the Horseman of the Muslims – though this was in name and not in deed. And it was certainly said about him that when he went from

Cairo to the tents that had been pitched for him by the Abyssinian Lake,[26] he was overtaken by fear, so he crossed to the Gīza bank with the soldiers and troops who were with him, and made camp in the district of Gīza.[165b]

News then arrived that Shāwar had reached the house of Ibn Furayj al-Sunbusī, and he had found [Ibn Furayj's] wife hidden in the rooms while Ibn Furayj was absent. She would give refuge to those who sought it, so she gave him refuge also. When Ibn Furayj arrived and found [Shāwar] there, he was at a loss, for he was not capable of making trouble for the sultan, nor of undermining the protection [given by] his wife. When his wife saw him confused, she scolded him, saying 'O Ibn Furayj! Why do I see you confused?' He replied: 'You've fallen into a huge dilemma; if you give refuge to this man, I don't have the power to disobey the sultan [al-'Ādil]. Yet I do not want to wrong those under my protection.' She said: 'You [should rather] die, you, your family and your cousins before you ruin your [reputation for] protection. The Bedouin will say that you corrupted your high status and surrendered your protégés, and this cannot be. The Bedouin tribes would gossip about it forever.' So she emboldened him, and he warned his nephew Ibn Sunbusī and all of them.

It was a great talking-point in Egypt that the Horseman of Syria [Ibn Nāṣir al-Dawla Yāqūt] was in the entourage of Shāwar, and when [news of] this reached Badr, the Horseman of the Muslims and the uncle of al-'Ādil Ruzzīk, his muscles trembled and his insides were in turmoil, and he knew that he did not have strength to match him. So he withdrew, and Shāwar advanced with his party towards Cairo. The emirs of Cairo had written to Shāwar, because of the grudges they bore in their hearts against the house of Ruzzīk and their envy of the authority attained by [the Banū Ruzzīk].

When Shāwar neared Cairo, the emirs came out to him, and news of this reached al-'Ādil Ruzzīk, who was overtaken by the fear that had gripped his uncle. When the army knew of this, a group [of troops] hastened to meet Shāwar, among them the children of the Chamberlain, and Mulhim, Dirghām, Humām and Ḥusām, men who had a great reputation for valour and horsemanship. [But] all those who were fired up about going out returned and dismounted from their horses. When the army and Dirghām went out [to Shāwar], not one of them went beyond Kawm al-Fuḍūl, and they did not stop going to and from Gate to Gate. So al-'Ādil Ruzzīk gathered his wealth, tied it in purses around the waists of his *mamlūk*s and said to them: 'Ride on the road to Syria.' [165b, l.24]

[166a, l.11] [Shāwar] rode to al-Ḥawf[27] and sought refuge with Ṭarīf b. Maknūn, a Bedouin chief, who gave him sanctuary and took him by sea to the city of our master and prophet Muḥammad the messenger of God, the salutations and peace of God descend upon him, and he stayed there.

The emir Fakhr al-Dīn b. Shams al-Khilāfa **relates**: Once, the emir Sayf al-Dīn Ḥusayn b. Abi 'l-Hayjā' fell ill in Madina – may the best of salutations and peace descend on its Inhabitant – and he thought that he was dying, so he summoned all the 'Alawites [Prophetic descendants] and divided everything he owned among them until nothing was left, and then he recovered. Then it was necessary for him to write to Egypt, to the home of his parents, asking for some money, and [his father] sent some money to him. When the emir Sayf al-Dīn Ḥusayn wanted to go out to Madina the Ennobled city, he was entrusted with wealth in the way we have set out, and it was considerable. Then it was transported to him when he took up residence in Madina, and he spent all of it on the people of Madina. He resided in Madina until he died and was buried in the Baqīʿ [cemetery], may God most high have mercy on him. This is what we know of the emir Sayf al-Dīn Ḥusayn b. Abi ʾl-Hayjāʾ.

As for al-ʿĀdil Ruzzīk, he asked after the emir Sayf al-Dīn b. Abi ʾl-Hayjāʾ, and [people] told him: 'He has gone – his heart was broken – and his relatives left too, in secret.' So [al-ʿĀdil] set out on the trail of his family, heading in an easterly direction, under cover of darkness, but he lost his way, and ended up in Iṭfīḥ,[28] in the tents of one of the Bedouin known as Sulaymān [166b] b. al-Nayṣ al-Lakhmī. Then the people of his house, who had been keeping warm by a fire, attacked and then arrested him.

The emir Shāwar **entered** Cairo with a large crowd, and lodged in the House of al-Saʿīd al-Suʿadāʾ – which these days is the Sufi lodge by the square of the Gate of ʿĪd[29] – along with his sons Ṭayy, Shujāʿ and al-Ṭārī. It is said that al-ʿĀdil came upon [some] Bedouin warming themselves by a fire, who attacked him, and he was made to flee to the Red Mountain.[30] Then the Bedouin took his men and their wealth and jewels. The Bedouin named this year the Year of the Adulteration, because they had mixed up the gold with the jewels. And it is [also] said that among the *dīnār*s were *rubāʿiyyāt*,[31] and that they called it [the year of] the Adulteration because of this.

Al-ʿĀdil was alone at the Red Mountain, and did not know which way to turn. Then he saw a fire, headed towards it and found a group of shepherds near it. He asked them which way to go, but they were suspicious of him, and could smell the odour of perfume on him. So they grabbed him, threw him off his mount, took what jewels he had left – and he still had jewels worth more than a million *dīnār*s with him – and eventually pulled off his slippers. He was dragged along the ground stripped, so that his back was lacerated, and they carried him to their chief, Sulaymān b. al-Nayṣ al-Lakhmī.

It is said that al-ʿĀdil left Cairo with a group of his men, with many mules loaded with wealth, jewels and special robes. But he did not know which way to go, and they ended up on the outskirts of Iṭfīḥ, near the chief emir of the Bedouin, who was known as Ibn al-Nayṣ, and [the Bedouin] took everything they had.

When al-ʿĀdil Ruzzīk left Cairo, the emir Shāwar entered and took it over. The robes of the vizierate were then conferred on him on the authority of al-ʿĀḍid, the ruler of Egypt, and he was given the honorific Chief of the Army. He received the oath of allegiance from the emirs, and he held a session of congratulation. ʿAlim al-Mulk al-Naḥḥās wrote about him [in verse]… [l.24]

[166b, l.30] **When** the emir Shāwar reached Cairo and consolidated his rule as vizier, [167a] he recovered all the wealth of [al-ʿĀdil] Ibn Ruzzīk and his deposits from the people. Ibn al-Nayṣ al-Lakhmī {…} al-ʿĀdil Ruzzīk. He knew him and had known his father al-Ṣā[liḥ] {…} and he {…} Shāwar in Cairo.

When [al-ʿĀdil] reached [Shāwar], he treated him nobly and paid him allowances, and his reason for honouring him was that Shāwar had asked for the governorship of Qūṣ from the vizier Ṭalāʾiʿ b. Ruzzīk during the beginning of his rule, but [the vizier] had denied him that because of what he knew of Shāwar's inner strength. Then Shāwar asked [for help] from Ruzzīk, who interceded with his father in [Shāwar's] matter, and persisted in this until [Ṭalāʾiʿ] appointed him over Qūṣ, and Shāwar had recognised this [help] from [al-ʿĀdil]. It said that al-Ṣāliḥ b. Ruzzīk said to his son Ruzzīk: 'I have accepted your counsel in respect of Shāwar, even though I know very well that he is the one who will divest you of rule.' And the matter turned out just as he said.

The vizier then summoned Sulaymān b. al-Nayṣ al-Lakhmī, who had brought Ruzzīk to him, and said to him: Woe unto you! How have you allowed yourself to bring the son of al-Ṣāliḥ to me [as a captive] when he and his father gave you such gifts and favours that are beyond reckoning? I do not think that al-Ṣāliḥ did this to you and kept you for the sake of his son except [to end] in harm. And I will, without a doubt, conceal you and store you away for my son. Then, on his orders, [al-Lakhmī] was crucified, and it was announced that 'This is the recompense for he who does not observe good behaviour.' He was crucified in Kawm al-Fuḍūl. **[l.16]**

[l.20] Al-Ṭuwayr **said**: al-'Ādil came and took up office as vizier for a little over a year, and the people had hardly seen such good behaviour towards them. He waived the [tax] arrears, recorded in the *dīwān*s, owed by his subjects,, and he didn't hasten their [payment].

When he was put to flight by Shāwar, the latter entered Cairo in the year 558. He drew up salaries and extra pay for the armies, the Bedouin and palace servants, the equivalent of ten times their [previous] pay. But he was not visible to the people and remained shut away in fear. [l.28]

[167b, l.5] **It is said** that when Shāwar became vizier of Egypt, and his dominion grew powerful and great, and as his sons' and brothers' influence over the people increased – he had three sons: Ṭayy, al-Kāmil and Sulaymān – they spread themselves [in oppression] over the populace. They were arrogant towards them, and the people rejected them [as rulers]. Al-Kāmil was the strongest of them, was disdainful of the [Fatimid] dynasty, spread his hands over the [public] wealth, and exceeded all bounds in his tyranny and pride. And he set his sights on taking over as ruler.

The emir Mulhim and his brother the emir Dirghām had been the protégés of al-Ṣāliḥ b. Ruzzīk, and when they witnessed people's antipathy towards the vizier Shāwar, on account of his sons, they began a correspondence with al-'Ādil Ruzzīk b. al-Ṣāliḥ Ṭalā'i', who was in prison, and plotted to restore him to the vizierate. Knowledge of this came to Ṭayy, the son of Shāwar, and he went to his father Shāwar and said to him: 'You are unaware that Mulhim and Dirghām are perverting your rule and destroying your position. They have thrown in their lot with Ruzzīk, and taken the oath of allegiance on his behalf from a group of emirs. It is not possible to rectify your situation except by killing Ruzzīk.' Shāwar replied: 'My son! Don't pay attention to what is said, take things easy and don't reveal your secret to anyone.' [Ṭayy] said to him: 'There can be no doubt about the [need for] killing Ruzzīk. If you kill him, you'll be safe.' Shāwar said to him: 'The father of Ruzzīk did me a good turn, and it is because of [his appointment] that I've occupied this office [of the vizierate].' Then his son left him and went to Ruzzīk and killed him in prison. His father heard of this, then all hell broke loose, and then what we shall relate, God-willing, took place. It is said that all this happened in the year [5]57, which was the previous year [168a], and it is more obvious that it was in the year,[5]58, as we have set out. And God knows best.

Account of the agreement between the noblemen of Egypt to wage war on the vizier Shāwar; his flight to Syria; and the vizierate of Dirghām over Egypt

Al-Ṣāliḥ Ṭalā'i' b. Ruzzīk, who **was** the vizier of Egypt, had created [a corps of] emirs known as the Barqiyya,[32] whose chief was known as Dirghām. He was a horseman and an author. When news of the murder of al-'Ādil Ruzzīk b. al-Ṣāliḥ Ṭalā'i' b. Ruzzīk reached him, he brought together his troops, his brother Mulhim and those emirs from whom they had taken the oath of allegiance, and they marched with the army towards the vizier Shāwar.

It is said that the reason for the emirs' rebellion against Shāwar was his sons' conduct against them, and what was known of al-Kāmil's plans.

It is [also] said that the reason for it was that when he became vizier, Shāwar reduced the wages of the soldiers and treated them unjustly, so they plotted to kill him.

It is said that al-Kāmil, son of the vizier Shāwar, employed a sun-shade that was carried over his head the way it was carried for caliphs. His father was written to about this, but he did nothing, so the emirs rebelled against him.

And it is said that at the beginning of his rule, Dirghām was one of the chamberlains of the Commander of the Armies, the vizier Shāwar. [Dirghām] had partisans and a family, and he lived in Barqiyya, where there was a group of soldiers who thought highly of him and took orders from him. He was a man of great intelligence, excellent penmanship and good expression. He loved knowledge and literature, was fond of poetry and loved the poets. It was for this reason that al-Qāḍī al-Fāḍil[33] gained advancement. When he intended to rebel against the vizier Shāwar, he gathered a great number [of men] and challenged Shāwar for the vizierate in the month of Ramaḍān of the year [5]58. Then he became the ruler and the vizier Shāwar was routed from there to Syria.

When Shāwar fled towards Syria and exited at the Gate of Cairo with his sons following him, the army caught up with them and killed Ṭayy b. Shāwar. The one who caught up with him and killed him was Ghanīm, the servant of al-'Ādil Ruzzīk. Ṭayy had not taken pleasure in life after his murder of Ruzzīk. [The soldiers] then killed [168b] his brother Sulaymān b. Shāwar, and took al-Kāmil b. Shāwar prisoner. Mulhim took him, detained him personally, stopped his brother Dirghām from killing him, set him up with himself in his house and remembered well the favours [al-Kāmil] had previously done to him.

When Shāwar fled, heading for Syria, and some of his sons had been murdered and others taken prisoner, the emir Dirghām took up the vizierate bestowed on him by al-'Āḍid the sovereign of Egypt. He entitled him al-Malik al-Manṣūr, and the armies gave him the oath of allegiance. The vizierate of Shāwar this time had lasted seven months.

The *qāḍī* Nāṣir al-Dīn Shāfi' b. 'Alī, the grandson of the *qāḍī* Muhy al-Dīn b. 'Abd al-Ẓāhir, along with some other historians, **said**, in his book *Arrangement of Conduct in the History of Caliphs and Kings*, the following: Shāwar, the vizier of al-'Āḍid the sovereign of Egypt, **proceeded** to Damascus on the sixth of the month of Rabī' al-Awwal of the year 558, and met with al-Malik al-'Ādil Nūr al-Dīn, the ruler of Syria, and described Egypt for him, and the weakness of its population. He guaranteed that if he sent an army with him, he would take [Egypt] for him. But the first account appears to be more clear.

After being routed from Egypt, and the appointment of Dirghām over it, and after he knew for sure about the murder of his two sons, the vizier Shāwar **had** set out towards Syria [to] the service of al-Malik al-ʿĀdil Nūr al-Dīn Maḥmūd b. al-Malik al-Manṣūr ʿImād al-Dīn Atabeg Zengī, the ruler of Syria, seeking refuge with him and protection from him. When he arrived at Buṣrā, news about him reached al-Malik al-ʿĀdil Nūr al-Dīn. He appointed a group to meet him and to set him up at the palace on the Maydān al-Akhḍar [Green Hippodrome]. He excelled in his reception of [Shāwar] and in honouring him, but al-Malik al-ʿĀdil Nūr al-Dīn did not go out to meet him [personally]. When a week had passed since [Shāwar's] arrival in Damascus, al-Malik al-ʿĀdil Nūr al-Dīn summoned Ibn al-Ṣūfī and a group of Damascene noblemen and said to them: 'Go to this man, greet him and inform him of our excuses for our inadequacy in his regard. Ask him why has come, and what his aim and his need are. If he has come into our hands choosing to stay [here], we assign to him, from our resources, whatever suffices him. We'll accomplish his aim, be a help to him for all of his life and apportion [funds] for him, so that he can go to any length in his *jihād* in the way of God most high. If he has come for some other [reason] than this, clarify his need and his objective, so that we can take him towards his desire.'

So the group **went out** to him with the letter [outlining the above], and he expressed gratitude for al-Malik [169a] al-ʿĀdil Nūr al-Dīn's kindness that had reached him, and he praised the favour he had heaped upon him, [but] was silent about what was behind this [his aim]. So the people asked for his response, and he said: 'If [my] objectives are not fixed {...}' So the people returned to al-Malik al-ʿĀdil Nūr al-Dīn and informed him and repeated what they'd heard from [Shāwar]. [Al-Malik al-ʿĀdil Nūr al-Dīn] ordered them to go back to him on the following day, and to hear what he said to them. So they went back to him and sought an answer, but he was silent again for a long time. Then he said: 'If Nūr al-Dīn, may God lengthen his life, sees fit to meet with me, then I am happy to agree.' So then they returned to al-Malik al-ʿĀdil Nūr al-Dīn and acquainted him with what he had said.

Al-Malik al-ʿĀdil Nūr al-Dīn agreed to a meeting at the Maydān on horseback. Al-Malik al-ʿĀdil Nūr al-Dīn rode out the next morning, leading the noblemen of his state and the elite of his kingdom, in their finest costumes and their best appearance. When he entered the Maydān, Shāwar rode from the palace, and they met with salutations only in the middle of the Maydān. Neither of them dismounted for his counterpart, then they went from the meeting-place, which was in the centre of the Maydān, to the edge. Then they separated at that point, and the duration of their meeting was only as long as it took to get to the middle of the Maydān, and it is not known what passed between them. Al-Malik al-ʿĀdil Nūr al-Dīn returned to the citadel and, at that very moment, set about gathering troops, choosing warriors, collecting weapons and [organising] the pay of the soldiers. Asad al-Dīn Shīrkūh b. Shādhī b. Marwān, the paternal uncle of Sulṭān Ṣalāḥ al-Dīn Yūsuf, son of the Father of Kings Najm al-Dīn Abi 'l-Shukr Ayyūb b. Shādhī b. Marwān, was [then] in Raḥba,[34] which he held. So al-Malik al-ʿĀdil Nūr al-Dīn sent for him and summoned him from there. [Al-Malik al-ʿĀdil Nūr al-Dīn] had had good luck with Asad al-Dīn, and he was blessed in the good fortune that came with him, for he had never sent him on any mission except that he succeeded. And he had never put him into any narrow scrape without him opening it up. So he ordered him to [169b] take what was needed for the journey, since he had no responsibility [at that time]. So Asad al-Dīn came to him with everything that was needed for the journey, and then what we shall relate, God-willing, came to pass. [l.3]

[170a l.4] Someone else **said** that news reached Dirghām about a group of noblemen who were envious of him, deemed him insignificant, and had written to Shāwar when he was in Syria, summoning him [to take over in Egypt]. So [Dirghām] set about effecting a strategy against them. He summoned them to the vizieral palace one night – and they consisted of al-Khalwāṣ, Asad al-ʿĀrī, the sons of Munīr al-Dawla, Abu Aṣbaʿ, ʿAlī b. al-Zayd and ʿAyn al-Zamān b. ʿAyn al-Zamān – and ambushed them in the store-rooms of the house. The men were armed, and each one who entered [the store-rooms] was an emir. [Dirghām] said [to his men]: 'Go out with [each] to the store-room and dispatch him', and they would go out with him and kill him. Then he sent for the remainder of that group [of rebels], who were absent from Cairo, and killed all of them. He did not lay hands on the wealth of those he killed, nor their honour.

The author of *Arrangement of Conduct in the History of the Caliphs and Kings* **said**: Dirghām killed more than seventy noblemen who were with Shāwar, not including their followers. **Someone else said**: It is said that he killed ninety emirs. **And it is said** that he placed them in caskets, and wrote the name of each one on his coffin, and ordered that each one be handed over to his family. Among those he killed were three brothers who were some of the greatest noblemen. Their mother faced him and said: 'O Dirghām! You've killed my sons! May God orphan your children!' He said to her: 'O lady! I do not rejoice in what I have done to them. It is them today and us tomorrow!'

This was the greatest factor in his own demise, for he weakened the Egyptian army by killing these noblemen. Then Dirghām wrote a letter to al-Malik al-ʿĀdil Nūr al-Dīn, the ruler of Syria, [delivered] by the hand of ʿAlam al-Dīn b. al-Naḥḥās, manifesting obedience, and proposing that [Nūr al-Dīn] forsake Shāwar. Then al-Malik al-ʿĀdil [170b] Nūr al-Dīn outwardly indicated to ʿAlam al-Dīn b. al-Naḥḥās that he accepted this, but inwardly he was with Shāwar. He replied to the letter, and ʿAlam al-Dīn b. al-Naḥḥās left Damascus. When he reached the outskirts of Kerak,[35] he was intercepted by Philip b. al-Rafīq the Frank,[36] and he robbed him of whatever he had. ʿAlam al-Dīn b. al-Naḥḥās himself fled and made for the coast, and then travelled to Egypt. And God knows best. [l.6]

[184a, l.1] *sub anno 559/1163*

Account of the journey of the vizier Shāwar and the Syrian army to Egypt; the murder of the vizier Dirghām; the continuation of Shāwar's vizierate in Egypt; and his treachery towards the Syrian army

We have related that al-Malik al-ʿĀdil Nūr al-Dīn Maḥmūd, the ruler of Syria, ordered the army to be prepared for going out to Egypt in the company of Shāwar, and that he summoned the emir Asad al-Dīn Shīrkūh from Raḥba. On the day that he reached him, [Shīrkūh] found the army disposed to illness and making excuses for [forsaking] the journey. So he went to al-Malik al-ʿĀdil Nūr al-Dīn and met him alone, and [al-Malik al-ʿĀdil] entrusted certain things about Egypt to him. [Shīrkūh] was pleased by this; he had courage and strength of character and paid no attention to fear. Shāwar **had** made al-Malik al-ʿĀdil Nūr al-Dīn, the ruler of Syria, covetous of the wealth of Egypt, excited his interest in ruling and being the one in power there. When news of the army's completion [of preparation] reached Shāwar, he asked who would be leading it, and was told that it was the emir Asad al-Dīn Shīrkūh. This did not please him, because he thought that [Shīrkūh] would take precedence over him and command the army towards his aim. When he was caught by this force [Shāwar] was at a loss, and his strength was weakened, but he could not avoid the journey. So they travelled together with the army on Jumāda al-Ūlā of the year 559. **This was said** by the *qāḍī* of *qāḍī*s Sham al-Dīn Aḥmad Ibn Khallikān. **Another author said**: This was on the 20th of Jumāda al-Ākhir of this year. **And it is [also] said**: in the year [5]58.

Al-Malik al-ʿĀdil Nūr al-Dīn **travelled** out with them to the borders of the Muslim lands that adjoined Frankish territory, leading the remainder of the army of Damascus, in order to divert the Franks from opposing the emir Asad al-Dīn Shīrkūh. The utmost the Franks could manage was to protect their lands from al-Malik al-ʿĀdil Nūr al-Dīn. Then Asad al-Dīn separated from al-Malik al-ʿĀdil Nūr al-Dīn and headed for Egypt with those accompanying him. The road at that time went east of al-Kerak and al-Shawbak[37] towards ʿAqabat Ayla, then towards Ṣadr and Suez, and thence to the lake that is near the Gate of Cairo the Protected. **And it is said** that when the army reached the borders of Egyptian territory, they camped at a hill in the interior near Bilbays, known as the hill of Basṭa.

News of the arrival of Shāwar and the emir Asad al-Dīn Shīrkūh with the Syrian army **reached** al-Malik al-Manṣūr [184b] Dirghām, the vizier of Egypt. So he brought together the noblemen and consulted with them, and Shams al-Khilāfa Muḥammad b. Mukhtār urged him to mobilise the army, and to go out without a heavy baggage train and meet the Syrian army [in battle] by Ṣadr, which was two days' [ride] from Cairo. [The Syrians] would not have spent the night there because people came out there from the desert, weak from the scarcity of water that afflicted them, as they would carry water from Ayla, a journey of three days. But they did not follow this opinion. They were minded to meet [the Syrians in battle] at Bilbays.

The vizier Dirghām then **ordered** the emirs to go out [to battle], and they went out looking their best, with perfect equipment, and proceeded until they surrounded the hill where the emir Asad al-Dīn Shīrkūh had stopped. When Asad al-Dīn saw the magnitude of the Egyptian army, and that they had control of all routes and had blocked the openings to the road, he said to the vizier Shāwar: 'You have trapped us in a noose, and deceived us! You said there was hardly an army to speak of in Egypt, so we came out leading this small group!' [Shāwar] replied: 'Don't be frightened by what you perceive of the size of this group: most of them are weavers and farmers gathered by the drumbeat, and the stick will disperse them! Do not think them [capable of] fierce fighting or that the battle will become violent. As for the noblemen, their contracts [of allegiance] are with me and their oaths are to me, and this will be demonstrated to you when we meet them [in battle].' [Shāwar] then said: 'I would like you to command the army to prepare and to mount up.' So Asad al-Dīn called out [the order] to ride, and the troops flew to arms, mounted [their horses] and fell into line for battle. Then Shāwar forbade them from combat [yet], and the army of Egypt also drew up in ranks for the battle.

The morning grew warm, and the mail-coats burned against the bodies of the men, and the men of Egypt waited for the Syrian army to come out for combat. But not one of them came out to them, so most of them ordered their comrades to pitch their small and large tents. They came off their horses and sat in the shade, and most of them took off their armour. **When** the vizier Shāwar saw this, he ordered [his] people to attack and to launch an assault on them. And the most fortunate of emirs was he who could mount his charger and loosen his reins in flight. They abandoned their tents and left their possessions unprotected, and the men of the emir Asad al-Dīn Shīrkūh seized them and took all that they had left as booty. Then Asad al-Dīn and Shāwar drove on [185a] in pursuit, heading for Cairo.

At the heart of the Egyptian army **was** Nāṣir al-Dīn, the brother of Dirghām; leading the right wing was Shams al-Khilāfa Muḥammad b. Mukhtār; and leading the left wing was the Horseman of the Muslims. Shams al-Khilāfa and a group of Egyptians were taken prisoner, and when they approached Cairo, all those who had been captured escaped because the vizier Shāwar was not able to bind them [properly], or to guard them. And they came to Cairo at the end of Jumāda al-Ākhir. **Or it is said** at the end of Jumāda al-Ūlā of this year.

I saw in a small fragment which its author has called *Reports of the Egyptian Dynasty, and the Trials and Wars that Took Place Among the Kings and Caliphs from the Time of al-Āmir to the Time of Shīrkūh* – though the author's name is not mentioned – and I copy **from it** that: al-Ṣāliḥ b. Ruzzīk, the vizier of Egypt, had settled that money from the salaries of the employees and from the administrative districts of the emirs and others would be taken to the Franks annually [as a tribute], and it was 33,000 *dīnār*s every year. Then when Ṭalā'i' died and his son al-'Ādil Ruzzīk became vizier after him, and Shāwar deposed him from the vizierate, it was paid from a large amount of wealth belonging to Ṭalā'i' b. Ruzzīk and his son – and it was more than 500,000 *dīnār*s. For his sons, who were Ṭayy [and] al-Kāmil, [Shāwar] took a great deal of money, utensils, pack-horses and weapons. And al-Ṭārī [his third son] was in a powerful position, for he also had great wealth. They obtained, during their tenure, more wealth than was obtained by anyone before them.

None of the wealth that Shāwar obtained during his regency was placed in his house – not even a single *dirham*. Rather, he deposited it with the Bedouin, fulfilled their needs [from it] and advanced their interests. The Bedouin grew so wealthy that it was said about them that they measured [money] by *qadaḥ*s [dry measures], and [people] would remark: 'So-and-so has two *qadaḥ*s [of coins] and so-and-so has three *qadaḥ*s, and so-and-so has such-and-such.' [185b] During [Shāwar's] tenure, the Bedouin did not quit the al-Futūḥ and al-Naṣr Gates.

[Shāwar] appointed one of his brothers over al-Sharqiyya and another over al-Gharbiyya; his sovereignty grew firm and the world was his oyster. That year, he put Bedouin in charge of the revenues of al-Ḥawf, who plundered it and coveted the fiefholders' titles, and they were not denied these by the vizier Shāwar, for he [wanted] in himself to set them up as a refuge and 'protection', just as the vizier Riḍwān had set them up them before him. Shāwar had been among the vizier Riḍwān's group of emirs, and he preserved the status quo established by Riḍwān. The envoys of the Franks continued [to come], seeking tribute from the vizier Shāwar.

When the month of Ramaḍān came along in year 558, and eight months and a few days of his vizierate had elapsed, Shāwar's son Ṭayy incited him against al-ʿĀdil Ruzzīk b. al-Ṣāliḥ Ṭalāʾiʿ. God had put something of fear in their hearts, and they hated [the idea] that Ruzzīk filed away at his shackles and wanted to escape, and that his brother made signals to him. So Ṭayy entered Ruzzīk['s cell] and murdered him. Fear of Dirghām, the brother of his chamberlain Mulhim, then descended upon the heart of Shāwar, and this became evident so that Shāwar exacted an oath from Dirghām that he would not betray him, be disloyal to him or make common cause [with others against him], and Shāwar considered apprehending Dirghām.

[Dirghām] spent the night at the royal palace and when morning came, he rode to his house, gathered his men, and sent for Ibn Shāhanshāh, Asad al-ʿĀrī and ʿAyn al-Zamān, who had arrived from the Ḥijāz after the murder of Ṭalāʾiʿ and al-Khalwāṣ. They all gathered with their men and the Barqiyya troops, and travelled leading a great army, with Dirghām among them. Shāwar then thought – and he was proved right and did not doubt – that they came to seize him. The report did not lie, and he exited from al-Naṣr Gate as if prepared for that. His sons al-Kāmil and al-Ṭārī were with him, and he carried as much wealth as he could. His son [186a] al-Kāmil Ṭayy was then killed in Bayn al-Qaṣrayn [Street], and his corpse remained discarded for two days. The same [happened] to his nephew, and a man named Ḥassān who was with him at his son's house was also killed. The house of Shāwar was plundered, as were those of his sons and his in-laws, and he slipped away from sovereignty as if he had never existed. All that he had obtained from the Ruzzīk family also went. Shāwar left and came to the administrative district of al-Fāqūsiyya,[38] and stayed with the Banū Manẓūr and others. Dirghām sent no-one to him, and his vizierate on that ccasion had been for nine months.

Dirghām became vizier, was officially appointed to [the post], and his support grew strong. The next thing he was aware of was that the Franks had set out for Egypt, and he came to know that they had reached al-Sadīr.[39] So he sent out his brother Humām, who was very brave, who reached the Franks and met them [in battle]. He prevailed, defeated the Franks and killed a great number of them. Then the accursed ones marched to the fortress of Bilbays and took part of the wall, but Humām repelled them from it [along with] the Banū Kināna.[40] As for the army, most of it headed for al-Ḥawf, by virtue of the fact that the Bedouin had interposed between themselves and Cairo. And over each one that they gained victory, they cried 'Defeated!', and then killed him and took whatever he had. As for those soldiers who sought al-Ḥawf, they were met by local peasants who inflicted a worse blow on them than any they would have had from the Bedouin. A great many [troops] were killed, and because of this, the army returned, defeated.

The Franks returned to Syria while Shāwar was between Bilbays and Cairo on the eastern side, with the Bedouin who were with him rather than with the [Egyptian] army or the Franks. In fact, at times they sided with the Muslims and were useful to them.

The news had reached the Franks that the sulṭān [Shāwar] interposed between themselves and Cairo, so they journeyed from Bilbays and returned to Syria with those Muslims they had captured. Among them was an emir [186b] called al-Qaṭūrī, who was one of the greatest men of the state. When Humām, brother of the vizier Dirghām, returned to Cairo after the departure of the Franks [back to Syria], he and his brother Dirghām were in harmony as if they shared the vizierate; each of them signing [orders] and running affairs of government, and whatever this one did, the other confirmed. No welath was obtained by Dirghām during his vizierate because the wealth meant for viziers would be given away, wasted and taken away. Whatever he acquired, he began to squander it, give it away, bestow it [as gifts], did not save any of it and bribed the emirs with it [from going] against himself, for he had no avidity for the vizierate. He would win the hearts of the people by whatever means he could.

Murtafiʿ al-Khalwāṣ[41] had been **appointed** over the port of Alexandria, and felt himself disgusted by [Dirghām]. Ibn Shāhanshāh was of his group, and he was the greatest and most venerated of them; and also ʿAyn al-Zamān, Asad al-ʿĀrī and Ibn al-Zayd. It is mentioned that [the latter] was the one who planned out who would leap on al-Khalwāṣ in Alexandria, and that Murtafiʿ seized the group sent to him by Dirghām and tortured them, and they confessed. And each of those aforementioned emirs thought in himself that he was more entitled to the vizierate than Dirghām, for he was the least of them and was never celebrated the way they were celebrated. It seemed proper to Murtafiʿ in himself that he should gather his men and his tribesmen. Murtafiʿ al-Khalwāṣ was aware that the people of Alexandria followed what took place between himself and their governor, who was known as Ibn al-Ḥājib, and [was aware of] their revolt against him, the murder of his men and his secretary, the looting of his house,and all that had ensued when he treated them with shameful conduct. So the emir Murtafiʿ al-Khalwāṣ set out and travelled from Alexandria, and news of this reached the vizier Dirghām, [but] he did not say a word until he had seized Asad al-ʿĀrī, Ibn Shāhanshāh and the son of ʿAyn al-Zamān. Then his brother, the emir Humām, went with an army to meet Murtafiʿ al-Khalwāṣ.

After the army left Cairo, the vizier Dirghām attacked Asad al-ʿĀri, Ibn Shāhanshāh and the son of ʿAyn al-Zamān, killed them [187a] and threw their corpses out into the street. When the people awoke in the morning and saw the corpses, they broadcast it, and the news spread. Their news reached the emir Murtafiʿ al-Khalwāṣ, whose campaign was cancelled, for without doubt, before his exit from Alexandria, [this] group had promised to help him, except that the vizier Dirghām had got to them first and murdered them before the arrival of the army and Humām at al-Buḥayra.[42] The party of the emir Murtafiʿ al-Khalwāṣ fell apart when news reached them of the murder of the emirs, and of the army's exit towards Murtafiʿ al-Khalwāṣ. When the Bedouin saw the collapse of the emir Murtafiʿ al-Khalwāṣ' men, and that he now led a very small group, they set their sights on him, seized him from Sunbus and used him to show their goodwill to the emir Humām after the latter had seized those who were with him in the army. Among these was Ibn al-Zayd. Then the emir Humām, who had already overcome the emir Murtafiʿ al-Khalwāṣ and taken him prisoner, returned with the army,. When they reached Cairo, his brother Dirghām rejoiced, fell upon Murtafiʿ al-Khalwāṣ, decapitated him outside Zuwayla Gate and crucified him.

The vizier Dirghām and his brothers persisted in [the conduct] we have mentioned. The Franks repeatedly sent envoys seeking the money [entailed by] the treaty, and [Dirghām] resisted this, and delayed the messengers, sometimes telling them: 'I have nothing but the sword, and I do not honour the truce,' and at other times saying 'I uphold the truce.' [This went on] until the [carrier] birds sent by his brother the emir Ḥusām from Bilbays came down. [Ḥusām] was the governor of al-Sharqiyya who had oppressed the populace before his brother Dirghām became vizier, and more so during [Dirghām's] vizierate. The rest of his brothers were better than him in [governance].

When the vizier Dirghām read what was in the letters he received from the birds, he found they contained [news of] the arrival of the vizier Shāwar and the emir Asad al-Dīn Shīrkūh the Turk at al-Karā'im, and a great party of Turks with them. The vizier Dirghām was alarmed, and prepared for sending out the army [187b]. Then morning came on the 29th of Jumāda al-Ūlā of the year [5]59, and [news of the arrival of Shāwar *et al*] had spread among the people, who were frightened. They began moving about from place to place according to their habit, collecting sweet water, foodstuffs and firewood. Fear descended on the people.

The emir Humām **set out** with the army on the first of Jumāda al-Ākhira of the year [5]59, and an army of six thousand horsemen, most of them with freely-grazed horses and precious suits of armour and weapons not possible to be found in other lands, went out with him. The people saw this army, their alacrity, their setting out with hearts at ease and ample expectation, and they thought that they would be helped, for they saw an army the like of which had not been seen before. The army reached Bilbays on Sunday the second of the Jumāda al-Ākhira we mentioned, and the vizier Shāwar and the emir Shīrkūh arrived with the Syrian army on Monday the third of this month, and they met [in battle] on Tuesday the fourth of the aforementioned month, Jumāda al-Ākhira.

Some of the Turks in the Syrian army **were heard** to say: 'By God, we despaired of staying alive when we saw the size of the [opposing] army, a group on horses while we are foot-soldiers, well-dressed [in armour] while we are bare [of protection], and rested, while we are tired, hungry and thirsty. Most of us have come to a stop, and our horses have died. Among us are ones whose nag has died, and whose feet are swollen. We are near the end! Shāwar has reproached us, and we say to him: "O you, you say that your sultan sent for and summoned you, that the army of Egypt will not confront you, and that they are happy with you and your arrival. You have tossed us into a calamity which you brought upon us!" Then he said: "Be firm! For help comes from God." And thus it happened. When they came to us again, we rose up a hill and looked down over them in great fear at their magnitude.'

Then when the two parties met, the emir Nāṣir al-Dīn Humām and the emir Fakhr al-Dīn Ḥusām, the brothers of the vizier Dirghām, attacked the army of the emir Shīrkūh and the vizier Shāwar. The emir Humām went out from the side after being overtaken by injuries from arrows, and turned around [188a] seeking one of his soldiers, but did not find one. This was because the left flank of the emir Humām's army had Bedouin in it, and when they saw the arrows, they fled, and their flight caused the defeat of the [whole] army. So they all retreated to Bilbays with the army of Shāwar on their heels, and they entered the Syrian Gate with the Turks on their tracks. A group of [Egyptians] and all their accompaniments – horses, weapons, tools and equipment – were captured and taken. None of them escaped [capture] except the emir Humām, who reached Cairo on the dawn of Wednesday the fifth of the aforementioned Jumāda al-Ākhira, wounded, with an arrow still in him, and he was most unfortunate.

As for his brother, the emir Fakhr al-Dīn Ḥusām, he hid in Bilbays in a place which was pointed out [to his pursuers] by some of the [Banū] Kināna, because they had experienced oppression from him, and this is what results from oppression. He was taken prisoner, shackled and carried with the vizier Shāwar, and then with Shāwar and Shīrkūh. They arrived in Cairo early in the morning of a Thursday in Jumāda al-Ākhira, and they came down by al-Tāj[43] on the outskirts of Cairo the Protected. Shāwar had sent some of the Turks to Minyat al-Sīraj[44] to protect those soldiers who were there, and not harm them. The army had spread through the estates and al-Minya,[45] looking for food and fodder for their horses.

Dirghām had corresponded with [the local rulers in] all the administrative districts, calling upon them, summoning them and giving them the news. The people were extremely fearful of the Turks and said, 'They are foreigners, and we cannot be sure they will not introduce new arrangements. No-one has strength against their [strong] character.' When Shāwar arrived with his accompanying army and descended at al-Kharqāniyya and what adjoins it, the vizier Dirghām brought together all the foot-soldiers and the Rayḥāniyya, the Juyūshiyya and others, to the inside of Cairo. When Shāwar came down with his army at al-Tāj on the outskirts of Cairo, he stayed there a few days until those with him were rested. When they had rested, they acquired from the encounter at Bilbays horses, equipment and weapons [188b] that made them rich, and they were avid [for more], and their expectations persisted. So the vizier Shāwar gathered them, sought their oath of allegiance and extracted compacts from them, and contracts that they would not betray him, surrender him or be put to flight, unless defeated, and [that they] would be a help and an aid to him.

His vanguard, who were always from the Bedouin, skirmished with the army of the vizier Dirghām in the area of al-Ṭabbāla,[46] and when the chase took place, the people of al-Minya thought that the Egyptian army was strong and had help. So they sided with the army of Shāwar and killed the Turks. Then the vizier Shāwar ordered Minyat al-Sīraj to be plundered, so it was plundered and he inflicted an exemplary punishment on its people.

Shāwar and his men then stayed for some days in the regions of al-Kharqāniyya and Shubrā and Damanhūr.[47] Some of the Bedouin with him pursued some soldiers of Dirghām in the area of al-Ṭabbāla, and the army came out and did not go beyond Kawm al-Fuḍūl.

The vizier Shāwar and those with him **headed for** Cairo from the direction of al-Maqsim, and the army of the vizier Dirghām came out to them and attacked them as one man and routed them in a great defeat. The vizier Dirghām was greatly pleased by this and sent for the chief *qāḍī*, saying to him: 'Bring [me] all the wealth that has been deposited.' He said: 'O my lord, this is the wealth of the orphans, so how can it be taken?' He said: 'The matter is more serious than that.' So he took it. When the people found out that Dirghām had taken the orphans' wealth, they knew his weakness, and they knew that he was doomed for many reasons. The first of these was his taking of the orphans' wealth, the second was his killing of innocents and the third was his false oaths.

Then the vizier Shāwar travelled out, making for the Abyssian Lake. He advanced to the mosque of Sa'd al-Dawla, then headed for al-Raṣad[48] and what adjoined it. He seized Old Cairo and stayed there for some days, and neither the vizier Dirghām nor those with him had the power to drive him away. He began riding through Egypt, calming people and preventing the Turkish [troops] from harming them. Dirghām and his army threatened the people of Egypt and said: 'If we overcome Shāwar then we will burn Egypt and everything in it because you people [189a] have enabled him to enter it, pledged allegiance to him, and bought [his favour].' They replied to them: 'You are the masters of swords, and the caliph, the sultan and the army are among you. Even if you prevent [Shāwar] from reaching to us, you would be unable to [stop] his taking power over the land.' They sought the help of God most high, and asked Him to suffice them against their [opponents'] mischief.

Then Shāwar stayed for a few days more after this, stopped at al-Lūq[49] and pursued the horses of the vizier Dirghām. Then al-Manṣūra[50] and al-Hilāliyya were deserted and he advanced to al-Ansiya, and did not fight [its people] out of consideration for the jurist Raslān and 'Uthmān. He fought the people gently, then he and the emir Shīrkūh advanced to the Gate of al-Sa'āda, the Gate of al-Qanṭara and the house of the emir Jibrīl, and set fire to the house of Ibn Dalāl, and the fire reached all the way to al-Lu'lu'a.[51] There was then a terrible and well-known battle between both parties, and a number – known only to God the lofty and exalted – of soldiers were killed and injured. When night fell, the commanders of the Rayḥāniyya infantry gathered and said: 'We are fighting without the army of Egypt meeting us, or coming out. If victory is ours, what we have goes to them; and if it is against us, they stay intact. Many men have perished at our hands.' And they decided to go out to Shāwar and seek a truce with him. It is said that the vizier Shāwar sent [his people] to them every night, making them promises and suborning them.

It is said that when the caliph saw the vizier Dirghām – when fortune turned against him, and knew that he did not prosper, and that the Turks were strong against him – he sent for the archers and said to them: 'Do not fire – any of you – a single arrow.' When morning came, the foot-soldiers went out to the vizier Shāwar and surrendered themselves to him. He honoured them, and was gladdened and strengthened in himself. There came to the people of Egypt a [period of] calm, and their intentions cooled; each one who had been fired up to ride out [in battle] returned and dismounted. Then the army and the vizier Dirghām went out, and not one of them went beyond Kawm al-Fuḍūl. They continued coming and going from door to door. Among their number were horsemen renowned in battle, such as the son of Mulhim, brother of the vizier [Dirghām], Ibn Faraj Allāh, Ḥāzim b. Abī Khalīl and a group [of others]. They pursued those who had pursued them. When Dirghām wrote [a decree] for the people to be called out to war, none came to him from any direction [189b] except Ṭalḥa and Ja'far, who arrived leading 800 horsemen, and were involved in furious attacks and warfare. The Turkish companions of Shāwar ruined them [in the fight] with arrows, and they returned to their families defeated.

When the vizier Dirghām observed the seriousness of this matter, he ordered the drums and trumpets to be sounded on the [city] walls, to gather the people. But no-one emerged and no-one gathered, and the people were dented [in their spirits]. Then he thought the army would be with his brother, so he sent [people] to look for those with him, but he found no-one except 40 horsemen from the followers [of his family], while the noblemen, all of them, sat in their houses. So the vizier Dirghām returned to the Gate of al-Dhahab with 500 horsemen around him. He stopped under the window and asked the caliph to open up the window according to his usual habit, to speak to him and indicate to him [Dirghām] what he should do. It was the usual practice of the caliph of Egypt to issue commands and prohibitions from the window, to promise help, or to prevent fighting. Then at this point, news of this [conversation] reached Shāwar, and he ordered his son Sulaymān al-Ṭārī to enter [Cairo] from the Gate of al-Qanṭara, and not to advance a single step, but to take possession of the Gate and stop [there]. When the matter grew lengthy for the vizier Dirghām, he called out, 'I want the Commander of the Believers to speak with me so I can ask him about what I should do.' But no-one answered him. Then he shouted, 'O my lord, speak to me, my lord! Show me your noble face, my lord, by the sanctity of your forefathers before God!' And he was crying. Yet no-one answered him.

Then the sun grew stronger, so he changed position and moved towards the shade, until five hours of the morning had elapsed. [Then] he indicated to one of his men, saying to him: 'Gallop to the city and shout out "It was a plot against Shāwar!", for the Rayḥāniyya have killed a group of Shāwar's Turkish soldiers.' When the people heard this, they took their horses and returned to Cairo, and the horses and foot-soldiers hurried from every side, from [all] the alleyways and passages, such as al-Sayl al-ʿAẓīm [the Great Channel]. When they arrived and saw the vizier Dirghām in that situation, and that the window had not been opened, and that the caliph had not addressed a single word to him, all who had hurried there returned, gloomy, saying, 'Go back, for it was a big lie, and victory is Shāwar's.' The vizier Dirghām remained [190a] in this state until the ninth hour of that morning, and none remained with him except thirty horsemen. He [then] despaired of life.

Then the vizier Shāwar wrote to al-ʿĀḍid bi-Llāh about mending the situation, and to permit him to enter Cairo, and he permitted it. So Shāwar sent [word] to his son that he should enter Cairo, and he entered it. The vizier Dirghām heard a strange trumpet call, the like of which he had not heard before, from the trumpets of the Turkish soldiers who were the troops of Shāwar's son. [The latter] then suddenly appeared from the direction of al-Tabbānīn [Gate].[52] [Dirghām] asked about him and [his men], saying to him: 'It is al-Ṭārī the son of Shāwar who has marched on you.' So [Dirghām] fled, making for the Gate of Zuwayla. Then the people knew for sure that he was routed, so they seized some equipment from those with him, and shouted out at him. For this reason, they were called hypocrites, finding happiness at these misfortunes and rejoicing at them, for they were envious of [Dirghām's family's] good fortunes. Now blessing the emir for no reason, and now cursing him, being 'brothers' of those whose benefactions continued.

When Dirghām exited from the Gate of Zuwayla, with the people cursing him and shouting at him, one of the Syrians overtook him and Dirghām said to him: 'Take me to the emir Asad al-Dīn Shīrkūh, and name your desire!' But he did not agree to this and charged him, speared him and killed him. He dismounted, went to him, **then cut off his head** by the shrine of our lady Nafīsa, the daughter of al-Ḥasan b. Zayd b. al-Ḥasan b. ʿAlī b. Abī Ṭālib, may God be pleased with them, at the end of Jumāda al-Ākhira. **Or it is said** at the end of Jumāda al-Ūlā of this year. **And it is said** that Dirghām was by a pillar of the Garden of ʿAbbās,[53] opposite the Ṭūlūnid mosque. **He was killed by** the son of a Bedouin, who took [Dirghām's] head to Shāwar. [Shāwar] ordered him to parade it around Cairo. We seek refuge in God from the changing of one's state towards evil. **And it is said** that Dirghām came out of Cairo, after the Gates of the palace were locked in his face, and came to the Great Dike[54] and was killed there. He was killed by a manservant of Ṭayy, the son of Shāwar.

The *qāḍī* Nāṣir al-Dīn Shāfiʿ **said** in his book *The Arrangement of Conduct* [190b] *in the History of Caliphs and Kings* that when the emir Shīrkūh arrived in Egypt and Shāwar was in his service, Dirghām knew that he was trapped, so he came to the caliphal palace and called out: 'O my lord!' But he got no answer and was met with a written message stating: 'Look to yourself and save yourself!' So he went away, a fugitive. Then Shāwar's men overtook him, killed him and killed his brothers with him.

It is said that Mulhim ended up as a fugitive by the mosque of al-Tibn,[55] and was killed there. He was killed by some of the Turkish troops, who took his armour from his person, after which someone found him abandoned, murdered. [This man] cut off his head and went with it to Shāwar, who ordered that he put it on a spear and it was paraded. **It is said** that Nāṣir al-Dīn, brother of Dirghām, was killed by the Elephant Lake,[56] as was the Horseman of the Muslims. **It is also said** that when the Syrian carried the head of the vizier Dirghām to the emir Asad al-Dīn Shīrkūh and informed him of what had happened between himself and Dirghām, [Shīrkūh] found this deed hard to swallow, and he dealt [the Syrian] a painful blow and thought of killing him, but the vizier Shāwar interceded for him. The body of Dirghām remained discarded for two days, then it was carried away and buried in Qarāfa cemetery. So look, all those who have a heart, at these deeds that are mutually similar. The son of Shāwar was killed on Friday the 21st of the month of Ramaḍān of year 558, and [Shāwar] was killed on Friday the 28th of Ramaḍān, the same aforementioned month. His nephew Ḥassān was killed with [Shāwar's son], and the vizier Dirghām killed Ibn Shāhanshāh, Ibn ʿAyn al-Zamān and Asad al-ʿĀrī.

It is said that the mother of [Ibn] ʿAyn al-Zamān came out to him and said: 'O Dirghām, you have made my heart burn by [your murder of] my son. May God not take my life until your mother tastes what you have given me to taste, and cool my heart and make her heart burn!' And this is just what happened: they killed him and his brother on a Friday, and God made their mother's heart burn.

When Shāwar left Egypt and set off for Damascus, his son Shujāʿ, known as al-Kāmil, Shāwar's sons-in-law and his brother sought safety with Dirghām, with the help of [his brother] Humām. Shāwar's first vizierate was for nine months, and Dirghām's vizierate was for nine months, precisely. Dirghām **was** a leader of the emirs, a splendid horseman, and was very good at polo and archery and spear-throwing. His [written] hand was that of Ibn Muqla, and [Dirghām] wrote excellent *muwashshaḥ*s [stanzas of verse].

Account of Shāwar's entry to Cairo; his restoration to the vizierate [191a]; the disagreement between Shāwar and Shīrkūh; and Ṣalāḥ al-Dīn Yūsuf's possession of Bilbays

The vizier Shāwar **entered** Cairo, and al-ʿĀḍid the ruler of Egypt bestowed the vizieral robe on him at the start of the month of Rajab of this year. He restored him to the vizierate over Egypt and gave him power therein. When the vizier Shāwar got to Cairo, his son al-Kāmil came out to him from the house of Mulhim the brother of Dirghām, where he had been detained, and al-Qāḍī al-Fāḍil also came out with him. He, too, had been detained there. Friendship and harmony had cemented between the two of them [al-Qāḍī al-Fāḍil and al-Kāmil]. Then [al-Kāmil] brought him to his father the vizier Shāwar, praised [al-Qāḍī al-Fāḍil] and extolled his virtues; and news about him and the progress of his affairs got out. It was from this time on that he was called al-Qāḍī al-Fāḍil; before this time, al-Qāḍī al-Fāḍil was known as al-Qāḍī al-Asʿad. On the subject of Shāwar's **return** to the vizierate after his removal from it, ʿUmāra b. ʿAlī al-Yamanī praised him in a poem .... **[l.15]**

[l.19] It is said that when the vizier Dirghām was killed, the vizier Shāwar and the emir Shīrkūh stayed in their camp outside Cairo on the al-Maqsim side for Saturday and Sunday. Shāwar entered Cairo on Monday, and presented himself to the caliph al-ʿĀḍid at the Gate of al-Malik in the vaulted hall, who congratulated him on his security and victory, so [Shāwar] was happy and cheerful. He exited from the Gate of Zuwayla and returned by the Gate of al-Qanṭara and lodged at the vizieral house. The emir Shīrkūh **rode** to Old Cairo, looked around, and went to see jurists such as Ibn al-Kayzānī, Ibn al-Ḥaṭiyya and Ibn Marzūq, greeted them, and then returned to [191b] his tent.

The decree of Shāwar's [appointment to the] vizierate was read out on the fourth of the month of Rajab of that year, while the emir Shīrkūh remained in his tents, and [the caliph, al-ʿĀḍid] continued the supply of hospitality: [he sent] twenty dishes of all kinds of foods each day and night, and two hundred weights of bread and eighty dry measures of barley. And to each person who brought this hospitable treatment to him, [Shīrkūh] made prayers for the caliph and was profuse in his thanks and supplications. The caliph had prepared clothes and a seat for him, which the emir had left behind for some of his men, adorned with jewels of great value. The caliph ordered [Shīrkūh] to enter [the city] so he could bestow [honour] upon him and clothe him with the robes he had prepared for him, according to custom. But he refused. And the people coming to him with hospitality came with [the request] but he took no interest in it and did not accept it from them. This is because he stayed with the army outside Cairo at al-Maqsim, awaiting the order of the vizier Shāwar regarding his previous guarantee to al-Malik al-ʿĀdil Nūr al-Dīn Maḥmūd and to also himself [Shīrkūh], concerning Egypt.

But [Shāwar] betrayed them both and reneged on what he had previously agreed in their favour. So the emir Shīrkūh wrote to Shāwar saying: 'Our staying here in tents grows long, and the army is troubled by heat and dust.' So Shāwar sent him thirty thousand *dīnārs* and said: 'Leave now, under the protection of God and His tranquility.' When the emir Shīrkūh heard this, he wrote to him saying: 'Al-Malik al-ʿĀdil Nūr al-Dīn gave me instructions when I left him, stating "If Shāwar becomes ruler of Egypt, take up residence with him there, and you will have a third of the [revenues from] the fertile land, another third will be for Shāwar and the army, and the last third will be for the ruler of the Palace [the caliph], to be paid to him for his own purposes."' Shāwar said: 'I did not arrange anything of what you say; I sought the aid of al-Malik al-'Ādil Nūr al-Dīn, and when my work was finished, [the Syrians were to] return to Syria. I have sent financial support to you; take it and depart. I part company with Nūr al-Dīn.' The emir Asad al-Dīn replied: 'I am not able to oppose Nūr al-Dīn, and I cannot depart except on completion of his command.'

When the vizier Shāwar heard this, he began preparations for a siege and for fighting Asad al-Dīn, and the emir Asad al-Dīn Shīrkūh also made preparations and sent the emir Ṣalāḥ al-Dīn Yūsuf, the son of his brother Najm al-Dīn Ayyūb b. Shādhī b. Marwān al-Ayyūbī, [192a] leading a small section of the army, to Bilbays. [Shīrkūh] ordered him to gather the annual crops and fodder and whatever was needed, and to make all he acquired ready in Bilbays, so that it could form their provision if the need arose.

Then [Shīrkūh] set about fighting the people of Cairo, and Shāwar locked the Gates of Cairo. Ṣalāḥ al-Dīn set out, subdued and took control of all of al-Ḥawf. He sent out his cavalry here and there, ordered the collection of revenues and wealth and took possession thereof. Then his ambition extended, and he advanced to the Island of Quwaysnā with his men intending to plunder Minyat Ziftā.[57]

When news of this reached the caliph al-'Āḍid billāh, he sent three palace eunuchs to call the people of Upper Egypt to war. On the Island of Quwaysnā was a governor known as Ibn Shās. The people [of Quwaysnā] joined forces to fight the Turkish troops: they fought them, overcame them and drove the remainder into the Nile, drowning most of them. If the people of Egypt had been united of purpose, obedient to God and those with power, they would not have met any obstacle. The armies and battalions returned to their places while the emir Asad al-Dīn remained under duress, unable to achieve his aim, and with no power to return to his country.

Shāwar ordered the army and soldiers and all of the groups and commanders to move out, and stationed them next to al-Bustān al-Kabīr. The emir Asad al-Dīn Shīrkūh returned to the outskirts of Cairo. The vizier Shāwar marched on and confronted him, and enticed a group from his army to advance. They approached until they were within reach of an ambush of the vizier. He triumphed over them, and some of those with Shīrkūh were made to flee. At this point, all of the army of Shīrkūh turned on the army of Shāwar, but they routed them until they reached the Gates of Cairo. The emir Asad al-Dīn Shīrkūh arrived at Cairo, but its [gates] were locked, and he stayed there until the end of the day. When night fell, the emir Shīrkūh set alight [the section] from the Gate of al-Sa'āda to the area of the canal, just as he had on a previous occasion, and the matter grew grave [192b]. As often as one of the Egyptian troops came out, he eliminated and killed him.

The vizier Shāwar came out, then went back, and the people crowded upon the walls to see what was happening. Then a battlement fell down upon the head of Shāwar, who had not protected his head, and this injured him and made him faint. So [the crowd] took him to al-Kāfūrī [Hospital], though they despaired of him [recovering].

The chief physician was summoned, who squeezed [juice from] unripe grapes into his nose, and he recovered. Then he sent for a beverage for him from the caliph, and he drank it and rode. He dismounted at his house, having acquired a swelling on his face.

The emir Asad al-Dīn Shīrkūh intensified the fighting at the Gate of al-Qanṭara, and set alight all of the canal-front. As often as Shāwar saw what he did, he did the same [in] burning the houses in the quarter of al-Zuwayla. The Banū Kināna and a large number of Egyptian troops helped him, then his men returned to the quarter of the Rayḥāniyya, where the fighting grew worse. A breach was opened up and the violent fighting continued until midday.

Then the caliph al-ʿĀḍid billāh **sat down** by the Gate of al-Dhahab and ordered the people to go out [to fight]. The equestrian guards and others rushed to the breach, making for [Shīrkūh's troops], and continued to fight the Turks and the Kināniyya and the emir Shīrkūh's men until they had made them retreat to their camps, and they barricaded the breach. Before his death, on the arrival of the vizier Shāwar and the emir Shīrkūh and the Syrian troops who were with them, vizier Dirghām **had** sent [word] to the Franks and asked them to direct themselves towards Egypt, to help the caliph against this serious enemy, which had already reached Bilbays, and stipulated an increase in the tribute they would receive. But the Frankish leader declined to do this until the order came from the caliph, because he would not receive orders from viziers since their rule was not established: every so often, one vizier was killed and another took his place. And then what we shall relate, God-willing, took place.

Account of the vizier Shāwar's invitation to the Franks, their arrival in Egypt and their seige of Asad al-Dīn Shīrkūh at Bilbays

It is said that once the vizier Shāwar was convinced that he did not have the power to fight the emir Asad al-Dīn Shīrkūh, he wrote to Amalric, king [193a] of the Franks, on the coast, seeking his aid. He said to him: 'Truly, Asad al-Dīn Shīrkūh did show me help, [but] when they reached [this] land, they coveted it. Once they take it over, they will remove you from your land and do to you what they did to us.' He settled that 1,000 *dīnār*s would be paid to [Amalric] for each stage he travelled. And he agreed an amount for his horses' barley, and something [for his household expenses.] The Franks were certain that their destruction would be wrought if al-Malik al-ʿĀdil Nūr al-Dīn, ruler of Syria, attained power in Egypt. When the vizier Shāwar wrote to them asking them to expel the emir Asad al-Dīn Shīrkūh from the land [of Egypt], they felt a relief that they had not anticipated from him. They hastened to comply with his request, and go to his aid. They were avid for rule over Egypt, so they made ready and set out.

Then Amalric the Frankish king **set out** from Ascalon, leading his hosts to Qābūs in 27 stages, and collected 27,000 *dīnār*s from there. **It is said** that when the Franks heard about Nūr al-Dīn's army's heading towards Egypt, they were extremely fearful, and were certain of their [own] destruction and that their land would be annihilated. When Shāwar's emissaries reached them asking them to help him, they were gladdened by this and hastened to him, moving towards compliance with him. They were avid for Egypt, and prepared themselves after an agreement was made between themselves and

Shāwar for a large sum that would be paid to them if the army of al-Malik al-ʿĀdil Nūr al-Dīn departed that land.

When the emir Asad al-Dīn Shīrkūh was certain that the Franks were near Cairo, he left it for Bilbays and stayed there. He found that the emir Ṣalāḥ al-Dīn Yūsuf b. Najm al-Dīn Ayyūb had made excellent preparation, so he entered Bilbays and its people the Kināniyya joined him. The vizier Shāwar left [Cairo] leading the Egyptian army and joined with the Franks, proceeding until he set up camp at Bilbays and surrounded it, besieging Asad al-Dīn and waging war morning and evening. They continued in this for eight months, and news from Egypt and those there was cut off from al-Malik al-ʿĀdil Nūr al-Dīn, the ruler of Syria. Then [news] reached him that the Frankish army had travelled to Egypt, and then he knew for sure about Shāwar's treachery, and he set about mobilising his army. [193a, l.29]

[193b, l.20] Shaykh Muḥammad b. ʿAlī b. ʿAbd al-ʿAzīz b. Naẓīf al-Ghassānī al-Ḥamawī, the scribe of al-Malik al-Ḥāfiẓ Arslān Shāh b. al-Malik al-ʿĀdil Sayf al-Dīn Abū Bakr b. Ayyūb, **said: In** the year 559, the master Asad al-Dīn Shīrkūh went to Egypt with Shāwar and the Syrian army. The sultan of the land at that time was al-Malik al-ʿĀdil Nūr al-Dīn Maḥmūd b. Zengī, and Asad al-Dīn was one of his foremost noblemen, from the elite of his dynasty and well-known. He took power in Egypt, and [Shīrkūh and Shāwar] killed Dirghām. Then Shāwar was false to Asad al-Dīn Shīrkūh and was afraid of him. So he wrote to the Franks, and the Frankish king came to him with a huge number of men. Asad al-Dīn went out to Bilbays, and the Franks besieged him there for six months, and then what we shall relate, God-willing, took place. [l.30]

[196a, l.3] Account of the truce struck between the emir Asad al-Dīn Shīrkūh, the Egyptians and the Franks

When al-Malik al-ʿĀdil Nūr al-Dīn Muḥammad b. al-Malik al-Manṣūr ʿImād al-Dīn Zengī, the ruler of Syria, conquered Bāniyās,[58] he set about instilling weakness in the Franks. He summoned a courier called Faḍl al-Fayḍī, gathered the banners of the Franks and their scalps, put them in his bag and handed them to [al-Fayḍī]. Then he said: 'I want you to force march through night and day, and devise entry into Bilbays. When you get there, greet Asad al-Dīn and inform him of the victory God has given to the Muslims, give him these banners and scalps and ask him to display them on the walls of Bilbays. For this will undermine the vigour of the disbelievers and plant fear in their hearts.' And he did this.

When the Franks witnessed the banners, they grew anxious, were fearful for their land, and asked Shāwar to permit them to withdraw. Shāwar was alarmed by this and frightened of Asad al-Dīn Shīrkūh, so he asked them to delay [departure] for some days, and he gathered his noblemen for consultation. They advised him to make a truce, and its completion was undertaken for him by the emir Shams al-Khilāfa Muḥammad b. Mukhṭār. So Shāwar appointed him an emissary to Asad al-Dīn, and he went to him, and the truce was brokered by his hand.

It is related that Shāwar wrote to the emir Asad al-Dīn Shīrkūh while he was besieged at Bilbays, saying to him, 'Know that I have spared you, and I have not empowered the

Franks to take you – for they are powerful enough to take you in the least amount of time. I have only done this for two reasons. The first of them is that I do not desire to shatter the prestige of the Muslims, or to give the Franks strength against them; and secondly because I am fearful that if the Franks capture Bilbays, they will covet it, and say "This is ours, for we conquered it by our swords." And not a day passes without my sending a sum of money to the most senior Franks and my asking them to break the determination of the [Frankish] king to attack, whenever he decides upon it, and other matters of this sort.' So he sought a truce from [Amalric] on condition that he convey 30,000 *dīnār*s more to him, and the emir Asad al-Dīn Shīrkūh consented to the truce.

It is said that the emir Asad al-Dīn Shīrkūh became weak at Bilbays, and was fearful for himself because a group of his men had been killed. His provisions grew meagre and he had [196b] thought that al-Malik al-ʿĀdil Nūr al-Dīn would support him with an army, but he did not support him with even a single man. So he wrote to Amalric the Frankish king, and sought a truce from him. [News of] this came to the vizier Shāwar, and Asad al-Dīn wrote to Ibn al-Rafīq, one of the Frankish rulers, and Humphrey[59] and other [Frankish] noblemen, and the truce was established without them paying attention to the vizier Shāwar. The emir Asad al-Dīn Shīrkūh exited Bilbays in Dhul Ḥijja of that year. A group of his men had been killed, among them Sayf al-Dīn Muḥammad b. Barān, the ruler of Ṣarkhad,[60] who was hit by an arrow. He recited **as he was dying** .... [l.9]

[l.12] **It is said** that [Shīrkūh] had a large group of the Kināniyya of Bilbays with him, and that the Franks attained great wealth from the vizier Shāwar, for he gave them a thousand *dīnār*s each day. The emir Shīrkūh stayed on the outskirts of Bilbays for three days, and then what we shall relate later, God-willing, took place. **About the siege** of Bilbays and the victory over Asad al-Dīn Shīrkūh, Shaykh ʿUmāra b. ʿAlī al-Yamanī says in a *qaṣīda* praising al-ʿĀḍid the caliph of Egypt and his vizer Shāwar .... [l.18]

[200b, l.19] *sub anno 560/1164*

Account of what happened to the emir Asad al-Dīn Shīrkūh on his route from Egypt and his safe arrival in Damascus

When the emir Asad al-Dīn Shīrkūh set out from Egypt, he travelled through desert while the Franks travelled along the coast. **It so happened** that the accursed Prince Reynald [de Chatillon], the ruler of Kerak and Shawbak, a despot, 'interpreted' his vow and applied subtle arguments to his oath, may God most high curse him, saying: 'I have made an oath that I will not follow Asad al-Dīn Shīrkūh or his army on land, but intend to meet him at sea!' Then he, may God curse him, took to the sea and travelled to Ascalon in one day, then left it for Kerak and Shawbak. Then he mobilised his army that was stationed there, and set down in anticipation of Asad al-Dīn Shīrkūh's emergence from the desert, to pounce on him. But the emir Asad al-Dīn Shīrkūh, may God most high have mercy on him, **knew** intuitively and by his own guesswork of the Frankish prince's plot, so he went [201a] to the place known as al-Mizza and Umm Kaʿb, and traversed into the Jordan rift valley. He came out at al-Balqā',[61] and it was as if he came out beyond the place where Reynald, may God most high curse him, was. So he was saved, and Reynald had no knowledge of him, and God most high safeguarded [Asad al-Dīn Shīrkūh] against his plot. [l.4]

[l.10] The emir Asad al-Dīn **reached** Damascus safely at the start of this year, met with al-Malik al-ʿĀdil Nūr al-Dīn, the ruler of Syria, and informed him of what had happened with Shāwar and how he had betrayed him. He also informed him of the weakness of the [defence of] Egypt, and awakened [Nūr al-Dīn's] desire for it. After his return from Egypt, the emir Asad al-Dīn Shīrkūh did not stop talking about it and urging attack on it, until what we shall relate, God-willing, took place.

Account of what befell the vizier Shāwar after the emir Asad al-Dīn Shīrkūh's journey from Egypt

It is said that when the emir Asad al-Dīn Shīrkūh left Egypt and the vizier Shāwar returned to Cairo, he had no aim but the pursuit of those whom he knew had acquaintance and companionship with the emir Asad al-Dīn Shīrkūh. Shāwar had suborned a group of Asad al-Dīn Shīrkūh's troops, among them Khashtarīn al-Kurdī, and granted him the fiefdom of Shaṭṭanawf.[62]

It is related by al-Idrīsī who said: The vizier Shāwar intensified his search for my uncle al-Sharīf al-Muḥannak [the eunuch], because he had been a companion of Dirghām, and he was the one whom Dirghām had sent as an emissary to al-Malik al-ʿĀdil Nūr al-Dīn, the ruler of Syria, to turn his opinion away from helping the vizier Shāwar. When he reached Nūr al-Dīn, he had showed him favour, and there was friendliness between himself and Nūr al-Dīn because [201b] the vizier al-Ṣāliḥ b. Ruzzīk had [previously] sent him as an emissary to him on many occasions. The Franks intercepted him on the road, seized him and his men and took them to Ascalon. Then it so happened that he fled from them and went to al-Malik al-ʿĀdil Nūr al-Dīn, attended on him and conveyed the missive to him about the matter of the vizier Shāwar. Al-Malik al-ʿĀdil Nūr al-Dīn **was** well-disposed towards the vizier Shāwar for certain reasons, **one of which** was that he related to him in terms of confession [Sunnism], and he disliked the Fatimids. **Another** was that [Shāwar] had promised him rule over Egypt. **Another** was that he had guaranteed him great wealth and the same to a group of his noblemen.

The vizier Shāwar **knew** that al-Sharīf al-Muḥannak had exaggerated about him in the presence of al-Malik al-ʿĀdil Nūr al-Dīn, and this induced his rancour against him. Al-Idrīsī **relates**: The vizier Shāwar proposed to al-Malik al-ʿĀdil Nūr al-Dīn that there should be a meeting between him and my uncle al-Sharīf al-Muḥannak, and he sent him to him. [Al-Idrīsī] said: 'I was with him, and we entered his [presence] up to the kiosk of the Green Hippodrome in Damascus. Then he rose in honour of my uncle al-Sharīf al-Muḥannak and treated him with deference, and then began censuring him. [Shāwar] said to him, amongst other things, 'You, O Sharīf, know that the reason for my rising up against the house of Ruzzīk is only on account of Dirghām and his brothers, and for a group of noblemen among whom are al-Mufaḍḍal Shāhanshāh, ʿAyn al-Zamān, Asad al-ʿĀrī and other emirs of the Barqiyya. Their aim is to pursue revenge on the son of al-Ṣāliḥ [b.] Ruzzīk. When I arrived in Cairo, I raised their ranks, increased their income and fulfilled their expectations of me. I achieved their desires for them, so much so that they had no ambitions after I had done for them what I did, other than to remove me from my place. But this did not satisfy them, so they murdered my children, plundered my wealth and scattered my men, and they wielded the sword among my personal household and my men. Do you know of any wrong I committed against them?'

Then my uncle al-Sharīf al-Muḥannak said to him: 'You know, O emir, that your son Ṭayy exceeded his limit and overstepped the boundary, to the point where he was arrogant even towards you, and fulfilled his plan to the exclusion of yours. After Ruzzīk b. al-Ṣāliḥ was killed, he loosened his tongue against the noblemen, and stretched his hand over their wealth and their women. He slandered them in courtly gatherings and shouted at them in the processions until they hated this, and they complained to you of him. You did not complain of them. They sought your help against his deeds, and he did nothing but [202a] detest them. Your companions and men treated the people with every [kind of] bad conduct, and so the hearts of the public and the elite were turned against you, and they turned towards what they [then] did to you.' Then he recited some verses during **his speech** … . [l.3]

[l.4] **When** the vizier Shāwar heard this, he was quiet and we [al-Idrīsī and his uncle] stood and left him. This was what Shāwar held against my uncle al-Sharīf al-Muḥannak in his heart. When he returned to Cairo, he had no aim but to pursue him. So al-Sharīf al-Muḥannak fled to the Jaʿfarī Sharīfs. Al-Idrīsī **relates**: 'I was with him when we arrived at al-Ushmūnīn, and he was venerated with [the title] 'al-Sharīf' there. He took what he was able, then travelled with the Bedouin to Syria and stayed with al-Malik al-ʿĀdil Nūr al-Dīn, ruler of Syria. As for his two sons, al-Riḍā and al-Murtaḍā, they took ship to Makka the Noble, went from there to al-Jarān and then to their father in Damascus. [l.12]

[203b, l.4] Muḥammad b. ʿAlī b. Naẓīf al-Ghassānī al-Ḥamawī the scribe, **said** in the small history he authored: **In** the year 560, Asad al-Dīn Shīrkūh went up to Egypt for a second time, almost conquered it and then returned. Here **ends** his account. What seems clearest is that his return to Egypt a second time was in the year [5]62, as we shall relate, God-willing. [l.9]

[211a, l.11] *sub anno 562/1166*

Account of the emir Asad al-Dīn's journey to Egypt

When the emir Asad al-Dīn Shīrkūh returned from Egypt and arrived in Damascus, the desire of al-Malik al-ʿĀdil Nūr al-Dīn Maḥmūd b. al-Malik al-Manṣūr ʿImād al-Dīn Atabeg Zengī, the ruler of Syria, for rule over Egypt grew strong. This was because the emir Asad al-Dīn Shīrkūh did not stop talking about it and urging attack on it. In this year, al-Malik al-ʿĀdil Nūr al-Dīn ordered the emir Asad al-Dīn Shīrkūh to mobilise the army to set out for [Egypt], so he prepared it and went out leading a strong force. Al-Malik al-ʿĀdil Nūr al-Dīn, ruler of Syria, sent a group of emirs with him. [Nūr al-Dīn] was not in favour of this but when he saw the seriousness of Asad al-Dīn regarding the journey, he could do nothing but send a group with him, for fear that an accident might be unleashed on them, and that Islam would [thereby] be weakened.

The emir Asad al-Dīn **set out** from Damascus in the month of Rabīʿ al-Awwal, or it is said in the month of Rabīʿ al-Ākhir of this year, and al-Malik al-ʿĀdil Nūr al-Dīn went with him to the borders of the land, fearful of trouble from the Franks. Ṣalāḥ al-Dīn Abu ʾl-Muẓaffar Yūsuf b. Najm al-Dīn Ayyūb b. Shādhī b. Marwān al-Ayyūbī was with his uncle Asad al-Dīn Shīrkūh on this expedition. ʿArqala al-Dimashqī said about this, in praising [211b] the emir Salah al-Dīn .... [l.1]

[l.7] Asad al-Dīn Shīrkūh then **travelled** towards Egypt, left the land of the Franks on the right hand, and arrived in Egypt. The first of this that the vizier Shāwar in Egypt was aware of was the arrival of a letter from Amalric, the Frankish king, informing him that the emir Asad al-Dīn Shīrkūh had departed from Damascus with an army, heading for Egypt. So Shāwar returned his reply to him, praising him and asking him for a return his splendid army's help, and that the agreed sum would reach him as it had the previous year. So Amalric set out leading the Frankish army, intending to help Shāwar, avid for the rule of Egypt and fearful that the emir Asad al-Dīn might gain power over it – and then there would remain no place for [the Franks] in their lands alongside [Shīrkūh] and al-Malik al-ʿĀdil Nūr al-Dīn.

So Amalric went to Egypt, leading his army along the coast, while the emir Asad al-Dīn Shīrkūh journeyed by land. The Franks got there first and halted outside Bilbays. Then the Egyptian army came out – the vizier of Egypt Shāwar among them – and met with the Frankish king. Then they all settled down to await Asad al-Dīn. The emir Asad al-Dīn knew of the Franks' rendezvous with Shāwar and their presence in Bilbays, so he deviated from their route and took the mountain path. He left the Franks on the right side and emerged at Iṭfīḥ, which is in the south of Egypt, and launched an attack there. News of him reached the vizier Shāwar, so he set out on his tracks, along with the Franks. The emir Asad al-Dīn Shīrkūh learned of this and withdrew before them, until he arrived at Sharawna[63] in Upper Egypt. He then employed artful means [to acquire] boats on which he embarked and crossed to the western bank [of the Nile].

It is said that a man named [212a] Riḍwān, one of al-Sharīf al-Muḥannak's men, pointed them towards a ford for them to cross. When they had completed the crossing, the vizier Shāwar overtook some of [Shīrkūh's] rear-guard, then separated from his army and destroyed them. Shāwar summoned boats and crossed the Nile in pursuit of the emir Asad al-Dīn Shīrkūh, with all of [Shāwar's] army and the Frankish army. The emir Asad al-Dīn Shīrkūh went on to Gīza, opposite Egypt the Protected, and set up camp there for the duration of fifty days.

The *qāḍī* Nāṣir al-Dīn Shafiʿ, the grandson of the *qāḍī* Muhy al-Dīn b. ʿAbd al-Ẓāhir and an historian, **said: In the year** [5]62, Asad al-Dīn's second expedition to Egypt took place, with a sizeable contingent of Nūriyya forces. He had informed Nūr al-Dīn of the conditions in Egypt and the weakness of its army. So [Nūr al-Dīn] sent him out a second time leading a number of soldiers, and this was in the month of Rabīʿ al-Awwal. They travelled to Egypt and stopped at Gīza, staying there blockaded for 57 days. His nephew Ṣalāḥ al-Dīn Yūsuf was with him. Shāwar sought help from the Franks and they made their way to help Shāwar, aiming for Egypt.

Someone else said: He stayed there for 50 days and more, and when the emir Asad al-Dīn Shīrkūh arrived in Gīza, he sent al-Riḍā Abū ʿAbd Allāh al-Ḥusayni b. al-Muḥannak to the Jaʿfarī, the Ṭalḥī and the Qurayshī Sharīfs, and called on them [for help], for the vizier Shāwar had wronged them, and they came to his service at great speed. **It is said** that when the vizier Shāwar came with the Frankish army on the western side, the emir Asad al-Dīn Shīrkūh wrote to him saying: 'I swear by God before you by binding oaths that I will not stay in Egypt, and none of my men will harm you. Let us come together, you and I, against the enemies of God, the accursed Franks, and avail ourselves of a chance that has become possible [against them], and the spoils that are available. I do not think that the like of this [chance] to profit Islam will ever return.' When the messenger travelled to the vizier Shāwar and delivered the letter, he ordered [the messenger] to be killed. He said: 'These are not "Franks", these are a release [for us].'

When [news of] this reached the emir Asad [212b] al-Dīn, he bit his hands in regret at the vizier Shāwar's opposition to him in his stance. [Nūr al-Dīn] said, 'May God curse him! If [Shāwar] had followed me, there would not remain a single Frank in Syria after that.' And he besieged Cairo for 50 days and more and fled to Dalja.[64] The vizier Shāwar descended at al-Lūq and al-Maqsim, and set about building a bridge between Gīza and the Island. Then he called for boats, which were filled with men, and he ordered them to come in the rear of the army of the emir Asad al-Dīn Shīrkūh. Then what we shall relate, God-willing, took place.

Account of the Battle of the Two Gates: An historian **said**: The emir Asad al-Dīn Shīrkūh wrote to the people of the port of Alexandria, seeking their help against the vizier Shāwar because of his aiding the Franks, and their squandering the wealth of Muslims. So [the Alexandrians] rose up with him, and they appointed Najm al-Dīn Ibn Maṣāl over [their army], one of the descendants of the Egyptian viziers who had fled to Alexandria under cover, and who emerged during this crisis.

Al-Idrīsī **reports**: I was then in Alexandria and Ibn Maṣāl wrote a letter for me to deliver to the emir Asad al-Dīn. [Ibn Maṣāl] said to me: 'Tell him when he gives you attendance that the weapons and armour will arrive.' He had sent Asad al-Dīn a store of weapons. [Al-Idrīsī] said: I preceded them by two days and I came before Asad al-Dīn and gave him by word of mouth the message of Najm al-Dīn Ibn Maṣāl regarding the purpose of the weapons and equipment, which arrived two days later with the nephew of the jurist Ibn 'Awf.

[Al-Idrīsī] said: We stayed at Giza for two days, then the messenger from Ibn Madāfi' came to us, informing the emir Asad al-Dīn that the vizier Shāwar was near him, and he ordered [us] to flee. Then the emir Asad al-Dīn left the tents, field kitchens and whatever would be heavy to carry, and went off at great speed until he approached Dalja. The emir Asad al-Dīn ordered it to be plundered, and it was; the army seized many things from it. Then the troops dismounted for the grazing of the animals, and they had not finished feeding when the emir Asad al-Dīn ordered the people to travel again. So the torches were lit at night and we set out. But there was the marshall [213a] calling the people to return, because the vizier Shāwar and the Franks did not drive forward with decisiveness, since they had separated from the coast {…} seeking the emir Asad al-Dīn.

Asad al-Dīn returned to Dalja and settled there, while the vizier Shāwar camped at al-Ushmūnīn. Then the emir Asad al-Dīn ordered the men to stand in battle order before morning came. He informed them that Shāwar and the Franks had caught up with them, and that they [had nothing left] except to [form] battle lines and fight them. When morning came, the people were drawn up. [Al-Idrīsī] said: [I saw] that the army of the Franks was like the teeth of a comb in soft sand. Shāwar sent some of his men ahead and they attacked the people, and 'Izz al-Dīn al-Jawālī [was defeated]. Nothing could stop ['Izz al-Dīn] except Alexandria. Then he {...} the Egyptian, and he arrived at Asyūṭ,[65] defeated.

As for the emir Asad al-Dīn, he was the first to withdraw from his position and fled when he saw the lack of fight in his men, until Ibn Talīl came, and he had been in the centre. As for the ruler of Qaysāriyya, he had taken it upon himself to chase the defeated men on exhausted horses, most of which had halted.

A large number of the emir Asad al-Dīn's men were killed, especially from among the Alexandrians. The reason for this was that the emir Asad al-Dīn Shīrkūh had divided his men into two groups, one of which was with him and the other with Ṣalāḥ al-Dīn Yūsuf, the son of his brother Najm al-Dīn Ayyūb. Then when the time for *al-ẓuhr* came, the emir Asad al-Dīn's men gathered together with one another and said: 'Know that you are bait for these [people], and there is no safety for you except in death, and in seeking martyrdom at the hands of these disbelievers.' So they prepared themselves to be patient, swarmed [together] and attacked Shāwar and the Egyptian and Frankish armies that were with him. Ṣalāḥ al-Dīn then turned up leading an army, and they killed [Egyptians and Franks], [in] a great massacre. The master of this battle was Ṣalāḥ al-Dīn Yūsuf, for he had uncovered his head, attacked from the right wing, drove the ranks back and broke their cohesion. He had made his aim [213b] and his purpose a group of Franks whom he knew were the ones whose efforts had wreaked havoc and caused harm to the Islamic army. So he wielded his sword among them until he had rocked them on their heels.

Asad al-Dīn saw this, and Shāwar and the Franks were discouraged in their hearts. [Asad al-Dīn] returned from the right side and did his utmost and used his sword until night fell upon the two parties. Then the Frankish and Egyptian parties turned their backs and took to flight. The rest of the Franks, who were behind Asad al-Dīn's men who had fled, **returned**. They found their army spent, and their troops defeated. They found the men of the emir Asad al-Dīn were waiting for them, and they had no refuge except in flight, and the God-forsaken king of the Franks was nearly captured on this day, were it not for his comrades.

The *qāḍī* Nāṣir al-Dīn Shāfi', grandson of the *qāḍī* Muhy al-Dīn Ibn 'Abd al-Ẓāhir, author of *Arrangement of Conduct in the History of the Caliphs and Kings*, and others, **said: When** Asad al-Dīn Shīrkūh knew of the arrival of the Franks, he travelled to a place known as the Two Gates [al-Bābayn], then he arranged his men for battle and met the Franks [in battle]. Then engagements took place in which Asad al-Dīn was victorious against the Franks. He killed a host of them and took 70 knights as captives. [l.17]

[214b, l.2] Account of Asad al-Dīn Shīrkūh's taking control of the port of Alexandria

When the emir Asad al-Dīn Shīrkūh and his men were victorious over the vizier Shāwar and those of the Egyptian and Frankish armies who were him, and routed them as we have set out, the emir Asad al-Dīn Shīrkūh went to Alexandria by way of al-Fayyūm.[66] When he reached al-Buḥayra, he ordered the army to plunder it, and they made away with the revenues and cattle belonging to the people. He proceeded until they entered Alexandria, came to the palace, and made a prison there for the Franks they had captured. Ibn Zubayr was then in charge of the administrative bureau there, to which he brought money and he strengthened it with weapons. The emir Asad al-Dīn was fearful that the vizier Shāwar and the Franks would aim for him and besiege him, and he would perhaps be harmed by the siege. So he left the emir Ṣalāḥ al-Dīn Yūsuf, his nephew, with the people of Alexandria because they stood by him for the sake of religion [Sunnism], and out of hatred for the vizier Shāwar and the Egyptians. So he dispatched the strongest in his army, and they set out aiming for Upper Egypt. [**I.15**]

[I.23] Account of the Egyptian army and the Franks' siege of the emir Ṣalāḥ al-Dīn at the port of Alexandria

When the vizier Shāwar and those with him of the Egyptian army and the Franks were routed by the emir Asad al-Dīn Shīrkūh and his men as we have set out, the Egyptian army and the Franks returned to Cairo the Protected, defeated. Then they improved their condition, prepared [themselves], [215a] gathered and went to the port of Alexandria where they besieged the emir Ṣalāḥ al-Dīn. The siege intensified and the food within became scarce, and the people had to endure this.

It is said that the vizier Shāwar and the Franks arrived and descended at Alexandria, and besieged Ṣalāḥ al-Dīn there for a period of {...} months.

The *qāḍī* Nāṣir al-Dīn Shāfiʿ, author of *Arrangement of the Conduct*, and other [historians], **said**: They besieged Alexandria for four months, and the people of Alexandria disliked the Egyptian [Fatimid] dynasty. **As for** the emir Asad al-Dīn Shīrkūh, when he reached Upper Egypt, he seized it, its wealth and its revenues, collected the land-tax and took possession of whatever he could. He continued staying there until he had fasted the month of Ramaḍān of that year and celebrated the ʿĪd there. Then news that the situation of the people of Alexandria had grown more difficult reached him, so he arrived via Qūṣ, [heading] in the direction [of Alexandria]. [News of] this reached Shāwar [also], so he and the Franks made their way towards Cairo, for the [information] had reached them that the emir Asad al-Dīn was besieging Cairo. There was an encounter between them, and then what we shall relate, God-willing, took place.

Account of the truce between Asad al-Dīn, the Egyptians and the Franks

The emir Asad al-Dīn Shīrkūh had **written** to the emir Ṣalāḥ al-Dīn Yūsuf, his nephew, with orders to establish a truce, so the emir Ṣalāḥ al-Dīn Yūsuf sent a letter to the king of the Franks seeking a truce from him. He acceded to this and it was settled that the vizier Shāwar would recompense the emir Asad al-Dīn all the expenditure he had sustained on this departure, give the Franks 30,000 *dīnār*s, and that all of them would return to their land. And oaths to this effect followed.

The emir Ṣalāḥ al-Dīn **wrote** to the king of the Franks saying: 'I have companions among whom are those who are strong and those who are weak. As for those who are strong, they will follow us on the land, but as for the weak, we want boats to transport them.' So the king ordered a number of boats for them and [Salah al-Dīn's] men left in them.

Al-Idrīsī **narrates**: 'I was among the group that left Alexandria on the boats [215b] with the emir Ṣalāḥ al-Dīn, and he met with the emir Asad al-Dīn Shīrkūh. The vizier Shāwar sent for and seized every Egyptian who was with the emir Ṣalāḥ al-Dīn Yūsuf, among them Najm al-Dīn Ibn Maṣāl. News of this reached the emir Ṣalāḥ al-Dīn, who met the Frankish king and said to him: 'Truly, Shāwar has [violated] the oaths.' He said: 'How is that?' He replied: 'He has seized {…} to us.' [The Frankish king] said: 'He cannot do this.' Then he wrote to Shāwar, who denied that he had done that deed, and he got him to swear an oath [protecting] all those who had taken refuge with the emir Ṣalāḥ al-Dīn and the emir Asad al-Dīn. He forbade [his] people from staying in Egypt, and they departed for Syria. Then the vizier Shāwar himself came out, gathered all of his noblemen who had decided to make the journey from Egypt, and swore an oath to them that he would treat them well and double their wealth. Among them were those who trusted his oaths and stayed put, and those who were not reassured and made the journey to Syria. **As for** the men on the boats, they reached Acre and were seized and imprisoned in a cane-press [factory] until the Frankish king arrived and set them free. [215b, l.16]

Notes

1 *Qur'ān* 13:38.
2 A place outside the Gate of Futūḥ, Cairo: *Itti'āẓ* 3:143.
3 Ibn al-Furāt refers here to al-Ma'mūn al-Baṭā'iḥī (d. 1125) the vizier, rather than his son, the author Ibn al-Ma'mūn al-Baṭā'iḥī (d. 1192).
4 An island on the Nile opposite the fortress of Cairo: *Khiṭaṭ* 2:5.
5 A dyke stretching from the coast of Cairo at Fustat to the Rawḍa Island: *Itti'āẓ* 3:126.
6 The large city between Cairo and Damietta: *Mu'jam al-buldān* no. 10792, 5:76.
7 For the Gates of Cairo, see Bloom (2007), 122–8.
8 A fortified stronghold and a rural district north of Aleppo: *Mu'jam* no. 2565, 2:47.
9 A large district between Basra and Wasit, near Maysan: ibid. no. 12231, 5:369.
10 The governorate in N. Egypt.
11 A village in Upper Egypt on the west bank of the Nile: *Itti'āẓ*, 3:279.
12 The Atabeg of Damascus between 1138 and 1149.
13 Eilat, a city on the coast of the Qulzum (Suez) river near the Syria/Hijaz border: *Mu'jam* no. 1196, 1:347.
14 Or Minya Ibn Khaṣīb, a part of Ushmunin: *Itti'āẓ* 3:216.
15 Or the exponents of free will.
16 Al-Qarāfa, below the Muqattam Hills.
17 A fortress city in the southern Nile Delta, in the modern governorate of Qalyubiya.
18 An Imami Shi'i emir who was one of Ibn Abī Ṭayy's oral informants; see Morray (1994), 96–7.
19 Two governorates of Lower Egypt.
20 Or Hermopolis, a city in the Upper Egyptian governorate of al-Minya, in medieval times a governorate in itself.

21 The brother-in-law of Ṭalā'i', as mentioned in 153a above.
22 Upper Egyptian city in the Suhaj governorate.
23 An emir who had served the previous caliph but one al-Ḥāfiẓ: *Itti'āẓ* 3:221.
24 A city in Upper Egypt on the west bank of the Nile: *Itti'āẓ* 3:92.
25 A village in the governorate of Buhayra: *Itti'āẓ* 3:257.
26 An open reservoir on the outskirts of Fustat: Levanoni (2008), 184.
27 The semi-deserted tracts of land on either side of the Nile Delta: Kennedy (2001), 125.
28 A town in Giza, Upper Egypt known in ancient times as Aphroditopolis: Gil (2004), 81.
29 In N. E. Cairo: *Khiṭaṭ* 2:217.
30 A mountain near the straits of Cairo: *Khiṭaṭ* 2:207.
31 Coins with a value of one sixth of a *dīnār*, acc. to Ibn Ṭuwayr: *Nuzhat*, 127.
32 The name of both a district of Cairo, designated as such by Jawhar (d. 992) after the people of Barqa (Cyrenaica) who had settled there, and a corps of Mamluks: *Khiṭaṭ* 2:212.
33 The well-known author and Ayyubid vizier (d. 1199), whose career in high office began under the Fatimids.
34 An *iqṭā'* (land-grant) held by Shīrkūh alongside Ḥims for a town of that name in Syria: Richards, 'Shīrkūh', *EI*².
35 One of two Crusader fortresses south of the Dead Sea (the other being Shawbak): *Itti'āẓ* 3:230.
36 Identified by Richards (2007, 2:148, n.6) as Philip of Milly, according to the *Rawḍatayn* of Abu Shāma.
37 See n. 35 above.
38 An area of Lower Egypt: *Khiṭaṭ* 1:194.
39 A village in the administrative district of Tarabya, L. Egypt: *Khiṭaṭ* 1:194.
40 One of the Bedouin tribes mentioned by al-Maqrīzī: *Khiṭaṭ* 1:708.
41 An emir from the Barqiyya regiment: *Itti'āẓ* 3:256.
42 The coastal governorate in Lower Egypt.
43 A town in Giza: *Khiṭat* 2:143.
44 In Lower Egypt, east of the Nile: *Khiṭaṭ* 2:210.
45 Egyptian governorate west of the Nile.
46 Tract of land between the Nile and the Cairo canal: Levanoni (2008), 185.
47 A Lower Egyptian city in al-Buhayra governorate.
48 The observatory near Old Cairo: Levanoni (2008), 185.
49 An area of land to the west of Fatimid Cairo: *Khiṭaṭ* 1:467-9.
50 The largest city in the coastal Lower Egypt governorate of al-Daqhaliyya.
51 The name of a Fatimid beauty spot on the Cairo straits, where a palace with the same name is located: *Itti'āẓ* 3:40; *Khiṭaṭ* 1:467-9.
52 A Gate at the northern side of the Western Palace of the Fatimids: *Itti'āẓ* 3:144; Walker (1997), 192.
53 For more on this garden, see Levanoni (2008), 199.
54 The embankment separating the two lakes of Birkat al-Fīl (Elephant Lake) and Birkat Qārūn in S. E. Cairo: Levanoni (2008), 186, 192.
55 A mosque outside Cairo, by the Trench: *Itti'āẓ* 3:270-1; *Khiṭaṭ* 2:458–9.
56 A lake in S. E. Cairo: Levanoni (2008), 186, 192.
57 A small town on the eastern Nile delta.
58 A city in north western Syria.
59 Identified by Richards (2007, 2:148, n.6) as Humphrey of Toron, according to the *Rawḍatayn* of Abu Shāma.

60 A fortified town east of Bosra.
61 The plain of Balka, acc. to Hava, 46; Cf. *Itti'āẓ* 3:279.
62 In the governorate of al-Gharbiyya: *Itti'āẓ* 3:279.
63 An Upper Egyptian town east of the Nile: *Itti'āẓ* 3:283.
64 A town in the governorate of Ushmunin: *Itti'āẓ* 3:283.
65 A large Upper Egyptian town on the Nile, south of Cairo.
66 The Egyptian governorate to the west of the Nile.

Bibliography

Primary sources

al-ʿAynī, Maḥmūd Badr al-Dīn, *ʿIqd al-jumān fī taʾrīkh ahl al-zamān – al-ʿaṣr al-Ayyūbī*, ed. M. R. Mahmud (Cairo, 2003).

al-ʿAzīmī, Muḥammad b. ʿAlī, *Taʾrīkh Ḥalab*, ed. I. Zarur (Damascus, 1984).

Baybars al-Manṣūrī, *Zubdat al-fikra fī taʾrīkh al-hijra*, ed. D. S. Richards (Beirut, 1998).

Baybars al-Manṣūrī, *al-Tuḥfa al-mulūkiyya fi ʾl-dawla al-Turkiyya*, ed. A. S. Hamdan (Cairo, 1987).

Hajji Khalīfa, *Kashf al-ẓunūn ʿan asāmī ʾl-kutub wa ʾl-funūn*, 2 vols (Istanbul, 1941, 1943).

al-Hidāyatu ʾl-Āmiriyya, *Being an Epistle of the Tenth Fatimid Caliph al-Āmir bi-aḥkāmi ʾl-lāh*, ed. A. A. A. Fyzee (Oxford, 1938).

Ibn ʿAbd al-Ẓāhir (d. 1292), *al-Rawḍat al-bahiyyat al-ẓāhira fī khiṭaṭ al-Muʿizziyya al-Qāhira*, ed. A. F. Sayyid (Cairo, 1996).

Ibn al-Athīr, *Al-Kamil fi ʾl-taʾrikh*: (i) ed. C. J. Tornberg (Leiden, 1867–71); (ii) ed. in 11 vols by M. Y. al-Daqqāq (Beirut, 2003).

Ibn al-Athīr, *The Chronicle of Ibn Al-Athir for the Crusading Period from Al-Kamil Fiʾl-Taʾrikh: Years 491–541/1097–1146: The Coming of the Franks and the Muslim Response*, Part 1, ed. and trans. D. S. Richards (Aldershot, 2006).

Ibn al-Athīr, *al-Bāhir fi ʾl-dawlat al-atābakiyya*, ed. A. A. Tulaymat (Cairo, 1963).

Ibn al-Dawādārī, *Kanz al-durar*, ed. S. al-Munajjid (Cairo, 1961).

Ibn Duqmāq, *al-Jawhar al-thamīn fī siyar al-mulūk wa ʾl-salāṭīn*, ed. M. K. I. Ali (Beirut, 1983).

Ibn Duqmāq, *Kitāb al-intiṣār*, ed. K. Vollers, 2 vols (Cairo, 1891–2).

Ibn al-Furāt, *Taʾrīkh al-duwal wa ʾl-mulūk*: Volume 2 unpublished edition by M. F. Elshayyal (PhD thesis, Edinburgh University, 1986).

Ibn al-Furāt, *Taʾrīkh al-duwal wa ʾl-mulūk*: Volume 4 edited in 2 parts by M. H. al-Shammāʿ (Basra, 1968–9).

Ibn al-Furāt, *Taʾrīkh al-duwal wa ʾl-mulūk*: Volume 5 (first half only, covering 600–15/1203–18): by M. H. al-Shammāʿ (Basra, 1970). Volumes 6 and 7: by C. Zurayk and N. ʿIzz al-Dīn (Beirut, 1939, 1942).

Ibn al-Furāt, *Taʾrīkh al-duwal wa ʾl-mulūk*: Volume 9 (first half, covering 789–92/1387–89)): by C. Zurayk (Beirut, 1936).

Ibn al-Furāt, *Taʾrīkh al-duwal wa ʾl-mulūk*: Volume 9 (second half, covering 792–9/1389–96): by C. Zurayk and N. ʿIzz al-Dīn (Beirut, 1938).

Ibn al-Furāt, *Taʾrīkh al-duwal wa ʾl-mulūk*: Extracts from volumes 5–7 (641–76/1243–77) appear in *Ayyubids, Mamlukes and Crusaders: Selections from the* Taʾrīkh al-duwal wa ʾl-Mulūk *of Ibn al-Furāt*, 2 vols, U. and M. C. Lyons (eds) with introduction and notes by J. S. C. Riley Smith (Cambridge, 1971).

Ibn Ḥajar al-ʿAsqalānī, *al-Durar al-kāmina fi aʿyān al-miʾa al-thāmina*, ed. M. S. J. al-Ḥaqq in 5 vols (Cairo, 1966–7).

Ibn Ḥajar al-ʿAsqalānī, *Inbāʾ al-ghumr bi abnāʾ al-ʿumr*, 3 vols (Cairo, 1969–72).
Ibn Ḥajar al-ʿAsqalānī, *al-Majmaʿ al-muʾassas biʾl-muʿjam al-mufahras*, ed. Yusuf Abd al-Rahman al-Marʿashli in 4 vols (Beirut, 1992–4).
Ibn Ḥajar al-ʿAsqalānī, *Rafʿ al-isr ʿan quḍāt Miṣr*, ed. A. M. ʿUmar (Cairo, 1998).
Ibn al-ʿImād, *Shadharāt al-dhahab fī akhbār man dhahab* (Cairo, 1932).
Ibn al-Jawzī, *al-Muntaẓam fī taʾrīkh al-umam*, ed. M. A. Ata et al. (Beirut, 1992).
Ibn Khalaf, *Mawādd al-bayān*, ed. Fuat Sezgin (Frankfurt, 1986).
Ibn Khaldūn, *Kitāb al-taʿrīf bi Ibn Khaldūn wa riḥlatuhu gharban wa sharqan*, ed. T. M. T. al-Tanji (Cairo, 1951).
Ibn Khaldūn, *Kitāb al-ʿibar wa dīwān al-mubtadāʾ wa ʾl-khabar*, ed. in 7 vols (Cairo, 1867).
Ibn Khaldūn, *The Muqaddimah: An Introduction to History*, trans. F. Rosenthal (New Jersey, 1967).
Ibn Khallikān, *Wafayāt al-aʿyān*, ed. I. Abbas in 8 vols (Beirut, 1968–72).
Ibn al-Maʾmūn al-Baṭāʾiḥī, *Passages de la Chronologie d'Egypte d'Ibn al-Maʾmūn, Prince Jamāl al-Dīn Abū ʿAlī Mūsā b. al-Maʾmūn al-Baṭāʾiḥī*, ed. A. F. Sayyid (Cairo, 1983).
Ibn Muyassar, *Akhbār Miṣr*: (i) ed. H. Massé as *Annales d'Égypte* (Cairo, 1919); (ii) ed. A. F. Sayyid as *Chronique d'Égypte* (Cairo, 1981).
Ibn Naẓīf, al-Ḥamawī, *al-Taʾrīkh al-Manṣurī talkhīṣ al-kashf waʾl-bayān fī ḥawādith al-zamān,* (or Taʾrīkh-i Mansūrī), ed. P. Gryaznevich (Moscow, 1963).
Ibn Qāḍī Shuhba, *al-Muntaqā min Ta ʾrīkh Ibn al-Furāt*, Chester Beatty MS Arab 4125, ff. 1–196.
Ibn al-Qalānisī, *The Damascus Chronicle of the Crusades. Extracted and Translated from the Chronicle of Ibn al-Qalānisī*, ed. H. A. R. Gibb (London, 1932).
Ibn al-Ṣayrafī, *al-Qānūn fī dīwān al-rasāʾil:* (i) ed. ʿAlī Bahjat (Cairo, 1905); (ii) ed. A. F. Sayyid (Cairo, 1990).
Ibn al-Ṣayrafī, *Kitāb al-wuzarāʾ li ʾl-dawla al-Fāṭimiyya bi ʾl-Qāhira al-Muʿizziyya* (= *al-Ishāra ilā man nāla ʾl-wizāra*), ed. A. Mukhlis, *BIFAO* 35 (Cairo, 1924), 49–1.
Ibn Shaddād, Bahāʾ al-Dīn, *The Rare and Excellent History of Saladin: Or al-Nawadir al-Sultaniyya wa ʾl-Mahasin al-Yusufiyya by Bahaʾ Al-Din Ibn Shaddad*, ed. and trans. D. S. Richards (Aldershot, 2001).
Ibn Taghrībirdī, *al-Nujūm al-zāhira fī mulūk Miṣr wa ʾl-Qāhira*, ed. in 16 vols by M. H. Shams al-Dīn (Beirut, 1992).
Ibn Taghrībirdī, *al-Manhal al-ṣāfī wa ʾl-mustawfā ba ʿd al-wāfī* (Cairo, 1958).
Ibn Ṭūlūn, Shams al-Dīn Muḥammad b., ʿAlī, *al-Ghuraf al-ʿaliyya fī tarājim mutaʾakhkhirī al-Ḥanafiyya*', Süleymaniye Library, MS Şehid Ali Paşa, 1924, ed. T. Wollina, available online at: https://f.hypotheses.org/wp-content/blogs.dir/3349/files/2016/12/Ibn-Tulun_Ghuraf-al-Aliyya.pdf (accessed October 2017).
Ibn Ṭuwayr, *Nuzhat al-muqlatayn fī akhbār al-dawlatayn*, ed. A. F. Sayyid (Beirut, 1992).
Ibn Wāṣil, *Mufarrij al-kurūb fī akhbār Banī Ayyūb*, vols 1–3, ed. J. al-Shayyal (Cairo, 1953–60); vols 4–5, ed. S. A. Ashur and H. Rabie (Cairo, 1972–7).
Ibn Ẓāfir, *Akhbār al-duwal al-munqaṭiʿa: La section consacrée aux Fatimides*, ed. A. Ferré (Cairo, 1972).
Ibn al-Zayyāt, *al-Kawākib al-sayyāra fī tartīb al-ziyāra* (Cairo, 1907).
Idrīs ʿImād al-Dīn, *ʿUyūn al-akhbār wa funūn al-āthār*, vol. 7, ed. A. F. Sayyid as *The Fatimids and Their Successors in Yaman. The History of an Islamic Community* (London and New York, 2002).
ʿImād al-Dīn al-Iṣfahānī, *Bustān al-jāmiʿ*: (i) ed. Cl. Cahen, *Bulletin d'Etudes Orientales*, 7–8, 1937–8; (ii) ed. U. A. Tadmuri (Beirut, 2002).
al-Imām al-Mustanṣir, *al-Sijillāt al-Mustanṣiriyya*, ed. A. M. Majīd, 2nd edn (Cairo, n.d.).

al-Maqrīzī, *al-Mawā'iẓ wa 'l-i'tibār fī dhikr al-khiṭaṭ wa 'l-āthār* [also known as the *Khiṭaṭ*]: (i) Bulaq edition in 2 vols (Cairo, 1893); (ii) partial edition in 4 vols by G. Wiet (Cairo, 1906, 1911); (iii) ed. K. al-Manṣūr (Beirut, 1998); (iv) an early draft of the *Khiṭaṭ*, ed. A. F. Sayyid, 3 vols (London, 2002–4).

al-Maqrīzī, *Kitāb al-sulūk li ma'rifat duwal wa al-mulūk*, 4 vols (Cairo, 1936–58, 1970–3).

al-Muṣabbiḥī, *Tome quarantième de la chronique d'Egypte de Musabbiḥī, 366–420/ 977–1029, Vol. I, Partie historique*, ed. A. F. Sayyid and T. Bianquis (Paris, 1978).

al-Muṣabbiḥī, '*Nusus da'i'a min* Akhbār Miṣr *li'l-Musabbiḥī*', ed. A. F. Sayyid, *AI* 17 (1981), 1–54.

Nāṣir-i Khusraw, *Naser-e Khosraw's Book of Travels (Safarnāma)*, trans. and with an introduction by W. M. Thackston (New York, 1986).

Nicetas Choniates, *Chronicles*, translated as *O City of Byzantium: Annals of Niketas Choniatēs*, by H. J. Magoulias (Detroit, 1984).

al-Nuwayrī, *Nihāyat al-arab fī funūn al-adab*, ed. M. H. M. Ahmad et al., 31 vols (the rest in progress) (Cairo, 1923–to date).

Qāḍī al-Nu'mān, *Da'ā'im al-Islām*, ed. A. A. A. Fyzee (Cairo, 1951–61).

Qāḍī al-Nu'mān, *Kitāb iftitāḥ al-da'wa wa ibtidā' al-dawla*, ed. W. al-Qaḍi (Beirut, 1970).

Qāḍī al-Nu'mān, *Kitāb al-majālis wa 'l-musāyarāt*, ed. H. Faqi, I. Shabbuh and M. Ya'lawi (Tunis, 1978).

al-Qalqashandī, *Ṣubḥ al-a'shā fī ṣinā'at al-inshā'*, ed. M. A. Ibrahim in 14 vols (Cairo, 1913–20).

al-Qalqashandī, *Selections from Subh al-A'shā by al-Qalqashandi, Clerk of the Mamluk Court: Egypt: "Seats of Government" and "Regulations of the Kingdom", From Early Islam to the Mamluks*, ed. Tarek Galal Abdelhamid and Heba El-Toudy (London, 2017).

Shāfi' b. 'Ali, *Ḥusn al-manāqib al-sirriyya*, ed. A. al-Khuwaytir (Riyad, 1976).

Abū Shāma, *Kitāb al-rawḍatayn fī akhbār al-dawlatayn*: (i) ed. in 2 vols (Cairo, 1870–1); (ii) ed. in 5 vols, I. al-Zibaq (Beirut, 1997).

al-Sulamī, *Ṭabaqāt al-ṣūfiyya*, ed. J. Pedersen (Paris, 1938).

al-Ṣuyūṭī, *Ḥusn al-muḥāḍara fī ta'rīkh Miṣr wa 'l-Qāhira* (Cairo, 1967).

al-Sakhāwī, *al-I'lān bi 'l-tawbīkh li man dhamma 'l-ta'rīkh* (Cairo, 1349 H); trans. F. Rosenthal, *A History of Muslim Historiography* (Leiden, 1952).

al-Sakhāwī, *al-Ḍaw' al-lāmi' li ahl al-qarn al-tāsi'* (Cairo, 1355 H).

Ṭalā'i' b. Ruzzīk, *Dīwān*, ed. A. A. Badawī (Cairo, 1958).

Usāma b. Munqidh, *Memoirs of an Arab-Syrian Gentleman or An Arab Knight in the Crusades. Memoirs of Usamah Ibn-Munqidh* (*Kitāb al-I'tibār*), trans. P. K. Hitti (Beirut, 1964).

Usāma b. Munqidh, *Dīwān*, ed. A. A. Badawi and H. Abd al-Majid (Cairo, 1953).

William of Tyre, *Historia rerum in partibus transmarinis gestarum*, translated by J. Brundage, as *The Crusades: A Documentary History* (Milwaukee, 1962).

Yāqūt al-Ḥamawī, *Mu'jam al-buldān*, ed. in 7 vols by F. A. al-Jundī (Beirut, 1990).

Secondary sources

Allouche, A., 'The Establishment of Four Chief Judgeships in Fatimid Egypt', *JAOS* 105:2 (April-June 1985), 317–20.

Amitai, R., 'In the Aftermath of 'Ayn Jalut: The Beginnings of the Mamluk-Ilkhanid Cold War', *al-Masāq* 3 (1990), 12–13.

Amitai, R., *Mongols and Mamluks: The Mamluk-Īlkhānid War, 1260–1281* (Cambridge, 1995).

Amitai, R., review of *The Cambridge History of Egypt, Vol. 1: Islamic Egypt, 640–1517*, ed. C. F. Petry, *JAOS* 121:4 (October-December 2001), 707–09.

Amitai, R., 'Al-Maqrizi as a Historian of the Early Mamluk Sultanate (or: Is al-Maqrizi an Unrecognized Historiographical Villain?)', *MSR* 7:2 (2003), 99–118.

Ammur, A. and Binbin, A. S., *Kashshāf al-kutub al-makhṭūṭa bi 'l-khizānat al-Ḥasaniyya* (Rabat, 2007).

Arjomand, S. A., 'The Law, Agency, and Policy in Medieval Islamic Society: Development of the Institutions of Learning from the Tenth to the Fifteenth Century', *CSSH* 41:2 (April 1999), 263–93.

Ashtor, E. 'Some Unpublished Sources for the Bahri Period', in *Studies in Islamic History and Civilisation*, ed. U. Heyd (Jerusalem, 1961), 11–30.

Assaad, S. A., *The Reign of al-Hakim bi Amr Allah (386–411): A Political Study* (Beirut, 1974).

Atiyeh, G. N. (ed.), *The Book in the Islamic World* (New York, 1995).

Attiya, H. M., 'Knowledge of Arabic in the Crusader States in the Twelfth and Thirteenth Centuries', *JMH* 25:3 (1999), 203–13.

Auchterlonie, P., *Arabic Biographical Dictionaries: A Summary Guide and Bibliography* (Durham, 1987).

Ayalon, D., 'Studies on the Structure of the Mamluk Army I', *BSOAS* 15:2 (1953), 203–28.

Ayalon, D., 'Studies on the Structure of the Mamluk Army II', *BSOAS* 15:3 (1953), 448–76.

Ayalon, D., 'Studies on the Structure of the Mamluk Army III', *BSOAS* 16:1 (1954), 57–90.

Al-Azmeh, A., 'Muslim History: Reflections on Periodisation and Categorisation', *The Medieval History Journal*, 1:2 (1998), 195–231.

Al-Azmeh, A., *Ibn Khaldun: A Reinterpretation* (London, 2012).

Bacharach, J. L., 'Circassian Mamluk Historians and Their Quantitative Economic Data', *JARCE* 12 (1975), 75–87.

Bashir, S., 'On Islamic Time: Rethinking Chronology in the Historiography of Muslim Societies', *History and Theory* 53 (December 2014), 519–44.

Bates, M. L., 'The Function of Fatimid and Ayyubid Glass Weights', *JESHO* 24:1 (January 1981), 63–92.

Bauden, F., 'Maqriziana I: Discovery of an Autograph Manuscript of al-Maqrīzī: Towards a Better Understanding of His Working Method Description: Section 1', *MSR* 7:2 (2003), 21–68.

Bauden, F., 'Mamluk Era Documentary Studies: The State of the Art', *MSR* 10:1 (2005), 15–60.

Bauden, F., 'Maqriziana I: Discovery of an Autograph Manuscript of al-Maqrīzī: Towards a Better Understanding of His Working Method, Description: Section 2', *MSR* 10:2 (2006), 81–139.

Bauden, F., 'Maqriziana II: Discovery of an Autograph Manuscript of al-Maqrīzī: Towards a Better Understanding of His Working Method, Analysis', *MSR* 12:1 (2008), 51–118.

Bauden, F., 'Maqriziana XII: Evaluating the Sources for the Fatimid Period: Ibn al-Ma'mūn al-Baṭā'iḥī's History and Its Use by al-Maqrīzī (with a Critical Edition of his Resumé for the Years 501–515 AH)', in B. Craig (ed.), *Ismaili and Fatimid Studies in Honor of Paul E. Walker* (Chicago, 2010), 33–85.

Bauden, F., 'Du destin des archives en Islam. Analyse des données et éléments de réponse', in D. Aigle and S. Péquignot (eds), *La correspondance entre souverains, princes et cités-États. Approches croisées entre l'Orient musulman, l'Occident latin et Byzance (XIIIe–début XVIe siecle)* (Turnhout, 2013), 27–49.

Bauden, F., 'Taqī al-Dīn Aḥmad Ibn 'Alī al-Maqrīzī', in A. Mallett (ed.), *Medieval Muslim Historians and the Franks in the Levant* (Leiden and Boston, 2014), 161–200.

Bauer, T., 'Mamluk Literature as a Means of Communication', in S. Conermann (ed.), *Ubi sumus? Quo vademus?: Mamluk Studies-State of the Art* (Göettingen, 2013), 23–56.

Bauer, T., *Warum es kein islamisches Mittelalter gab* (Munich, 2018).

Bausi, A., Brockmann, C., Friedrich, M. and Kienitz, S. (eds), *Manuscripts and Archives: Comparative Views on Record-Keeping* (Berlin, 2018).

Behrens-Abouseif, D., 'The Façade of the Aqmar Mosque in the Context of Fatimid Ceremonial', *Muqarnas* 9 (1992), 29–38.

Behrens-Abouseif, D., *Islamic Architecture in Cairo: An Introduction* (Leiden, 1997).

Behzadi, L., 'Introduction: The Concept of Polyphony and the Author's Voice', in L. Behzadi and J. Hämeen-Anttila (eds), *Concepts of Authorship in Pre-Modern Arabic Texts* (Bamberg, 2016).

Berkey, J., 'Women and Islamic Education in the Mamluk Period', in N. Keddie and B. Baron (eds), *Women in Middle Eastern History: Shifting Boundaries in Sex and Gender* (New Haven, 1991), 143–57.

Berkey, J., *The Transmission of Knowledge in Medieval Cairo* (New Jersey, 1992).

Berkey, J., 'The Mamluks as Muslims: The Military Elite and the Construction of Islam in Medieval Egypt', in T. Philipp and U. Haarmann (eds), *The Mamluks in Egyptian Politics and Society* (Cambridge, 1998).

Berkey, J., 'Culture and Society during the Late Middle Ages', in C. F. Petry (ed.), *The Cambridge History of Egypt*, vol. 1 (Cambridge, 1998), 375–411.

Berkey, J., 'The Transmission of Religious Knowledge', *The Formation of Islam* (Cambridge, 2003), 224–30.

Berkey, J., 'There Are ʿulamāʾ and Then There Are ʿulamāʾ: Minor Religious Institutions and Minor Religious Functionaries in Medieval Cairo', in R. E. Margariti, A. Sabra and P. M. Sijpesteijn (eds), *Histories of the Middle East Studies in Middle Eastern Society, Economy and Law in Honor of A. L. Udovitch* (Leiden, 2011), 9–22.

Berque, J., 'The Koranic Text: From Revelation to Compilation', reprinted in *The Book in the Islamic World* (ed. Atiyeh).

Bierman, I. A., *Art and Politics: The Impact of Fatimid Uses of Tirāz Fabrics* (Chicago, 1980).

Bierman, I. A., *Writing Signs: The Fatimid Public Text* (Berkeley, 1998).

Black, A., *The History of Islamic Political Thought: From the Prophet to the Present* (London, 2001).

Blochet, E., *Catalogue des Manuscrits Arabes des Nouvelles Acquisitions, 1884–1924* (Paris, 1926).

Bloom, J. M., 'The Origins of Fatimid Art', *Muqarnas*, 3 (1985), 20–38.

Bloom, J. M., *Arts of the City Victorious: Islamic Art and Architecture in Fatimid North Africa and Egypt* (New Haven, 2007).

Bonner, M., review of Brett's *The Rise of the Fatimids*, *JAH* 44 (2003), 145–94.

Bora, F., 'An Historiographical Study of al-Quḍāʿī's *Taʾrīkh*', MPhil thesis, Oxford University, 1998.

Bora, F., 'Mamluk Representations of Late Fatimid Egypt: The Survival of Fatimid-Era Historiography in Ibn al-Furāt's *Taʾrīkh al-duwal wa 'l-mulūk* (History of Dynasties and Kings)', DPhil thesis, Oxford University, 2010.

Bora, F., 'A Mamluk Historian's Holograph. Messages from a *Musawwada* of *Tarīkh*', *Journal of Islamic Manuscripts* 3:2 (2012), 119–53.

Bora, F., 'Did Salah al-Din Destroy the Fatimids' Books? An Historiographical Enquiry', *JRAS* 25:1 (2015), 21–39.

Bosworth, C. E., 'A Medieval Islamic Prototype of the Fountain Pen', *JSS* 26:2 (1981), 229–34.
Bradley, H., 'The Seductions of the Archive: Voices Lost and Found', *History of the Human Sciences* 12:2 (1999), 107–22.
von Brandt, A., *Werkzeug des Historikers*, 15th edn (Stuttgart, 1998).
Brett, M., 'Fatimid Historiography: A Case Study – The Quarrel with the Zirids, 1048–58', in D. O. Morgan (ed.), *Medieval Historical Writing in the Christian and Islamic Worlds* (London, 1982), 47–59.
Brett, M., review of A. F. Sayyid's edition of Ibn Muyassar's *Akhbār Miṣr*, *JRAS* 2 (1983), 293–5.
Brett, M., 'The Way of the Nomad', *BSOAS* 58:2 (1995), 251–69.
Brett, M., 'The Battles of Ramla (1099–1105)', in U. Vermeulen and D. de Smet (eds), *Egypt and Syria in the Fatimid, Ayyubid and Mamluk Eras*, vol. I (Leuven, 1995), 17–37.
Brett, M., 'The Realm of the Imam: The Fatimids in the Tenth Century', *BSOAS* 59:3 (1996), 431–49.
Brett, M., *The Rise of the Fatimids: The World of the Mediterranean and the Middle East in the Fourth Century of the Hijra, Tenth Century CE* (Leiden, 2001).
Brett, M., '*Lingua Franca* in the Mediterranean: John Wansborough and the Historiography of Medieval Egypt', in H. Kennedy (ed.), *The Historiography of Islamic Egypt (c. 950–1800)* (Lieden, 2001), 1–11.
Brett, M., 'Abbasids, Fatimids and Seljuqs', in D. Luscombe and J. Riley-Smith (eds), *The New Cambridge Medieval History, vol. 4, part 2: c.1024–c.1198* (Cambridge, 2004), 675–720.
Brinner, W. M., review of 'Mark R. Cohen's *Jewish Self-Government in Medieval Egypt: The Origins of the Office of Head of the Jews. ca. 1065–1126*', *AJS Review* 10:2 (Autumn 1985), 237–8.
Broadbridge, A. F., 'Academic Rivalry and the Patronage System in Fifteenth-Century Egypt: al-'Aynī, al-Maqrīzī, and Ibn Ḥajar al-'Asqalānī', *MSR* 3 (1999), 85–107.
Brockelmann, C., *Geschichte der Arabischen Litteratur*, 2 vols (Leiden, 1943–9) and *Supplementbänden*, 3 vols (Leiden, 1937–42).
Brundage, J. (trans.), William of Tyre, *Historia rerum in partibus transmarinis gestarum*, XX, 5–10, *Patrologia Latina* 201, 788–9, in *The Crusades: A Documentary History* (Milwaukee, 1962), 139–40.
Busse, H., review of 'A. F. Sayyid's edition of Ibn al-Ma'mūn's chronicle' (1983), *IJMES* 18:3 (August 1986), 397–8.
Cahen, C., 'Quelques Chroniques Anciennes Relatives aux derniers Fatimides', *BIFAO* 37 (1937), 1–27.
Cahen, C., 'Une chronique syrienne du VIe/XIIe siècle: Le *Bustān al-Jāmi*', *Bulletin d'études orientales de l'Institut français de Damas* vii–viii (1937–8).
Cahen, C., 'La Chronique Abrégée, d'Al-'Azīmī', *JA* 230 (1938), 353–448.
Cahen, C., *La Syrie du Nord a l'époque des Croisades* (Paris, 1940).
Cahen, C., 'Editing Arabic Chronicles', *IS* (1962), 1–25.
Cahen, C., 'Un récit inédit de vizirat de Dirgham', *AI* 8 (1969), 27–46.
Cahen, C., 'Ibn al-Furāt', *EI*², vol. 3, 768–9 (1971); P. Bearman, Th. Bianquis, C. E. Bosworth, E. van Donzel and W. P. Heinrichs (eds) (Leiden, 1960–2007).
Calder, N., review of 'Stern's *Studies in Early Isma'ilism*' (Leiden, 1983), *BSOAS* 50:1 (1987), 133–4.
Canard, M., 'Une lettre du Calife Fatimite Al-Hafiz (524–44/1130–49) à Roger II (Roi de Sicile)', in *Atti del Convegno Internaxionale di Studi Ruggeriani*, I (Palermo, 1955), 125–46.

Canard, M., 'Fāṭimids', in *EI*², ed. P. Bearman et al. (Leiden, 1960–2007).
Çetin, A., 'Oghuz Turks in the account of a Mamluk Historian', *JIS* 20:3 (2009), 376–82.
Chamberlain, M., 'The Crusader Era and the Ayyubid Dynasty', in C. F. Petry (ed.), *The Cambridge History of Egypt*, vol. 1 (Cambridge, 1998), 198–242.
Chamberlain, M., *Knowledge and Social Practice in Medieval Damascus, 1190–1350* (Cambridge, 2002).
Cohen, M., 'Goitein, the Geniza, and Muslim History' (2001), available online only at: www.dayan.org/mel/cohen.pdf (accessed 31 July 2015) [broken link].
Comes, M., 'Umayya b. ʿAbd al-ʿAzīz, Abi 'l-Ṣalt al-Dānī al-Ishbīlī', in *EI*², ed. P. Bearman et al. (Leiden, 1960–2007).
Conermann, S., 'Ibn Ṭulūn (d. 955/1548): Life and Works', *MSR* 8 (2204), 115–39.
Conermann, S. and Seidensticker, T., 'Some Remarks on Ibn Ṭawq's (d. 915/1509) Journal *al-Taʿlīq*', *MSR* 11:2 (2007), 121–36.
Conrad, L. I., 'Recovering Lost Texts: Some Methodological Issues', *JAOS* 113:2 (April-June 1993), 258–63.
Cortese, D. and Calderini, S., *Women and the Fatimids in the World of Islam* (Edinburgh, 2006).
Crone, P., *Medieval Islamic Political Thought* (Edinburgh, 2005).
Dadoyan, S., *The Fatimid Armenians* (Leiden, 1997).
Daftary, F., *The Isma'ilis: Their History and Doctrines*, 2nd edn (Cambridge, 1990, 2007).
Daftary, F., 'A Major Schism in the Early Isma'ili Movement', *SI* 77 (1993), 123–39.
Daftary, F., *The Assassin Legends: Myths of the Isma'ilis* (London, 1994).
Daftary, F., *A Short History of the Isma'ilis* (Edinburgh, 1998).
Daftary, F., 'Sayyida Hurra: The Isma'ili Sulayhid Queen of Yemen', in Gavin R. G. Hambly (ed.), *Women in the Medieval Islamic World: Power, Patronage and Piety*, reprinted in *The New Middle Ages* 6 (New York, 1998), 117–30.
Daftary, F., *Isma'ili Literature* (London, 2004).
Daftary, F., *The Isma'ilis: Their Doctrines and History* (Cambridge, 2007).
Daftary, F., 'Isma'ili Historiography', *Encyclopaedia Iranica* 14 (2007–8), 176–8.
Dajani-Shakeel, H., 'Egypt and the Egyptians: A Focal Point in the Policies and Literature of Al-Qāḍī Al-Fāḍil', *JNES* 36:1 (January 1977), 25–38.
De Blois, F. C., Van Dalen, B., Humphreys, R. S., Marin, Manuela, Lambton, Ann K. S, Woodhead, Christine, Athar Ali, M., Hunwick, J. O., Freeman-Grenville, G. S. P., Proudfoot, I., et al., 'Taʾrīk͟h, in *EI*², ed. P. Bearman et al. (Leiden, 1960–2007).
Déroche, F., 'The Copyists' Working Pace: Some Remarks towards a Reflexion on the Economy of the Book in the Islamic World', in L. Pfeiffer and M. Kropp (eds), *Theoretical Approaches to the Transmission and Edition of Oriental Manuscripts* (Würzburg, 2007), 203–13.
Derrida, J., *Archive Fever. A Freudian Impression*, trans. E. Prenowiz (Chicago and London, 1995).
de Slane, W. M. G., *Catalogue des Manuscrits arabes* (Paris, 1883–95).
de Vivo, F. and Donato, M. P. (eds), 'Scholarly Practices in the Archive (16th-18th Centuries)', special issue of *Storia della Storiografia*, 68 (2015).
Edbury, P. W. and Rowe, J. G., *William of Tyre: Historian of the Latin East* (Cambridge, 1991).
Ehrenkreutz, A. S., 'Saladin's coup d'etat in Egypt', in Sami A. Hanna (ed.), *Medieval and Middle Eastern Studies: In Honor of Aziz Suryal Atiya* (Leiden, 1972).
Ehrenkreutz, A. S., *Saladin*, Albany (New York, 1972).
Elayyan, R. M., 'The History of the Arabic-Islamic Libraries: 7th to 14th Centuries', *ILR* 22 (1990), 119–35.

Elbendary, A., 'The Worst of Times: Crisis Management and Al-Shidda Al-'Uzma', in *Money, Land and Trade: An Economic History of the Muslim Mediterranean* (London, 2002), 67–83.

Elbendary, A., 'The Historiography of Protest in Late Mamluk and Early Ottoman Egypt and Syria', *International Institute of Asian Studies Newsletter* 43 (2007), 9.

Elbendary, A., *Crowds and Sultans. Urban Protest in Late Medieval Egypt and Syria* (Cairo, 2015).

El-Hibri, T., *Reinterpreting Islamic History: Hārūn al-Rashīd and the Narrative of the 'Abbāsid Caliphate* (Cambridge, 1999).

El-Leithy, T., 'Living Documents, Dying Archives: Towards a Historical Anthropology of Medieval Arabic Archives', *al-Qantara: Revista de Estudios Arabes* 32:2 (2011), 389–434.

El Shakry, O., 'History without Documents': The Vexed Archives of Decolonization in the Middle East', *The American Historical Review* 120:3 (2015), 920–34.

Elshayyal, M. F., 'A Critical Edition of Volume II of *Tarikh al-duwal wa 'l-Mulūk* by Muhammad b. 'Abd al-Rahim b. 'Ali Ibn al-Furat', *IQ* 47 (2003), 197–216.

Ernst, H., *Die mamlukischen Sultansurkunden* (Wiesbaden, 1960).

Fähndrich, H. E., 'The *Wafayāt al-A'yān* of Ibn Khallikān: A New Approach', *JAOS* 93:4 (October-December 1973), 432–45.

Fernanades, L., 'On Conducting the Affairs of the State: A Guideline of the Fourteenth Century', *AI* 24 (1988), 81–91.

Fischel, W. J., 'The Spice Trade in Mamluk Egypt: A Contribution to the Economic History of Medieval Islam', *JESHO* 1:2 (April 1958), 157–74.

Fischel, W. J., 'Ibn Khaldūn's Use of Historical Sources', *Studia Islamica* 14 (1961), 109–19.

Fischel, W. J., *Ibn Khaldūn in Egypt, His Public Functions and His Historical Research (1382–1406): A Study in Islamic Historiography* (Berkeley and Los Angeles, 1967).

Flügel, G., *Die Arabischen, Persischen und Türkischen Handschriften der Kaiserlich-Koeniglichen Hofbibiliothek zu Wien*, II (Vienna, 1869).

Foucault, M., *Les Mots et les choses* (1966), translated as *The Order of Things: An Archaeology of the Human Sciences* (Hove, 2002).

Foucault, M., *The Archaeology of Knowledge and the Discourse of Language*, trans. A. M. S. Smith (New York, 1972).

Frenkel, Y., 'Political and Social Aspects of Islamic Religious Endowments (*awqāf*): Saladin in Cairo (1169–73) and Jerusalem (1187–93)', *BSOAS* 62:1 (1999), 1–20.

Friedrich, M., *The Birth of the Archive. A History of Knowledge*, trans. J. N. Dillon (Michigan, 2018).

Friedrich, M., 'Epilogue: Archives and Archiving across Cultures–Towards a Matrix of Analysis', in A. Bausi et al. (eds), *Manuscripts and Archives: Comparative Views on Record-Keeping* (Berlin, 2018).

Gacek, A., 'Some Remarks on the Cataloguing of Arabic Manuscripts', *BRISMES* 10:2 (1983), 173–9.

Gacek, A., 'Taxonomy of Scribal Errors in Arabic Manuscripts', in J. Pfeiffer and M. Kropp (eds), *Theoretical Approaches*, 217–35.

Gacek, A., *Arabic Manuscripts – A Vademecum for Readers* (Leiden, 2009).

Ghersetti, A., Editor's introduction: 'The Book in Fact and Fiction in Pre-Modern Arabic Literature', in A. Ghersetti and A. Metcalfe (eds), *Journal of Arabic and Islamic Studies* 12 (2012), 1–15.

Gibb, H. A. R., 'Historiography', *EI*, 1st edn, Supplement (Leiden, 1938), 233–45.

Gibb, H. A. R., 'Al-Barq al-Shami: The History of Saladin by the Katib 'Imad al-Din al-Isfahani', *WZKM* 52 (1952–5), 93–115.

Gil, M., 'Institutions and Events of the Eleventh Century Mirrored in Geniza Letters', *BSOAS* 67:2 (2004), part 1: 151–67; part 2: 168–84.
Görke, A. and Hirschler, K., *Manuscript Notes as Documentary Sources* (Würzburg, 2012).
Goitein, S. D., 'The Cairo Geniza as a Source for the History of Muslim Civilisation', *SI* 3 (1955), 75–91.
Goitein, S. D., 'The Documents of the Cairo Geniza as a Source for Mediterranean Social History', *JAOS* 80:2 (April-June 1960), 91–100.
Goitein, S. D., *A Mediterranean Society*, 5 vols (Berkeley, 1967).
Goldziher, I., *Muslim Studies (Muhammedanische Studien)*, vol. 2, ed. S. M. Stern, trans. C. R. Barber and S. M. Stern (Chicago and New York, 1971).
Gosh, A., 'The Slave of Ms. H. 6', Occasional Paper No. 125 (1990), Centre for Studies in Social Sciences, Calcutta.
Gottheil, R., 'Al-Ḥasan ibn Ibrāhīm ibn Zūlāq', *JAOS* 28 (1907), 254–70.
Guest, A. R., 'A List of Writers, Books and Other Authorities mentioned by El Maqrizi in His *Khitat*', *JRAS* (1902), 103–25.
Guest, A. R. and Richmond, E. T., 'Miṣr in the Fifteenth Century', *JRAS* (1903), 791–816.
Guo, L., 'Mamluk Historiographic Studies: The State of the Art', *MSR* I (1997), 15–43.
Guo, L., *Early Mamluk Syrian Historiography: Al-Yūnīnī's Dhayl mir'āt al-zamān* (Leiden, 1998).
Guo, L., 'History writing', in R. Irwin (ed.), *The New Cambridge History of Islam* (Cambridge, 2010), 444–57.
Haarmann, U., *Quellenstudien zur fruhen Mamlukenzeit* (Freiburg, 1969).
Haarmann, U., 'Mamluk Endowment Deeds as a Source for the History of Education in Late Medieval Egypt', *al-Abhath* 28 (1980), 31–47.
Haarmann, U., review of *The Civilian Elite of Cairo in the Later Middle Ages* by Carl F. Petry, *BSOAS* 47:1 (1984), 133–5.
Haarmann, U., 'Rather the Injustice of the Turks Than the Righteousness of the Arabs: Changing 'Ulamā' Attitudes towards Mamluk Rule in the Late Fifteenth Century', *SI* 68 (1988), 61–77.
Haarmann, U., 'Mamluk Studies – A Western Perspective', *Arab Journal for the Humanities* 13:51 (1995), 329–47.
Hachmeier, K., 'Private Letters, Official Correspondence: Buyid Inshā' as a Historical Source', *JIS* 13:2 (2002), 125–54.
Haji, H., *Inside the Immaculate Portal: A History from the Fatimid Archives* (London, 2012).
Hallaq, W. B., 'The "*qāḍī's dīwān (sijill)*" before the Ottomans', *BSOAS* 61:3 (1998), 415–36.
Halm, H. 'Der Treuhander Gottes', *DI* 63 (1986), 11–72.
Halm, H. *Das Reich des Mahdi* (Munich, 1991), translated by Michael Bonner as *The Empire of the Mahdi* (Leiden, 1996).
Halm, H. *The Fatimids and Their Traditions of Learning* (London, 2001).
al-Hamdani, H. F., 'The Letters of Al-Mustanṣir bi'llāh', *BSOAS* 7:2 (1934), 307–24.
Hamdani, S. F., *Between Revolution and State: The Path to Fatimid Statehood* (London, 2006).
Hanaoka, M., *Authority and Identity in Medieval Islamic Historiography: Persian Histories from the Peripheries* (Cambridge, 2016).
Harber, J., *Medieval Creation Commentary as Literary Interpretation: St. Augustine's De Genesi ad Litteram and at-Tabarī's Tafsīr of Sūra 2:29–38* (Wisconsin-Madison, 1979).
Hartmann, A., 'A Unique Manuscript in the Asian Museum, St. Petersburg: The Syrian Chronicle *at-Ta'riḥ al-Manṣūrī* by Ibn Naẓīf al-Ḥamawī from the 7th AH/13th

Century', in U. Vermeulen and D. De Smet (eds), *Egypt and Syria in the Fatimid, Ayyubid and Mamluk Eras*, I (Leuven, 1995), 89–100.
Hava, J. G., *Arabic English Dictionary* (Beirut, 1899).
Head, R. C., 'Preface: Historical Research on Archives and Knowledge Cultures: An Interdisciplinary Wave', *Archival Science* 10 (2010), 191–4.
Hillenbrand, C. 'Some Medieval Islamic Approaches to Source Material: The Evidence of a 12th Century Chronicle', *Oriens* 27 (1981), 197–225.
Hillenbrand, C. *The Crusades: Islamic Perspectives* (London and New York, 2000).
Hirschler, K., *Medieval Arabic Historiography: Authors as Actors* (London and New York, 2006).
Hirschler, K., *The Written Word in the Medieval Arabic Lands: A Social and Cultural History of Reading Practices* (Edinburgh, 2011).
Hirschler, K., 'Islam: The Arabic and Persian Traditions, Eleventh–Fifteenth Centuries', in S. Foot and C. F. Robinson (eds), Chapter 13 of *The Oxford History of Historical Writing, Vol. 2:400–1400* (Oxford, 2012).
Hirschler, K., "Catching the Eel' – Documentary Evidence for Concepts of the Arabic Book in the Middle Period', *JAIS* 12 (2012), 224–34.
Hirschler, K., 'Studying Mamluk Historiography: From Source-Criticism to the Cultural Turn', in S. Conermann (ed.), *Ubi sumus? Quo vademus?: Mamluk Studies-State of the Art* (Göettingen, 2013), 159–86.
Hirschler, K., 'From Archive to Archival Practices: Rethinking the Preservation of Mamluk Administrative Documents', *JAOS* 136:1 (January–March 2016), 1–28.
Hirschler, K., *Medieval Damascus: Plurality and Diversity in an Arabic Library* (Edinburgh, 2016).
Hirschler, K., 'Document Reuse in Medieval Arabic Manuscripts', *Comparative Oriental Manuscript Studies Bulletin* 3:1 (2017), 33–44.
Hirschler, K. and Savant, S., 'What Is in a Period? Arabic Historiography and Periodization', *DI* 91:1 (2014), 6–19.
Hodgson, M. G., *The Venture of Islam*, 3 vols (Chicago, 1977).
Hoffman, A. and Cole, P., *Sacred Trash: The Lost and Found World of the Cairo Geniza* (New York, 2011).
Holt, P. M., 'Qalāwūn's Treaty with Acre in 1283', *English Historical Review* 91:361 (October 1976), 802–12.
Holt, P. M., 'Saladin and His Admirers: A Biographical Reassessment', *BSOAS* 46:2 (1983), 235–9.
Holt, P. M., 'Some Observations on Shāfi' b. 'Alī's Biography of Baybars', *JSS* 29:1 (Spring 1984), 123–30.
Holt, P. M., review of *Passages de la Chronique d'Egypte d'ibn al-Ma'mūn, Prince Gamāl al-Dīn Abū 'Alī Mūsā b. al-Ma'mūn al-Baṭā'iḥī, m. 588 h.* by A. F. Sayyid, *BSOAS* 48:2 (1985), 424.
Holt, P. M., 'A Chancery Clerk in Medieval Egypt', *The English Historical Review* 101:400 (July 1986), 671–9.
Holt, P. M., 'Literary Offerings: A Ggenre of Courtly Literature', in T. Philipp and U. Haarmann (eds), *The Mamluks in Egyptian Politics and Society* (Cambridge, 1998).
Hrbek, I., 'Egypt, Nubia and the Eastern Deserts – The Fatimids', in R. A. Oliver (ed.), *The Cambridge History of Africa*, vol. III (Cambridge, 1977), 10–26.
Humphreys, R. S., 'The Emergence of the Mamluk Army I', *SI* 45 (1977), 67–99.
Humphreys, R. S., 'The Emergence of the Mamluk Army II', *SI* 46 (1977), 147–82.
Humphreys, R. S., *Islamic History: A Framework for Inquiry* (New Jersey, 1991).

Humphreys, R. S., 'Egypt in the World System of the Later Middle Ages', in C. F. Petry (ed.), *The Cambridge History of Egypt*, vol. 1(Cambridge, 1998), 445–61.
Humphreys, R. S., 'Turning Points in Islamic Historical Practice', in Q. Edward Wang and Georg G. Iggers (eds), *Turning Points in Historiography: A Cross-Cultural Perspective* (Woodbridge, 2002), 89–100.
Imad, L. *The Fatimid Vizierate* (Berlin, 1990).
Irwin, R., review of *The Cambridge History of Egypt* (1998) in *MSR* 4 (2000), 271–7.
Irwin, R., 'Al-Maqrīzī and Ibn Khaldūn, Historians of the Unseen', *MSR* 7:2 (2003), 217–30.
Irwin, R., 'Mamluk History and Historians', in R. Allen and D. S. Richards (eds), *Arabic Literature in the Post-Classical Period* (Cambridge, 2006), 159–70.
Irwin, R., *Ibn Khaldun. An Intellectual Biography* (New Jersey, 2018).
Jackson, S., 'Discipline and Duty in a Medieval Muslim Elementary School: Ibn Ḥajar al-Haytamī's *Taqrīr al-maqāl*', in J. E. Lowry, D. J. Stewart and S. M. Toorawa (eds), *Law and Education in Medieval Islam: Studies in Memory of Professor George Makdisi* (Cambridge, 2004), 18–32.
Jiwa, S., 'The Initial Destination of the Fatimid Caliphate: The Yemen or the Maghrib?', *BRISMES* 13:1 (1986), 15–26.
Jiwa, S., 'Fatimid-Buyid Diplomacy during the Reign of al-'Azīz Billāh (365/975–386/996)', *JIS* 3:1 (1992), 57–71.
Jiwa, S., *The Founder of Cairo: The Fatimid Imam-Caliph Al-Mu'izz and His Era* (London, 2013).
Johns, J., *Arabic Administration in Norman Sicily: The Royal Dīwān* (Cambridge, 2002).
Kaegi, W. E., 'Egypt on the Eve of the Muslim Conquest', in C. F. Petry (ed.), *The Cambridge History of Egypt*, vol. 1 (Cambridge, 1998), 2–61.
Kaḥḥāla, U., *Mu'jam al-mu'allifīn* (Beirut, 1993).
Kaptein, N. J. G., *Muhammad's Birthday Festival: Early History in the Central Muslim Lands and Development in the Muslim West Until the 10th/16th Century* (Leiden, 1993).
Kennedy, H., *The Armies of the Caliphs: Military and Society in the Early Islamic State* (Abingdon and New York, 2001).
Kennedy, H., *An Historical Atlas of Islam*, 2nd edn (Leiden, 2002).
Kennedy, H., 'Caliphs and Their Chroniclers in the Middle Abbasid Period (Third/Ninth Century)', in *The Byzantine and Early Islamic Near East* (Farnham, 2006), 17–35.
Khalidi, T., *Arabic Historical Thought in the Classical Period* (Cambridge, 1994).
Khan, G. A., 'A Copy of a Decree from the Archives of the Fatimid Chancery in Egypt', *BSOAS* 49:3 (1986), 439–53.
Khan, G. A., 'The Historical Development of the Structure of Medieval Arabic Petitions', *BSOAS* 53:1 (1990), 8–30.
Kohlberg, E., 'From Imāmiyya to Ithnā-'ashariyya', *BSOAS* 39:3 (1976), 521–34.
Kohlberg, E., *A Medieval Muslim Scholar at Work: Ibn Ṭāwūs and His Library* (Leiden, 1992).
König, J. and Whitmarsh, T. (eds), *Ordering Knowledge in the Roman Empire* (Cambridge, 2007).
Koselleck, R., 'Representation, Event, and Structure', in *Futures Past: On the Semantics of Historical Time*, 2nd edn (New York, 2004), 105–14.
Krey, A. C., 'William of Tyre: The Making of an Historian in the Middle Ages', *Speculum* 16:2 (April 1941), 149–66.
Landau-Tasseron, E., 'On the Reconstruction of Lost Sources', *al-Qanṭara* 25 (2004), 45–91.

Lapidus, I., 'The Grain Economy of Mamluk Egypt', *JESHO* 12:1 (January 1969), 1–15.

Lapidus, I., Mamluk Patronage and the Arts in Egypt: Concluding Remarks', in *Muqarnas* 2 (1984), 173–81.

Lapidus, I., *Muslim Cities in the Later Middle Ages* (Cambridge, Mass., 1967; repr. Cambridge, 1984).

Lassner, J., *Islamic Revolution and Historical Memory* (New Haven, Connecticut, 1986).

Leder, S., *Story-Telling in the Framework of Non-Fictional Arabic Literature* (Wiesbaden, 1998).

Leiser, G., 'The Restoration of Sunnism in Egypt: Madrasas and Mudarrisūn 495–647/1101–1249', unpublished PhD dissertation, University of Pennsylvania, 1976.

Leiser, G., 'The Madrasa and the Islamization of the Middle East: The Case of Egypt', *JARCE* 22 (1985), 29–47.

Leiser, G., 'The Madrasa and the Islamization of Anatolia before the Ottomans', in J. E. Lowry, D. J. Stewart and S. M. Toorawa (eds), *Law and Education in Medieval Islam: Studies in Memory of Professor George Makdisi* (Cambridge, 2004), 174–91.

Le Strange, G., 'The Story of the Death of the Last 'Abbāsid Caliph from the Vatican MS of Ibn al-Furāt', *JRAS* (1900), 293–300.

Lev, Y., 'The Fatimid Princess Sitt al-Mulk', *JSS* 32 (1987), 319–28.

Lev, Y., 'The Fatimids and Egypt 301–358/914–969', *Arabica* 25 (1988), 186–96.

Lev, Y., 'The Fatimid Imposition of Isma'ilism on Egypt (358–386/969–996)', *ZDMG* 138 (1988), 313–25.

Lev, Y., *State and Society in Fatimid Egypt* (Leiden, 1991).

Lev, Y., *War and Society in the Eastern Mediterranean, 7th–15th Centuries* (Leiden, 1996).

Lev, Y., *Saladin in Egypt* (Leiden, 1999).

Lev, Y., 'Symbiotic Relations: Ulama and the Mamluk Sultans', *MSR* 13:1 (January 2009), 1–26.

Levanoni, A., 'The Mamluk Conception of the Sultanate', *IJMES* 26:3 (August 1994), 373–92.

Levanoni, A., *A Turning Point in Mamluk History: The Third Reign of al-Nasir Muhammad Ibn Qalawun (1310–1341)* (Leiden, 1995).

Levanoni, A., 'Water Supply in Medieval Middle Eastern Cities: The Case of Cairo', *al-Masāq* 20:2 (2008), 179–205.

Lewis, B., 'Saladin and the Assassins', *BSOAS* 15:2 (1953), 239–45.

Lewis, B. (with P. Holt, eds), *Historians of the Middle East* (London, 1962).

Lewis, B., review of *Die Chronik des Ibn ad-Dawādārī. Sechster Teil. Der Bericht über die Fatimiden* by Ṣalāḥ al-Dīn al-Munajjid, *BSOAS* 26:2 (1963), 429–31.

Lewis, B., 'An Interpretation of Fatimid History', in *Colloque International sur l'histoire du Caire* (Cairo, 1969).

Lewis, B., Letter, 'The Vanished Library', *The New York Review of Books*, 37:14 (27 September 1990).

Lewis, B., 'Reflections on Islamic History', *From Babel to Dragomans: Interpreting the Middle East* (Oxford, 2004).

Lindsay, J. E., 'Prophetic Parallels in Abu 'Abd Allah al-Shi'i's Mission among the Kutama Berbers', *IJMES* 24 (1992), 39–56.

Lindsay, J. E., 'Ibn 'Asākir as a Preserver of the "Qiṣaṣ al-Anbiyā": The Case of David B. Jesse', *SI* 82 (1995), 45–82.

Little, D. P., *An Introduction to Mamluk Historiography: An Analysis of Arabic Annalistic and Biographical Sources for the Reign of Al-Malik-An-Nāṣir Muḥammad Ibn Qalā'ūn* (Stuttgart, 1970).

Little, D. P., 'An Analysis of the Relationship between Four Mamluk Chronicles for 737–45', *JSS* 19:2 (1974), 252–68.

Little, D. P., 'The Recovery of a Lost Source for Bāḥrī Mamlūk History: Al-Yūsufī's Nuzhat Al-Nāẓir Fī Sīrat Al-Malik Al-Nāṣir', *JAOS* 94:1 (January-March 1974), 42–54.

Little, D. P., 'The Haram Documents as Sources for the Arts and Architecture of the Mamluk Period', *Muqarnas* 2 (1984), 61–72.

Little, D. P., 'The Use of Documents for the Study of Mamluk History', *MSR* 1 (1997), 1–13.

Little, D. P., 'Historiography of the Ayyubid and Mamluk Epochs', in C. F. Petry (ed.), *The Cambridge History of Egypt*, vol. 1 (Cambridge, 1998), 412–44.

Little, D. P., 'A Comparison of al-Maqrīzī and al-'Aynī as Historians of Contemporary Events', *MSR* 7:2 (July 2003), 205–15.

Lyons, M. C. and Jackson, D. E. P., *Saladin: Politics of the Holy War* (Cambridge, 1982).

Mackensen, R. S., 'Moslem Libraries and Sectarian Propaganda', *AJSLL* 51:2 (1935), 83–113.

Madelung, W., 'A Treatise on the Imamate of the Fatimid Caliph al-Manṣūr bi-Allāh', in C. F. Robinson (ed.), *Texts, Documents and Artefacts: Islamic Studies in Honour of D. S. Richards* (Leiden, 2003).

Mai, A., *Codices Vaticani Orientali* (Rome, 1831).

Makdisi, G., 'Madrasa and University in the Middle Ages', *SI* 32 (1970), 255–64.

Makdisi, G., *The Rise of Colleges: Institutions of Learning in Islam and the West* (Edinburgh, 1981).

Margoliouth, D. S., review of the *History of Ibn al-Furat, Vol. IX, JRAS* 3 (July 1938), 460.

Marlow, L., 'Kings, Prophets and the "Ulama" in Mediaeval Islamic Advice Literature', *SI* 81 (1995), 101–20.

Marshall, M., 'Engaging History: Historical Ethnography and Ethnology', *American Anthropologist* 96:4 (December 1994), 972–4.

Marwick, A., *The New Nature of History: Knowledge, Evidence, Language* (Chicago, 2001).

Marzolph, U., 'Coining the Essentials: Arabic Encyclopedias and Anthologies of the Pre-Modern Period', in Anja-Silvia Goeing, Anthony T. Grafton and Paul Michel (eds), *Collectors' Knowledge: What Is Kept, What Is Discarded* (Leiden, 2013).

Massoud, S. G., *The Chronicles and Annalistic Sources of the Early Mamluk Circassian Period* (Leiden, 2007).

Mayer, H. E., review of *Saladin* by A. S. Ehrenkreutz (1972), *Speculum* 49:4 (1974), 724–7.

Mbembe, A., 'The Power of the Archive and Its Limits', in Carolyn Hamilton, Verne Harris, Michele Pickover, Graeme Reid, Razia Saleh and Jane Taylor (eds), *Refiguring the Archive* (Dordrecht, 2002), 19–27.

McSheffrey, S., 'Detective Fiction in the Archives: Court Records and the Uses of Law in Late Medieval England', *History Workshop Journal* 65:1 (2008), 65–78.

Meisami, J. S., 'History as Literature', *Iranian Studies*, 33:1/2 (2000), 15–30.

Mejcher-Atassi, S. and Schwartz, J. P. (eds), *Archives, Museums and Collecting Practices in the Modern Arab World* (London, 2016).

Melvin-Koushka, M., 'Of Islamic Grammatology: Ibn Turka's Lettrist Metaphysics of Light', *al-'Usur al-Wusta* 24 (2016), 42–113.

Meri, J. (ed.), *Medieval Islamic Civilization: An Encyclopedia*, 2 vols (Abingdon and New York, 2006).

Michel, N., project on 'Private Archives in Ottoman and Contemporary Egypt', http://www.ifao.egnet.net/axes-2012/ecritures-langues-corpus/2012-archives-privees//#en (accessed October 2017).

Mitha, F., *Al-Ghazali and the Ismailis: A Debate on Reason and Authority in Medieval Islam* (London, 2001).
Möhring, H., *Saladin und der Dritte Kreuzzug* (Wiesbaden, 1980).
Möhring, H., *Saladin: Der Sultan und seine Zeit, 1138–1193* (Munich, 2005); trans. as *Saladin: The Sultan and His Times, 1138–1193* by D. S. Bachrach (Baltimore, 2008).
Mojaddedi, J., *The Biographical Tradition in Sufism: The Tabaqat Genre from al-Sulami to Jami* (Abingdon and New York, 2001).
Moosa, M., 'The Crusades: An Eastern Perspective, with Emphasis on Syriac Sources', *MW* 93 (April 2003), 249–89.
Morray, D., *An Ayyubid Notable and His World: Ibn Al-Adim and Aleppo as Portrayed in His Biographical Dictionary of People Associated with the City* (Leiden, 1994).
Muhanna, E., 'Why Was the Fourteenth Century a Century of Arabic Encyclopaedism?', in Jason König and Greg Woolf (eds), Chapter 16 of *Encyclopaedism from Antiquity to the Renaissance* (Cambridge, 2013), 343–56.
Muhanna, E., *The World in a Book: Al-Nuwayri and the Islamic Encyclopedic Tradition* (New Jersey, 2017).
Müller, C., 'The Power of the Pen: Cadis and Their Archives', in A. Bausi, C. Brockmann, M. Friedrich and S. Kienitz (eds), *Manuscripts and Archives: Comparative Views on Record-Keeping* (Berlin, 2018), 361–85.
Munro, D. C., 'Letters of the Crusaders', *Translations and Reprints from the Original Sources of European History* 1:4 (Philadelphia, 1896), 14–17; reprinted in Leon Bernard and Theodore B. Hodges (eds), *Readings in European History* (New York, 1958), 105–07.
Munro, D. C., 'The Western Attitude toward Islam during the Period of the Crusades', *Speculum* 6:3 (July 1931), 329–43.
al-Musawi, M., 'Pre-Modern Belletristic Prose', in R. Allen and D. S. Richards (eds), *Arabic Literature in the Post-Classical Period* (Cambridge, 2006), 101–33.
al-Musawi, M., *The Medieval Islamic Republic of Letters: Arabic Knowledge Construction* (Notre Dame, Indiana, 2015).
al-Nabarāwī, F., *'Ilm al-ta'rīkh: Dirāsah fī manāhij al-baḥth* (Alexandria, 1993).
Nagel, T., *Frühe Isma'iliya und Fatimiden im Lichte der Risālat iftitāḥ ad-da'wa: Eine religionsgeschichtliche Studie* (Bonn, 1972).
Nashabi, H. 'Educational Institutions', in R. B. Sergeant (ed.), *The Islamic City* (Paris, 1980).
Nicolle, D., *Historical Atlas of the Islamic World* (London, 2004).
Northrup, L. S., 'The Baḥrī Mamlūk sultanate 1250–1390', in C. F. Petry (ed.), *The Cambridge History of Egypt*, vol. 1 (Cambridge, 1998), 242–89.
Ouerfelli, M., *Le Sucre Production, commercialisation et usages dans la Méditerranée médiévale* (Leiden, 2008).
Paul, J., 'Archival Practices in the Muslim World Prior to 1500', in A. Bausi et al. (eds), *Manuscripts and Archives: Comparative Views on Record-Keeping* (Berlin, 2018), 339–60.
Pedersen, J., *The Arabic Book*, trans. Geoffrey French (New Jersey, 1984).
Petry, C. F., 'Geographic Origins of Dīwān Officials in Cairo during the Fifteenth Century', *JESHO* 21:2 (May 1978), 165–84.
Petry, C. F., 'Geographic Origins of Academicians in Cairo during the Fifteenth Century', *JESHO* 23:1/2 (April 1980), 119–41.
Petry, C. F., 'Geographic Origins of Religious Functionaries in Cairo during the Fifteenth Century', *JESHO* 23:3 (October 1980), 240–64.
Petry, C. F., *The Civilian Elite of Cairo in the Later Middle Ages* (New Jersey, 1981).

Petry, C. F., 'A Paradox of Patronage', *MW* 73:3–4 (1983), 182–207.

Petry, C. F., 'Travel Patterns of Medieval Notables in the Near East', *SI* 62 (1985), 53–87.

Petry, C. F., 'Scholastic Stasis in Medieval Islam Reconsidered: Mamluk Patronage in Cairo', *Poetics Today* 14:2 (1993), 323–48.

Petry C. F. and Mendenhall, S., 'Geographic Origins of the Civil Judiciary of Cairo in the Fifteenth Century', *JESHO* 21:1 (January 1978), 52–74.

Philipp, T. and Haarmann, U. (eds), *The Mamluks in Egyptian Politics and Society* (Cambridge, 1998).

Poonawala, I. K., *Bibliography of Isma'ili Literature* (Malibu, California, 1977).

al-Qadi, W., 'Biographical Dictionaries: Inner Structure and Cultural Significance', in George N. Atiyeh (ed.), *The Book in the Islamic World: The Written Word and Communication in the Middle East* (Albany, 1995), 93–122.

al-Qadi, W., 'How Sacred Is the Text of an Arabic Medieval Manuscript?', in J. Pfeiffer and M. Kropp (eds), *Theoretical Approaches to the Transmission and Edition of Oriental Manuscripts* (Würzburg, 2007), 13–53.

Rabbat, N. O., *The Citadel of Cairo: A New Interpretation of Royal Mamluk Architecture* (Leiden, 1995).

Rabbat, N. O., 'Al-Azhar Mosque: An Architectural Chronicle of Cairo's History', *Muqarnas* 13 (1996), 45–67.

Rabbat, N. O., 'Representing the Mamluks', in H. Kennedy (ed.), *The Historiography of Islamic Egypt (c. 950–1800)* (Lieden, 2001), 59–75.

Rabbat, N. O., 'Who Was al-Maqrizi? A Biographical Sketch', *MSR* 7:2 (2003), 1–19.

Reisman, D. C., 'A Holograph MS of Ibn Qāḍī Shuhbah's *Dhayl*', *MSR* 2 (1998), 19–49.

Richards, D. S., 'The Early History of Saladin', *IQ* 17 (1973), 140–59.

Richards, D. S., 'A Fatimid Petition and "Small Decree" from Sinai', *Israel Oriental Studies* 3 (1973), 140–58.

Richards, D. S., 'A Consideration of Two Sources for the Life of Saladin', *JSS* 25:1 (1980), 46–65.

Richards, D. S., 'Imād al-Dīn al-Iṣfahānī: Administrator, Littérateur and Historian', in M. Shatzmiller (ed.), *Crusaders and Muslims in Twelfth-Century Syria* (Leiden, 1993), 133–46.

Richards, D. S., *The Rare and Excellent History of Saladin: Or al-Nawadir al-Sultaniyya wa'l-Mahasin al-Yusufiyya by Baha' Al-Din Ibn Shaddad* (Farnham, 2001).

Richards, D. S., *The Chronicle of Ibn Al-Athir for the Crusading Period from Al-Kamil Fi'l-Ta'rikh*, ed. in 3 vols (Farnham, 2007).

Robinson, C. F., *Islamic Historiography: Religion and society in the Near East, 600–1800* (Cambridge, 2003).

Robinson, C. F., *Texts, Documents and Artefacts: Islamic Studies in Honour of D. S. Richards* (Leiden, 2003).

Roffe, D., *Decoding Domesday* (Suffolk, 2015).

Rosenthal, F., *A History of Muslim Historiography* (Leiden, 1952).

Rosenthal, F., '"Of Making Many Books There Is No End": The Classical Muslim View', in G. N. Atiyeh (ed.), *The Book in the Islamic World: The Written Word and Communication in the Middle East* (New York, 1995).

Rosenthal, F., 'Ibn al-ʿImād', in *EI*[2], ed. P. Bearman et al. (Leiden, 1960–2007).

Rustow, M., 'A Petition to a Woman at the Fatimid Court (413–414 AH/1022–23 CE)', *BSOAS* 73:1 (2010), 1–27.

Rustow, M., 'Fatimid State, Documents, Serial Recyclers and the Cairo Geniza', Mellon Sawyer Seminar, U. of Iowa (28 April 2017), https://www.youtube.com/watch?v=eM7FpQjGlvU (accessed October 2017).

Ryzova, L., 'The Good, the Bad, and the Ugly: Collector, Dealer and Academic in the Informal Used-Paper Markets of Cairo', in Sonia Mejcher-Atassi and John-Pedro Schwartz (eds), *Archives, Museums and Collecting Practices in the Modern Arab World* (London, 2011).
Salaymeh, L., *The Beginnings of Islamic Law: Late Antique Islamicate Legal Traditions* (Cambridge, 2016).
Sanders, P., 'Claiming the Past: Ghadīr Khumm and the Rise of Hafizi Historiography in Late Fatimid Egypt', *SI* 75 (1992), 81–104.
Sanders, P., *Rituals, Politics and the City in Fatimid Cairo* (New York, 1994).
Sanders, P., 'The Fatimid State, 969–1171', in C. Petry (ed.), *The Cambridge History of Egypt*, vol. 1 (Cambridge, 1998), 151–74.
Sartain, E., *Jalal al-Din al-Suyuti, Vol. 1: Biography and Background* (Cambridge, 1975).
Sartori, P., 'Seeing Like Khanate: On Archives, Cultures of Documentation, and Nineteenth-Century Khvarazm', *Journal of Persianate Studies* 9 (2016), 228–57.
Sayeed, A., 'Women and Ḥadīth Transmission: Two Case Studies from Mamluk Damascus', *SI* 95 (2002), 71–94.
Sayyid, A. F., 'Lumieres nouvelles sur quelques sources de l'histoire Fatimide en Egypte', *AI* 13 (1977), 1–41.
Sayyid, A. F., *La capitale d'Egypte jusqu'à l'époche Fatimide, al-Qahira et al-Fustat. Essai de reconstruction topographique* (Beirut, 1998).
Scanlon, G. T., review of 'Andrew S. Ehrenkreutz's *Saladin*' (1972), *JSS* 20 (1975), 276–8.
Schacht, J., review of 'Samuel Stern's *Fatimid Decrees*' (1964), *Speculum* 40:3 (July 1965), 553.
Schauer, A., *Muslime und Franken: Ethnische, soziale und religiöse Gruppen im* Kitāb al-i'tibār *des Usāma ibn Munqiḍ (sic)* (Berlin, 2000).
Schultz, W. C., 'The Monetary History of Egypt, 642–1517', in C. F. Petry (ed.), *The Cambridge History of* Egypt, vol. 1 (Cambridge, 1998), 318–38.
Schultz, W. C., review of 'Sami G. Massoud' (2007), *Speculum* 84 (2009), 184–5.
Segal, J. B., Poonawala, I. K., Fehérvári, G. and Robinson, B. W., 'Notes and Communications', *BSOAS* 36:1 (1973), 109–18.
al-Shayyal, J., *Majmū'āt al-wathā'iq al-fāṭimiyyīn: I wathā'iq al-khilāfa wa wilāyat al-'ahd wa 'l-wizāra* (Cairo, 1958, reissued 1965).
al-Shayyal, 'The Fatimid Documents as a Source for the History of the Fatimids and Their Institutions', *Bulletin of the Faculty of Arts*, Alexandria University, 8 (1954), 3–12.
Shenoda, M. M., 'Displacing Dhimmī, Maintaining Hope: Unthinkable Coptic Representations of Fatimid Egypt', *IJMES* 39 (2007), 587–606.
Sijpesteijn, P. M., 'The Archival Mind in Early Islamic Egypt: Two Arabic Papyri', in P. M. Sijpesteijn, L. Sundelin, S. Torallas Tovar and A. Zomeno (eds), *From al-Andalus to Khurasan: Documents from the Medieval Muslim World* (Leiden, 2006), 163–87.
Smoor, P., 'Fatimid Poets and the 'Takhallus' that Bridges the Nights of Time to the Imam of Time', *DI* 68 (1991), 232–62.
Smoor, P., 'Palace and Ruin, a Theme for Fatimid Poets?', *WO* 22 (1991), 94–104.
Smoor, P., 'Wine, Love, and Praise for the Fatimid Imams, The Enlightened of God', *ZDMG* 142 (1992), 90–104.
Smoor, P., 'The Poet's House: Fiction and reality in the works of the 'Fatimid' poets', *QSA* 10 (1992), 45–62.
Smoor, P., "The Master of the Century': Fatimid Poets in Cairo', in U. Vermeulen and D. De Smet (eds), *Egypt and Syria in the Fatimid, Ayyubid and Mamluk Eras*, vol. I (Leuven, 1995), 139–63.

Smoor, P., 'Al-Mahdi's Tears: Impressions of Fatimid Court Poetry', in U. Vermeulen and D. De Smet (eds), *Egypt and Syria in the Fatimid, Ayyubid and Mamluk Eras*, vol. II (Leuven, 1998), 131–70.
Smoor, P., "Umara's Elegies and the Lamp of Loyalty', *AI* 34 (2000), 467–564.
Smoor, P., "Umara's Odes Describing the Imam', *AI* 35 (2001), 549–626.
Stern, S. M., 'The Epistle of the Fatimid Caliph al-Āmir (*al-Hidāya al-Āmiriyya*): Its Date and Its Purpose', *JRAS* (1950), 20–31.
Stern, S. M., 'The Succession to the Fatimid Imam al-Āmir, the Claims of the Later Fatimids to the Imamate, and the Rise of Ṭayyibi Isma'ilism', *Oriens* 4 (1951), 193–255.
Stern, S. M., 'Heterodox Isma'ilism at the Time of al-Mu'izz', *BSOAS* 17 (1955), 10–33.
Stern, S. M., 'A Fāṭimid Decree of the Year 524/1130', *BSOAS* 23:3 (1960), 439–55.
Stern, S. M., *Fatimid Decrees: Original Documents from the Fatimid Chancery* (London, 1964).
Stern, S. M., *Documents from Islamic Chanceries* (edited volume) (Oxford, 1966).
Stewart, D. J., 'Popular Shiism in Medieval Egypt: Vestiges of Islamic Sectarian Polemics in Egyptian Arabic', *SI* 84 (1996), 35–66.
Stewart, D. J., 'The Structure of the *Fihrist*: Ibn al-Nadīm as Historian of Islamic Legal and Theological Schools', *IJMES* 39 (2007), 369–87.
Stilt, K., *Islamic Law in Action: Authority, Discretion, and Everyday Experiences in Mamluk Egypt* (Oxford, 2011).
Stoler, A., 'Colonial Archives and the Arts of Governance', *Archival Science* 2 (2002), 87–109.
Studi Orientalistici in onore di Giorgio Levi della Vida (Rome, 1956).
Szombathy, Z., 'Genealogy in Medieval Muslim Societies', *SI* 95 (2002), 5–35.
Thomson, K., *Politics and Power in Late Fatimid Egypt. The Reign of Caliph al-Mustansir* (London and New York, 2016).
Traboulsi, S., 'The Queen Was Actually a Man: Arwā bint Aḥmad and the Politics of Religion', *Arabica* 50:1 (2003), 96–108.
Treadwell, W. L., 'Ibn Ẓāfir al-Azdī's Account of the Murder of the Samanid *amīr* Aḥmad b. Ismā'īl and the Succession of His Son, Naṣr', in C. Hillenbrand (ed.), *Studies in Honour of Clifford Edmund Bosworth*, Vol. 2: *The Sultan's Turret* (Leiden, 2000), 397–419.
Treadwell, W. L., 'The Account of the Samanid Dynasty in Ibn Ẓāfir al-Azdī's *Akhbār al-duwal al-munqaṭi'a*', *Iran* 43 (2005), 135–71.
Trouillot, M., *Silencing the Past: Power and the Production of History* (Boston, 1995).
Udovitch, A. L., 'Theory and Practice of Islamic Law: Some Evidence from the Geniza', *SI* 32 (1970), 289–303.
Van Berkel, M., 'Reconstructing Archival Practices in Abbasid Baghdad', *Journal of Abbasid Studies* 1 (2014), 7–22.
Van Berkel, M., Buskens, L and Sijpestein P. M. (eds), *Legal Documents as Sources for the History of Muslim Societies. Studies in Honour of Rudolph Peters* (Leiden, 2017).
Van Steenbergen, J., *Order Out of Chaos – Patronage, Conflict and Mamluk Socio-Political Culture, 1341–1382* (Leiden, 2006).
Van Steenbergen, J., Wing, P. and D'hulster, K., 'The Mamlukization of the Mamluk Sultanate? State Formation and the History of Fifteenth Century Egypt and Syria: Part I – Old Problems and New Trends', *History Compass* 14 (2016), 549–59.
Vollers, K., *Description de l-Égypte par Ibn Doukmak* (1893; repr. Beirut, n.d.).

Von Hees, S. 'Mamlukology as Historical Anthropology. State of the Art and Future Perspectives', in S. Conermann (ed.), *Ubi sumus? Quo vademus?: Mamluk Studies-State of the Art* (Göttingen, 2013), 119–30.
Waldman, M., *Toward a Theory of Historical Narrative: A Case Study in Perso-Islamicate Historiography* (Columbus, Ohio, 1980).
Walker, P. E., 'Succession to Rule in the Shi'ite caliphate', *JARCE* 32 (1995), 239–64.
Walker, P. E., 'Fatimid Institutions of Learning', *JARCE* 34 (1997), 179–200.
Walker, P. E., 'The Ismā'īlī Da'wa and the Fāṭimid caliphate', in C. Petry (ed.), *The Cambridge History of Egypt*, vol. 1 (Cambridge, 1998), 120–50.
Walker, P. E., *Exploring an Islamic Empire: Fatimid History and Its Sources* (London, 2002).
Walker, P. E., 'Al-Maqrīzī and the Fatimids', *MSR* 7:2 (July 2003), 83–97.
Walker, P. E., *Orations of the Fatimid Caliphs: Festival Sermons of the Ismaili Imams* (London, 2009).
Wollina, T., 'Ibn Ṭawq's Ta'līq. An Ego-Document for Mamluk Studies', in S. Conermann (ed.), *Ubi sumus? Quo vademus?: Mamluk Studies-State of the Art* (Göttingen, 2013), 337–62.
Wollina, T., 'News and Rumor – Local Sources of Knowledge about the World', in Stephan Conermann (ed.), *Everything Is on the Move: The Mamluk Empire as a Node in (Trans-) Regional Networks* (Göttingen, 2014), 284–309.
Wordsworth, W., Preface to *Lyrical Ballads, 1798* (London and New York, 1991).
al-Zirikli, Khayr al-Din, *al-A'lām: Qāmūs tarājīm li ashhar al-rijāl wa 'l-nisā' min al-'arab wa 'l-musta'ribīn wa 'l-mustashrifīn*, 15th edn in 8 vols (Beirut, 2002).

Index

Page references in *italics* refer to figures and tables; and references in **bold** refer to selected extracts from *Ta'rīkh al-duwal* in Arabic.

'Abbās al-Ṣanhājī, vizier 103, 109, 110, 111–12, 113, 114, 115–16, 117, **154–6**, **157**, 182–7, 188
al-'Āḍid al-'Ubaydī, caliph 64, 103, 118, 119, *144*, **157**, **168**, 188, 209
al-'Ādil Ruzzīk, vizier 103, 118, 124, *144*, **158–62**, **164**, 190–6, 202
administrative manuals 19, 76, 90, 129–30
al-Afḍal, vizier 68, 74 n.70, 89–97, 104, 105, *138*, 149, **150–1**, 175–7
al-Afḍal Kutayfāt, vizier 103, 107, 108, *139–40*, **151–2**, 178–80
Akhbār al-dawla al-miṣriyya wa mā jarā bayn al-mulūk wa 'l-khulafā' min al-fitan wa 'l-ḥurūb min ayyām al-āmir ilā ayyām shīrkūh 60, 61, *63*, 69, 77, 81, 82, 122, 124–5, *144*, **151**, 177
Akhū Muḥsin 59
Aleppo 62, 80, 82, 92, 105, 113
al-Āmir, caliph *63*, 68, 80, 89, 91, 92, 93, 98, 104–6, *139*, **150**, **151**, 175–6, 177–8
Amitai, R. 41, 45
al-Anṭākī, Yaḥyā 20, 58, 59, 80
Arabic historiography. *See* historiography
archival approach 2, 3, 7, 14–15, 16, 134
archivalia 6–7, 8, 12–13, 45–7, 130
  defined xvi
  Fatimid-era works in post-Fatimid accounts 58–9
  from late Fatimid Egypt 55–6, 59–64
  Ibn al-Furāt's 76–8, 131, 132
archivalism 15–16, 96, 133–4
archivality 2, 3–4, 8, 46, 47–8, 129–30
  defined xvi
  as conservation 2, 6, 45–7, 83
  of Ibn al-Furāt 84, 93, 96–7
  material signs of 29–36, 49 n.17
  of state documents 65–6
archive 3–4
  defined xv–xvi
  Arabic terms for 2
  building of 21–3
  epistemic environment 14–16
archivistics 15, 22, 75
  defined xvi
'Arqala al-Dimashqī 120–1, *146*
Ashtor, E. 41, 44, 46, 128 n.49
Auchterlonie, P. 13
'authenticity' debate 20–1, 83
autograph
  defined xv
  Ibn al-Furāt's 12, 23 n.1, 29–36, 42, 43, 46–7, 48, 49 n.13, 60, 107, 129, 133–4, 148, 149
  Ibn Ḥajar's *39*
  Ibn Zūlāq's 72 n.36
al-'Aynī, Maḥmūd Badr al-Dīn 41, 45, 47
  Iqd al-jumān 81
Ayyubid-era sources 7, 12, 13–14, 58–9, 77–8, 83, 99, 122, 125

Bacharach, J. L. 44
Bahrām, vizier 103, 107, *141–2*, **152–3**, 180–1
Abu Bakr b. Sannāj 38
Bauden, F. 18–19, 22
Bauer, T. 76, 132
Baybars al-Manṣūrī 81, 104, 106
  on al-Āmir caliphate and succession crisis 104, 105, 106, *139*
  appellation of 96
  on al-Ḥāfiẓ caliphate 107, *140*

al-Tuḥfa al-mulūkiyya fī 'l-dawla al-turkiyya 78
Zubdat al-fikra fī ta'rīkh al-hijra 78, 93–4, 105, 106, *139*, *140*, *141*, *142*
biographical dictionaries 4, 13, 17, 19, 77, 83, 94–5, 123
biography/ies
of caliphs and viziers 12, 60, 94
of Ibn al-Furāt 38
of al-Ma'mūn al-Baṭā'iḥī 97
See also memoirs
al-Birzālī 64
Brett, M. 6, 67, 69
Brockelmann, C. 38, 51 n.44

Cahen, Cl. 44
Cairo 1, 12
archival historiography 46
authors based in 13, 31, 41, 45, 85 n.34
authors based in Damascus and 38, 77
'Cairo narrative style' 39, 98, 120, 134, 149
literary output from 13
patterns in the works of authors based in 46
caliphs/caliphates
al-Āmir 104–6, *139*, **150**, **151**, 175–6, 177–8
biographies on 12, 60, 94
al-Fā'iz 109, 117, *143*, **155–6**, 184–6
al-Ḥāfiẓ 106–8, *139*, *140–1*, *142*, **151**, **152**, 178, 179–81
and historians' relations 55–6, 66–8, 69–70, 73 n.64, 134
list of 103
official or semi-official works 64–6, 68–9, 123
al-Quḍā'ī's works on 57
al-Ẓāfir 109–16, *142*, *143*, **153–6**, 181–6, 187
See also viziers/vizierates
catchwords (*istikhrāj*, *ta'qībāt*) 30, 34, 35, *37*, 49 n.18
Chamberlain, M. 22
chronicles xv
archival dimension of 2, 3, 5–6, 16, 17–18, 21, 30, 75–6, 129–35
as documentary narrative 3–4, 5
citations 23, 60, 125–6
Egyptian and non-Egyptian 82–3
Ibn al-Dawādārī's 81, 90
to Ibn al-Furāt 34, 36, 40, 45, 126
Ibn al-Furāt's 12, 42, 44–5, 47, 68, 77 n.3, 82–3, 90, 93, 95–6, 104, 105, 107, 108, 113, 114, 119–20, 121–2, 123, 137, *138–47*
Ibn Khallikān's 94–5, 96
Ibn Taghrībirdī's 107, 114–15, 126
al-Maqrīzī's 96, 107, 125, 126, 127 n.16
rubrication use 30, 34
codex/codices (AA/AB) 43, 49 nn.9, 13, 18, 131, 148–9
defined xv
authorship claim in 31
autographic nature of 31
clean copy or draft 39–42
material signs of archivality in 29–36
missing sections 32
original title *30*, 32
scribal copy 32, *33*, 37–8
sealing off notation 31
sources in 46–7
colophon 31
commemoration 3, 4, 12–13, 15, 16, 22, 55, 59
compilation 45–6, 47–8, 78–9, 108, 123–5
Conermanm, Stephan 17
conservation 2, 6, 16, 42, 43, 45–7, 57, 75–6, 79, 83, 124–5, 131
Crusades 46, 67, 80

Daftary, F. 56
al-Dallasī, Abū Futūḥ 38
Damascus 1, 32
authors based in 13, 31, 45, 86 n.39, 112–13
authors based in Cairo and 38, 77
dating 2, 9 n.4
decrees. *See sijillāt/sijill*
Derrida, J. 15, 55
de Vivo, F. 4–5
al-Dhahabī 38, 68, 99
Ta'rīkh al-Islām 114
diplomatic edition 8, 128 n.52, 148–9
Arabic text extracts **150–74**
English translation 175–220
direct speech 111, 113, 125
Ḍirghām, vizier 103, 122, 125, *144–5*, **161**, **162**, **163–8**, **169**, **170**, **171**,

196, 197, 198, 199, 200–1, 202–8, 211, 212, 214
document
 defined 18
 life cycle of 47–8, 64–6, 75–6, 84, 126, 129–30
 narrative as 3–4
 and narrative dichotomy 18–20, 132
 output in late Fatimid Egypt 8, 55–6
documentation 65
 historiography as 2, 7, 121
Donato, M. P. 4–5

Egypt 7
 Fatimid migration to 56–7
 historiographical agency 8, 12, 66–8, 69–70
 late Fatimid historiography scope and survival 12, 55–6, 59–64
 sources from 81–3, 119, 122–4
El-Leithy, T. 4–5, 15, 17, 65
Elshayyal, M. F. 38, 46–7, 127 n.33
encyclopedism 15–16, 21–3, 94, 120–1, 133–4
episteme 2, 13, 22, 65, 76–7, 129, 133
 defined xvi
epistemic archive 5–6, 17, 20, 29–30, 34–6, 45
 defined xvi
epistemology 6–7
ethnography 21, 123
Eurocentrism xv, 15, 129
eyewitness accounts
 of al-ʿĀdil Ruzzīk vizierate 122
 of al-Afḍal vizierate 90–2, 95
 of Ḍirghām vizierate 124–5
 of late Fatimid-era 48, 58, 59–64, 68–70, 80, 81, 82, 92, 122, 133
 on Ṭalāʾiʿ vizierate 118–19, 121
 of al-Ṭayyib's birth 105
 of Ṣalāḥ al-Dīn 123, 125
 of Shāwar and Shīrkūh power struggle 77, 125
 of al-Ẓāfir caliphate 110

Abu 'l-Faḍl Bayhaqī 3
al-Fāʾiz al-ʿUbaydī, caliph 91, 98, 103, 109, 111, 112, 113, 117, 119, *143*, **155–6**, **157**, 184–6, 188
Abu 'l-Faraj Ibn ʿAbd al-Hādī 38
Fatimid history 6–7, 8, 55–6, 130–1
 archival origins 68–70
 caliph and historian's agency 66–8, 69–70, 73 n.64, 134
 continuity/gaps in 58, 64
 three ages in 56–7, 71 n.8
 through Mamluk lens 11–13
 See also individual caliphs and viziers, e.g. ʿAbbās al-Ṣanhājī, vizier; al-Ḥāfiẓ, caliph
Ferré, A. 78
Fischel, W. J. 46
Flügel, G. 31
Friedrich, M. 4–5, 8, 15, 71 n.12

Geniza/Cairo Geniza 26 n.49, 49 n.17, 57, 65, 66, 68, 71 n.12, 73 n.58, 74 n.70
genre 2–3, 4, 13, 19, 62, 77, 129–30
al-Ghazālī 130
Goitein, S. D. 66
Gryaznevich, P. A. 78
Guo, L. 82

hadith 3, 13, 31, 38, *39*, **157**, 188
al-Ḥāfiẓ, caliph 73 n.58, 81, 95, 103, 104, 106–8, *139*, *140–1*, *142*, **151**, **152**, 178, 179–81
Ḥājjī Khalīfa 38, 51 n.44, 90
al-Ḥalabī, Khalīl b. Khumārtakīn 61–2, *63*, 77, 81, 82, 120, 122, **157**, 189
Hallaq, W. B. 22
Halm, H. 6, 20, 56
al-Hamdani, H. F. 66
Abu 'l-Ḥasan al-Bandanījī 38
Ḥasan b. al-Ḥāfiẓ, vizier 103, *141*, **152**, 180
Hātim b. Ibrāhīm 105
Hazārmard (Hizabr al-Mulūk), vizier 103, 107, *139–40*, **151**, 178
hermeneutics 6, 15, 17, 20–1, 75
hierarchization 6, 22, 92, 94, 96, 99, 115, 119, 120, 121, 125
Hirschler, K. 4–5, 15, 17, 22, 58–9, 75–6, 123
historians 12
 agency of 55–6, 66–70, 73 n.64, 134
 of late Fatimid-era 59–61, 92–3
 multidisciplinary approaches of 21, 220 n.3
 'serving the dynasty' 60–1, 62, 67–9

historical anthropology 17
historiography 1
  defined xv
  as archives 12–13
  as documentation 2, 7
  elitist/hegemonic discourse 4, 12, 14, 17, 24 n.17, 55–6, 60–2, 64, 123, 134
  epistemic facets of 15–16
  volume and variety of output 8, 13–14
history (dynastic, regional, confessional) xvi–xvii, 14, 17, 56–7, 59, 78, 81–3, 95, 130–1
holographs xv, 17–18

Ibn ʿAbd al-Ẓāhir *63*, 78, 82, 86 n.44, 124, 129
Ibn Abi ʾl-Ṣalt 58, 61, 62
  Risāla al-Miṣriyya 60, *63*
Ibn Abī Ṭayy 12, 62, 68, 69, 77, 81, 122, 125, 128 n.47, 130, 148
  on al-ʿĀdil Ruzzīk vizierate 124
  on al-Afḍal Kutayfāt 107, **151–2**, 178–80
  on al-Afḍal vizierate 89, 92–3, *138*, **150, 151**, 175–6, 177
  on al-Āmir caliphate and succession crisis 104, 105–6, *139*, 177–8
  on al-Ḥāfiẓ caliphate 106–8, *139*, *141*, *142*, **151**, **152**, 178, 180–1
  on Hazārmard (Hizabr al-Mulūk) vizierate 107, *140*
  Maʿādin al-dhahab fī taʾrīkh al-mulūk wa ʾl-khulafāʾ wa dhawi ʾl-rutab *63*, 77, 89, 92–3, 97, 98, 104, 105–8, 109, 110, 111, 113, 117, 122, *138, 139, 140, 141, 142, 143, 144*
  on al-Maʾmūn al-Baṭāʾiḥī vizierate 97, 98, *138*
  sources/informants of 82
  on Ṭalāʾiʿ vizierate 117, 119, 120, 121, **157**, 189
  textual accessibility 45–6
  on al-Ẓāfir 110, 111, 113, *142*, **153**, 181–2
Ibn Abī Uṣaybiʿa 60
Ibn ʿAsākir 122
Ibn al-Athīr 41, 67, 81, 83, 86 n.35, 100 n.33, 101 n.40, 110, 148
  on al-Afḍal vizierate 89, 93–4, *138*
  on al-Āmir caliphate and succession crisis 104, 105, *139*
  appellation of 96
  attributions by 96
  al-Bāhir fī taʾrīkh atābakāt al-Mawṣil 77
  on al-Ḥāfiẓ caliphate 106, 107, *139*, *140*
  hegemonic leanings of 123
  al-Kāmil fi ʾl-taʾrīkh 21, 60, 77, 81, 89, 93–4, 97, 98, 104, 105, 106, 107, 108, 113, 114, 116, *138*, *139*, *140*, *141*, *142*
  on al-Maʾmūn al-Baṭāʾiḥī vizierate 97, 98, *138*
  on Shāwar-Ḍirghām era 124
  sources of 90, 119
  on al-Ẓāfir assassination 113, 116
Ibn al-Dawādārī 16, 59, *63*, 72 n.43, 81, 127 n.40
  Kanz al-durar 90, 99
Ibn Duqmāq 38, 44, 52 nn.73–4, *63*, 120
  al-Durr al-munaddad fī wafayāt aʿyān ummat Muḥammad 47
  al-Jawhar al-thamīn fī siyar al-mulūk wa ʾl-salāṭīn 114
  Nuzhat al-anām 79, 86 n.35, 99
  on al-Ẓāfir assassination 111, 114, 116
Ibn al-Furāt 1, 4, 5, 7, 11, 12, 17, 57, 58
  analytical approach of 33–4
  appellations for other authors 96
  archival mindset/proclivity of 2–3, 22, 96, 115–16
  archival practices of 6, 84, 100 n.33, 132–4
  attributions 44–5, 83, 93, 95, 107, 120
  authorship claim by 31
  biographical sketch of 38
  contributions to later historiography 43–5
  epistemic environment 29–30
  exhibitor of documentary specimens 18
  handwriting of *39*
  hierarchization 22, 92, 94, 96, 99, 121, 125
  historiographical intelligence of 46, 95–6
  sources of (*see* sources)

suspension of writing 27 n.6, 30
textual strategization 21
See also Ta'rīkh al-duwal wa 'l-mulūk
Ibn Ḥabīb al-Ḥalabī 85 n.34
Ibn Ḥajar al-'Asqalānī 31, 41, 51 n.44, *63*, 130
Inbā' al-ghumr bi abnā' al-'umr 36
al-Musalsalāt *39*
sources of 38, 39–40, 44
Ibn al-'Imād 38, 51 n.44
Ibn 'Imād al-Ḥanbalī 41
Ibn Iyās 41
Ibn al-Jawzī 81
al-Muntaẓam fī ta'rīkh al-umam 77, 117, 119–20, 127 n.33, *143*
Ibn Khaldūn 4, 7, 13, 45, 47, *63*, 86 n.35, 110, 119, 120, 130–1
historigraphical intelligence of 46
Kitāb al-'ibar wa dīwān al-mubtada' wa al-khabar fī ayyām al-'arab wa al-'ajam wa al-barbar, wa man 'āṣarahum min dhawī al-sulṭān al-akbar 2, 46, 79, 114
sources of 91, 98–9, 116
on al-Ẓāfir assassination 114, 116
Ibn Khallikān *63*, 78, 81, 82, 83, 90, 100 n.33, 110, 119, 127 n.40, 148
on al-Afḍal vizierate 90, 94–5, 96, *138*, **150**, **151**, 176, 177
on al-Āmir caliphate and succession crisis 104, 105–6, *139*
appellation for 96
attributions 60, 94–5, 96
on al-Ḥāfiẓ caliphate 106, 107, 108, *142*
on al-Ma'mūn al-Baṭā'iḥī vizierate 97, 98, *138*
on Shāwar-Ḍirghām era 123, 124, 125, *144*, *145*, *146*, 200
on Ṭalā'i' vizierate 117, 119, 127 n.40
Wafayāt al-a'yān 77, 90, 94–5, 96, 97, 98, 104, 105–6, 107, 108, 109, 113–14, 115, 117, 120, 122, *138*, *139*, *142*, *143*, *144*, *145*, *146*, *147*
on al-Ẓāfir assassination 113–14, 115
Ibn al-Ma'mūn al-Baṭā'iḥī 10 n.26, 60, *63*, 64, 72 n.35, 76, 89, 97, 99, 100 n.14, **150**, **151**, **155**, 176, 184, 220 n.3
Ibn Maṣāl, vizier 103, 110, 114, *142–3*, **153**, **173**, **174**, 181–2, 217, 220
Ibn Muyassar 60, 67, 68, 69, 77, 79, 81, 101 n.40, 119, 122
Akhbār Miṣr *63*, 79
on al-Āmir caliphate and succession crisis 104, 105, 106
historiographical transmission of 10 n.26, 108
on al-Ma'mūn al-Baṭā'iḥī vizierate 97, 99
sources of 115, 125
on Ṭalā'i' vizierate 117, 118
on al-Ẓāfir assassination 110, 113, 114, 115, 116
Ibn al-Nadīm 12
Ibn Naẓīf al-Ḥamawī 81, **172**, 215
Ta'rīkh-i Mansūrī 78, 122, 123, 125, *145*, *146*
Ibn Qāḍī Shuhba 31, 36–7, 38, 41, 45
Ibn al-Qalānisī 67, 80
and Ṭalā'i' vizierate 118, 127 n.24
on al-Ẓāfir assassination 110, 111, 112, 113, 114–15, 119, 127 n.24
Ibn Ṣa'īd al-Maghribī 80
Ibn al-Sālār, vizier 103, 110, 111–12, 113, 114, 115, *143*, **153–4**, 181–2, 183
Ibn al-Ṣayrafī 61, 62, 66, 73 n.58, 74 n.70, 93, 96, 100 n.8
on al-Afḍal vizierate 89, 90–1, *138*
hegemonic leanings of 123
al-Ishāra ilā man nāla 'l-wizāra 76, 90, 97
Kitāb al-wuzarā' li 'l-dawla al-fāṭimiyya bi 'l-qāhira al-mu'izziyya 76, 89, 90–1, *138*
official wordsmith 67–8, 69
al-Qānūn fī diwān al-rasā'il 68, 76, 90, 91
as resource 13, 58, 59, 60, *63*, 64, 65, 72 n.43, 81, 98
sijillāt 91
textual accessibility 133
Ibn Shaddād 58
Ibn Taghribirdi 12, 17, 38, 45, 47, 51 n.44, 57, 58, *63*, 119, 128 n.54, 130
hierarchisation 115
al-Nujūm al-zāhira fī mulūk Miṣr wa 'l-Qāhira 41, 79, 125

sources of 41, 44, 91, 98–9, 107, 110, 114–15, 126
on Ṭalā'i' vizierate 120
on al-Ẓāfir assassination 114–15, 116
Ibn Ṭawq 3
Ibn Ṭūlūn 31, 38, 41, 49 n.5
Ibn Ṭuwayr 13, 64, 86 n.35, 93, 148
on al-Afḍal vizierate 89, 91–2, *138*
on al-Āmir caliphate and succession crisis 104–6, *139*
appellation of 96
on al-Ḥāfiẓ caliphate 106–8, *139*, *142*
on Hazārmard (Hizabr al-Mulūk) vizierate 107, *139*, *140*
on al-Ma'mūn al-Baṭā'iḥī vizierate 97, 98, *138*
Nuzhat al-muqlatayn fī akhbār al-dawlatayn *36*, *63*, 77, 83, 89, 91–2, 97, 98, 104–8, 109–10, 111, 113–14, 115, 117–18, *138*, *139*, *140*, *141*, *142*, *143*
as resource 58, 59, 60, 65, 68, 69, 81, 83, 119, 122
sources/informants of 107, 108
on Ṭalā'i' vizierate 117–18, 119, 121, *143*
textual accessibility 45–6, 133
on Yānis and Bahrām vizierates 107, *141–2*
on al-Ẓāfir assassination 109–10, 111, 113–14, 115, 116, *143*
Ibn Wāṣil 13, *63*, 81, 82
Mufarrij al-kurūb fī akhbār Banī Ayyūb 78, 81, 122, 123, 124, 125, 128 n.54, *144*, *145*
Ibn Ẓāfir 60, *63*, 79, 81, 96
on al-Afḍal vizierate 90, 95
Akhbār al-duwal al-munqaṭi'a 78, 79, 90, 95, 108
as resource 104
on Ṭalā'i' vizierate 117, 118, 119
on al-Ẓāfir assassination 110, 111, 112, 113, 114, 115
Ibn al-Zayyāt *63*, 91
Ibn Zūlāq 60, 64, 72 n.36, 86 n.44, 94
al-Idrīsī, emir 61–2, *63*, 77, 81, 82, 122, 123, 124, 125–6, 128 n.47, *146*, *147*, **171–2**, **173**, **174**, 214–15, 217–18, 220
Idrīs 'Imād al-Dīn *63*, 70 n.1, 104, 105
'Uyūn al-akhbār 12, 80
'Imād al-Dīn al-Iṣfahānī 3
al-Barq al-Shāmī 58
Bustān al-jāmi'/Kitāb al-bustān fī ḥawādith al-zamān 80, 99, 105, 109, 111, 112, 113, 117, 127 n.18
Kharīdat al-qaṣr wa jarīdat al-'aṣr 108
on Shāwar-Ḍirghām era 122
on al-Ẓāfir assassination 111, 112, 113, 119
Imad, Leila 97
Irwin, R. 44, 70
al-Iskandarānī 107, 108, *140*, **152**, 179
Islamicate 2, 22, 25 n.29
defined xv
archives 3–4, 129–30
'documentary turn' 18–20
rubrication use 34
text reuse 84
Isma'ili/Isma'ilism xvi, xvii, 6, 12, 43, 57, 59, 70 n.1, 73 n.64, 80, 96–7, 100 n.8, 105, 130
al-Jabartī 86 n.44
al-Jawharī 41
al-Jazarī 64
al-Kalbī, Hishām 46

Khalidi, T. 22
Khan, G. A. 66, 73 n.58
al-Khaṭṭāb 105
al-Khilāfa, Fakhr al-Dīn b. Shams 122, 124, **160–1**, 194–5
khuṭbas (Friday/festival sermons) 64, 66
König, J. 22, 84
Kropp, M. 47

Le Strange, G. 47
letters 109, 114, 115
See also sijillāt/sijill
Lewis, B. 6, 56
libraries 70 n.6, 126, 131–2
life cycle (of documents) 47–8, 64–6, 75–6, 84, 126, 129–30
'second life' 132
Little, D. 5–6, 21, 44, 79, 131

McSheffrey, S. 4–5
madrasa 4, 11, 38, *40*, 129, 133

al-Malaṭī 41
Mamluk-era sources 7, 12, 13-14, 78, 79, 83, 129
Mamluk historians 12, 14, 15, 130
  as archivists 2–3, 116
  attributions 83
  political and religious alignments of 24 n.17
  priorities of 6–7
  subject range of 52 n.63
al-Ma'mūn al-Baṭā'iḥī, vizier 97–9, *138*, 177
manuscript 13, 51 n.54, 79, 81, 95, 96, 133
  defined xv
  Bodleian Hunt 198 93–4
  Chester Beatty MS 36–7, 50 n.30
  Paris MS 97
  Paris MS Blochet 5990 *30*, 49 nn.9, 13, 18, 50 n.23
  Paris MS Blochet f. 214r 49 n.16
  Paris MS De Slane 1595 32, *33*
  precarity of 48, 51 n.45
  Vienna MS 32, 49 n.9
  Vienna MS AF 117 *35*, *36*, *37*, 49 n.16, *61*
  See also codex/codices
al-Maqrīzī 1, 4, 13, 17, 18, 22, 27 n.67, 31, 38, 52 n.73, 58, 59
  attributions 96, 107, 125, 126, 127 n.16
  confessional history 12
  Ibn al-Furāt cited by 40–1, 44, 45, 51 nn.50, 52, 83, 126
  Itti'āẓ al-ḥunafā' 7, 21, 40–1, 43, 51 n.52, 57, 79, 90, 96, 99, 104, 114, 125, 127 n.16, 130, 131, 149
  Khiṭaṭ 7, 77, 79, 86 n.44, 96, 97, 99, 104, 120, 125, 126, 127 n.16, 129, 130, 149, 221 n.40
  Kitāb al-sulūk 17, 40, 45, 51 n.50
  sources of 51 n.52, 60, 62, *63*, 67, 72 n.36, 77, 81, 83, 86 n.44, 90, 91, 96, 97, 98–9, 104, 107, 110, 125
  on Ṭalā'i' vizierate 119, 120
  on al-Ẓāfir assassination 114, 116
Massoud, S. 36–7, 41, 44–5, 58–9, 79, 131
material culture 29–36, 42, 49 n.17
memoir 62, 112, 117, 127 nn.16–17
memorialization 3, 5, 8, 13, 16, 130
al-Mizzī 38
al-Muhannak 60, *63*, 69, 95, **171**, 214, 215
  as resource 104, 105, 108
Mu'īn al-Dīn Unar, emir 109, 113, 114, 115, **154**, 182
al-Mu'izz, caliph 60, 64, 72 n.36
mukhlaqāt (official documents) 58, 64, 65, 66–7
al-Mundhirī 68
al-Musabbiḥī 60–1, 64, 69, 86 nn.35, 44, 94, 95, 108
al-Musta'lī, caliph 18, 68, 89, 90–1, 92
al-Mustanṣir, caliph 59, 66, 68, 71 n.8, 80, 89

narrative
  as documentary material 3–4
  and document dichotomy 18–20, 132
  new uses of 17
  output in late Fatimid Egypt 55–6
Naṣr b. 'Abbās (Nāṣir al-Dīn Naṣr) 110, 111–12, 113, 116, 117, **153**, **154–5**, **156**, 181, 183–4, 185, 186–7
al-Nu'mān, Qāḍī 58
  Iftitāḥ al-da'wa wa ibtidā' al-dawla 12
numismatics 57, 109
Nūr al-Dīn, Emir of Damascus and Aleppo 94, *147*, **162–3**, **169**, **170**, **171**, **172**, 189, 197–200, 209–10, 211–12, 213–14, 215–17
al-Nuwayrī 20, 22, 59, *63*, 83, 101 nn.37, 40, 127 n.40, 136 n.28
  Nihāyat al-arab 79, 95, 114, 128 n.49
  on Shāwar-Ḍirghām era 124
  sources of 98, 99, 119
  on al-Ẓāfir assassination 114

obituaries 17, 30, 31, 34, *36*, 38, 43
Ottoman 3, 19

paper
  reuse 18–19, 65, 129–30
  types used 31, 49 n.17
patronage 45, 55, 82
  See also caliphs/caliphates: and historians' relations

Paul, J. 76
poetry 62, 107, 108, 121, *140*, *142*, *143*, *144*, *145*, *146*, **154**, 182–3
preservation xv, 2, 12–13, 15, 16, 19, 22, 47–8, 58–9, 62, 65–6, 68, 70, 71 n.12, 76, 84, 98, 111, 116, 129–30, 131–2
prioritization. *See* hierarchization
prose 46–7, 62, 76–8, 81–3, 95–6, 108, 148
prosopography 14, 17, 22

al-Qāḍī, W. 13, 148
al-Qāḍī al-Fāḍil 58, 68, 69, 72 n.40, **162**, **168**, 197, 209, 221 n.33
  Mutajaddidāt 62
Qāḍī al-Nuʿmān 67, 69
  Iftitāḥ al-daʿwa wa ibtidāʾ al-dawla 12, 73 n.64
al-Qalqashandī 2, *63*, 66
  on Shāwar-Ḍirghām era 124
  sijillāt preserved in 104
  sijillāt term usage by 64–5
  sources of 13, 67, 91
  Ṣubḥ al-aʿshā 81, 90
  textual strategization 133
al-Qifṭī 60
al-Quḍāʿī 57, 60–1, 62, 64, 78, 86 nn.38, 44, 95, 124, 129
  ʿUyūn al-maʿārif 56, 58
al-Qurṭī 60, 80

al-Rashīd Ibn al-Zubayr 86 n.44, 107
  Kitāb al-jinān wa riyāḍ al-adhhān 108, *142*
al-Rawḥī 80, 86 n.38
redactions 23
  of *Akhbār al-duwal al-munqaṭiʿa* 95
  of Ibn al-Ṣayrafī's work 90
  of *Taʾrīkh al-duwal* 36–7, 99
  of *ʿUyūn al-maʿārif* 56
  of *Wafayāt al-aʿyān* 95, 104
  of *Zubda* 93–4
reflexive/reflexivity 3, 16, 110, 116, 121, 132–3
repository 2, 5, 6, 14, 15, 16, 39, 47, 57, 75, 92, 132
research priorities 7, 135
Riḍwān b. al-Walakhshī, vizier 103, 108, *142*, **153**, **164**, 181, 202

rubrication 30, 34, 35, 49 n.18, 83, 149
rubrics 13, 14, 49 n.13, 130
Rustow, M. 20, 65, 66

al-Ṣābī, Hilāl 80
al-Ṣafadī 68
al-Sakhāwī 31, 38, 40, 44, 51 n.44, 90, 131
  Iʿlān 40, 41
Ṣalāḥ al-Dīn, Sultan of Egypt and Syria 58, 64, 122, 123, 125, 128 n.42, **169**, **172**, **173**, **174**, 210, 216, 218, 219–20
Salaymeh, L. 19
Sanders, P. 116
Sartori, P. 4, 20
Sayyid, A. F. 6
Shāfiʿ b. ʿAlī 43, 81, 82, **172**, 216
  Arrangement of Conduct in the Histories of the Caliphs and Kings **162**, **163**, **168**, **174**, 197–8, 199, 208, 218, 219
  Ḥusn al-manāqib al-sirriyya 78, 85 n.26
  Naẓm al-sulūk fī taʾrīkh al-khulafāʾ wa ʾl-mulūk 78, 122, 124, 125, *145*, *146*, *147*
Shafiʿi 38
Abū Shāma 12, 13, 47, 58, 62, *63*, 77, 84, 122
  Kitāb al-rawḍatayn fī akhbār al-dawlatayn 77, 92, 126, 127 n.17, 128 n.47
Shāwar al-Saʿadī, vizier 103, 118, 122–3, 125, *144–5*, *146*, **159–74**, 192–220
al-Shayyal, J. 66, *144*
Shiʿi/Shiʿite 56, 57, 96, 127 n.40, 130
Shīrkūh, vizier 103, 123, 125, *145–6*, **163–4**, **165–6**, **167**, **168–71**, **172–4**, 198–201, 204, 205, 206, 208, 209–14, 215–20
Sibṭ b. al-Jawzī 80, 86 n.39, 110, 113, 114, 115
sijillāt/*sijill* (imperial instructive letters/ decrees) 21, 64–5, 66–7, 68, 73 nn.58, 62, 76, 80, 91, 98, 104, 105, 107, 206, 209
Sijpestein, P. 22
Sīrat al-khalīfa al-Mustanṣir 60

Sīrat al-wazīr al-Afḍal 60, *63*, 95
Sīrat al-wazīr al-Yāzūrī 60
Smith, R. 46
sources 52 nn.73–4, 65, 75, 86 n.35, 128 nn.40, 47, 49
  on al-ʿĀdil Ruzzīk vizierate 118, 124, *144*, **158–62**, 190–6
  on al-Afḍal Kutayfāt 107, 108, *139–40*, **151–2**, 178–80
  on al-Afḍal vizierate 89–97, *138*, **150–1**, 175–7
  on al-Āmir caliphate 104–6, *139*, 177–8
  Ayyubid-era 7, 12, 13–14, 58–9, 77–8, 83, 99, 122, 125
  comparison of contemporary sources 78–81
  on al-Fā'iz caliphate and Ṭalā'iʿ vizierate 62, 117–21, 127 n.40, *143*, **155–8**, **159**, **161**, **164**, 184–90, 191–2, 195–6, 201
  Fatimid-era 58-9, 76–7, 99
  on al-Ḥāfiẓ caliphate 106–8, *139*, *140–1*, *142*, **151**, 178, 179–81
  on Hazārmard (Hizabr al-Mulūk) vizierate 107, *139–40*
  on Ibn Maṣāl vizierate 110, 114, *142–3*, **153**, 181–2
  Mamluk-era 7, 12, 13-14, 78, 79, 83, 129
  on al-Ma'mūn al-Baṭā'iḥī vizierate 97–9, *138*, **150**, **151**, **155**, 176, 177, 184
  most cited 92, 95–6, 127 n.33
  quasi-courtly 123
  on Riḍwān b. al-Walakhshī vizierate 108, *142*
  Shāwar and Ḍirghām era 121–5, *144–5*, **159–68**, 192–208
  Shāwar and Shīrkūh power struggle 123, *145–7*, **168–74**, 209–20
  transregionality of 81–3
  on Yānis and Bahrām vizierate 107, *141–2*
  on al-Ẓāfir caliphate 109–16, *142*, *143*, **153–5**, 181–4
  See also under individual authors; eyewitness accounts
state documents 58, 64–7, 68–9, 73 n.64, 123
Stern, S. M. 66
Sulaymān b. al-Ḥāfiẓ, vizier 103
Sunni 12, 62, 70 n.6, 126, 131
survival bias 47–8, 129
al-Ṣuyūṭī 38, 44, 51 n.44, *63*, 90, 130
Syria 37–8, 66, 79, 80, 81–3, 112–13, 119

al-Ṭabarī 94
Ṭalā'iʿ b. Ruzzīk, vizier 62, 117–21, 127 nn.24, 40, 130, *143*, **156–8**, **159**, **161**, **164**, 186–90, 191–2, 195–6, 201
Ta'rīkh al-duwal wa 'l-mulūk (Ibn al-Furāt) 1, 3, 6, 7, 8, 14, 15–16, 21, 58, 71 n.7, 119, 121, 128 n.42
  additions to text 31
  archival dimension of 17–18, 129, 130–1, 132–5
  authority of 41
  authorship statement 31
  chapters 34
  copies of 45
  criticism of 39
  documentary and narrative qualities of 20
  introductory matter 32–4, *35*
  musawwada 41–2
  original title of 9 n.3, 29, *30*, 32
  as resource 36–7, 38, 39–41, 44, 45–6, 51 nn.50, 52, 83, 126
  significance of 43–5
  subject matter and spatial aspects 42–3, 92, 106, 109, 122
  See also Ibn al-Furāt
al-Ṭayyib (son of caliph al-Āmir) 16, 80, 104–6, **151**, 178
texts
  loss/precarity of 47–8, 51 n.45, 75, 131–2
  transmission of 6, 10 n.26, 12–13, 15, 16, 22, 44, 47–8, 58–9, 62, 64, 107–8, 83, 116, 118, 119, 120, 121, 124, 128 n.49, 133, 134
textual witness 11, 12, 23, 47–8, 82, 92, 97, 119, 129, 134
topography 46, 78
transmission. *See* texts: transmission of

al-Ṭuwayr 124, **161**, 196
Twelver 12, 92, 120, 130

'Umāra al-Yamanī 58, 62, *63*, 69, 80, 82, 105, 120–1, *145*
Abū 'Umar al-Kindī 86 n.44
unicum 36–7, 78, 129
Usāma b. Munqidh 62, 109
  Kitāb al-i'tibār *63*, 110, 117, 127 nn.16–17
  sojourn in Egypt 80, 110, 111–12, 113, 114, 115, 116, *143*, **154–5**, **156**, 182–4, 186, 187

Van Berkel, M. 15, 22
viziers/vizierates 94
  al-'Ādil Ruzzīk 118, 124, *144*, **158–62**, **164**, 190–6, 202
  al-Afḍal 89–97, *138*, **150–1**, 175–7
  al-Afḍal Kutayfāt 107, 108, *139–40*, **151–2**, 178–80
  Bahrām 107, *141–2*, **152–3**, 180–1
  Ḍirghām 122, 125, *144–5*, **161**, **162**, **163–8**, **169**, **171**, 197, 199, 200–1, 202–8, 211, 214
  Ḥasan b. al-Ḥāfiẓ *141*, **152**, 180
  and historians' relations 64, 66, 68–70
  Ibn Maṣāl 110, 114, *142–3*, **153**, **173**, **174**, 181–2, 217, 220
  Ibn al-Sālār and 'Abbās al-Ṣanhājī 109–16, *143*, **153–6**, 182–7
  list of 103
  al-Ma'mūn al-Baṭā'iḥī 97–9, *138*
  Riḍwān b. al-Walakhshī 108, *142*
  Shāwar and Ḍirghām 121–5, *144–5*, **159–68**, 192–208
  Shāwar and Shīrkūh power struggle 123, *145–7*, **168–74**, 209–20
  Ṭalā'i' and al-'Ādil Ruzzīk 117–21, 127 n.24, *143*, *144*, **156–62**, **164**, 186–96, 201
  Yānis 107, *141*, **152**, 180
  See also caliphs/caliphates
Von Hees, S. 17

Waldman, M. 17, 135
Walker, P. E. 59
Whitmarsh, T. 22, 84

Yānis, vizier 103, 107, *141*, **152**, 180, 191
Yāqūt al-Ḥamawī 60
  Mu'jam al-buldān 149
al-Yunīnī 64
al-Yūsufī 131

al-Ẓāfir al-'Ubaydī, caliph 80, 103, 109–16, 117, 118, 119, 127 n.24, *142*, *143*, **153–6**, 181–6, 187
al-Ẓāhir, caliph 57, 69
al-Ziriklī 38, *39*, 51 n.44